INDIAN EDUCATION
IN THE AMERICAN
COLONIES, 1607–1783

INDIGENOUS EDUCATION

Series editors

Margaret Connell Szasz
University of New Mexico

Brenda J. Child
University of Minnesota

Karen Gayton Swisher
Haskell Indian Nations University

John W. Tippeconnic III
The Pennsylvania State University

INDIAN EDUCATION
IN THE AMERICAN
COLONIES, 1607–1783

Margaret Connell Szasz

With a new introduction by the author

UNIVERSITY OF NEBRASKA PRESS
LINCOLN AND LONDON

With gratitude to Robert Jim
and his people
for starting me on the path

First Nebraska paperback printing: 2007

An earlier version of a part of chapter 1 was originally published as
"Native American Children," in *American Childhood, A Research
Guide and Historical Handbook,* Joseph M. Hawes and N. Ray
Hiner, Eds. (Greenwood Press, Inc., Westport CT, 1985), pp. 185–233.
Copyright © 1985 by Joseph M. Hawes and N. Ray Hiner. Reprinted
with permission.

An earlier version of chapter 9 appeared as "'Poor Richard' Meets
the Native American: Young Indian Women at School in Eighteenth-
Century Connecticut," *Pacific Historical Review* 49 (May 1980):
215–235. Reprinted with permission.

Maps by Carol Cooperrider

Library of Congress Cataloging-in-Publication Data
Szasz, Margaret.
Indian education in the American colonies, 1607–1783 / Margaret
Connell Szasz; with a new introduction by the author.—Bison
Books ed.
    p. cm.—(Indigenous education)
Originally published: Albuquerque: University of New Mexico
Press, c1988.
Includes bibliographical references and index.
ISBN-13: 978-0-8032-5966-9 (pbk.: alk. paper)
ISBN-10: 0-8032-5966-2 (pbk.: alk. paper)
1. Indians of North America—Education.   2. Indians of North
America—Missions—History.   3. Indians of North America—
Cultural assimilation.   4. Missions—United States—History.   I.
Title.
E97.S94   2007
370.89'97—dc22   2007004971

INTRODUCTION TO THE
BISON BOOKS EDITION

"Underneath what looks like loose stone,
there is stone woven together."[1]

In his poem "A Story of How a Wall Stands," Acoma poet Simon J. Ortiz reminds us of how "stone woven together" forms the inner core of a wall. In 1988, when the first edition of *Indian Education in the American Colonies, 1607–1783* appeared, I hoped that the book rested on such a well-woven core. It had been ten years in the making. Almost two decades later, the core remains essentially in place. In the years following the volume's first publication, however, research and writing on American Indians during the colonial era virtually exploded. Even though the new scholarship extended well beyond Native issues, the world of Native Americans often remained a central theme. In this new introduction, I will review some of the literature on colonial America that has been published since the late 1980s, and I will also evaluate its impact on the assessment of Indian education that I first presented almost twenty years ago.

Since the late 1980s, American colonial history has been experiencing a dynamic metamorphosis. As the editors of *Historically Speaking* declared in the spring of 2005, "No field has attracted more attention in recent decades than early American History." Moving in different directions from their predecessors, recent historians of the colonial era have rejuvenated an interest in the entire Atlantic world. Within this world, according to David Armitage, scholars have begun to examine "'the movement of people, ideas of empire, cultural encounters, the circulation of ideas,' and the Atlantic slave trade."[2] Jack Rakove agrees. He positions "the new interest in the nature of empires and imperialism . . . as a collateral branch of Atlantic history." Similarly, Edward G. Gray argues that empire remains the key issue, noting that "what is relatively new is the notion that empire and all that it implied in the 18th century—the imperial bureaucracy, commercial networks, a distinct form of subjecthood, hierarchical legal and political regimes, etc.—allows us to view the whole disjointed 18th-century American past as a single, unified field of historical investigation."[3]

The expanding focus on Native people within the empire remains integral to the revitalized scholarship on America's colonial and revolutionary history. Gray contextualizes this fascination with empire by suggesting that research on American Indians, which has been "animated in part by a desire to incorporate native peoples into the early American narrative, tends to focus on so-called backcountry or peripheral regions of the British Empire." Rakove provides a less flattering motivation for American Indian research, suggesting that "the tendency of the 1960s and 1970s to treat social history as a story from the bottom up has given way to the cultural historians' propensity to view the world from the margins out." In contrast, Pauline Meier praises this approach: "The most novel work in recent years has . . . been outside the political—on trade, migrations both voluntary and coerced, the relationship of colonizers to indigenous peoples, and social structures, with particular reference to class, race, and gender." Whether scholars of Native people have engaged the field of American colonial history in order to address issues of empire, to mainstream the Native experience, or to reconsider the concept of "peripheral" versus "core" cultures, as Daniel Richter does in his study *Looking East from Indian Country*, these academics, known collectively as *ethnohistorians*, have left an imprint on our understanding of this era that cannot be ignored.[4]

The ethnohistorians who have reshaped our perception of Natives before and during the American Revolution have ranged widely in their interests. Even so, their publications concentrate overwhelmingly on Native people in the Northeast, primarily on the eastern Algonquians of New England or on the League of the Iroquois.[5] Only a small number of ethnohistorians have studied Natives in the Chesapeake region. These include J. Frederick Fausz, Thomas E. Davidson, and Helen C. Rountree, who remains the best-known scholar of the Powhatan and the eastern shore Indians of Virginia and Maryland.[6]

Several ethnohistorians have cast their research net far more widely, encompassing relations between Native American nations and the Spanish, French, and Dutch empires, as well as Native relations with the English and within Indian Country among different Native tribes and nations. In their edited volume, *Empire and Others: British Encounters with Indigenous Peoples: 1600-1850*, Martin Daunton and Rick Halpern underline the international approach to the topic by ranging across North America, Africa, Australia, and other continents also influenced by the British Empire.[7] Gregory Evans Dowd, among others, celebrates this recontextualizing of American Indian history. In "seeking a more panoramic vision," he observes, recent historians have sought to reintegrate American Indian history "into the broad sweep of American history." Looking back, Dowd suggests that the works of these scholars "have returned Native Americans to a larger, and perhaps more visible, early American drama."[8]

The prolonged 1992 quincentenary commemoration of the first encounter between Native Americans and Christopher Columbus sparked the new approaches to colonial American history. As Karen Ordahl Kupperman writes, the quincentenary "brought scholars from a wide variety of disciplines together and spurred continuing exchange." In 2000 she noted, "This is a propitious moment to consider the confrontation between American and European peoples at the time when North America was being colonized." In *Beyond 1492, Encounters in Colonial North America* James Axtell observes, "The quincentenary of Columbus's voyage is a perfect time for the citizens of the 'global village' he helped create to reassess the initiation, conduct, and long- and short-term results of those encounters." Axtell reasons that ethnohistorians remain well suited for this assignment since "they try to view intercultural encounters from both (or all) sides of the frontier. . . . Their major subject of study is 'otherness,' the often ineluctable differences perceived in one group by another." As in his previous study *After Columbus: Essays in the Ethnohistory of Colonial North America*, Axtell's *Beyond 1492* ranges widely, looking at Native-Spaniard confrontations and Native-Jesuit encounters in the Americas.[9]

Richard White's seminal study *The Middle Ground: Indians, Empires, and Republics in the Great Lakes Region, 1650–1815* exemplifies this mode of comparative history. In *Indians and English, Facing Off in Early America* Karen Ordahl Kupperman offers an astute assessment of the earliest decades after Indian-European contact, relying on a remarkable selection of Native and European immigrant voices to recall the moods of the time. The appearance of Colin G. Calloway's groundbreaking look at American Indians during the era of the Revolution, *The American Revolution in Indian Country: Crisis and Diversity in Native American Communities*, reminds us of the molasses-like pace of scholarship on Native America. More than two centuries after the American Revolution, an ethnohistorian finally crafted the first major work on this important, yet largely ignored, aspect of the war.[10]

Given the belatedness of this scholarly attention to American Indians between 1492 and 1783, any theoretical framework for American Indian studies has to remain preliminary. Scholars—from all ethnic backgrounds—have much work ahead of them before they can construct a comprehensive matrix of analysis. In her recent collection of essays *Clearing A Path: Theorizing the Past in Native American Studies*, anthropologist (and ethnohistorian) Nancy Shoemaker concludes that the field still remains skeptical about the use of theory. Even though she credits the "New World" concept introduced by James Merrell in *The Indians' New World* and the "Middle Ground" model that Richard White crafted in *The Middle Ground* as having "a tremendous impact on Native, frontier, and borderlands scholarship in the 1990s," she maintains that "theory has not figured prominently in discussions of research, writing, and teaching about the past in American Indian studies." The largely interdisciplinary method of ethnohistory serves primarily as a type of methodology, rather than a theory. In Shoemaker's words, "Most of us prefer not to call it anything at all."[11]

In this brief survey of the recent literature on Native Americans during the American colonial era it is clear that three key issues dominate: the importance of relations among Native American nations themselves and between those nations and the colonial outposts of European nations; the critical need to mainstream Native experiences from the sixteenth through the eighteenth centuries; and the "centrality" rather than the "marginality" of Native peoples throughout this era. The need for change remains daunting. As Daniel Richter reminded us in 2001, "The 'master narrative' of early America remains essentially European focused."[12]

Despite this impressive burst of scholarship, few authors have addressed the issues of Euroamerican schooling for Native Americans. Within this small group, most have directed their attention solely to New England. Foremost among these authors are Richard W. Cogley, *John Eliot's Mission*; Ives Goddard and Kathleen Bragdon, *Native Writing in Massachusetts*; Laura J. Murray, *To Do Good to My Indian Brethren*; Hilary E. Wyss, *Writing Indians*; and several studies not discussed here because they cover a much greater time period. (These include Helen Jaskoski, ed., *Early Native American Writing: New Critical Essays*, which incorporates three essays that focus on the colonial era; David Murray, *Forked Tongues: Speech, Writing and Representation in North American Indian Texts*, a broad-based assessment of American Indian texts heavily based on literary theory; and Bernd C. Peyer, *The Tutor'd Mind: Indian Missionary Writers in Antebellum America*, also more inclusive.[13]) Moving beyond the colonial Northeast, in *Pocahontas's People* Helen C. Rountree intermittently mentions the English attempts to educate the Indians in Virginia in the English modes of learning.

Since the 1980s scholars writing within this subfield of colonial Indian education have aided in our understanding of this world. Expanding on the position taken in *Indian Education in the American Colonies*, these scholars have concentrated on the voices of the Native people who negotiated the cultural encounter between the American Indians and the English. When *Indian Education in the American Colonies* appeared, it offered the first broad synthesis of the education that Euroamericans introduced to American Indians wherever they crafted some form of Christian schooling for Native youth. In this study I juxtaposed voices from different peoples. Hence, the narrative alternated between listening to the Indian voice and recovering the words of outside missionaries and schoolmasters.

Much of the recent scholarship focuses on the Indian voice. None of these authors, however, provide widespread coverage of Indian education within the thirteen colonies, nor do they seize on education as one of the core themes of the cultural exchange. Instead, they have directed their attention almost exclusively toward interpreting the written words of Native people in the seventeenth and eighteenth centuries. In most instances these scholars have tailored their individual interpretations to reflect the theoretical frameworks of their respective disciplines, notably American studies and English. Their assessments have often been driven by the perceived need to contextualize Native words via literary theory, but some of their works rely on the methodologies of ethnology, history, and sometimes ethnohistory. Limiting themselves largely to the narratives of colonial Christian Indians, they assess a variety of documents ranging from Algonquian annotations in the seventeenth-century Massachusett/English Bible and conversion narratives of the Wampanoag or Pawkunnakut people of Martha's Vineyard to the letters, journals, and published works of the Brothertown Algonquians, who lived among the Oneidas in New York. Assessing the value of these Native documents, Hilary Wyss writes, "The narratives of the Christian Indians are a testament to their struggle to find a place for themselves in a colonial system that often seemed to exclude them."[14]

By focusing on the words of indigenous people, these scholars have enlarged our understanding of the tremendous variety of Native voices in the subregions of colonial America. Through the efforts of Goddard and Bragdon, who collected and translated the annotations of Algonquians writing responses in their Massachusett/English bibles, we have gained a remarkable source for these Native Christians who learned to read in the vernacular.[15] Wyss observes, however, that we cannot have access to "'authentic Native communities' because the act of writing and the possibility of recording the authenticity of nonliterate peoples ultimately contradict each other." On the other hand, Bragdon notes that "for many of these 'paraliterate' cultures, there is some evidence to suggest that literacy did not change the nature of native world view, but was rather compartmentalized, as were other non-native imports, and used in specific contexts without 'spilling' over into other conceptual arenas."[16] Still, Wyss reminds us of the significance of this vernacular commentary: when Christian Indians recorded their words in the bibles, they provided "a record of the experience and world view of Native Americans . . . participating in a newly developing culture which threatens to exclude them entirely if they do not accept its terms."[17] Wyss's argument hearkens back to James Merrell's concept of "The Indians' New World." As Merrell suggests, "By the close of the colonial era, native peoples as well as whites and blacks had created new societies, each similar to, yet very different from, its parent culture."[18]

Other scholars writing in this field have interpreted the voices of eighteenth- and nineteenth-century Native intermediaries, those influential individuals who received some Euroamerican schooling and often became multilingual. These included figures such as Hendrick Aupaumut, Mahican Christian leader of the Stockbridge Indian nation of western Massachusetts, whose people eventually settled on Menominee lands in Wisconsin; and Moses Tatamy, Delaware interpreter for Presbyterian missionary David Brainerd and his brother, John Brainerd. Historian William A. Hunter wrote an earlier biographical account of Tatamy's life, but Richard W. Pointer has recently shifted the focus of attention from Brainerd to Tatamy. Pointer constructs a persuasive argument for Tatamy's influence over David Brainerd's life during their two-and-a-half-year relationship. "Once employed, Tatamy soon became indispensable to Brainerd. . . . At the same time, Brainerd never thought of Tatamy as anything but an Indian. . . . Still, the Indian interpreter was a crucial presence for Brainerd. . . . No wonder Brainerd felt comforted by Tatamy. He was living proof that, with God's grace, the ideal could be realized."[19]

In her recent collection of the writings of Joseph Johnson, the Mohegan son-in-law of Native American Presbyterian minister Samson Occom, Laura J. Murray has provided further access to the thoughts of another intermediary who served as a catalyst for the founding of Brothertown, the southern New England Algonquian community formed directly after the American Revolution. Less well known than his illustrious father-in-law, Joseph Johnson played a crucial role among the Indians who attended Moor's Indian Charity School, the mid-eighteenth-century school established by Eleazar Wheelock in Lebanon, Connecticut. Later, the young Mohegan ultimately helped his people by providing a means of escape for the Christianized Natives of this region.[20] Laura J. Murray also published writings of two other figures of this southern New England Algonquian world—Hezekiah Calvin and David Fowler—both of whom lived in Iroquois communities during the 1760s, where they attempted to teach the Iroquois youth some of the subjects and the world view they had absorbed at Wheelock's school. Murray analyzes their writings, assessing their use of "textual resistance" to rebel against Wheelock. She argues that their letters "demonstrate an elaborate combination of deference and defiance," a combination that enabled them to "retain or regain some degree of autonomy from his authority."[21]

These explorations into the lives of Christian Indians have also enlarged our understanding of Samson Occom, the most important figure of the mid to late eighteenth-century southern New England Algonquian world. At the turn of the twenty-first century, Occom has attracted the attention of several scholars. Since the 1980s there have been three short biographies of Occom: an essay I wrote titled "Samson Occom: Mohegan as Spiritual Intermediary"; a chapter by Bernd C. Peyer, "Samson Occom and the Vision of a New England Christian Indian Polity," included in his book *The Tutor'd Mind*; and a second essay by me, "Samson Occom, Mohegan Leader and Cultural Broker."[22] Most scholars of Occom rely on the late nineteenth-century biography of the minister written by W. Deloss Love, but none of them seem aware of the reprint of this book that the University of Syracuse Press published in 2000. I wrote a new introduction for the volume that seeks to evaluate Love's analysis of Occom in the historical context of his generation.[23]

Several other scholars have employed literary theory to interpret Occom's writing. These include David Murray, whose analysis of Occom carries overtones of the complexities that Laura J. Murray finds in the letters of Hezekiah Calvin and David Fowler. In his evaluation Murray concludes that "in dealing with Occom I have tried to show how he actually exploits the ambiguities of his position as civilized Indian in his writing, even if he was less able to do so in his life." In a further reflection on Occom that focuses exclusively on his "Short Narrative of My Life," literary scholar Dana D. Nelson suggests that Occom's autobiographical piece "highlights the psychological complexities that arise out of oppressive economic and social practices." In another analysis of the minister that looks at the writings of the Algonquian emigrants who settled Brothertown, Hilary E. Wyss finds common themes shared by both Occom and Joseph Johnson. Wyss assesses the complexities of their dual identities as Native people who were Christian by faith, arguing that "Johnson and Occom simultaneously celebrate Native identity and reject Anglo-American colonial control by invoking a powerful rhetoric of Native manhood."[24]

Returning to the themes that appeared in the review of recent literature on Native Americans in the colonial era, I would like to address the need to mainstream Native experiences and the centrality of those experiences. The intensive efforts of scholars to interpret specific Native experiences within their encounters with missionaries and schoolmasters, as well as the broader studies of Natives during the colonial era, may have catapulted Native communities and individuals, if not to center stage then at least to the perimeters of center stage. The sheer abundance of writing on American Indians during this era may serve to attract the attention of historians who focus on other aspects of colonial America. If the recent studies contribute to the mainstreaming of American Indian experiences, then they shall have achieved a remarkable breakthrough.

Two classic accounts of the British Empire—*Strangers Within the Realm* and *Empire and Others*—remind us of the persistence of "core" and "periphery" or Natives and "others" in our vocabulary. In *Strangers Within the Realm* Bernard Bailyn and Philip D. Morgan entice us with the promise of a new approach to the Empire, one that is "transnational in spirit, pluralist and multicultural in approach." Yet the tack they intend to replace—the old British imperial history, which encompasses "the center and the margins"—clings in our memory with haunting persistence. Daunton and Halpern propose a link between the historiographies of both sides of the Atlantic, postulating that "British historiography has much to gain from this dialogue. Unlike American historians, who have long dealt with indigenous peoples as a part of their own national history, historians of Britain have been able to avoid including encounters with colonized peoples within their domestic history."[25]

The perception of "center and margins" has enjoyed a healthy lifespan. For this reason, perhaps, it has come under attack by the authors discussed in this survey of colonial scholarship. In his assessment of the relationship between David Brainerd and Tatamy, Richard Pointer turns the argument for "center and margins" on its head. He suggests that historians have viewed Brainerd as the "center" and consequently reduced the Delawares to the "margins." Pointer argues for the opposite: "Delaware men, women and children molded the character of the young missionary." He asserts that the Delawares "were the chief cause of Brainerd's much-noted soul searching. . . . They prompted him to reassess why he was among them and what he could accomplish. They provoked him consciously and unconsciously to wonder about the nature of God and his power. They left him perplexed and perturbed about the workings of native life and thought."[26] In this important revision of the dialogue between Indian and missionary or schoolmaster, the argument for "center and margins" can cut both ways.

In his research on John Eliot's relationship with the Algonquians of Massachusetts, Richard Cogley has reached similar conclusions. Cogley enhances the missionary's reputation, suggesting that "Eliot had a greater respect for the Indians' intelligence than did his contemporaries, and he had a stronger sense of justice than they did." Still, he asserts that Eliot "was transformed by his exposure to the natives: he learned to appreciate their humanity and to sympathize with their problems." In this context Laura J. Murray suggests that the "textual resistance" of Eleazar Wheelock's students caused "great uneasiness" on the part of the minister, giving the students "some degree of autonomy from his authority."[27]

In a similar fashion, in her evaluation of Samson Occom's "Short Narrative," Dana Nelson emphasizes the centrality of Occom's essay to early American literature. In Nelson's view Occom's life had a powerful influence on the "center." Occom's experiences were not "marginal" in colonial America; they remained "*central* to the constitution of life for those in the 'center.'" Contrasting Occom's writings with those of Benjamin Franklin, Nelson argues that the "'Short Narrative' represents the [Native American communal] social fabric that is literarily repressed, and literally oppressed, by Franklin's celebratory individualism."[28]

Recent scholars writing on the Indians who participated in Euroamerican schooling have helped revitalize the literature on the
colonial era. Their imaginative assessment of Native influence on
the cultural frontiers of early America has allowed them to question the power structure of these colliding worlds. They have
shifted our perception of the balance from the controlling power
of the "outsider" to the subtle influence emanating from within
the indigenous cultures. Whenever this relationship appears to
be in balance, the "otherness" that James Axtell describes will
have the double meaning that he intended.

I am pleased that the University of Nebraska Press has agreed
to reprint *Indian Education in the American Colonies*, and I am
especially pleased that the recent scholarship has enlarged upon
the Native voice that appeared in my original edition. As Native
people gain further recognition through careful rereading of the
words they left for us to peruse, the balance of center and periphery may eventually be restored.

NOTES

I would like to thank Shawn G. Wiemann, my invaluable research assistant during the
preparation of this new introduction.

1. Simon J. Ortiz, "A Story of How a Wall Stands," in *Woven Stone* (Tucson: University
of Arizona Press, 1992), 145.

2. Armitage is quoted in Pauline Meier, "Disjunctions in Early American History," *Historically Speaking* 6, no. 4 (March–April 2005): 20. Meier's essay was delivered at a forum sponsored by the National Endowment for the Humanities (NEH), "The State of Early
American History: A Forum," held on April 30, 2004. The Historical Society invited
several "prominent early Americanists" to respond to Meier's essay and published these
responses, in addition to her edited essay and rejoinder, in the above issue of its bulletin,
19-32. On the growing interest in Atlantic history, see Barry Gewen, "Forget the Founding
Fathers," *The New York Times Book Review* 110, no. 23 (June 5, 2005): 32–33.

3. The historians who responded to Meier's essay included Jack Rakove, "An Agenda
for Early American History," *Historically Speaking* 6, no. 4 (March–April 2005): 30; and
Edward G. Gray, "The Promise of Empire," *Historically Speaking* 6, no. 4 (March–April
2005): 23.

4. Gray, "The Promise of Empire," 23; Rakove, "An Agenda for Early American His-
tory," 31; Meier, "Disjunctions in Early American History," 20; Daniel K. Richter, *Facing
East from Indian Country: A Native History of Early America* (Cambridge MA: Harvard
University Press, 2001).

5. See, for example, Daniel K. Richter, *The Ordeal of the Longhouse* (Chapel Hill: University of North Carolina Press, 1992); Robert S. Grumet, ed., *Northeastern Indian Lives*
(Amherst: University of Massachusetts Press, 1996); Daniel R. Mandell, *Indians in Eigh-*

teenth-Century Eastern Massachusetts (Lincoln: University of Nebraska Press, 1996); Ives Goddard and Kathleen Bragdon, Native Writing in Massachusetts, 2 vols., (Philadelphia: American Philosophical Society, 1988); Richard W. Cogley, John Eliot's Mission to the Indians before King Philip's War (Cambridge MA: Harvard University Press, 1999); Hilary E. Wyss, Writing Indians: Literacy, Christianity, and Native Community in Early America (Amherst: University of Massachusetts Press, 2000); Michael Leroy Oberg, Uncas: First of the Mohegans (Ithaca NY: Cornell University Press, 2003); Colin G. Calloway, ed., After King Philip's War: Presence and Persistence in New England (Hanover NH: University Press of New England, 1997); Colin G. Calloway, The Western Abenakis of Vermont, 1600–1800: War, Migration, and the Survival of an Indian People (Norman: University of Oklahoma Press, 1990); Yasuhide Kawashima, Igniting King Philip's War (Lawrence: University Press of Kansas, 2001); Jill Lepore, The Name of War: King Philip's War and American Identity (New York: Knopf, 1998); Laurie Weinstein, Enduring Traditions: The Native Peoples of New England (Westport CT: Bergin and Garvey, 1994); Kathleen J. Bragdon, Native People of Southern New England, 1500–1650 (Norman: University of Oklahoma Press, 1996); Ruth Wallis Herndon, Unwelcome Americans: Living on the Margins in Early New England (Philadelphia: University of Pennsylvania Press, 2001); Ann Marie Plane, Colonial Intimacies: Indian Marriage in Early New England (Ithaca NY: Cornell University Press, 2000); Matthew Dennis, Cultivating a Landscape of Peace: Iroquois-European Encounters in Seventeenth-Century America (Ithaca NY: Cornell University Press, 1993); Jean M. O'Brien, Dispossession by Degrees: Indian Land and Identity in Natick, Massachusetts, 1650–1790 (Cambridge: Cambridge University Press, 1997); Laura J. Murray, ed., To Do Good to My Indian Brethren: The Writings of Joseph Johnson, 1751–1776 (Amherst: University of Massachusetts Press, 1998); Alden T. Vaughan, ed., New England Encounters: Indians and Euroamericans, 1600-1850 (Boston: Northeastern University Press, 1999); Timothy Shannon, Indians and Colonists at the Crossroads of Empire: The Albany Congress of 1754 (Ithaca NY: Cornell University Press, 2000).

6. J. Frederick Fausz, "'An Abundance of Blood Shed on Both Sides': England's First Indian War, 1609–1614," Virginia Magazine of History and Biography 98 (1990): 3–56; Helen C. Rountree, The Powhatan Indians of Virginia (Norman, University of Oklahoma Press, 1989); Helen C. Rountree, Pocahontas' People: The Powhatan Indians of Virginia Through Four Centuries (Norman: University of Oklahoma Press, 1990); Helen C. Rountree and Thomas E. Davidson, Eastern Shore Indians of Virginia and Maryland (Charlottesville: University of Virginia Press, 1997).

7. Martin Daunton and Rick Halpern, Empire and Others: British Encounters with Indigenous Peoples, 1600–1850 (Philadelphia: University of Pennsylvania Press, 1999). Another volume that looks at "The Margins of Britain," Bernard Bailyn and Philip D. Morgan, eds., Strangers Within the Realm: Cultural Margins of the First British Empire (Chapel Hill: University of North Carolina Press, 1991), juxtaposes Native Americans with Scots, Irish, Scots-Irish, and several other groups seen as "marginal with respect to the conquering power." Yet the editors argue that "these peripheral worlds . . . formed core worlds of their own that . . . generated margins even more complex than they themselves had been" (1). Drawing on the theme of his earlier study The Indians' New World, James H. Merrell writes in his chapter on Native Americans, "'The Customs of our Country': Indians and Colonists in Early America," that "learning to survive as a conquered people by combining European and aboriginal ways . . . was the fate in store for every native group" (156). Merrell also includes a section on interactions between Euroamerican missionaries and educators and Native Americans (146–52).

8. Gregory Evans Dowd, A Spirited Resistance: The North American Indian Struggle for Unity, 1745–1815 (Baltimore: The Johns Hopkins University Press), xii, 206n8. Some of the historians Dowd cites include James H. Merrell, The Indians' New World: Cataw-

bas and Their Neighbors from European Contact through the Era of Removal (Chapel Hill: University of North Carolina Press, 1989); Daniel K. Richter and James H. Merrell, eds., *Beyond the Covenant Chain: The Iroquois and Their Neighbors in Indian North America* (Syracuse NY: Syracuse University Press, 1987); and J. Leitch Wright, *Creeks and Seminoles: The Destruction and Regeneration of the Muscogulge People* (Lincoln: University of Nebraska Press, 1986).

9. Karen Ordahl Kupperman, *Indians and English: Facing Off in Early America* (Ithaca NY: Cornell University Press, 2000), ix; James Axtell, *Beyond 1492: Encounters in Colonial North America* (New York: Oxford University Press, 1992), viii, x; James Axtell, *After Columbus: Essays in the Ethnohistory of Colonial North America* (New York: Oxford University Press, 1988).

10. Richard White, *The Middle Ground: Indians, Empires, and Republics in the Great Lakes Region, 1600–1815* (Cambridge: Cambridge University Press, 1991); Kupperman, *Indians and English*; Colin G. Calloway, *The American Revolution in Indian Country: Crisis and Diversity in Native American Communities* (Cambridge: Cambridge University Press, 1995).

11. Nancy Shoemaker, ed., *Clearing A Path: Theorizing the Past in Native American Studies* (New York: Routledge, 2002), viii–x. Citing Linda Tuhuwi Smith, *Decolonizing Methodologies: Research and Indigenous Peoples* (New York: Zed Books, 1999), Shoemaker notes, "The possibility of something called 'indigenous theory' is in the air . . . but it is not clear what shape these discussions will take or what impact they will have."

12. Richter, *Facing East from Indian Country*, 8.

13. Helen Jaskoski, ed., *Early Native American Writing: New Critical Essays* (Cambridge: Cambridge University Press, 1996). See especially chapters 1–3. David Murray, *Forked Tongues: Speech, Writing and Representation in North American Indian Texts* (Bloomington: Indiana University Press, 1991). Samson Occom appears in chapter 4. Bernd C. Peyer, *The Tutor'd Mind: Indian Missionary-Writers in Antebellum America* (Amherst: University of Massachusetts Press, 1997). See chapter 3, "Samson Occom and the Vision of a New England Christian Indian Policy."

14. Wyss, *Writing Indians*, 51.

15. Goddard and Bragdon, *Native Writing in Massachusetts*.

16. Wyss, *Writing Indians*, 10; Kathleen J. Bragdon, "Vernacular Literacy and Massachusett World View, 1650–1750," in *Algonkians of New England: Past and Present*, The Dublin Seminar for New England Folklife, Annual Proceedings, June 29 and 30, 1991, vol. 16 (Boston: Boston University, 1993), 31. Bragdon suggests that seventeenth-century native vernacular literacy in Massachusetts appeared in "two specific contexts," which were "bureaucratic affairs, particularly associated with land sales and exchanges, and the practice of Christianity, both of these accommodations to the unavoidable English presence."

17. Wyss, *Writing Indians*.

18. Merrell, *The Indians' New World*, ix.

19. William A. Hunter, "Moses (Tunda) Tatamy, Delaware Indian Diplomat," in *A Delaware Indian Symposium*, ed. Herbert C. Kraft, 71–88 (Harrisburg: The Pennsylvania Historical and Museum Commission, 1974); Richard W. Pointer, "'Poor Indians' and the 'Poor in Spirit': The Indian Impact on David Brainerd," in Vaughan, *New England Encounters*, 243–44. Pointer argues that the Delaware Indians "were the chief cause of Brainerd's much-noted soul searching. . . . Delaware men, women and children molded the character of the young missionary" (242).

20. Laura J. Murray, *To Do Good To My Indian Brethren*. On Joseph Johnson, also see Peyer, *The Tutor'd Mind*, 101–10.

21. Laura J. Murray, "'Pray Sir, Consider A Little': Rituals of Subordination and Strate-

gies of Resistance in the Letters of Hezekiah Calvin and David Fowler to Eleazar Whee-lock," in Jaskoski, *Early Native American Writing*, 32-33.

22. Margaret Connell Szasz, "Samson Occom: Mohegan as Spiritual Intermediary," in *Between Indian and White Worlds: The Cultural Broker*, ed. Margaret Connell Szasz, 61–78 (Norman: University of Oklahoma Press, 1994; Norman OK: Red River Books, 2001). Citations are to the University of Oklahoma Press edition; Peyer, "Samson Occom and the Vision of a New England Christian Indian Polity," 54–101; and Margaret Connell Szasz, "Samson Occom, Mohegan Leader and Cultural Broker," in *The Human Tradition in American History*, eds. Nancy Rhoden and Ian K. Steele, 237–56 (Wilmington DE: Scholarly Resources, Inc., 1999).

23. W. DeLoss Love, *Samson Occom and the Christian Indians of New England*, (1899; repr., Syracuse NY: Syracuse University Press, 2000), xv–xxxi.

24. David Murray, *Forked Tongues*, 57; Dana D. Nelson, "'If I Speak Like A Fool, But I Am Constrained': Samson Occom's Short Narrative and Economies of the Racial Self," in Jaskoski, *Early Native American Writing*, 61; Wyss, *Writing Indians*, 135.

25. Bailyn and Morgan, *Strangers Within the Realm*, 30; Daunton and Halpern, *Empire and Others*, 1.

26. Pointer, "'Poor Indians' and the 'Poor in Spirit,'" 242.

27. Cogley, *John Eliot's Mission to the Indians before King Philip's War*, 249; Laura J. Murray, "'Pray Sir, Consider A Little,'" 33.

28. Nelson, "'I Speak Like A Fool,'" 62.

CONTENTS

ILLUSTRATIONS

MAPS

ACKNOWLEDGMENTS

The preparation of this monograph has covered the span of about ten years. In the process, I have relied on the assistance of family, friends, colleagues, librarians, and archivists in the United States and England.

First, I would like to express my appreciation to those who have read all or part of the manuscript. These include Ferenc Morton Szasz, James Ronda, Mel Yazawa, Robert A. Trennert, and William Dabney.

In the preliminary stages of research, L. Madison Coombs and Brewton Barry offered encouragement. Throughout the last decade I have received continuing support from Francis Paul Prucha, Robert A. Trennert, Peter Iverson, Lawrence C. Kelly, Richard N. Ellis, L. G. Moses, and Norris Hundley. Neal Salisbury and James Axtell have also provided their able counsel. For many years Dave Warren, Myron Jones, and Martha Yallup have nudged my thinking in new directions. I have appreciated the support of Wilcomb E. Washburn and William T. Hagan. During an academic year at the University of Exeter, England, I found that my colleagues in American and Commonwealth Arts offered new perspectives. I am especially grateful to Mick Gidley, Richard Maltby, and David Horn at the University of Exeter, and Jacqueline Fear at the University of East Anglia.

I have accumulated many debts to librarians and archivists. I would like to thank Kenneth C. Cramer at Special Collections, Baker Library, Dartmouth College, and Harold F. Worthley, director of the Congregational Library in Boston, for their continuing patience and good humor. Their aid made it possible to bridge the vast distances separating New Mexico from the Atlantic coast. I also received able assistance from Frank K. Lorenz, curator of archives and special collections at Hamilton College Library. In addition, Diane Yount, Special Collections librarian at Andover Newton Theological School, Mrs. Velma C. Clifford and Eleanor Kruse at the Congregational Library in Boston, Mr. David W. Riley at the John Rylands University Library of Manchester, England, Louis Charles Willard of the Speer Library, Princeton Theological Seminary, and Janet Halton at the library of the Moravian Church House in London assisted my research.

It would have been impossible to complete this monograph without the superb staff at Zimmerman Library, University of New Mexico. Once again, I acknowledge the remarkable sleuthing skills of Dorothy Wonsmos, who has procured many an elusive volume through her Inter-library Loan office. I would also like to thank librarians Beatrice Hight, Linda K. Lewis, and Jan D. Barnhart. At the University of Exeter library I relied on the skills of David Horn, Heather Eva, and Andrew Lacey. Their efficiency and pleasantness contributed greatly to my esprit. I also would like to acknowledge the secretaries at the Department of History, University of New Mexico, including Mariana Ibanez, Yolanda Martinez, and Pat Devejian. At the University of Exeter, I enjoyed the skills of Vi Palfrey, Patricia Dowse, and Sandi De Solla.

To Penny Katson, I owe a boundless debt of gratitude. As typist, editor, and friend, she has stuck by me through many travails. Her wide-ranging talents have left their impress of excellence.

I am grateful to all those at the University of New Mexico Press who assisted in the publishing of this book.

A special thanks is extended to Jerry Ingram for again doing an original painting to serve as a jacket for one of my books.

To Frank, Eric, Chris, and Maria, my appreciation overflows. Their warmth and their bantering have given me immeasurable support. As Emily Dickinson once wrote:

A little Madness in the Spring
Is wholesome even for the King
But God be with the Clown—
Who ponders this tremendous scene—
This whole experiment of Green—
As if it were his own!

1

INTRODUCTION

In 1975, Francis Jennings jolted the world of American colonial history with the appearance of his book *The Invasion of America: Indians, Colonialism, and the Cant of Conquest*.[1] As James P. Ronda later noted, "Jennings mounted a frontal assault on the myth of the happy Thanksgiving and by so doing, marked the coming of age of a major reinterpretation of Indian and European interaction in early America."[2] The publication of Jennings's *Invasion* provoked extensive debate, thus adding further yeast to the theme that William N. Fenton had introduced in 1957, in *American Indian and White Relations to 1830: Needs and Opportunities for Study*.[3] Now, almost two decades after Fenton's call for further study in the fields of Indian history and Indian–white relations, the first major, dynamic response had appeared, and others soon followed. In searching to achieve that balance between history and ethnology known as ethnohistory, Ronda, James Axtell, Neal Salisbury, Bruce Trigger, and Nancy O. Lurie have reinterpreted colonial North American Indian history and Indian–white relations through an ethnohistorical framework.[4]

For well over a decade, therefore, a small group of scholars have employed the techniques of this mixed discipline.

Once defined by Axtell as "the use of historical and ethnological methods and materials to gain knowledge of the nature and cause of change in a culture defined by ethnological concepts and categories," ethnohistory enables scholars to move beyond traditional methods in providing a balanced assessment of cultures meeting in the arena of contact.[5] The ethnohistorian is not restricted by the inherent moralism of the "civilized–savage" dichotomy, in which "the Indians have been assigned the role of a mere foil, an opposing and distinct element whose only contribution was to stimulate the energy and ingenuity of European dispossessors."[6] In using the tools of ethnology and history, the ethnohistorian subjects both cultures to equally intense scrutiny.

Trigger's *The Children of Aataentsic* and Salisbury's *Manitou and Providence* epitomize the method's potential. In his two-volume study of the Huron, Trigger suggests that ethnohistorical writing should "promote a genuine understanding of the Indians as people." "One can argue," Trigger says, "that the aim of an Indian history should be to make Indians sympathetic figures. Sympathy, however, does not always imply understanding and without a clear understanding of peoples' motives, respect is impossible." Shifting his focus to the other culture, Trigger suggests that "if we are to understand the total situation, we must attempt to achieve a similar dispassionate understanding of the motives of European groups."[7] Salisbury, writing in a similar vein, observes that ethnohistorians have begun "to see both Indians and Europeans as rational human beings and their interactions as a process of contact between societies and cultures."[8]

In 1957, the same year that Fenton's pioneering study appeared, American educational history was startled by the appearance of Bernard Bailyn's essay *Education in the Forming of American Society: Needs and Opportunities for Study*.[9] A reassessment of traditional views on colonial education, this seminal work also encouraged the adoption of a broad interpretation of education. Bailyn, like Fenton, challenged students to adopt a new approach, arguing that education should be seen as "the entire process by which a culture transmits itself across the generations."[10]

A modified form of Bailyn's definition serves as the framework for the interpretation of education provided in chapter 2. This introductory chapter offers an overview of colonial Euroamerican education: concepts, institutions, and methods for rearing children and youth. Following this background chapter, however, my interpretation of education narrows its focus. Thus, chapters 3 through 11 provide a history of specific efforts to school the Indians in the American colonies, experiments ranging from the initial attempts by Virginians to educate Powhatan youth in the early 1600s to the efforts of Indian schoolmasters who taught among the Iroquois during the decade preceding the American Revolution.

Lawrence A. Cremin once suggested that Bailyn's definition of education was simply too "latitudinarian," and in his study *American Education: The Colonial Experience, 1607–1783,* Cremin adopted a modified version of Bailyn's concept.[11] Like Cremin, I too have found Bailyn's definition so broad as to be unwieldy. Had this study included the entire process of cultural transmission, it might have expanded infinitely. Hence, I focus on formal schooling as a single, crucial dimension of the larger process of cultural interaction.

Indian schooling in colonial America was continuously immersed in the constant flux that characterized the exchange between cultures. Where this cultural exchange occurred, it affected all peoples involved—Indian, Afroamerican, and Euroamerican.[12] The exchange was both overt and subtle, and it took place on many levels. It rubbed religion against religion; it was caught up in the ubiquitous traumas of land ownership, disease, alcohol, and warfare, and was often molded by the impact of the fur and hide trade, as well as by the trade in Indian slaves; it was affected by the exchange in food goods and material culture—weapons, utensils, even luxury items; and it altered the role of the family and community, disrupting cultural heritage, attitudes, and values. All of those involved were molded and remolded as they found themselves continually thrust into the cultural arena.

The various dimensions of the exchange also influenced each other. Indian schooling in the southeast, for example, was hindered by the hide and slave trade and virtually destroyed by constant warfare. Indian schooling in the Housatonic Valley was engendered, in part, by the actions of the Dutch and the Iroquois, which served to push a small group of Mahican east to the valley that later attracted the missionary and schooling efforts at Stockbridge. The impetus for Moor's Indian Charity School in the 1750s emanated from the Great Awakening, which had a direct impact on the two pivotal figures of the school—the Rev. Samson

Occom and the Rev. Eleazar Wheelock. In each of these instances, the story of Indian schooling was interwoven with one or more of the other dimensions of cultural interaction.

Colonial Indian schooling took place within the framework of this broad cultural exchange. Indeed, it lay at the cutting edge of cultural interaction in the sixteenth and seventeenth centuries. A number of colonial Euroamericans and Indians deemed Indian schooling as the ultimate tool for achieving cultural change among Indian people. The colonial schoolmasters to the Indians viewed their efforts as honest attempts to change Indian youth, hoping that Indian schooling would redirect the lives of those who held the future of their people in their hands. Schoolmasters reasoned that if these youth could be taught to read and write, to cipher, to comprehend the Bible, and to change their ways accordingly, they might teach their own people to do likewise. It was this elusive goal that attracted figures such as Thomas Mayhew, Jr., Benjamin Ingham, John Brainerd, and Francis LeJau. Thus, from this ethnocentric view, those youth who had the opportunity for schooling held the key for potential change among Indian groups. This contemporary interpretation of Indian schooling suggests that for these Euroamericans, and, indeed, for some of their Indian counterparts, the efforts to school the Indian lay at the core of the cultural exchange. What was achieved, however, was a different matter.

When one concentrates on these seventeenth- and eighteenth-century Indian schooling experiments (as I have done for a decade), the first pattern that emerges is one of tremendous diversity in which there appears to be no common ground. Apparently few links connected seventeenth-century New England, for example, with the turmoil that prevailed in the early Carolinas. In a similar manner, the conditions that dictated the expansion of Indian schools in southern New England during the Great Awakening appear to be completely different from those that dominated early seventeenth-century Virginia. Clearly, tremendous differences separated these varied experiments in educating the Indian. The nature of the Euroamerican, the nature of the Indian, and the conditions in the given colony all led to widespread diversity; and here, Indian schooling shared some parallels with mainstream colonial history. The diversity of the colonies, in terms of ecology, settlement patterns, education, and government, was clearly reflected in this crucial dimension of seventeenth- and eighteenth-century America. One of the most obvious parallels between Indian schooling and colonial history lies in the general availability of schooling for a given region. New England, which is often considered the strongest area of formal schooling in colonial America, also opened the greatest number of Indian schools. By contrast, the region with the fewest number of schools and the highest rate of illiteracy—the Carolinas and Georgia—also witnessed only marginal success in Indian schooling.

Thus, the diversity that characterized the colonies was also a prominent characteristic of colonial efforts to school the Indians. Nonetheless, most colonial Indian schooling experiments shared a heretofore unheralded commonality. In each instance—regardless of whether it occurred in the seventeenth or eighteenth century or in Massachusetts or Georgia—a clear-cut pattern of events led to the formulation of plans for formal Indian education. Whether or not the schools actually materialized is another matter. The plans for their inception, however, followed a common pattern. First, either the colony or a missionary organization established the fundamental principle necessary for Indian schooling: the need to Christianize and civilize the natives. In a colony such as Virginia, this purpose might be incorporated in the charter. Massachusetts Bay also registered its commitment on the colonial seal. In the missionary societies, the goals of Christianization and civilization were synonymous with their founding. The three great Protestant colonial missionary organizations— the Company for Propagation of the Gospel in New England (the New England Company, 1649), the Society for the Propagation of the Gospel in Foreign Parts (the SPG, 1701), and the Society in Scotland for Propagating Christian Knowledge (the SSPCK, 1709)—all figure prominently in efforts to school the Indians. In the second step, one or more Euroamericans, either missionary or pious layman, emerged as the catalyst for the schooling movement. Invariably, this individual bore several personality traits, including a strong sense of self-motivation, perseverance, and financial acumen as well as a certain amount of aggressiveness. His personal direction of the plans was crucial. Notwithstanding all of his efforts, however, he stood a good chance of failing unless one other condition prevailed. The third essential ingredient of the planning stage demanded the involvement of at least one

Indian. When this individual displayed some degree of compe-
tence in the basic tenets of Christianization and civilization, the
success of the project was almost assured. The Indian's skills
provided the exemplary model, which was then advertised by the
missionary/schoolmaster for the express purpose of attaining financial support. Yet even the completion of all of these steps did
not guarantee success. As illustrated in seventeenth-century Virginia and later in the Carolinas, other dimensions of the cultural
exchange could dictate disaster for Indian schooling; but when
Indian schools were established, they tended to follow this se-
quence of events.

The preceding analysis is largely limited to the role of the
Euroamericans involved in Indian schooling. The other side of
the study is much less well known: How did the Indians perceive
the potential for schooling? Indians in the colonial period were
pressured to attend school, and they responded generally in one
of several ways to the educational opportunities offered by Euroamericans. In the first years of the Indian school at the College of
William and Mary, for example, the few students enrolled came
from distant tribes. They had been captured, often by Indians
from other tribes, and were brought to the school as captives. The
initial efforts of John Eliot to establish the praying villages in
Massachusetts Bay involved overt persuasion on his part to enlist
the necessary Algonquians. In addition to pressure, the straitened
circumstances of many Indian parents led them to choose Euroamerican schooling for their children. Widespread economic
changes, compounded by the impact of disease and alcohol,
forced many Indians into increasing poverty, and such conditions
occasionally dictated the necessity of choosing the free board and
room available in a charity school, a solution which offered the
only hope for some families that their children would survive.
Finally, some Indians chose schooling for other, less easily defined reasons. For these people, formal schooling offered a means
by which they could move across cultures, often enabling them to
serve their own people through a wider base of understanding.

These Indians deserve a more prominent role in colonial history, for they became cultural brokers for the colonial world.
However, with the exception of Pocahontas, their tale remains
largely untold. They lived in two worlds. Most made a conscious

decision to become bilingual; others, to become literate; most chose to adopt Christianity (some, like Joseph Brant or Thayendanegea, with more perseverance than others); yet most decided to live permanently among their own people and to serve as a liaison between cultures. Some accomplished this balancing act more successfully than others, and some were more fortunate than others, but almost all of these Indians achieved a degree of dignity and a sense of their own self worth, which was an uncommon feat in a period of staggering change.

It is not surprising, then, that colonial Indian schooling remains a story of individuals. These pages are filled with the lives of men such as Francis Le Jau, David Fowler, Benjamin Ingham, and Cockenoe; and women like Pocahontas, Mary Musgrove, and Hannah Garrett Fowler. The individualization is the result of the limited number of people who took part in the experiments. A handful of missionary/schoolmasters, their supporters in England and the colonies, and their schoolmasters and student counterparts among the Indians themselves stamped these experiments in colonial Indian education with the strength of their singular personalities.

When Native American youth were educated in white schools—whether in colonial, nineteenth-, or twentieth-century America—they brought to those institutions varying degrees of native culture. Formal schooling often served as an overlay for the attitudes and perceptions of the world that they had already acquired within the family and the community. Historically, then, the Indian child came to school with unique cultural traits. Educators, scholars, and students of Indian history cannot fully comprehend the responses of the Indian youth in a formal school environment without an awareness of the native child-rearing practices that preceded the educational process.

The following section focuses on traditional native child rearing in North America, and offers a brief glimpse of native education across the entire continent.

The Iroquois viewed babies on the cradleboard as "barely separated from the spirit world." They said that "an infant's life is as the thinness of a maple leaf."[13] The Omaha shared similar attitudes. Like the Iroquois, when these prairie people made a pair of moccasins for an infant, they cut a small hole in the side of one to insure that

> if a messenger from the spirit world should come and say to the child "I have come for you," the child could answer, "I cannot go on a journey—my moccasins are worn out!"[14]

Moreover, when the relatives of an Omaha infant came to visit, they noted the hole in the moccasin and remarked, " 'Why he (or she) has worn out his moccasins; he has traveled over the earth!' " This was an "indirect prayer" that the child might "live long."

From newborn infants to young men or women on the threshold of adulthood, children held an important position in native American cultures. Their family and community gave them love and care, and reared them in an integrated educational environment designed to develop mature and responsible members of society. All native groups recognized the significance of child-rearing practices. Their children held the promise of their continued identity as a people. In their youth lay the kernel of their future.

Across the continent, native people have demonstrated their "wonderful affection" for their children. In 1639, a Jesuit wrote from Quebec to state that the natives of New France "love their Children above all things." Several decades later, another priest living among the Ottawa noted that these Indians were "passionately fond of their little children."[15] In the eighteenth century, visitors to the Creek villages commented on the parents' love for their children; while Robert Beverly, writing of the Indians of Virginia, observed, "Children are not reckon'd a Charge among them, but rather Riches."[16]

In the late fifteenth and early sixteenth centuries, the various European words for native Americans—los indios, the Indians, les Indiens, die Indianer—referred to a people who existed only in the European imagination. In reality, hundreds of different groups lived in a dozen or so distinct culture areas stretching across the continent. In the Southwest lived bands of Athabaskan-speaking Dinneh (Navajo) and Tinneh (Apache), and villages of Hopi and other horticulturalists. In the Southeast resided villages of Muskogean-speaking peoples and mountaineering bands of Aniyunwiya (Cherokee). In the Columbia River Plateau, bands of Sahaptin-speaking people, ranging from *Pish-wana-pum* and *Pah-qy-ti-koot* (northern and southern divisions of Yakima) to *Nu mi pu* (Nez Perce), lived in the shadows of the Cascades and Northern Rockies. In the northeastern woodlands, Iroquoian-speaking tribes were settled both north and south of the Great Lakes; and Algonquians, such as the Munsee and Unami and the Wampanoag and Narragansett, lived not far from the Atlantic Coast. Each people retained their own identity and their own culture, never identifying themselves as belonging to a broad, generalized group characterized by the misnomer "Indians."

Traditional native American child rearing reflected this diversity of cultures. Several common practices did cut across cultural boundaries, but they are difficult to identify because they were often expressed in forms unique to each group. Thus, it was not until the mid-twentieth century that an effort was made to explore these practices and their variations.

In the mid-1940s, George A. Pettitt, an anthropologist and University of California Ph.D., completed the first comprehensive study of native child rearing, entitled *Primitive Education in North America*.[17] In viewing his subject through the framework of Progressive-era education, Pettitt saw in traditional native American child rearing the concept of community so visibly absent from contemporary American education, and his account offered a modest cure for some of the ills of modern schooling. Like John Collier, the well-known reformer and commissioner of Indian affairs, Pettitt recognized numerous attributes of native child rearing long overlooked by Euroamericans. While his ideas provide much of the basis for this chapter, they caused scarcely a ripple when his monograph appeared in 1946.

Pettitt made some remarkable discoveries. He uncovered the surprising extent of commonality in child-rearing practices among native groups; and more important, as he studied and compared these practices he became convinced that every group had developed a holistic system for rearing its youth. This system relied on tested methods to encourage the growth of mature members of society, an idea that had already been introduced by pioneering ethnologists and others who had studied either specific individual groups or several groups. Thus, because earlier students had admired or at least noted the complexity of native child rearing, Pettitt's major contribution was to synthesize these con-

clusions. Pettitt explored several universal ideas about childhood, recognizing that they differed according to the customs of
the individual group.

In the prehistoric era, most native groups of North America
enjoyed an insularity largely impossible in modern industrial-
ized and urbanized societies, where we no longer live in the
isolated groupings that enabled native peoples to develop separate identities. Perhaps one of the keys to this insularity lay in the
name by which groups identified themselves. The names of many
native societies translate as "the people": Dinneh ("the people"),
Nu mi pu ("real people"), Kanye Keha Ka (Mohawk, "people of
the place of flint"), Yokuts ("the people"), Nunamiut ("inland
people"), Lenni Lenape (Delaware, "original people"), or Aniyunwiya ("real people" or "principal people"). From this perspective,
outsiders were viewed as nonentities. For example, when men
from the Tewa Pueblo Oke-oweenge (San Juan) returned from
their fall buffalo hunt on the southern plains, they subjected
themselves to ritual precautions designed to reintegrate them
fully into the Tewa world. They viewed their hunting sojourn as a
visit "among a people [Plains Indians] whom the Tewa did not
recognize as people."[18]

An Ottawa once described this sense of insularity and autonomy when he wrote that "our way of life was total, nothing was
outside of it, everything was within."[19] The dominance of insularity did not preclude cultural exchange, however. Raiding
and warfare served as one opportunity for the exchange of material goods as well as of some nonmaterial culture. But more important were the trade networks that crisscrossed the continent,
spanning mountain ranges and deserts and including Meso-
America, which for centuries served as a significant source of new
foods, art, and other cultural innovations.

Through these trade networks, individual groups absorbed aspects of other cultures and were influenced by them, but such
exchanges did not detract from their own distinctiveness. By and
large, each group lived in a separate and insular world which
immersed its youth in a homogeneous atmosphere, wherein everyone spoke a common language and shared a common spiritual
outlook, a common past, and a common set of customs. As a
Cherokee noted, life was "integrated and consistent from one

sphere to another."[20] Whether survival rested on an abundance of natural resources, as along Chesapeake Bay, or on a paucity of them, as in the Great Basin, everyone took part in the great challenge, surviving or faltering through the shared wisdom and heritage of the group. Within this group, the child was surrounded by expanding concentric circles of people who cared for him or her. The immediate family assumed basic guidance, but others were equally important, including, within the extended family, grandparents, maternal uncles or paternal aunts, and cousins.

Beyond the family, and depending on the complexity of the society, the child was influenced by clan or lineage groupings, by secret societies, by societal leaders and, finally, by the entire community. As Pettitt noted, "education was not consciously institutionalized." Rather, it was "a community project in which all reputable elders participated at the instigation of individual family."[21]

Every native group required that certain skills be mastered before a youth was accepted as a mature member of society. These requirements generally fell into three areas: economic skills, knowledge of cultural heritage, and spiritual awareness. A Tuscarora described the traditional training of native children as consisting of "three basic courses": "Survival," "Religion," and "Ethics." "They were, of course, interwoven," he added, "and were taught primarily by families, clans and leaders of sub-societies, religious and secular, within the tribe."[22]

Training for survival lay at the core of a child's growing years. Because of the tremendous variations in economic base for native groups, survival training was specifically geared to available resources. A wide gap separated the sedentary horticulturalists of the southwestern deserts from the hunters and gatherers of the subarctic. A sharply defined ecological boundary limited the raising of native maize, beans, and squash to latitudes roughly south of the Great Lakes. This did not mean, however, that all groups living south of this imaginary parallel were horticulturalists. Many natives living in these more temperate latitudes and with access to sufficient water—such as residents of California or of the Columbia River Plateau—failed to cultivate maize, beans, and squash.

Regardless of these basic economic differences, all native children learned at an early age that survival depended upon well-

tested knowledge of skills accompanied by proper attitudes toward the earth and all animate and inanimate life living on it. For
example, a Cree hunter advised:

> The man who earns his subsistence from hunting, who survives, as
> the Indians say, from the land, depends on knowing where he must
> stand in the strangely efficient and mysterious balance that is
> arranged for the propagation of all life. . . . In this scheme of things
> the man is not dominant; he is a mere survivor, like every other
> form of life.[23]

For Abenaki youth, survival training could not begin too early. In
the eighteenth century a Jesuit observed: "No sooner do the boys
begin to walk than they practice drawing the bow; they become so
adroit in this that at the age of ten or twelve years they do not fail
to kill the bird at which they shoot."[24] A counterpart for this
hunter-oriented economy existed in the maize-oriented society of
the Hopi. Here, on farming plots located below their stark mesas,
the Hopi relied on horticultural skills combined with a complex
ceremonial cycle. Hopi ceremonial leaders are still regarded as
possessing extraordinary powers. But not all Hopi figures of
power were ceremonial leaders. Thus, an exceptionally able
farmer, particularly one who had the "ability to manipulate the
natural environment with its correlated supernatural forces,"
might also be called a *pavansino* (a powerful man).[25] The Hopi
also acknowledged the need for combining economic skills with a
proper attitude toward the universe. A dual mastery echoed
among southeastern groups like the Cherokee, who sought to
maintain a harmonious relationship with nature. To sustain this
spiritual harmony, the Cherokee "not only performed daily personal prayers and rituals but also engaged in a series of festivals
and rites closely linked to the agricultural seasons."[26]

Knowledge of cultural heritage marked the second aspect of
childhood learning among the native peoples of North America.
Storytelling was one of the strongest means of imparting the
culture to children. An ancient and universal art, storytelling had
also remained a familiar part of the European heritage until the
late seventeenth century.[27] Cultures without a written language
depended totally on oral tradition. The Indians of New France
astounded a Jesuit priest with their facility to retain obscure
information. Their "tenacious memory," he noted, enables their

"Captains" to recall "a thousand other particulars, which we could not rehearse without writing."[28] Thus, members of the oldest living generation held in memory all that was retained of their people's past, and they bore the responsibilities for transmitting this store of knowledge to the next generation, who then became the teachers.

The Swampy Cree related the story of the porcupine to describe the need to learn of the past in order to inform future generations. In seeking to explain the intentions of the porcupine as he backs into a rock crevice, they note:

> The porcupine consciously goes backward in order to speculate safely on the future, allowing him to look out at his enemy or just the new day.

For the Cree, the art of storytelling was "an instructive act of self-preservation," inviting the listener to " 'go backward, look forward, as the porcupine does.' "[29]

As the transmitter of the cultural heritage, the storyteller wielded a significant influence on native American children. Pablita Velarde, renowned artist of Santa Clara Pueblo, portrays the storyteller of her Tewa people in her illustrated narrative, *Old Father, the Story Teller*. In opening her account with the legend of "The Stars," she writes:

> Many stars made bright holes in the clear, cold autumn sky. In the village place a fire danced and children danced around it. They were happy and excited because Old Father was in the village and would begin tonight to tell them the winter's stories.
>
> "Tell us a story, tell us a story." They loved Old Father and he loved them and understood them. His kindness made a warmth like the fire. He laughed and asked: "What kind of a story?" and a tiny voice came tumbling, "Why are some stars brighter than all the others? And why don't they ever fall where we can find them?"
>
> The children settled around the fire as Old Father gazed up at the stars with a faraway smile. Pointing first toward Orion in the east, he said: That is "long Sash."[30]

Storytelling taught on many levels, with the tales reinforcing cultural ideals learned in more daily and mundane lessons, and moral instruction punctuating the lives of native youth. Huron parents inspired "their children with certain principles of honour . . . by rehearsing to them the famous exploits of their ancestors or countrymen."[31] Kiowa children learned that only those who developed courage, generosity, and kindness could become leaders.[32] Winnebago girls were told: "When you are bringing up children . . . Let them see what love is by observing you give things away to the poor."[33] A Hopi child was taught to listen to the old people, to obey his parents, and to "work hard and treat everyone right."[34] An Arapaho child was instructed to be kind: those without pity for others were told, " 'You have no heart.' "[35] An Omaha youth was advised: " 'If you are lazy, nobody will have pleasure in speaking to you. . . . The energetic man is happy and pleasant to speak with; he is remembered, and visited on his deathbed. But no one mourns for the lazy man.' "[36] These daily reminders of ethical guidelines took on new meanings in the context of a story. Storytellers often masked the moral instruction in the enjoyment of the tales themselves, which, as Victor Barnouw points out "is one of the main reasons, after all, why they are told."[37] In his autobiography *Guests Never Leave Hungry*, James Sewid, a Kwakiutl, recalled winter evenings in the big community house at Village Island. Each family lived in one corner of the house, where they had their own fire and did most of their cooking. But at night they built a fire in the middle, and Sewid remembered that when it was time for sleep,

> we would all sit around the fire and some of the older people would be telling the stories. It was a big open fire and we were all little kids sitting around it. I remember best the stories about Tlisliglia which means little Mink, child of the sun.[38]

For Sewid, and for countless other native children across the continent, the winter evenings of storytelling emerged as a cumulative experience. When those evenings were repeated winter after winter, they cemented the cultural ideals in the minds of the young, a process particularly important for those who were to become the future storytellers.

In almost every group, a certain number of individuals stood out as potential storytellers, medicine men, or ritual leaders. These youth displayed unusually keen memories as well as a strong interest in the significance of these prestigious positions. A clear memory was imperative. As Pablita Velarde notes with regards to storytelling, "small details are likely to carry much meaning."[39] From the training of the universal storytellers to the discipline endured by Hopi ceremonial leaders, Navajo medicine men, holy men of the Teton Sioux, or ritual leaders of the Seneca, the education of these culture bearers was a lifelong process of crucial importance for each group,[40] and childhood training for these individuals marked only the beginning of a long apprenticeship.

The difficult path toward spiritual awareness—yet another facet of learning for native American youth—was not limited to those who were to become shamans, priests, or medicine men. This aspect of childhood permeated all others, and it was as significant a sign of maturity as knowing how to cultivate maize, to scrape and dress skins and to tan them, or to leach acorns properly to rid them of tannic acid. Moreover, it applied to all youth within each group, male and female, the wealthy as well as the poor.

Spiritual awareness provided the matrix for native American groups, pervading their cultures and giving shape to common life. Some groups worshipped a creator or Great Spirit (such as *Kee-shay-lum-moo-kawng* of the Delaware, or *Taiowa* of the Hopi); others saw a single and all powerful supernatural power (such as *Wakan Tanka* of the Teton Sioux); and most acknowledged an awareness of the creative force in all things on earth, which suggests that they did not separate the spiritual and the material, the natural and the supernatural, or the human and the animal. The Omaha expressed this belief in the "interdependence of all forms of life" through the ritual that announced the birth of an infant. On the eighth day after birth, a priest came to the child's dwelling. Standing just outside the door and with his right hand raised to the sky, the priest pleaded to the cosmos for the safety of the child as he traveled a rugged road stretching over four symbolic hills—infancy, youth, manhood, and old age. The supplication concluded:

> Ho! All ye of the heavens, all ye of the
>   air, all ye of the earth
> I bid you all to hear me!
>   Into your life has come a new life.
> Consent ye, consent ye all, I implore!
> Make its path smooth, then shall it travel
>   beyond the four hills![41]

For the Omaha, as well as for other native peoples, the path toward spiritual awareness began early. Youth absorbed spiritual attitudes through family and older members of the group as well as through ritual and ceremony, which provided an important dimension for all native cultures. The intensity of training increased dramatically, however, about the time of puberty.

Puberty symbolized the sharp dividing line between childhood and adulthood. Among the Clackamas Chinook, "children, especially boys, were supposed to mature and be ready at puberty to act in an adult manner." By this stage in life, a Chinook youth was expected to have become "so courageous, skillful, resourceful, and industrious that if necessary he could support himself and live alone."[42] Significant rituals often occurred during puberty, a period when some groups, such as the southeastern Algonquian of the Tidewater, tested their boys to determine which ones should be trained for the priesthood. Others, such as the Pueblo, initiated their youth into secret societies responsible for some aspect of the community's ceremonial life; still others, such as the Delaware, sent them on their guardian spirit quest. While certain groups incorporated both the initiation and spirit quest, most adopted just one of these rituals. As Pettitt suggests, the presence of one tended "to minimize the need for or acceptability of the other."[43]

Training for initiation into a secret society was a group-oriented experience. A Tidewater Algonquian town along Chesapeake Bay might have initiated as many as fifteen young men in the *Huskanawing*, a ceremonial event conducted over several months. The length of initiation varied among the eastern or Rio Grande pueblos. At San Juan, for example, it lasted for four days, while at Taos the boys' training spanned a period of a year and a half. During this time, boys were separated from their homes and lived in the kiva, where they were trained by spiritual leaders.[44]

Preparation for the guardian spirit quest required training over a period of several years prior to the event itself. Among Columbia River Plateau bands, the quest represented the culmination of years of fasting, cold morning baths in nearby streams, food taboos, and less strenuous physical hardships; and when the moment arrived, the Plateau youths were prepared. Like their counterparts among the Puget Sound Indians, they had been trained to endure extensive privation: solitary days of fasting, searching, and waiting. Some authors have stressed the physical discomfort of the quest, but in doing so they fail to observe that this was an integral part of maturing. The goal of the quest was to harden oneself sufficiently to overcome physical discomfort in order to obtain a guardian spirit—whether in the form of an animal or some other living creature—which would aid and guide the youth for the remainder of his or her life. Among the Yakima, the Nez Perce, and the Puget Sound Salish, for example, both boys and girls went on quests. This was the case too among the Ottawa, where fasting was also a prerequisite to a successful vision. The discovery of the spirit was crucial, for it determined the direction of the youth's life. Thus, in certain cultures, a favorable guardian spirit quest was one of the main keys to success.[45]

Spiritual awareness, then, ranked high within the integrated learning patterns for native American children. When E. Adamson Hoebel described the challenges faced by the Cheyenne, he synthesized conditions for many native people.

> The land of the Cheyenne is not a paradise . . . it is a land where people must hold together, or perish; . . . Where the Cheyenne have come to rely not only on technical skill but on mystique and compulsive ritual to bolster their sense of security and give them a faith which will engender courage.[46]

Native youth faced these challenges from early childhood on, and it was their training in economic skills, their absorption of the cultural heritage, and their quest for spiritual awareness that taught them to meet such hardship.

Of equal importance were the ingenious methods used by family and community for rearing children. Beyond the substance of what children learned was the means by which these skills were taught. In native American cultures, these methods generally evolved from the two extremes of discipline and incentive. Although seemingly polarized, in reality these two forces worked harmoniously toward the same goal.

No feature of native American child rearing evoked more criticism than an apparent lack of discipline. In 1657, a Jesuit wrote of the Iroquois: "There is nothing for which these people have a greater horror than restraint. The very children cannot endure it, and live as they please in the houses of their parents, without fear of reprimand or chastisement."[47] In the cultural context of the European or American observer, discipline was often viewed as synonymous with corporal punishment. From this context, therefore, the observer assumed that lack of corporal punishment meant lack of discipline.

What role did discipline play in traditional child rearing? Here again, the tremendous diversity of native cultures clouds the picture. On the one hand, some groups avoided all corporal punishment. Among the Aleut, for example, "corporal punishment with sticks did not exist."[48] Likewise, Delaware children were seldom, if ever, physically punished.[49] Thomas Wildcat Alford recalled that among his people, the Shawnee, "force seldom was used to enforce good conduct."[50] Dan George said of his Salishan people of British Columbia: "it is not among our people to lick a child or scold harshly."[51] A Jesuit observed that the Ottawa are "too indulgent toward their children and know not what it is to punish them."[52] Some tribes, however, did use corporal punishment. When Klallam youth, who lived on the southern shore of the Straits of Juan de Fuca, refused to go on their guardian spirit quest, they were whipped with a digging stick.[53] East of the Cascades, the Sanpoil and Nespelem carried punishment a step further. If one child disobeyed a rule, an old man was brought in to whip not only the offender but all of the children among the several families in the band.[54] "Mischievous or thievish" Chickasaw children "might be scratched on the back with dried snakes' teeth."[55]

The total absence of corporal punishment was, therefore, not an accurate picture. Even the Iroquois resorted to throwing water in the faces of children when it was deemed necessary.[56] But generally, physical punishment for misbehavior was not imposed frequently. The underlying reason for this behavior pattern lay in the attitude that native people displayed toward pain. Because most native cultures idealized the ability to withstand pain, it was logical that they should weave this societal ideal into their patterns for child rearing. Thus, a youth's ability to endure pain and suffering without flinching was almost universally touted as a sign of maturity. Among southeastern Indian groups boys competed with one another to see who could tolerate the most pain: who, for example, could stand the most yellow jacket stings.[57] Native autobiographies and early ethnological field studies are replete with accounts of childhood training in physical endurance. Ales Hrdlicka reported that the Aleuts "had a habit of bathing the children in cold water, or in the sea, at all times of the year, with the object of strengthening their body,"[58] a custom that was common to many groups. William A. Newcomb observed of Delaware children that as they grew older they were more and more "exposed to a toughening program."[59] In similar fashion, the Eskimo trained their youth to be in excellent physical condition so that they were able "to withstand physical discomfort" and "to perform difficult tasks over long periods of time."[60] Nuligak, an Inuit born in the 1890s, recalled one childhood hunting trip when he and his companions "had difficulty in getting back home" because none of them, he recalled, "had had anything to eat since the day before, when we left."[61]

One of the seldom-noted forms of childhood training for endurance was the ubiquitous cradleboard, which was found across the continent, from the Delaware of the northeastern woodlands to the Washoe of California and the Great Basin. "As soon as they are born," a Jesuit observed of Abenaki infants, "they put them on a little piece of board covered with cloth and with a small bearskin, in which they are wrapped, and this is their cradle."[62] The Iroquois' attitude toward infants, noted earlier, suggests a general feeling of apprehension toward very young children, a feeling shared by many native peoples. Infants were often believed to be closely linked to the supernatural world. In Taos Pueblo, if an infant were left alone before it was "old enough to eat," there was concern that a spirit might "come and thereafter the child always 'sees things' "[63] What better place for this fragile being than in a cradleboard: there, it was held securely and could be closely watched.

The cradleboard also provided the infant's introduction to discipline. In societies vulnerable to enemy attack, infants were a liability, and under such conditions the cradleboard was ideal: it could be moved quickly, and it was well suited to teaching the merits of quiet behavior. Groups adapted varying methods to deal with infant crying. When Arapaho children cried, they were "firmly but gently pinched on the nose and mouths, so that their sounds could not give away the village's location to an enemy."[64] When a Cheyenne infant complained, it was taken away from the camp and its cradleboard hung on a bush until it cried itself out.

A few such experiences taught that it was preferable to behave, for the "good baby" was "cuddled and constantly loved."[65] In the 1630s, William Wood praised the behavior of Massachusetts infants. The mothers' "musick," he noted, "is lullabies to quiet their children, who generally are as quiet as if they had neither spleene or lungs."[66] Wood probably was not aware of the training provided by the Massachusetts to produce this remarkable result.

In native cultures, where toughness of body and spirit were esteemed, frequent or excessive corporal punishment would have been contrary to a predominant feature of child rearing. One did not physically abuse a child who was being taught to withstand pain. The alternative, however, was not the apparent absence of total restraint. Instead, native cultures chose to rely on other forms of control, with most, if not all, of them emanating from outside the nuclear family.

Parents in native societies deliberately avoided the unpleasant duties that might lead to conflict with the child "by projecting the blame upon outside agencies."[67] Sometimes a relative assumed this task. Edward Goodbird, a Hidatsa, recalled that his uncle "Flies Low, a clan brother of my father, punished me when I was bad." One evening when Goodbird refused to go to bed, his mother turned to Flies Low and cried, "A patip. Duck him." Goodbird was promptly ducked head first into a bucket of water several times until he promised to obey."[68]

This type of discipline was augmented by an even more powerful form of behavioral control: the use of ridicule. As an incentive for individual reform, no more effective weapon was wielded by the community. If a Blackfeet youth committed an ill-advised act, the incident became the subject of community verbal abuse. Shouted from one tipi at night, the story was picked up and repeated by a chorus of voices until the night reverberated with the sound; and the youth was compelled to remain hidden until he had completed some great feat to erase the memory of his disgrace.[69] In most cases, however, joking cousins, or other relatives identified as "the joking relationship," performed this task of sanctioned societal control.[70] Whether the subject of derisive laughter by one's own sex, or the victim of taunts by the opposite one, the individual took prompt action to remove the focus of derogatory attention. A half-century ago, Clark Wissler concluded that among native Americans "the whole control of the local

group . . . seems to have been exercised by admonition and mild
ridicule instead of by force and punishment."[71]

Ridicule served not only as a means of censure. Like many
forms of behavior sanctioned among native societies, it had a dual
purpose, controlling unacceptable actions while also serving as a
goad toward praiseworthy behavior. Yet another facet of societal
control which profoundly affected children was the use of the
supernatural. In some instances, the impact of the supernatural
overlapped with that of ridicule. For example, masked clowns
among the Hopi, Zuni, and other Pueblos offered sharply aimed
barbs of ridicule that punctuated the festivals in the annual ceremonial cycle of these peoples. But the supernatural played on
still another human emotion very real to children—fear. Again,
like ridicule, threats of supernatural intervention or punishment
served both as a censure of unacceptable behavior and as an
incentive for good behavior.

Reliance on the supernatural as a means of controlling the
behavior of children was universal among native cultures. Frequently, threats called on the power of evil spirits which assumed the form of some animal, bird or reptile. The owl, for
example, was perhaps the most ubiquitous of the bad spirits,
feared in many groups not only by children but by adults as well.
The Choctaw believed that different varieties of owls caused
different kinds of malevolence. Hence, the small screech owl was
viewed as harmful to children because it was seen as a "baby
owl." For the Choctaw, the sound of a screech owl presaged the
death of a child under seven years of age.[72] The grandmother of
the well-known Santee Sioux Charles Alexander Eastman, who
raised him as a young child, also warned of the owl. "It was one
of her legends," Eastman wrote, "that a little boy was once standing outside the tepee . . . crying vigorously for his mother, when
Hinakaga swooped down in the darkness and carried the poor
little fellow up into the trees."[73] Other creatures also reputedly
carried away naughty children, but a more immediate threat appeared in the form of frightening masked beings, such as "living
Solid Face" of the Delaware or the hideous "Spotted Face" of the
Flatheads, both of whom were said to harm disobedient children.

Ridicule, discipline, and use of the supernatural served, then,
as the negative incentives for children to conform. But, as astute
judges of human nature, native people also provided clear-cut

positive incentives that encouraged children to work toward the goals of spiritual, economic and cultural maturity.

Pettitt suggests that native American cultures have been unusually perceptive in their "attention to praise, privilege, and prestige on a community basis, as a reward of achievement for culture pattern ideals."[74] Through these methods, the community offered the child well-defined steps of progress. Each accomplishment was worthy of praise and perhaps also provided some form of reward. Since economic skills were the most visible, so, too, were their rewards. A Yakima boy was given a feast in honor of his first deer; a Wishram girl gave away her first significant gathering of huckleberries to the old women of the community called together for the occasion. "This gave her good luck in picking berries and made her a rapid picker."[75] With maturity came privileges long denied to youth. Among the Blood, a people of the Northern Plains, a proven warrior no longer had to carry wood and water and tend the fire, which were the chores of a boy on his first war party.[76] In many groups, marriage was prohibited until the youth had met certain tests—the killing of the first seal, proven proficiency as a hunter, or the preparation of skins.

Noteworthy accomplishments often signaled the moment to bestow a new name on the youth. Among many native cultures, names played an important role in determining one's direction in life. Names were frequently bestowed at high points in life—at birth, when names were given by special relatives; following a successful war party; after a favorable guardian spirit quest; or following an unusually fortunate escape from danger. Thus, one individual might bear a number of names during a lifetime, as well as many names simultaneously. For some, names were seen as property. Among Puget Sound Indians, for example, each tribe had its own set of names, and within the tribe each family considered the use of certain names its own privilege. Particular clans among the Creek owned war titles, which were assigned to men in recognition of their bravery.[77] A name often held spiritual powers, sometimes acquired as an inheritance, as among the Iroquois, and passed down through generations as an heirloom. A new name was thus both an honor and an incentive.

In every native culture, therefore, the child could look forward to maturity. Although it meant increased responsibilities in all realms—spiritual, economic, and cultural—the child had been trained to understand and to accept these responsibilities as a prerequisite of maturity. Moreover, there were compensations because maturity offered rewards and privileges denied to the young and the untested.

Childhood, then, was to a large degree a time of learning and a time of testing. As the mother of a young Fox girl explained, " 'That is why I treat you like that. . . . No one continues to be taken care of forever. The time soon comes when we lose sight of the one who takes care of us.' "[78] Responsibility for the education of youth was a duty, and the rearing of children was everyone's concern. The lifeblood of the community itself depended on the strength of its future generations, on their ability to bear the burdens of survival, to maintain the traditions, and to uphold the pride of the people. Because children held an integral position in the community, the Euroamerican historic portrayal of them—as undisciplined children of the forest or plains—cannot withstand close scrutiny.

On the other hand, play was an important part of early childhood for native youth. Autobiographies recount numerous descriptions of general play—from winter tobogganing and games of tag and wrestling to foot races, hoop games, ball games, and swimming—as well as play which centered on imitating adult life.[79] For example, a Cheyenne woman recalled:

> In my girlhood days we played what we girls called "tiny play." This play imitated the customs and ways of grownup people. . . . After a time as I became a little older we played what we called "large play." The boys would go out hunting. . . . We girls would pitch our tipis and make ready everything as if it were a real camp life. . . . Some of the boys would go on the warpath, and always came home victorious.[80]

Imitative play, then, served both as recreation and reinforcement for the education of native youth.

The complex structure of native childhood was to be severely tested with the arrival of Europeans, for the greatest inroads upon native culture were made through their youth. For as long as anyone could remember, native child rearing had always met the needs of the people. Through all of the instruction and methods described here briefly, children had learned to become mature adults and responsible members of their own community as well

among the larger community of all natural life. Now these foreigners were to bring a new dimension, claiming that native
children must have further education and must acquire another
view of spiritual awareness. Native children had always learned
by word of mouth, through oral tradition; the whites taught their
children through a written heritage, some of which was sacred
and some not. Native Americans were not blind to the dangers
inherent in this threat, and many of them shrewdly assessed the
potential damage to their integrated childhood learning patterns.
The following chapters explore some of the native responses to
these new conditions during the seventeenth and eighteenth centuries.

Native Groups
of North America

2

EDUCATION FOR THE COLONISTS

In the summer of 1599, William Shakespeare's latest comedy *As You Like It* was performed in the newly opened Globe Theatre. The most vivid character in the play, the melancholy philosopher Jacques, delivered his famous speech, "All the World's a Stage." The often-quoted soliloquy depicts the life of man as a play, "his acts being seven ages." Thus, Shakespeare cast the classic description of the recalcitrant schoolboy:

> Then the whining schoolboy, with his satchel
> And shining morning face, creeping like snail
> Unwilling to school.[1]

If this image of youth was a familiar one for Elizabethan England, it was not as familiar in colonial America. In the colonies, schooling was frequently selective, sometimes haphazard, and often nonexistent. Its substance and character depended not only on the individual colony, but was also determined by density of population, community attitudes toward schooling, and the chronology of events between 1607 and 1783. Even in those instances where schooling achieved some degree of consistency, as in seventeenth-century New England, it still provided only one of several dimensions of a child's training for maturity. Thus, while Shakespeare's "whining schoolboy" did indeed cross the Atlantic, he was not as ubiquitous a member of colonial society as he is sometimes portrayed.[2]

26

While a persistent phenomenon, schools were only one of the educational institutions of colonial America. The early settlers brought with them other and probably more important institutions that reflected their European heritage.

The colonists viewed their world through a religious framework. In an assessment of the milieu of preindustrial England, Peter Laslett observed that "their world was a Christian world and their religious activity was spontaneous."[3] In the seventeenth century, both in Europe and in the colonies, religion was the most pervasive feature of everyday life. It permeated the vocabulary; it emerged as biblical allusion; it dominated calendar appointments, and it even provided useful deadlines for businessmen. A given period might fall "from Easter term [1669] . . . to Easter term [1672]." Payments due were reckoned, for example, in the following manner: "she promeseth to pay the somme of 400 li due for the arrears of rent at Michaelmas"; or a given bill would come due to be "paid at Candlemas."[4]

The minister and church, which had been the dominant force in education in the old world, were also a significant dimension of the cultural inheritance transferred to North America, and in most colonies, though not all, their influence remained pervasive. It was the clerics, Bailyn concludes, "who provided the continuing contacts with the explicit, articulate cultural inheritance."[5] In the communities of seventeenth- and eighteenth-century America, they continued to guide the people through the bewildering changes affecting their lives, and as educators they remained a consistent source of strength.

Despite the importance of church and minister, they were not as significant as the family, the pivotal institution of colonial society. Laslett clarified the English roots of the family in characterizing pre-industrial England as a place where "people came not as individuals but as families," and where "[f]ew persons . . . ever found themselves in groups larger than family groups." In the largely rural population of Tudor and Stuart England, where three-fourths of all people lived in villages, the family was the basic unit of society. "To every farm there was a family," Laslett wrote, "which spread itself over its part of the village lands." Moreover, the home encompassed both the place of living and the place of employment, for one's livelihood, whether husbandry, milling, baking, or textile work, was learned and obtained in the home. Thus, "the whole of life went forward in the family, in a circle of loved, familiar faces."[6]

The family also served as the colonists' basic social and economic unit. Cremin suggests, however, that the colonial family "assumed an educational significance that went considerably beyond its English counterpart."[7] Seventeenth-century colonial families not only had access to fewer institutions than their counterparts in England; they found that they had to bear even greater responsibilities. Thus, the colonial family wore numerous and varied hats.

In many areas, the family served either as a substitute for or as an adjunct to a formal school. In communities where schools had not been established or where settlements were too scattered, the family instituted its own school. J. William Frost notes that the wide dispersion of Quakers in the South and in New England meant that many Quaker children "probably learned to read and write in the home."[8] But even in Puritan New England—where compact towns, legislation mandating schools, and an unequalled motivation for learning led to the highest literacy rate in the colonies—Puritan leaders continued to urge the importance of education in the home.[9] Thus, Cotton Mather admonished parents:

> Learn, O Parents, learn this by the way, that if you Teach your Children the Things that are Good, there is Good hope that they may learn what you Teach them, and if you are Exemplary for any Virtue, it may be hoped that your Children will follow your Example.[10]

In the sixteenth century, the accessibility of the Bible for a growing body of Protestants had provided a tremendous stimulus to reading, and along with increased schooling and several other trends, had raised the level of literacy. Optimists had envisioned the day when "every ploughboy [could] be as well read in the Scriptures as the most learned clerk."[11] By the early seventeenth century a number of devotional works had become popular supplementary reading to the Bible, both in England and in the colonies. Led by the most widely known of these manuals, Lewis Bayly's *The Practise of Piety* (London, 1613), they offered guidelines on how to live a Christian life. In defining piety "as consistently Christian belief and behavior in the day-to-day business of living," these works filled a genuine need for colonial families. The most popular literature for colonial readers proved to be the Bible, the leading pamphlets and almanacs of the eighteenth century, a select number of school texts, and the works devoted to piety.[12] In New England, for example, the Puritans debated biblical interpretation during the interim between sermons, and by the middle of the week they attended evening lectures on similar topics, which were delivered to larger congregations by the minister solely in charge of education.

But the home remained the institution most responsible for teaching children to lead pious lives, and Puritan journals are replete with references to this dimension of family life. Samuel Sewall, a transitional Puritan figure, held this parental duty as a sacred obligation; and when his daughter Elizabeth was eight years of age, Sewall noted in his journal:

> It falls to my daughter Elizabeth's share to read the 24. of Isaiah, which she doth very well, and the Contents of the Chapter and Sympathy with her draw Tears from me also.[13]

The Puritans, however, held no prerogative on the teaching of piety. Quaker parents were counseled to rear their children in a "godly atmosphere," and to demonstrate pious living by exemplary behavior.[14] Philip Fithian, the young Presbyterian tutor to the Robert Carter children in northern Virginia, catechized his charges during their long day in the school room at Nomini Hall.[15]

As the many strands of seventeenth-century Christian thought merged into the growing rationalism of the Enlightenment, the idea of piety also began to undergo transformation. Thus, John Locke's "simple common sense piety," which was based on the application of Christ's teachings, slowly shifted to a secularized piety. Ironically, this eighteenth-century version owed some of its origins to Locke's own reliance on reason, which the influential English philosopher termed "our last judge and guide in everything."[16]

The piety that emerged in the 1700s extended its framework from Christianity and teaching in the home to a wider base for instruction, adding to the core institutions of home and church the innovative schools of the 1700s—academies and colleges, in particular—the press, and the world of public affairs. The once-exclusive domain of family and minister faced many competitors in the preaching and practice of eighteenth-century piety, but in spite of its altered view of the world, the remolded piety of Benjamin Franklin's era retained its Reformation roots. Nor did these roots wither when the plant added new growth. Had they done so, the exemplary Christian piety of the seventeenth century would have become anachronistic, while the family and home would have relinquished one of their vital functions in the education of colonial children.[17]

A corollary to the family's role in the teaching of piety was its mandate to nurture civility. In England, civility included the instruction of young gentry in the formation of character and in those qualities necessary to rule. In the colonies, this translated into the pragmatism adopted by youth who sought to move upwards in the relatively unstructured society of colonial America.[18]

In the eighteenth century, the idea of civility merged into the concept of republicanism, so characteristic of revolutionary America, which was rooted in the faith in an educated populace, as exemplified by Thomas Jefferson. Jefferson's confidence in the people ran as a steady, almost legendary thread throughout his life. In 1787, he wrote from Paris, "I am persuaded myself that the good sense of the people will always be found to be the best army."[19]

As piety was remolded its teachers began to emerge from institutions beyond the family and church, which became the case with civility as well. As republicanism superseded the earlier concept of civility, its instructors appeared in academies and colleges. In the decades preceding the American Revolution, however, perhaps the most influential educators of the populace became the press and the world of politics and public affairs that it analyzed. By 1775 the American colonists had access to thirty-eight weekly newspapers, whose limited circulation proved to be deceptive. Actual circulation bore little relation to the number of people who *learned* the news from one of these gazettes. As Carl Bridenbaugh points out, the post office in every large town served as "the center for all intelligence, domestic and foreign, and wherever and whenever the riders delivered a newspaper some obliging person usually read the contents aloud for all present to hear."[20] In addition, papers tended to reprint any items the editors considered as newsworthy. Hence, *Letters from a Farmer in Pennsylvania to the Inhabitants of the British Colonies*, by the Philadelphia lawyer John Dickinson, were extensively reprinted from their original publication in the *Pennsylvania Chronicle*, and eventually they appeared in almost all of the colonial newspapers as well as in book form.[21]

The combined thrust of the weekly papers and the widely circulated printed sermons and pamphlets offered a broad education in public affairs to mid-eighteenth-century colonists. Fully aware of the impact of the press on his countrymen, Jefferson noted shortly after the revolution that

> were it left to me to decide whether we should have a government without newspapers or newspapers without a government, I should not hesitate a moment to prefer the latter.[22]

Despite the astounding changes ushered in by the eighteenth century, the powerful competitors to the family's hegemony in the education of children did not destroy its role in this arena. In some areas, the family may even have gained strength as the winds of new ideas and revolution swept through the world outside. During this period, the family remained for most Americans what Lawrence Cremin has called "the decisive agency of deliberate cultural transmission."[23]

In bearing the responsibility for teaching children a way of viewing the world and of acting appropriately, the family also served for some as a center of vocational training; thus, throughout much of the colonial period, the family guided the child toward economic maturity.

For the majority of colonists, the economic choice available to their children was restricted to two avenues of opportunity. The minority attended grammar school, while an even smaller percentage of grammar school graduates went on to college.[24] Despite the disproportional influence of these graduates in colonial affairs, they remained only a small percentage of the colonial population.

Most colonial youth followed another path in moving toward their future. Whatever basic schooling they mastered was learned in the home or in the colonial equivalent of an elementary school. By the age of twelve or perhaps fourteen, this far more average colonial youth began or intensified some type of economic training, and in many instances the home served as the primary institution for receiving this experience. In the 1700s, however, other opportunities arose.

By the mid-eighteenth century, settlers had swelled the populations of the colonial towns. In 1776, over 108,000 people lived in the principal cities. By including the secondary towns, one can estimate that 1 of every 16 colonial residents lived in an urban environment.[25] With the exception of Charleston, the coastal cities of Boston, New York, Philadelphia, and Newport were all located north of Maryland. In these coastal commercial centers, where 6 percent of the mid-eighteenth-century colonials lived, circumstances discouraged education in the home. Here, family education was at a disadvantage because it could not compete with the availability of two phenomena: the presence of adequate schools and a thriving industry in trades and crafts.

The leading coastal towns, such as Philadelphia, which boasted some 40,000 residents at the outbreak of the revolution, supported a wide array of artisans and craftsmen, ranging from the ubiquitous cordwainer or shoemaker to Huguenot silversmiths and recently arrived tailors from London. Printers were well established in all of the major towns. As Bridenbaugh has noted, the coastal towns had developed the right conditions: "a large population, sufficient wealth to purchase luxuries as well as necessaries, and an ample supply of materials, and superior tools required for the fabrication of every kind of goods."[26]

Under these circumstances, then, family economic training paled beside the bewildering array of opportunities available to the boy willing to apprentice himself. The young town dweller of the mid-eighteenth century might have become a printer's devil, like the illustrious Dr. Franklin; he might have apprenticed himself to a Newport hatter who sold his Rhode Island "beavers" throughout New England; or he could have learned a specialization of the wood-working trade by signing an apprenticeship with a carpenter or a joiner, a cabinet maker or a coach maker.

For a young woman, the choice, while more sophisticated than that available to her rural counterpart, was far more limited. For most girls, training beyond the confines of the home was restricted to an apprenticeship in another home, a practice that occurred in both the northern and southern colonies. Recently, however, historians have indicated that such training was perhaps less customary than earlier supposed.[27] Edmund Morgan concludes that Puritan daughters could begin their training at an age much younger than boys "because there was little likelihood of their ever following any career but that of a housewife, whether as daughter, housewife, or mother."[28] Other opportunities for women did arise. In the southern colonies, some women operated general stores, while others managed ferries, sometimes in conjunction with taverns.[29] In both the northern and southern colonies, women became midwives; opened "dame schools," where they taught young children; and served as tutors or governesses. And frequently widows managed businesses established by their husbands. When Anne Franklin, the wife of Benjamin's older brother James, was widowed, she supported her family by directing the printing business established by her late husband. For girls, a few avenues were also open through the apprentice route. They might learn millinery work, dressmaking, hair dressing, embroidery, and the making of artificial flowers.[30]

Before turning to the rural counterpart to apprenticeship in the coastal towns, it may prove useful to review the theological overtones that guided career choices for Puritan youth. The Puritans envisioned that one's choice of occupation should be considered as a call from God, and as Morgan notes, the determination of this calling was necessarily "a solemn affair." One's choice of occupation should serve society, for only then could it serve God. The choice must also reaffirm the Puritan belief that when God called one to a certain occupation, God did so by giving that person the "talents and inclination for it."[31] This decision imposed a heavy burden on Puritan youth, and often on their parents as well. The potential for anxiety was illustrated in the difficulties shared by Samuel Sewall, Jr., and his father. The young Sewall finally became a book seller, but not until the failure of several earlier apprenticeships and the accompaniment of much prayer.[32]

Youth in rural New England, like their counterparts in other regions, did not enjoy the opportunities for apprenticeship in specialized arts and crafts available to the youth in coastal cities. While rural New England may have been less isolated than western Pennsylvania and Virginia, its villages remained self-sufficient. In each community, a small group of artisans and craftsmen—blacksmiths, cobblers, carpenters, wheelwrights, and others—served the basic needs of its residents. The independence of these rural folk is exemplified by the Connecticut Valley farmer who bought nothing "to wear, eat or drink," and in a single year purchased only a little over two pounds' worth of salt and nails, which he could not make at home.[33]

In western Pennsylvania and the Shenandoah Valley reaching down into Virginia, thousands of small farmers of German and Scotch-Irish background "raised their wool, cotton, flax, hemp, and hides, and made them into clothing, shoes and harnesses." Moreover, their mines, mills, and forges supplied them with utensils and implements, which the farmers often made themselves.[34] As "Poor Richard" would say, "necessity is the mother of invention."

The greater economic simplicity characterizing these areas translated into more extensive reliance on the home. In rural communities, training for economic maturity fell back upon the family, as it had in Elizabethan England. Sons learned husbandry and a craftsman's skill from their fathers, and daughters learned the mastery of all those skills that would enable them to nourish, clothe, and care for their families when they became wives and mothers.[35] The rural family also clung to its role as educator in piety and civility, for resistance to change throughout the colonial period was more prevalent among those rural Americans comprising over 90 percent of the colonial population.[36]

The changes that led to the rise of these two types of apprenticeship—rural and urban—also affected the availability of schooling for apprentices. In rural communities, families that trained apprentices in the home were expected to accept broad responsibilities for their young charges. They provided not only the essentials of food, lodging, and clothing; they taught rudimentary school subjects and religion as well. In a rural family, where children often learned their letters at home, apprentices merely participated in this informal learning environment, and along with their masters' children, they were taught to read the Bible and to cipher.

Beginning in the 1740s, however, the specialization of crafts and trades in towns discouraged this informality in urban areas. In towns, masters began to see their responsibilities toward their apprentices in more narrow terms. Here, the adaptability of colonial education reasserted itself. When urban apprentices found themselves busy from morning to dark, urban educators responded by introducing the night school. When urban adult workers—servants, journeymen, artisans, or clerks—heard of this opportunity, they also participated by taking classes either for "self improvement" or for "further vocational training."[37] Thus, like much of colonial education, the night school owed its existence and success to new needs and changed circumstances.

Urban apprentice schooling was not the only type of formal instruction that reflected special conditions. The school in colonial America took on many forms, with some areas supporting a number of schools while others relied on alternative means of education. The intrinsic fascination with colonial schooling, therefore, does not lie in its general abundance nor in its universal significance, for in these dimensions it failed to rival either home or church. Rather, colonial schooling offers intriguing insights into the heterogeneous nature of the colonists themselves.

New England town schools, with their horn book and ubiquitous *New England Primer*, probably symbolize education in colonial America. Almost everyone who has read some history can recite the first verse of the *New England Primer*:

> In Adam's Fall
> We sinned all.[38]

The Puritans' reputation as the educators of colonial America is well deserved. Although basic education for children burdened the minds of many colonial parents, the seventeenth-century Puritans surpassed other colonists in their devotion to learning.

There were several reasons for their concern with education. The Puritans viewed education as one of the many steps leading toward salvation. Convinced that Satan, the "Old Deluder," discouraged scripture reading, they deemed salvation impossible without Christian knowledge and understanding.[39] Moreover, the high level of education of settlers who arrived during the Great Migration contributed to the interest in schooling.[40] In addition, because the Puritan way of life required a well-educated ministry, Massachusetts Bay had founded Harvard College by 1636, and in the 1640s it passed its first education laws, which became a model for other seventeenth-century New England colonies.

Perhaps more than any other single homogeneous group in the English colonies, these "chosen people" viewed the land of

America and its "savages" as the antithesis of civilization and Christianity, but this theme reverberated like an echo throughout the colonial period. From Virginia planters to Puritan divines, the fear of barbarism or savagism donned innumerable phantom shapes to haunt these transplanted English.[41]

Although the Puritans viewed their early schools as a foothold for "civilization," the town reading schools, were, at best, rudimentary. The meeting house or private home often served as the first place of instruction. As Walter Herbert Small noted, when the community did build its schoolhouse it often amounted to little more than "a bleak carpenter's box, heated by fireplaces or not heated at all till after 1800." Both teacher and pupils managed "with no light, with no desks for the smaller pupils, with few books, no blackboards, globes, or maps, no lead pencils and in some places no paper, only birch bark."[42]

Classes were in session all year, although the length of the day varied with the season. In the year 1700, the Salem school followed this schedule: from March 1 to November 1, days extended from 7:00 A.M. to 5:00 P.M.; from November 1 to March, shorter daylight hours reduced the session by two hours, from 8:00 A.M. to 4:00 P.M. Vacations, which were minimal, included general election day, Commencement Day and the rest of that week, fasts, Thanksgiving, training days, and Wednesday and Saturday afternoons.[43] Children attended church services on Sunday, both in the morning and in the afternoon, and in the interim they were to meditate quietly at home.

Although the mastery of reading, writing, and ciphering provided the ostensible goal of these town-supported reading or English schools, actual results varied extensively. Reading school probably proved to be relatively easy for children who enjoyed the advantage of an educational environment in the home. Cotton Mather exemplified the concerned parent, formulating numerous educational goals for his own children, not the least of which was mastery of writing:

> As soon as possible I make the Children learn to *write*. And when they can *write*, I employ them in writing out the most agreeable and profitable Things, that I can invent for them. In this way, I propose to freight their minds with *excellent Things*, and have a deep impression made upon their Minds by such Things.[44]

Thus, Mather urged that the art of writing would provide a useful tool for inculcating the omnipresent ideals of piety.

Children who were raised by parents of more modest talents (and more modest egos as well) probably struggled through the rudimentary lessons of their first schools. For many, the reading school provided the extent of their education, but even those with minimal schooling—virtually all women and the majority of men—contributed to the remarkably high literacy rate for New England.[45]

Although the eighteenth-century grammar schools continued to offer a classical curriculum that prepared students for Harvard or Yale (established in 1701), they faced increasing competition from private secondary schools, which were better known as academies. As in England, academies in the colonies varied widely, with some offering classical instruction, like the grammar schools; others patronized their sponsors and the needs of the community they served; many, however, were also boarding schools. Thus "no other institutional form," Cremin concludes in assessing the academy, "so well expressed the fluid, flexible and loosely defined character of the [colonial] educational experience."[46]

As schooling became more diversified in eighteenth-century urban New England, opportunities opened for two groups that had been denied full access to schooling: women and Blacks.

In the seventeenth century, girls were permitted to attend the colonial equivalent of the kindergarten, the "dame school." Generally directed toward children under seven or eight years of age, dame schools were taught by women in their homes, although some received financial aid from the town. Some town or reading schools admitted girls, but most limited their enrollment to boys. Hence, girls seeking further education were forced to rely on individual study. In the eighteenth century, however, secondary schooling became an option, as private academies for girls gained in popularity in larger towns such as Boston. Some of these academies were limited to reading, writing, and ciphering, but others offered embroidery, quilting, flute, and spinet, as well as French.[47]

Schooling for Blacks, who comprised only about 3 percent of the population in New England, was encouraged by Quakers and by prominent Puritans such as John Eliot, the seventeenth-century divine, and Cotton Mather, who opened a short-lived charity school for Indians and Negroes. Anglican missionaries for the Society for the Propagation of the Gospel in Foreign Parts (SPG), founded in 1701, also sought to school the New England Negro.[48]

In the 1700s, New England towns continued to struggle with the responsibilities of their community-supported schools. Financial support for the schools was squeezed out of town budgets, with parents contributing firewood to heat the building. The teacher's reimbursement was another matter. While the rural and frontier sections of colonial America survived with a cashless economy, circumstances in more populated areas were not much better, and a devaluated paper currency circulating in the late seventeenth and eighteenth centuries was so scorned that town school directors found it more convenient to pay teachers in commodities. A schoolmaster's meager salary, therefore, might have been specified as "half in wheat and half in other corn."[49]

The New England schoolmaster wore many hats. While the community weighed the caliber of his substantive instruction, whether in basic skills or classics, it viewed the teaching of piety as his most serious charge. However, as piety merged into denominationalism in the eighteenth century, the correctness of a schoolmaster's theological position became increasingly important to the community that hired him. If a community were fortunate, its schoolmaster would be a graduate of Harvard or Yale. In this case, his college curriculum had prepared him both to teach and to preach. Hence, when the minister was unavailable, the community had no qualms about asking the schoolmaster to deliver the Sunday sermon.

The imprint made by schooling on most of New England was unequalled in other regions. That New England's prominence in this respect was at least partly due to its cultural homogeneity is amply demonstrated by the contrast in the central colonies.

In Pennsylvania, New Jersey, Delaware, and New York, the diverse religious and national origins of the populace discouraged the establishment of a public system of education like the New England town schools. The impetus for schools, therefore, came from the religious or nationalistic groups that settled this region. Reading schools were founded by virtually all of these groups, and by the mid-1700s some of them had also founded secondary schools.

The SPG was very active in the central colonies, particularly in New York and Pennsylvania. In towns such as Philadelphia and New York City, where slavery was more deeply rooted than in rural areas, the SPG opened schools for Negro children. New York City's Negro School was founded in 1705 and continued its program until the revolution; while Anglican clergymen also instructed Negro children throughout the colony of New York.[50] But the SPG probably achieved greater success in its educational endeavors for white children, and through its support of schoolmasters and missionaries its effort spread into almost all of the colonies. In New York, for example, it supported between five and ten English schools throughout much of the eighteenth century. The Society's charity school in New York City enrolled between forty-five and eighty pupils annually in the decades between 1704 and 1776. Between one-fourth and one-half of these pupils enrolled free of tuition, and beginning in 1716, girls formed a consistent minority.[51]

SPG schools offered the equivalent of an English school curriculum. Beginning with reading, nearly all of which was based on the Scriptures, pupils advanced to writing and then to ciphering. One SPG schoolmaster, William Huddleston, reported:

> I teach in the morning reading and writing till 11—then the Bell rings them to prayers, where they daily appear to the great growth of the Church—In the afternoon they spell, read, write, & cipher from 1 to 5, when they read the Psalms for the day, & every [one] answers that can read—then they sing a staff or two of the Psalms they have just read—thus ends the day.[52]

When boys completed this course they were apprenticed, while girls generally received little instruction beyond reading, religious teaching, and needlework.

SPG schools were opened to both dissenters and Anglicans. Other groups were more selective. The Dutch in Anglo-Dutch New York and the Germans—both pietist and Lutheran—in Pennsylvania founded elementary schools for their own children, which served primarily as a defensive means of preserving their own cultural heritage.

The Scotch-Irish brought with them a long tradition of education that traced its roots to the Scottish Reformation and the
establishment of the Presbyterian Church.[53] Because they were a
restless people, whose general uprootedness made it difficult for
them to establish permanent schools, many Scotch-Irish children
were educated in the home or in small schools conducted by their
Presbyterian ministers.[54] The Great Awakening marked a mile-
stone in the history of colonial Presbyterianism, leading to an
even greater interest in education, stimulated in part by the necessity to train an American-born clergy. The revival triggered the
founding of the "Log College" by the Rev. William Tennent, a
Neshaminy, Pennsylvania, school which educated an influential
group of American Presbyterian ministers. The founding of the
College of New Jersey in 1745 marked one of the high points in
Scotch-Irish educational influence; and by 1768, under the guidance of John Witherspoon, the Scottish divine and educator, the
College of New Jersey had become a strong center of influence for
the Scottish Enlightenment.[55] Because it was the only college that
attracted students from throughout the colonies, it became a true
intercolonial institution.

The Scottish Enlightenment also stimulated the turbulent educational changes that occurred in Philadelphia during this period, where the innovative College of Philadelphia was founded
under the influence of the Aberdeen-born educator William
Smith and the ingenious Dr. Franklin. The first secular college in
colonial America, it also became the parent institution for the first
colonial medical school, which was begun by American doctors
who had attended the renowned medical school of the University
of Edinburgh.

The Quakers were equally famous as educators in Pennsylvania
and in the middle colonies. Unlike the Puritans or Presbyterians,
the Quakers did not seek an educated ministry; consequently,
they did not share the anxiety for the establishment of colleges to
train the clergy. But the Friends were determined that their children be schooled in a Quaker environment. As William Frost has
noted, they "fervently believed in Proverbs 22:6, 'Train up a Child
in the way he should go, and when he is old, he will not depart
from it.' "[56] Thus, in Pennsylvania and New Jersey, where they
lived in sufficient numbers, the Friends began their own reading
schools as well as founding one of Philadelphia's earliest second-

ary schools, the famous "Friends Public School," which charged tuition to all but the poor. In the revolutionary period, the openness of Quaker schooling was epitomized by the efforts of the Huguenot-born Anthony Benezet, the most renowned Quaker educator of colonial America. Benezet supported education for all—the wealthy and the dispossessed, the Indians, the Blacks, and women. Between the 1730s and 1780s, he moved from one educational experiment to another, teaching, advising, and offering commitments to popular education.[57]

Benezet's reforms symbolize the unique schooling in the middle colonies, where despite the lack of public schools, religious and ethnic groups shaped an experiment in pluralistic education that was, in some ways, more representative of future American schooling than the town school system of New England could ever be.

Nonetheless, schooling in these central colonies continued to suffer one major drawback. Since all schools were sectarian or private, many youth, especially in rural areas, had no access to formal instruction and were forced to rely exclusively on the home. In the southern colonies, the lack of opportunity for schooling was even more pronounced.

By the time of the revolution the southern colonies of Maryland, Virginia, the Carolinas, and Georgia boasted over half of the population in the entire eastern seaboard. From the perspective of schooling opportunities, however, this population's uniqueness and its environment posed severe limitations.

By 1776, approximately a half-million Blacks lived in the colonies and most of these were southern slaves. Opportunities for schooling for Negro children were restricted to two sources: denominational interest in their education, and owner concern for their welfare as human beings.

Denominational interest was spearheaded by the SPG, which established schools for Negro children throughout the southern colonies. In 1743, the SPG opened the Charleston Negro School. Although the death of its Black teacher forced it to close in 1764, the Charleston School's annual enrollment of fifty to seventy pupils demonstrated that it had clearly filled a need.[58]

From the Great Awakening forward, other denominations, led by the Presbyterians, also joined the cause. Presbyterian efforts were personified by the work of the Rev. Samuel Davies, an influ-

ential New Light minister who served as president of the College
of New Jersey from 1759 until his death in 1761. Davies, a strong
advocate of education, tutored in his home a number of students
who later attended the College of New Jersey and became ministers. Although he did not open a formal school for Negroes in his
county of Hanover, Virginia, he did encourage them to learn to
read and to participate in church services. Whenever shipments
of books requested from England arrived, he distributed them
among Blacks and whites alike. The favorite of the slaves was a
hymnal of Isaac Watts. The Negroes, Davies noted, "above all the
human species I ever knew, have an ear for music, and a kind of
ecstatic delight in Psalmody."[59] Occasionally, a group of slaves
visited Davies and sang away most of the night in his kitchen.
"[S]ometimes," he wrote, "I have awakened about two or three
o'clock in the morning, a torrent of sacred harmony poured into
my chamber, and carried my mind away to Heaven."[60]

Davies urged other ministers to follow his example. He also
advised slave holders to be as concerned about the welfare of their
slaves as that of their own children. In encouraging owners to
provide schooling and religious worship for their slaves, Davies
echoed seventeenth-century admonitions toward families who
trained apprentices in the home, for in each case, parents were
admonished to treat all of those living in their household as
members of their own family.

The rural character of the southern colonies also mitigated
against a uniform school system like that of New England. While
portions of the middle colonies and New England were also rural,
neither of them experienced the wide dispersal of population that
characterized the southern colonies. But, as Richard Beale Davis
concludes, southern colonists shared "from the beginning a persistent desire for schools and colleges, suggested by legislative
acts in every colony, petitions and proposals of organizations and
individuals and bequests and donations."[61]

This desire for schooling in the South took many forms. Small
farmers opened cooperative elementary schools in an effort to
assure some basic learning for their families. Typically, they re-
modeled an old tobacco shed or built a one-room schoolhouse in
a tobacco field "long abandoned to pine and broom-straw" and
centrally located to serve a number of families. Thus, these grass-
roots institutions became known as "old field" schools. Philip

Alexander Bruce has suggested that in seventeenth-century Virginia the greatest percentage of children who were educated received their instruction in an old field school.[62]

Other schools in the southern colonies were funded through individual wills. The endowed free school, which generally was based on this form of charity, emerged early in seventeenth-century Virginia. Two of these Virginia schools—one established by the will of Benjamin Symmmes, and the other by Dr. Thomas Eaton (which later merged)—became quite famous. But the endowed free schools, which existed in every southern colony except Georgia, never educated more than a small number of children.[63]

Denominational schooling also spread throughout the region.[64] Most southern colonies urged the establishment of a school in each Anglican parish. In Maryland, Catholics opened grammar schools, while Protestant denominations from Germany founded reading schools; and the SPG introduced charity schools early in the 1700s. But the greatest educational impact of the denominations followed on the heels of the eighteenth-century revival movement. In the wake of the restless migration of the Scotch-Irish and Germans through Virginia, the Carolinas, and Georgia, the Presbyterians, Moravians, and others opened schools for their own people.

Families who could afford private tuition possessed a wider range of choice. The few communities of any size established grammar schools. In the eighteenth century, a variety of institutions, including several boarding schools, served Charleston. But these urban opportunities reached only a handful of children. Perhaps the most decisive indicator of education in the Carolinas and Georgia was their lack of a college. South of Virginia, youth had no access to a regional college. Shortly before the revolution, the residents of Charleston made an effort to remedy this situation, but before it could attain sufficient momentum the war erupted.[65]

The planter aristocracy enjoyed further choices for their children's schooling. Representative of this highly literate class, William Byrd of Westover read Latin, Greek, and Hebrew; wrote extensively; and accumulated a library of more than 3,600 titles, a total matched only by Cotton Mather.[66] Southern gentlemen such as Byrd were as concerned about the education of their children as the Puritans were. Like the Puritans, they too struggled with the forces of wilderness and "savagery." As Louis Wright has noted, the wealthy planter William Fitzhugh "surrounded himself with the trappings of gentility, but he was continually oppressed by the threat of a barbarizing environment." Writing to a correspondent in London in 1687, Fitzhugh observed, "Good education of children is almost impossible, and better be never born than ill-bred."[67]

Yet southern plantation owners responded very differently from their intellectual counterparts in New England. With no Harvard close at hand, many southern aristocrats chose to send their children to England, the way in which the first William Byrd educated all four of his children. Not even the founding of the College of William and Mary in 1693 deterred these planters from their faith in the superiority of a classical English education. The opening of the College of New Jersey led them to consider the domestic competition to Oxford or Cambridge, but it was not until the mid-eighteenth century that they finally acknowledged the advantages of an American education.[68]

Others accepted a more practical solution by employing a resident tutor, a choice made in accordance with the planters' general emulation of the English aristocracy where tutors were commonly employed. John Locke's experiences as a tutor provided him with the practical basis for his influential essay, Some Thoughts Concerning Education (1693).[69] American tutors taught both daughters and sons of plantation owners. In the eighteenth century, the daughters of these southern gentlemen were also encouraged to master the social accomplishments of music and dancing as well as French.[70] But the privileged class was an exception, for most girls in the southern colonies were offered little opportunity for schooling. Julia Spruill concluded that a "large majority of seventeenth century women in Virginia were totally illiterate," a condition which prevailed throughout the southern colonies.[71]

Access to formal schooling, therefore, varied extensively. It depended upon many circumstances, including location, sex, and ethnic or cultural background. But the basic institutions that educated colonial youth were more democratic, providing to everyone an access to learning. One did not have to attend school to achieve literacy, which was often mastered at home. Nor was it necessary to leave home to learn piety or civility or to acquire the skills for economic maturity. Many colonists were also affected by the educational influence of the church, which, in conjunction with the home, provided support for the family's role as educator. Through the liturgy, the sermon, music, or quiet contemplation, the church offered spiritual sustenance and counsel, and it often provided the cultural reinforcement sought by many colonists.

In colonial America, then, education relied heavily on the basic institutions borne from the old world—the family and the church. These provided the substance for colonial learning, along with the broadening influences that emerged in the eighteenth century and the stimulation of formal schooling. In rural and small-town America, where most settlers lived, these institutions molded the youth in their progress toward maturity, providing economic skills and cultural values for a rapidly changing, heterogeneous society. And from the beginning, a small number of colonists were determined to teach these skills and values to the Indians of the eastern seaboard.

3

VIRGINIA: INDIAN EDUCATION IN THE SEVENTEENTH AND EIGHTEENTH CENTURIES

When the *Susan Constant*, the *Godspeed*, and the *Discovery* limped into Chesapeake Bay on April 26, 1607, the event may have seemed to the contemporary eye as yet another stab at European settlement along this coastline, perhaps another potential Roanoke; but the passage of time would reveal the difference.

The Virginia colonists aboard the ships had come for several reasons, one of which was to spread the gospel among the "heathen." In the First Charter of Virginia, signed on April 10, 1606, James I commended the knights, gentlemen, merchants, and other adventurers for their desire to further "so noble a Work," and urged that the colony devote itself to the "propagating of Christian Religion to such People, as yet live in Darkness and miserable Ignorance of the true Knowledge and Worship of God." James suggested that the colony "may in time bring the Infidels and Savages living in those Parts, to human Civility, and to a settled and quiet Government."[1]

In the spring of 1607, the Virginia colonists knew little about the native people, and what sketchy knowledge they possessed prior to departure had come from the records of the Roanoke colony. From the final years of the sixteenth century to the end of the colonial period, however, visitors and residents of the region compiled an ethnographic account that gradually expanded their knowledge of the Indians of Virginia. Contributing to this cumulative portrait were Thomas Hariot of the Roanoke expedition; Captain John Smith, William Strachey, and others of Jamestown; as well as Robert Beverly in the eighteenth century.[2]

Colonial Virginians of the eighteenth century dealt with Iroquoian and Siouan people who lived west of the fall line in the Piedmont and in the mountainous southwest, the home of the Siouan Manahoac, Monacan, Saponi, Tutelo, Mohetan, and Occaneechi and the Iroquoian Meherrin, Nottoway, and Cherokee.[3] But the detailed accounts of encounters with Indians in the seventeenth century focused on the people of the Tidewater, for they had the most significant impact on early English colonization.

The Algonquian residents of the Tidewater migrated from a region to the north and west of Virginia. Both native tradition and archaeological evidence suggest that they arrived no earlier than three centuries before the founding of Jamestown.[4] For perhaps as many as ten generations the Tidewater Indians had adjusted well to the ecology of their adopted region, with their "aptitude for fishing" enabling them to adapt their economy to the "tidal stretches of coastal plain." English visitors who recorded their impressions of the Virginia Indians or their Carolina coastal counterparts noted their striking physical appearance. They were tall of stature and their skin was noticeably dark. "They are generally of a Coulour browne or rather tawnye," Strachey wrote on his return to England in 1611. Strachey and other observers attributed this skin color to the Indians' habit of applying a type of ointment that altered the skin's natural color and protected it against insects, heat, and cold. "[T]hey are born white," Captain John Smith noted.[5]

English criticism of many aspects of native culture was balanced by a grudging admiration for other characteristics. In the 1500s Thomas Hariot wrote of the Algonquian living near Roanoke:

> In respect of us they are a people poor. . . . Nothwithstanding . . . considering the want of such means as we have, they seeme very ingenious; For although they have no such tooles, nor any such crafts, sciences and artes as wee; yet in those things they doe, they show excellence of wit.[6]

The absence of metal—with the exception of copper, which was highly prized as ornamentation—restricted the development

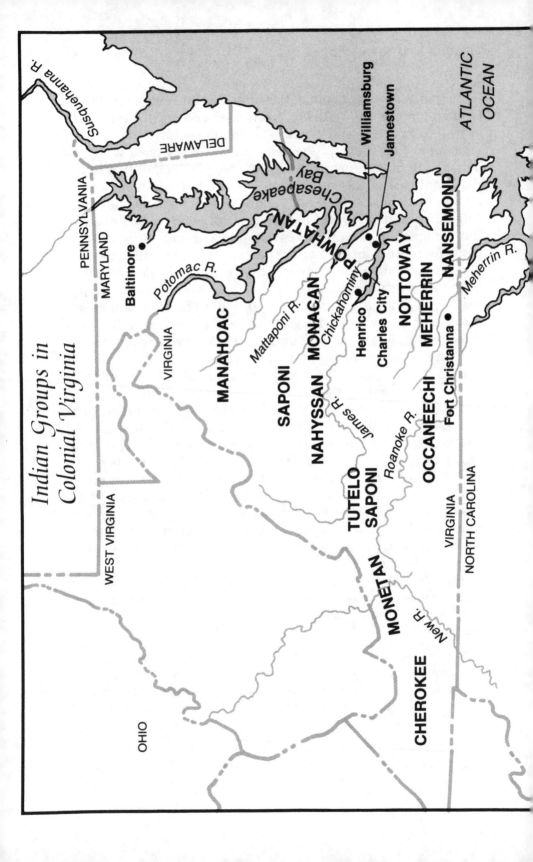

Indian Groups in Colonial Virginia

ATLANTIC OCEAN

Susquehanna R.

DELAWARE

PENNSYLVANIA

MARYLAND

Baltimore

VIRGINIA

Potomac R.

Chesapeake Bay

Williamsburg

Jamestown

POWHATAN

MANAHOAC

Mattaponi R.

SAPONI

MONACAN

NAHYSSAN

Chickahominy

Henrico

Charles City

NOTTOWAY

MEHERRIN

NANSEMOND

Meherrin R.

James R.

OCCANEECHI

Fort Christanna

Roanoke R.

TUTELO SAPONI

WEST VIRGINIA

MONETAN

VIRGINIA

NORTH CAROLINA

OHIO

New R.

CHEROKEE

Chesapeake Bay in the 17th Century

of native tools and weapons; and they quickly perceived the advantages of English hatchets, pots, and other metal items.

Through trade, metal tools could be added to the native technology, and English verbal and written skills could be learned. The greater challenge to the English lay in the attempt to alter attitudes that constituted the core of the native value system. Captain John Smith, who knew them better than perhaps any other early English observer, portrayed them as "inconstant on everie thing, but what feare constraineth them to keepe," adding that they were "[c]raftie, timerous, quicke of apprehension, and very ingenuous. Some are of disposition fearefull, some bold, most cautious, all Savage."[7] At the heart of the cultural conflict lay the issue of religion. Strachey echoed Captain Smith in attacking the Indians' religion; "their chief god they worship is no other indeed than the devill," he noted, "whom they make presentements of and shadow under the forme of an Idoll which they entitle Okeus."[8]

Despite the colonists' failure to understand native religion, the English did admire the Indians' ability to support themselves from the land, an area in which the colonists were clearly outwitted by their native counterparts. The Tidewater Algonquians relied on a mixed economy, balancing horticulture with fishing, hunting, and gathering. The mainstay crop was corn, which they knew by the name "Poketawes." Planted in three successive crops—in April, May, and June—its abundance was "one of the mervels of the New World."[9] Without a supply of Poketawes and other native crops, residents of early Jamestown probably would have starved.

Tidewater Indians were excellent fishermen, hunters, and gatherers. The English also admired the natives' knowledge of medicinal herbs. Captain Smith noted that "by their continuall ranging, and travel, they know all the advantages and places most frequented with Deare, Beasts, Fish, Foule, Rootes, and Berries."[10]

Employing nets, weirs, arrows tied with thread, and bone fish hooks, the Indians harvested sturgeon and herring as well as shell fish. "In March and April," Captain Smith noted, "they live much upon their fishing, Weares, and feed on fish, Turkies and squirrels." Almost three hundred years later ethnologist James Mooney observed of the Pamunkey, the modern descendants of the nucleus tribe of the Powhatan confederacy: "[t]hey derive their living almost entirely from the water, taking large quantities of herring and shad, according to the season, with duck, reed birds, and an occasional sturgeon." Theodore Stern stated that the Virginia natives formed such an intimate "adjustment to the Tidewater plains that their culture may be termed fluviatile."[11] Stern noted the persistence of the Chickahominy horticultural skills. "For the majority of the older men," he observed, "farming still makes up an important part of their activities." The Chickahominy, who resided in their own communities shortly after World War II, relied on the same communal ties that bound their ancestors. During the intervening centuries they had maintained a "persistent emphasis" on "kinship as an aligning and cohesive principle."[12]

Despite the abundance of contemporary accounts of these native peoples, the English observers recorded little on child rearing. Nonetheless, disjointed scraps of information yield an incomplete picture of native youth. The importance of kinship ties for these stable riverside communities suggests that adults relied on the extended family and the community as educators. Observers noted the widespread use of the cradleboard and the bathing of youth in cold water from infancy to maturity. From the evidence of such customs we can infer that the young were taught both endurance and a tolerance of pain. Indeed, Strachey said of the women: "[yet doe they love Children very dearely:] to make the Children hardeye, in the coldest morning they wash them in the Rivers."[13]

The clear-cut division of labor between the sexes meant that training for economic maturity—fishing and hunting for boys; and for the girls horticulture and household tasks, such as cooking, the preparation of skin or feather garments, or the making of mats, baskets, or pots—was a crucial aspect of education. One anonymous observer reported that Indian women "call the English men fools, in working themselves and keeping their wives idle."[14] Strachey described a method for the training of future hunters, whereby a boy's mother denied him his breakfast until his arrow had "hit a marke" that she had thrown into the "ayre."[15] Initiation for young men at the age of puberty was also the process by which future priests were selected. Hence, training in the spiritual dimension of life also served as an important aspect of education. The significance of names played a dynamic role, suggesting that these people recognized the need of using incentives for encouraging maturity. When boys were "able to travaile into the woods and to goe forth a hunting Fowling and Fishing, with their fathers," Strachey wrote, "their father gives him another name, as he fyndes him apt and of spirit, to prove toward and valiant." If a boy performed an unusual deed of bravery, the ruler or "weroance" awarded him with a "Present of Copper, or Chayne of Perle" and gave him a name "answerable to the attempt."[16]

Shortly before Jamestown was founded, the political life of these Tidewater people was altered through the meteoric rise to power of a local weroance ("he is rich") or king, as contemporary English understood the term.[17] Born in the 1540s as Wa-hun-son-a-cock, this weroance inherited at maturity the chieftaincy of his own town as well as that of five other villages. By 1607, through well-executed warfare and carefully chosen leadership, he had expanded this power base to include some twenty-eight tribes. In the meantime, he had become Momanatowick, or supreme chieftain, taking for himself the name of his own town Powhatan. When the English arrived, Powhatan controlled much of Tidewater Virginia. Captain Smith estimated that some 5,000 Indians, including 1,500 warriors, lived within sixty miles of Jamestown.[18] Three centuries later, James Mooney concluded that about 9,000 Algonquians lived in the Virginia Tidewater at the time of contact. Recent scholarship suggests that the total number of Virginia Algonquian may have been 14,000 to 21,000, while Powhatan's empire has been estimated at 12,000 people.[19]

Initial native–European point of contact, however, long predated the establishment of the Jamestown colony. Europeans had made their presence known to other coastal Algonquian at least eight decades before Jamestown. Indeed, prophecies bore testimony to the influence of this earlier contact, for according to Strachey, Powhatan's priests had warned him "that from the Chesapeake Bay a Nation should arise, which should dissolve and give end to his Empire." A second prophecy forecast that twice the Powhatan confederacy "should overthrowe and dishearten the Attempts . . . but the third tyme they themselves should fall into their Subjection and under their Conquest."[20]

With the exception of the Roanoke colony, most sixteenth-century contacts between these natives and the Europeans involved either Spaniards or Italians. Giovanni de Verrazano and Estevan Gómez paused here briefly in the 1520s; Sebastian Cabot may have sailed by in the 1590s. Throughout the remainder of the century, Spanish slave raiders from the West Indies anchored along the southern Atlantic coast. The best-known Hispanic–Indian episode, involving Don Luis de Velasco and the short-lived Jesuit mission, occurred between 1561 and 1571.[21] In 1607, therefore, the Powhatan confederacy demonstrated a wariness toward Europeans based on decades of experience. As Mooney once noted, "[T]he Jamestown colonists landed among a people who already knew and hated the whites."[22]

Thus, the naive Englishmen stumbled into a potential hornet's nest. Following Captain John Smith's shrewd dealings with the Algonquian people, relations between native and colonist degenerated, and from 1609 forward the two sides were at war. Not until the marriage between John Rolfe and Powhatan's favorite daughter Pocahontas, and a further strong attack by the English, did Powhatan accept a peace treaty in 1614.

The colonists' ethnocentrism made it impossible for them to compare their civilization to that of the native Virginians. Beyond the natives' ability to survive, their culture had little to recommend it in the eyes of the colonists. Roy Harvey Pearce states that "in Virginia, reasoning went: For giving God and civilization to the Indian, the colonial Englishman was to receive the riches of a new world,"[23] and to the Englishman this exchange seemed fair. Wesley Frank Craven has concluded that the English in seventeenth-century Virginia "had no solution for an accommodation of the two peoples that did not depend upon an assumption that the Indian in time would adapt to a European pattern of life."[24]

In early Stuart England, Christianization and civilization (or civility) were mutually interdependent,[25] and when these concepts were applied to the Indians they often came under the general rubric of "education." Throughout the early years of the Virginia colony, its official promoters in England urged that Indian youth be educated. Two years after Jamestown was founded, the Virginia company drafted a set of instructions to carry out the lofty principles set forth in the first charter. Sir Thomas Gates's relief expedition, sent to the starving colony in 1609, carried specific orders relating to education. Gates was instructed to "procure from them some convenient number of their Children to be brought up in your language and your manners," and in order to ensure the conversion of the natives, which remained "the most pious and noble end of this plantation," Gates was authorized to imprison the native priests. As long as the priests remained in a position "to poyson and infecte" the minds of the Indians, the Virginia Council believed that the colony could "never make any greater progress into this glorious work."[26]

The following spring, the Virginia Council repeated these orders in the instructions given to Lord De la Warr, whose arrival in June of 1610 cut short the exodus of the entire colony. Like Gates, De la Warr was authorized to imprison native priests, but his orders also provided for another option. "[I]n case they [the imprisoned priests] shall be willfull and obstinate," he was "to send over some three or foure of them into England we may endevour theire conversion here."[27]

The plan for educating Indian children in English homes was repeated in published tracts and official correspondence.[28] As late as 1619, Governor George Yeardley received instructions to "procure their [Indian] children in good multitude to be brought upp and to worke amongst us."[29] The directives given to Yeardley coincided with instructions about the establishment of the Indian college at Henrico. Therefore, while the half-decade between 1617 and 1622 witnessed the effort to establish formal schooling for Algonquians, sentiment in England continued to favor the rearing of Algonquian children in English homes, an informal method of conversion and civility.

From 1607 to 1622 and, to a lesser degree, throughout the rest of the century, policymakers in England pressed for Indian education in Virginia. The response within the colony itself was etched less clearly, for the colonists' reactions to the Indians varied. A number of colonists fled the English villages to settle with the Indians, by whom they were generally well treated. Others were deliberately placed among the Indians to learn the native languages and to become cross-cultural emissaries.[30]

A series of unwise decisions in these early years—including poor organization and direction, a collective labor system, the selection of colonists ill-prepared for the rigorous life, and particularly, the grievous lack of yeoman farmers and of women—precipitated the traumas of the Virginia colony.[31] Even the choice of site contributed heavily to the debilitating drain of disease and mortality. Strachey described Jamestown's location as "in some what an inwholesome and sickly ayre, by reason it is in a marish ground, low, flat to the River, and hath no fresh water springs, but what were drewe from a well . . . , fed by the brackish River oozing into it."[32] In writing of early Virginia, Edward Eggleston concluded: "Those who shaped the destinies of the colony had left little undone that inventive stupidity could suggest to assure the failure of the enterprise."[33] Edmund Morgan also suggests that the colonists themselves were partly to blame. They persisted, he says, in spending their leisure hours in "bowling in the streets," at least until John Rolfe's experiment with tobacco gave them some incentive to plant a crop.[34] The combination of these internal problems and the ongoing warfare with Powhatan's people suggests that in the early years the colonists probably did not have much time to devote to rearing Indian children in their homes.

Indian response to the educational policy was generally negative. During the decades of Powhatan's control, the growing stability provided by a "well-ordered and impressively complex system of government" had enabled the Algonquians to develop their institutions and to cultivate their arts and crafts. They were satisfied with their culture, and like the English, they saw little to emulate in the institutions, customs, and beliefs of their counterparts. Nancy Oestreich Lurie has suggested that "the degree of ethnocentrism was probably equal on both sides of the contact between Indians and Europeans in Virginia."[35]

The heritage of sixteenth-century contact with Europeans provided the Indians with further justification in assuming a cautious stance toward the English. With the exception of Captains Smith and Samuel Argall, very few Englishmen understood how to negotiate with the Indians, particularly with Powhatan himself. Strachey described Powhatan as an "able salvage . . . of a daring spirit, vigilant, ambitious, subtle to enlarge his dominions." Captain Smith, who knew Powhatan far better, said of his leadership, "What he commandeth they dare not disobey in the least thing." "It is strange to see," Smith mused, "with what great feare and adoration all the people doe obey this *Powhatan*."[36] How did Powhatan view the new situation created by the English settlement? Considering his position as an empire builder, it is likely that he tentatively cast the English in the role of a new ally that might assist him in expanding the confederacy.[37] To ensure the friendship of the English, he permitted Pocahontas, his favorite daughter, to marry the Englishman John Rolfe. Simultaneously, however, he feared the potential of the English to fulfill the prophecy that forecast the defeat of his people. Therefore, Powhatan practiced caution, and in the long run these Algonquian viewed the English as intruders. The longer the English remained, the more they disturbed the cultural florescence of the Powhatan confederacy. Indeed, the florescence may have stiffened their resistance to foreign education. Why should foreigners rear their children when they were so successful themselves?

For the Powhatan Algonquian, then, none of the arguments for foreign education of their youth convinced the parents that they should part with their children. Captain Smith and Strachey noted of the women: "Yet doe they love Children very dearly,"[38] and some years later, after more than two years of residence in Virginia, Governor George Yeardley wrote "The Spirituall vine you speak of will not so sodaynly be planted as it may be desired, the Indians being very loathe upon any tearmes to part with theire children." In view of this observation, Yeardley concluded that the "best course" would be to move entire Indian families to settle among the English.[39]

Governor Yeardley's three-year term of office, from 1619 to 1621, witnessed a general relaxation of the customary policy of vigilance toward the Indians. The ease with which the Indians then began to move among the English probably would have been viewed by Captain Smith, or by like-minded leaders such as Argall and Sir Thomas Dale, as an invitation to disaster.

During his first year as governor, Yeardley concluded two negotiations on Indian education with his Algonquian counterpart, Opechancanough, who had succeeded his half-brother when Powhatan died in 1618. The first agreement stipulated that Opechancanough would select the Indian families who would live within each corporation in the colony. The governor suggested that this plan would provide "the opportunity to Instructe theire Children and theire parents living amongst us."[40]

The second agreement dealt with the division of the spoils of battle. Yeardley was to provide Opechancanough with eight or ten men who would assist in an expedition of revenge against another group of Indians (evidently non-Algonquian). In a surge of generosity, Opechancanough even offered to furnish the English soldiers with "Indian shooes to march and to carry thire Armor for them." In exchange, the English would "share all the booty of male and female Children: of Corne and other things and to devide the Conquered land into two equall parts betweene us and them."[41]

Yeardley reported that the governor's council welcomed this proposal. As far as children captives were concerned, the council envisioned for them two potential roles. Some might serve "for privatt uses of pitular psons," which probably meant they would be made either slaves or servants; while others might "furnish ye intended Collidge this beinge a fayer opptunitye for the Advancement of this blessed worke seinge those Indians are in noe sort willing to sell or by fayer meanes to part with their children."[42]

There is little evidence to indicate that either agreement was carried out. Over two years later, when Opechancanough again agreed to an exchange of families, it seems that neither exchange had occurred yet. In any case, if some Algonquian families had settled among the colonists, the educational impact of the experiment must have been marginal.[43] Colonists usually recorded every thread of progress in education, which they directed toward the ears of potential supporters in England; but such correspondence from Virginia colonists has not survived.

One contemporary voice jars with the generally held opinion that Indian parents were unwilling to part with their children. In 1617, John Rolfe wrote to Sir Edwin Sandys, an influential member of the Virginia Company, regarding the state of the colony as Rolfe viewed it upon returning from England. Remarkably optimistic, the letter was so favorable in its description that it is hardly credible. Even Sandys may have been dubious about Rolfe's characterization of "[t]he Indyans" as "very loving, and willing to parte wth their children."[44] Rolfe, however, was writing from his own perspective; and as the widower of Pocahontas, who had died only three months earlier, and the father of a son who was half-Algonquian, he may have been given special consideration by the Indians. They may even have told him that they would be willing to send a child to him. After all, he had been married to a woman who had served as a living bridge between the two cultures.

It has been suggested that Pocahontas was directly responsible

for the movement that led to the proposal for Henrico College.[45]
To the degree that she served as a symbol for the potential Christianization and civilization of all of the Indians in Virginia, that
may well be true. In popular history, Pocahontas's fame rests on
the 1607 incident in which she reputedly saved the life of Captain
John Smith, as well as on her 1614 marriage to Rolfe. For the
contemporary Englishman of the early seventeenth century, however, Pocahontas represented a baffling, yet intriguing mixture of
"savagism" and civilities.

At the same time, she was a goad to the Christian conscience.
Had Pocahontas not visited England, it is possible that the propo-
sal for the Indian college at Henrico would have failed. Although
James I had initiated monetary collections through the Church of
England for "the erecting of some Churches and Schools, for the
education of the children of those Barbarians,'" the goal for the
collections remained vague by the time of Pocahontas's arrival in
London over a year later.[46]

The question that has intrigued historians is how to gauge the
impact of her ten-month visit to London. Between June 1616 and
March 1617, Pocahontas (dubbed "Lady Rebecca"), John Rolfe,
and their son Thomas, born in 1614, along with several Algonquian children sent to England to be educated, lived in the grimy
and overcrowded capital of the British Empire. As a converted
princess and daughter of a foreign emperor, Pocahontas attracted
a great deal of attention. During that winter, Simon van de Passe, a
young Dutch engraver, captured the only likeness of her.[47] Ben
Jonson took the opportunity to visit her, and her old friend Captain Smith paid her a call. Of her life in London, Smith wrote
later:

> divers Courtiers and others, my acquaintances, hath gone with mee
> to see her . . . and they have seene many *English* Ladies worse
> favoured, proportioned, and behavioured, and since I have heard,
> it pleased both the King and Queenes Majestie honourably to
> esteeme her, accompanied with . . . diverse other persons of good
> qualities, both publikely at the maskes and otherwise, to her great
> satisfaction and content.[48]

Pocahontas's presence served as a visible reminder of the noble
work in Virginia demanding attention. When she boarded the
ship to return to Virginia early in the following spring, London

and its courtiers and royalty might have forgotten the visiting princess had they not been startled by the sudden announcement of her death. Mortally ill aboard ship, Pocahontas was carried ashore to die at Gravesend, where she was buried on March 21, 1617. Less than a week later, on March 24, James sent another letter on the subject of Indian education to the archbishops. This letter provided for additional collections for the "education of ye children of those Barbarians," with the king asking "our people within their severall charges to contribute to so good a Worke in as liberall a manner as they may."[49]

Did the death of the remarkable Pocahontas smite the conscience of the king? If so, it may have also encouraged the process by which education in Virginia came to be translated into specific institutions. From this date forward until 1624, when the charter of the Virginia Company was revoked and Virginia became a royal colony, the English royalty, the pious gentry and merchants, the Virginia Company, and eventually the colonial government itself all supported the establishment of two institutions for Indian education: Henrico College and the East India School.

The story of this initial experiment in Indian schooling in the American colonies contains the classic features of colonial ventures in Indian education. All of the later experiments repeated a modified pattern of the characteristics of these early schools. In each instance, the given colony or religious group working within the colony established a policy to encourage Christianity and civilization among the native people. In Virginia, for example, the charter of 1606 incorporated these contemporary ideals, with two types of catalysts setting the experiment in motion: missionaries and/or pious laymen. These dedicated individuals progressed toward their goal through the successes of one or several "exemplary" Indians, whose conversion and educational achievement demonstrated the potential for the project.

In Virginia, missionaries or pious laymen played a secondary role. As the impetus for Indian schools in Virginia began to develop following Pocahontas's death, the only local minister who might have led the campaign within the colony also died. In 1617, Reverend Alexander Whitaker, who had lived in Virginia for five years, was drowned.

Captain George Thorpe was Virginia's equivalent to the pious layman concerned with Indian education. Thorpe's connection with Henrico College, however, came only after plans for the institution were well under way. In 1619, Virginia's first representative legislature, the General Assembly, endorsed the establishment of educational institutions in the colony. A year later, Thorpe was appointed deputy for the Indian college at Henrico.

Thorpe quickly acquired the reputation of being sympathetic toward the Indians. In defending his position, in 1621, he wrote to Sir Edwin Sandys that "if there bee wronge on any side [,] it is on ors who are not soe charitable to them as Christians ought to bee, they beinge, of a peaceable & vertuous disposition."[50] Thorpe's unusual attitude sharply contrasted with the views of men such as Captain Smith. Even in 1621 most Virginians derided any effort to educate Indian youth; but the deputy for the Indian college remained undaunted by such criticism, continuing to work toward the establishment of Henrico College until his death during the Indian uprising of 1622.

Wesley Frank Craven has suggested that Thorpe was a "worthy forerunner of Father Andrew White, John Eliot, and Eleazar Wheelock," all colonial educators of native peoples. J. Frederick Fausz put it in different terms: in his assessment, Thorpe "set out to undermine Powhatan religion and traditions and to alienate Indian youths from their elders by promoting English customs and Christianity among them."[51] While this interpretation put Thorpe in the same camp as White, Eliot, and Wheelock, it also thrust him into the role of a symbol for English culture, a fatal position on the eve of an anti-English uprising.

In this initial schooling experiment, as in later experiments in Virginia and elsewhere, the response to these two types of catalysts—missionary laymen and prominent Indians—emerged in the form of donations derived almost exclusively from European sources. When the corporation of Henrico College was formed in 1619, it received an amazing number of gifts sent by private sources. Often donated anonymously, these gifts ranged from a silver communion set to maps and several sets of books.[52] By 1620, the bishop's collection formally requested by James I had accumulated over two thousand pounds.[53]

The second educational institution planned for Virginia Indians, the East India School, a proposed feeder school for the college, also relied on donations. The East India School owed its name to the unusual circumstances of its birth, which occurred during a three-year voyage of a fleet of East Indian ships. On the return trip from Japan to England in 1621, the Rev. Patrick Copeland, chaplain of one of the ships, and Sir Thomas Dale, who had built the town of Henrico during the first year of his five-year military rule of Virginia, persuaded the passengers and crew to contribute to a charitable fund for the colony. This contribution provided the financial nucleus for what was envisioned as a public free school, to be located at Charles City. As a reward for his success in soliciting funds for the proposed East India School, the Virginia Company honored Copeland by appointing him rector of the proposed Henrico College.[54]

The Virginia Company suffered severe financial difficulties during its seventeen years of direction. Due to mismanagement, the company remained perpetually short on cash. Hence, its ingenious solution for economic support for Henrico College reflected the needs of its precarious financial situation. In 1619 the company determined to send groups of men to work for the college. Known as tenants-at-halves, these men, numbering 50 in each group, were to labor for seven years on college lands, donating half of their labor to the college. This plan enabled the company to borrow extensively on the cash donations for Henrico and, later, on those for the East India School. The number of men employed by the tenant project never totaled more than 150. Throughout its existence, it was poorly managed and failed to produce the anticipated income. Thus, the company did not achieve a sound financial basis for the planned institution.[55]

Virginia's plans for Indian schooling also included schooling for Euroamericans. Although the college at Henrico was built to educate only Indians, it held but one-tenth of the acreage that the company granted for education in 1619. The company had established ten thousand acres for the university at Henrico, which was to serve colonial white youth, and the thousand acres for the college were to be carved out of this larger grant.[56] The college at Henrico was not alone in its subsidiary relationship to the colony's university, for other experiments in colonial Indian education encountered a similar secondary status, with education for colonial white youth generally receiving preferential treatment.

Virginia's earliest experiment in Indian schooling was halted by the devastating Indian attack led by Opechancanough against the colony on March 23, 1622. The coup de grace for Henrico

College and the East India School came two years later, with the transfer of control of the colony to the crown in 1624.

By the mid-1620s, then, it was apparent that neither of the two civilizations—the Tidewater Algonquian or the English—had convinced the other of its own merits. The uprisings of 1622 and 1644 provided a vivid demonstration of the native attitude. Their goal, as Nancy Lurie has observed, was "to prevail over or remove the source of anxiety—the settlers—rather than to adapt themselves to the foreign culture. Certainly," Lurie concluded, "the Indians never felt that their difficulties would be resolved by assimilation among the whites."[57] Thus, the lack of any formal schooling for Indians in Virginia during the entire seventeenth century can be attributed, in part, to the strength and cultural cohesiveness of native society. Their message to the English was clear.

On the other side of the coin, the uprising of 1622 discouraged even the colonists' meager interest in Indian education. As Edmund Morgan noted, the uprising "released all restraints that the company had hitherto imposed on those who thirsted for the destruction or enslavement of the Indians." Within two or three years of the event, "the English had avenged the deaths of that day many times over."[58]

As the century wore on, with yet a second uprising in 1644, Bacon's Rebellion in 1676, and a "continuing toll" of Indian bloodshed, the colonists stubbornly maintained their singleness of purpose toward the native people. By the turn of the eighteenth century, Virginians' solution for the Indians remained what their English ancestors had advocated a century earlier. They still hoped "that the native ultimately would make the adaptation he so obviously and bitterly rejected."[59]

About a decade after the 1622 uprising in Virginia, James II granted to Lord Baltimore the land for a second colony on the Chesapeake. Envisioning Maryland as a refuge for Catholics, Lord Baltimore welcomed the services of the Society of Jesus. Andrew White, S.J. (1579–1656), an old friend of the Calvert family, helped to publicize the venture, writing a colonization tract, in 1633, and a description of the initial voyage to Maryland aboard the Ark.[60] Arriving "at the mouth of the Patomack" on the third of

March 1634, the colonists were met by the Piscataway, the Algonquian tribe who had lived in this region for some time.[61] "[T]he king of Pascatoway had drawne together 500 bowmen," White wrote: "gret fires were made by night over all the Country, and the bignesse of our ship made the natives reporte, we came in a Cannow as bigg as an Iland."[62] Here, among the natives of the Western Shore, Father White was to make his home, serving colonist and Indian alike for a decade, and earning the accolade of "Apostle of Maryland."

Born near London and educated on the Continent, the exigencies of the time had forced White to spend much of his earlier career in teaching theology at Jesuit colleges on the Continent. Like other early Marylanders, he found the colony to be a religious haven, and the respite for him remained unbroken until 1644 or 1645, when Virginia Puritans forced him to return to England where he was tried and acquitted. After another stint in Belgium, he spent his last years in England.[63]

During his decade in Maryland, Father White ministered to the Algonquian groups of the Western Shore. Before 1639 he focused on the Patuxent, who lived along the river that bore their name. In 1639 he began to work among the Piscataway, the tribe who had greeted the *Ark* five years earlier, and he remained among them until raids by the Susquehannock forced abandonment of the mission. At this time, other Jesuits were in Maryland, including Roger Rigbie, who lived with the Patuxent in the early 1640s and wrote a catechism in their language.[64] But no other Jesuit missionary in this region shared the limelight with Father White.

White's initial venture among the Patuxent yielded fewer converts than his later endeavors among the Piscataway. A year after his arrival at Piscataway, he baptized Kittamaquand, their "tayac" or "emperor," and his wife and daughter, in a ceremony witnessed by the governor and other colonial officials. White also convinced Kittamaquand to change certain aspects of his culture. The tayac renounced all but one wife, donned English clothing, and sent his daughter to the settlement at St. Mary's "to be educated amongst the English, and prepared for baptism."[65] During this time, the Jesuits baptized 130 Indians of the Western Shore. White also achieved sufficient mastery of the local Algonquian dialect to compile a dictionary and a grammar; and he translated a catechism for the Piscataway.[66] Then, in the mid-1640s, the work came to an abrupt halt; and though the Jesuits returned briefly in the 1650s, their influence had waned.

In the span of a single decade, Father White and his fellow missionaries were unable to make a significant impact on the lives of these Indians of the Western Shore. Recent scholars have questioned the long-term effectiveness of the Jesuits in achieving cultural change, arguing that the cultural persistence of the Piscataway enabled them to discard the temporary facade of Christianity and the English customs introduced by the Jesuits.[67] The question of Indian schooling, however, has received little attention. Since Father White translated a catechism for the Piscataway, he may have taught some of the native youth to read. The brevity of his stay, however, probably mitigated against a lasting effect.

Beyond the Jesuits, the story of Indian education in colonial Maryland falters. In 1673, during his travels among Friends living on the Eastern Shore, George Fox recorded that his audiences included some Indians. Fox also spoke to these Indians as a separate group, but there is no record of Eastern Shore natives (probably Nanticoke) becoming Friends at this time.[68] Shortly thereafter, between the late 1600s and the early 1700s, most of the Indians of Maryland migrated north to settle in the vicinity of the Susquehannock River in Pennsylvania, and by the 1740s few Indians remained in this Chesapeake Bay colony.[69]

In the interim period dividing Virginia's two major experiments in Indian schooling—Henrico and the East India School and the College of William and Mary—the colony reverted to the type of schooling proposed before Henrico: the placement of native children in private homes. Records of this experiment have eluded the most diligent researchers. Sadie Bell concludes: "It is impossible to gather from the records of this period any evidence of the extent to which Indian parents availed themselves of these provisions [of the legislation providing for Indian education]."[70] The legislation itself, however, suggests that the question of rearing Indian children in white homes continued to be a thorny issue in the middle years of the century.

In 1642, shortly before the second Algonquian uprising, the General Court granted "permission to keep an Indian boy, instructing him in Christian religion," but this single legalized instance may have been an isolated case. The 1644–46 uprising, the last military campaign of the aged Opechancanough, served as a dividing line in Indian–white relations. The treaty that ended the war, enacted by the Virginia legislature, reflected a measurably different attitude toward Indian youth. The treaty of 1646 provided "that such Indian children as shall or will freely and voluntarily come in and live with the English may remain without breach of the articles of peace, provided they be not above twelve years old."[71] The mood of Virginians had clearly changed: after a second uprising, they trusted only Indian youth. Despite its restrictive nature, this legislation left the door open for the Christian training of natives in the home, and evidence that this occurred is revealed in legislation of the late 1640s and 1650s.

In 1649, the General Assembly enacted a law to prevent the kidnapping of Indian children, with the assembly lamenting the fact that Virginians had persuaded Indians themselves to steal "other Indians' children," thereby "Renderinge Religion contemptible, and the name of Englishmen oidious." As punishment, the assembly fined any offender "500 [pounds of] tobacco to be Recovered in any Court of Justice within the Collonye."[72] A law passed in 1655 forbid the treatment of Indian youth as slaves, and it hinted at further abuse by permitting Indian parents to select those to whom they entrusted their children.[73] Evidently, some colonials were not to be trusted.

Three years later, the language of yet another law implied that previous illegalities had not been corrected. The 1658 law prohibited colonists from transfering an Indian child from one family to another for the purposes of education. As Bell notes, this measure attempted to counter "the practice of stealing Indians 'to the greate scandall of Christianitie.'" Further restrictions forbade colonials from altering the time of service that was due them. Indian "children" were to be set free at the age of twenty-five,[74] a restriction which suggests that youth ostensibly maintained in colonial homes for the purpose of education and Christianity were, for all practical purposes, serving as indentured servants. Furthermore, if colonials were retaining Indian services beyond the age of twenty-five, then the status of these "servants" was verging on the thin line separating indentured servants from slaves.

Given the attitude of Indians toward white education prior to the uprising of 1622, it is unlikely that many were willing to part with their children. Probably voluntary situations of this type were rare. Hostage Indian children, however, were another matter. Few restrictions hampered these arrangements. In fact, one colonial legislature in the 1660s passed a measure providing for the rearing of hostage Indians, authorizing an annual allowance of twelve hundred pounds of tobacco for "the maintenance and education of each when necessary."[75]

Whether they were white, native, or Black, most Virginia children enjoyed few schooling opportunities. In the 1660s, one Virginian assessed the irony of these poor educational conditions in a piece addressed to the Bishop of London. No "rationale Heathen," he noted, would "commit their children to the teaching and education of such Christians whom they shall perceive to want Schooles of learning . . . for their own."[76]

The persistent lack of basic schooling continued to be a dilemma for Virginia youth; nonetheless, the colony tackled the need for a college. Seemingly intent on putting the proverbial cart before the horse, some four decades after the failure of Henrico, Virginians renewed their efforts to establish a college in the 1660s. Twice during that decade, the General Assembly petitioned the crown for assistance in establishing such schooling.[77] In March of 1660–61, the Assembly passed an education measure requesting "that for the advance of learning, education of youth, supply of the ministry, and promotion of piety, there be land taken up or purchased for a college and free school."[78]

The next petition for a college was not drafted for nearly three decades. In the interim, the relations between Indians and colonials deteriorated to such an extent that tension between the two led to raids, retribution, frontier unrest, and the outbreak known as Bacon's Rebellion. During the peace following the 1644 uprising, the General Assembly had sought through legislation to establish an equitable coexistence with the tributary tribes.[79] Just as the Assembly began to pursue this approach, however, the colony of Virginia experienced a tremendous influx of new settlers. Between 1649 and 1666, the colony population grew from fifteen thousand to forty thousand, and by 1682 it was eighty thousand. This spelled disaster for Indian–white relations. As Wesley Craven concludes:

Not only were the natives divided politically and confronted by an immigration of such overwhelming proportions as to reemphasize each year their relative weakness, but over the preceding decades they themselves had suffered an extraordinary actual loss in numbers.[80]

John R. Swanton estimated that the population of the Powhatan Indians alone had fallen from Mooney's 1607 figure of eight or nine thousand to about two thousand in 1669.[81] Although these figures are only approximate, they suggest that in six decades of contact the native population had declined by 75 percent.

When the colony designed the peace treaty of 1677, following Bacon's Rebellion, it maintained its position of authority over the tributary Indians. Despite exoneration of the Pamunkeys, clearing them of their alleged aid to the Susquehannocks, the tributary tribes were again required to acknowledge their allegiance to the crown. Their numbers had shrunk drastically; their power had disappeared; their dependence on colonial goods had grown: would it be worthwhile to renew the old Christian dream of civilizing these native Virginians?

By the late 1680s some educators in the colony were convinced that the old dream, ostensibly dead in 1622, was still worth pursuing. Chief among these educators was the Rev. James Blair, a Scotsman who had sailed to the colony in 1685. As commissary for Virginia, Blair was the first to hold this position for the Anglican Church in the colonies, and he was the catalyst for the establishment of the long-awaited institution—the College of William and Mary. In 1691 he sailed to England on a successful mission to obtain a charter for the proposed college. When the college faculty wrote an institutional history in 1874, they described him as "the god-father of William and Mary College."[82] Blair also became the first president of the institution, serving in this capacity until his death in 1743.

Chartered in 1693, William and Mary College was partially dedicated to the education of Indian students, stating among its purposes

> that the Church of Virginia may be furnished with a Seminary of ministers of the Gospel, and that the youth may be piously educated in good Letters and Manners, and that the Christian faith may be propagated amongst the Western Indians, to the Glory of Almighty God.[83]

The college was supported by several funds, including a quit-rent fee on all tobacco exports from Virginia and Maryland. Funding for the Indian school was providentially arranged. In 1691, when the famous English chemist and natural philosopher Robert Boyle died, he left in his will a sum of £5400 to be devoted to "pious and charitable uses"[84] As was typical at that time, earnings were used to purchase a manor in Yorkshire owned by Sir Samuel Garrard. Income from the manor, known as the Brafferton Estate, was to be divided between two colonies. A total of £90 of the rent was allocated to the New England Company for the education of natives at Harvard College and for missionaries to be sent among the New England Indians. After this payment was expended, and as a direct result of Blair's urging, the remainder was slated to "be laid out for the advancement of the Christian religion in Virginia."[85]

Instructions regarding the Indian students at William and Mary College ordered that they be kept

> in sickness and health, meat, washing, lodging, clothes, medicine, books, and education from the first beginning of letters till they should be ready to receive orders and be thought sufficient to be sent abroad to preach and convert the Indians.[86]

Although the college opened its doors in the 1690s, the first Indian students did not arrive until the early 1700s. Little is known of those first years because a fire destroyed the college building in 1705.

The first commencement, held in 1700, attracted a large crowd from places as far away as New York. At this time, even though it was still largely a grammar school, William and Mary was the only college in colonial America located south of Pennsylvania, and the commencement was viewed as a novelty, for it was "a new thing in that part of America to hear graduates perform their exercises." Indians visiting Williamsburg joined the festivities, witnessing this major event in turn-of-the-century Virginia.[87]

It is difficult to determine the total Indian enrollment at the college. The faculty history of William and Mary, published in the 1870s, estimated that an average of eight to ten Indian students were enrolled each year.[88] More recent statistics, however, demonstrate a wide fluctuation in the enrollment. Karen A. Stuart, who has drawn upon a variety of sources to compile as complete a list as possible, concludes that the number of Indian students varied from as many as twenty-four to as few as one or two.[89] Even allowing for the duplication of names among those who remained longer than one year, it becomes apparent that William and Mary provided schooling for more Indians than any other institution of higher education in colonial America.

Indian enrollment in the college crested during the period when Alexander Spotswood served as lieutenant governor for Virginia between 1710 and 1722. Spotswood formulated his Indian policy during a tempestuous period on Virginia's frontier. The Tuscarora War broke out shortly after he began his term of office, and no sooner was it quelled than the conflict known as the Yamasee War inflamed the Carolinas. Fought in North Carolina, the Tuscarora War also embroiled Virginia, in part because these Iroquoian-speaking people lived along the rivers bordering the two colonies. Spotswood, on the lookout for a wedge to improve Indian–white relations, saw the war as an opportunity for establishing firm relations with all of the Virginia Indians. During negotiations with some Tuscarora bands seeking to ensure peace with Virginia, he proposed that they "deliver two Children of the great men of each town to remain as Hostages, and to be educated at our College." Not only would this plan "prove the most effectuall Security for their fidelity," Spotswood reasoned that it might also 'be a good step towards the Conversion of that whole Nation to the Christian faith."[90] Due to a number of circumstances, Spotswood's dealings with the Tuscarora proved disappointing, but he was able to salvage the initial hostage plan introduced to the Tuscarora and to adapt it to Virginia's tributary Indians.

Virginia's Indians had become tributaries in the treaty of 1646, which spelled out their subsidiary position. In the first act of the treaty, the Indian leader Necotowance, dubbed by the British as "King of the Indians," acknowledged that he held "his Kingdome from the King's Majestie of England, and that his successors be appointed or confirmed from the King's Governours." Thus, at this point, the British had firmly denied any further political independence to these groups. The General Assembly had agreed to protect the Indians, but in return for this protection, the Indians had promised "to pay unto the King's Governor the number of twenty beaver skins at the goeing away of the Geese yearly."[91] By 1712, according to Spotswood, the tributary Indians numbered perhaps 700, including 250 fighting men. But only three of Spotswood's contemporary "nine Indian nations"—the Pamunkey, Chickahominy, and Nansemand—were descended from the Tidewater Indians who had comprised the Powhatan confederacy. The remaining six groups were Iroquoian or Siouan. Thus, the population of the Powhatan people, who had numbered perhaps 2,000 in 1669, had diminished to probably less than half of the 700 Indians described by Spotswood.[92]

In 1711, Spotswood adopted his Tuscarora plan to suit the tributary Indians. His goal was to enlarge the Indian enrollment at the college and to improve relations with these remnant groups. Spotswood offered "to remit their annual Tribute of Skins as long as they Kept their Children at the College," and after some deliberation the Indians agreed. Shortly thereafter, Spotswood noted with undisguised pleasure:

> The King of the Nanserands has already sent his son and Cousin, the Nottoways and Meherrins have sent each two of their chiefs men's sons to be brought up to Learning and Christianity, and the Queen of Pamunkey, upon seeing how well these Indian children are treated has engaged to send her son and the son of one of the Chief man upon the same foot, and I also expect another boy from the Chickahominys.[93]

The favorable response by the tributary groups resulted in one immediate effect, a vast jump in Indian enrollment at the college. By December 1711, the college had received hostages from all the tributary Indians. By the following summer, the number of Indian students had increased from the earlier total of four, all of whom had been purchased through warfare with distant tribes, to twenty-four, with the tributary Indians adding twenty students to the total.[94] Suddenly, the lieutenant governor encountered a new problem. The Boyle fund, which provided in annual income about £200, was totally inadequate to support twenty students. The council had encouraged the enrollment of the additional students, but the House of Burgesses showed no indication of providing the funds to make their attendance feasible. Presuming that funds would be forthcoming from either the General Assembly or from private sources, the council then quarreled with the Assembly over another funding matter, with the end result a stalemate on Indian educational support. Spotswood then turned for aid to the Bishop of London, and in attempting to persuade the bishop of the significance of such schooling, he described the favorable reaction of Indians who visited the students: "Their parents and others of their Nations who come frequently to see them express much satisfaction with the care that is taken of them, and frequently lament their own misfortune in not having the like advantages in their youth." Spotswood pleaded with the Bishop of London and the Archbishop of Canterbury to intercede on his behalf to procure funding from the SPG.[95] Despite their efforts, no funding appeared. Ironically, the problem was to resolve itself internally, with the decline in Indian enrollment.

During the next two years, Spotswood negotiated further with the Tuscarora and the Iroquoian and Siouan groups of Virginia, but again the Tuscarora negotiations failed. By the late fall of 1714, however, he had relocated several of the other groups on two reservations that lay on opposite shores of the Meherrin River. On the south side of the river, where the Saponi were located, Fort Christanna, one of two frontier posts constructed at this time, was to serve as a base for colonial and Indian rangers guarding the area across the Roanoke and the Appomattox from Tuscarora attacks.[96] The fort would also include a school for Indian children, provided for under the Act for the Better Regulation of the Indian Trade, which also stipulated that the fort was to be the sole location of all Indian trade north of the James River.

Spotswood had a number of reasons for urging the passage of this Indian trade measure. He saw it as a lever for counteracting both French and Carolinian influence in the lucrative skin trade, but he also viewed it as a means for increasing the dependency of the tributary Indians as well as providing funding for a schoolhouse for Indian children at Fort Christanna. One of the highest priorities of Spotswood's Indian policy was the Christianization and education of the tributary Indians, and to this end, he himself paid the salary of the schoolmaster at the fort. Control of the Indian trade would be placed under the direction of the Virginia Indian Company, which was established under the Indian trade act and granted a twenty-year monopoly. Despite this optimistic beginning, opposition to the act was sufficient to bring about its demise within a few years. In 1717, crown officials disallowed the act because it established a monopoly; and the experiment, including the school, came to an end.[97]

During its several years of operation, however, the school at Fort Christanna enrolled a significant number of Indian youth, due largely to the personality of its schoolmaster. The Rev. Charles Griffin had been teaching for about a decade when Spotswood appointed him to the position. In 1705, he had settled in North Carolina, where he taught at two locations before moving to Virginia. In the first location he had been influenced by Quakers, and in the second assignment he had become a Quaker himself.[98] Thus, as a teacher of Indians in Virginia, he can be seen as a symbol of the historic role in Indian–white relations played by Quakers in colonial America, a role highlighted by the years when William Penn led his colony. In 1715, when Griffin began teaching at the fort, Spotswood anticipated dramatic results. Describing Griffin, Spotswood noted that since "ye Person I have pitch'd on for this Emyloym't is heartily inclined to the Service, and the fittest I could have found, I cannot but have great hopes of the good Success of these, my endeavours."[99] Other Virginians also praised Griffin. William Byrd described the schoolmaster as "a man of good family who by the innocence of his life and the sweetness of his temper was perfectly well qualified for that pious undertaking."[100]

By June 1715, Griffin had enrolled seventy Indian students. Spotswood himself had assisted in the selection of pupils, whom he described as "boys and Girls, who for their years are the most susceptible of Learning."[101] Griffin was diligent in his instruction throughout the summer, and by fall, Spotswood boasted that the "great part" of his pupils "could recite the Lord's Prayer and the Creed."[102] In the following year, Griffin substantiated this claim. In describing the progress of the Indian students in a letter to the Bishop of London, he noted that "the greatest number of my scholars can say the belief, the Lord's prayer, & ten Commds perfectly well, they know that there is but one God."[103] Griffin had introduced an appealing kind of approach to Indian education. Hugh Jones observed that the Saponi "so loved and adored him that I have seen them lift him up in their arms." Had he given permission, they "would have chosen him for a king of the Saponi Nation."[104]

Concerning the Christian teachings at Griffin's school, Spotswood declared that "both these Children and their Parents seem much delighted with the hopes of their being made Christians and taught to read." At the same time, Spotswood himself appeared to be forecasting the school's short life when he wrote: "I look upon the education of these Indians to be so feasible that I should be very sorry if it miscarry for want of a suitable support."[105]

One year after the school opened, its enrollment had climbed to one hundred pupils. As an added bonus for "permitting their Children to be educated in the Christian religion," Spotswood furnished the Indians at the fort with goods "at a Cheaper rate than any foreign Indians." He noted that the Indians at Fort Christanna are "well pleased with their circumstances."[106] Sadie Bell has commented on the Fort Christanna School: "Of all ventures in behalf of Indian education in colonial Virginia, this seems to have been the happiest."[107] Even William Byrd's assessment of Charles Griffin's teaching concluded that "he had so much the secret of mixing pleasure with instruction that he had not a scholar who did not love him affectionately."[108]

When the trade act providing for the school was disallowed, Byrd joined others in lamenting the removal of Griffin to the Indian Grammar School at William and Mary. Hugh Jones echoed this opinion when he described the closure of the school at Fort Christanna as "a pious design" that was "laid aside through the opposition of trade and interest."[109] But no one reflected on the end of the experiment as bitterly as Spotswood himself. Writing to the Board of Trade, he concluded:

> Thus, my Lords, by the prevalence of a party, and by their Assiduity in debauching the minds of weak, inconsiderate Men, all the Measures w'ch have been projected for the Defence of the Country are not overturned. . . . The Christianizing the Indians, w'ch was in so fair a way of being compassed, defeated, the King's Authority encroached on, his Interest thwarted and opposed, His Recommendation slighted, and common Justice denied to those who have laid out their Estates for the public Service of the Government and on the public Faith.

The hopes had come to naught, and the Indian school at the college offered the only remaining opportunity for instruction. Spotswood shifted Griffin there in 1718.[110]

When schoolmaster Griffin became master for the Indian students at the college, enrollment in the Boyle School, as it was

sometimes called, was already declining from the maximum figure of twenty students attained by Spotswood's offer of 1711. By
1716 only a few Indians remained there, but by 1723 sufficient
funds had accumulated in the Boyle fund to enable the college to
construct a separate building for the Indian students, known as
the Brafferton after the Brafferton Manor in England. Hugh Jones
pointed out that the building was a major change, since the Indian
students "were formerly boarded and lodged in the town." There,
however, he recalled that "abundance of them used to die, . . .
through sickness, change of provision and way of life."[111] In
1724, he praised the advantages of the Brafferton:

> The Indians who are upon Mr. Boyle's foundation now have a
> handsom apartment for themselves and their master, built near the
> College, which . . . ought to be carried on to the utmost advantage
> in the real education and conversion of the infidel.

A handsome, Georgian-style brick structure, with two main floors
and a third under the roof, the Brafferton lay opposite the home of
the college president.[112]

In the 1720s and during the decades before the American Revolution, the Boyle School was one of four maintained by the college. These included the grammar, philosophy, divinity, and Indian schools. The master of the grammar school prepared youth
for the philosophy and divinity schools. At the age of fifteen, after
studying Latin and Greek for five years, boys took the examina-
tion that enabled them to pursue their studies in divinity and
philosophy. On the other hand, the master of the Indian school
presided over what was essentially a common school, teaching
"reading and writing and vulgar arithmetic." William and Mary
also encouraged youth from Williamsburg to enroll in the Indian
school. Not included in the Boyle fund, these local youth paid the
Indian school master a fee of twenty shillings a year.[113]

Although the Brafferton was completed after Indian enrollment
at the school had peaked, statistics indicate that it continued to
house a small number of Indian students.[114] Within a short time,
however, these Indian boys began to share their building with the
college library.

In 1732, yet another surplus of funds in the Boyle endowment
led the college to request permission to furnish a library in the

room over the Indian school. The Brafferton contained one large and two smaller rooms on each of the first two floors. Stuart speculates that the large room on the first floor housed the classroom; its counterpart on the second floor, the library; and the small rooms on either the first or second floors, the living quarters of the Indian school master. If this is the case, the living quarters of the Indian students themselves may have been on the third floor, directly under the roof. It is very likely that the initial books for the library were purchased with Boyle funds; it is unlikely that the Indian students used the books, since neither their schooling nor that of the grammar school students was of the appropriate level for the collection.[115]

About a decade after the library addition, the rivalry between British and French interests in the Ohio Valley sharpened as both imperial powers tried to exert their influence over the Indians who dominated this strategic region. In treaty negotiations with the Iroquois and other tribes, the English offered gifts and further incentives in exchange for the Indians' land and their loyalty. One of these incentives was English education, which, from the Indians' perspective, was not always perceived as an attraction. In less than a decade, the Iroquois twice rejected offers to have their youth educated at William and Mary: first at Lancaster, Pennsylvania, in 1744; and then at Logg's Town, Pennsylvania, in 1752. Following the English military disasters of 1754–55, Virginia, Maryland, and eventually Pennsylvania responded to the desperate needs of frontier settlers by constructing forts and blockhouses. Once again, the colonials attempted to add schooling for Indian children to the package. In 1756, Virginia Governor Robert Dinwiddie wrote to the Lords of Trade to inquire if he might build a number of forts on the frontier and, to encourage Indian allegiance to the British, supply each of the forts with two blacksmiths "to mend the Guns of the Indians, &c" and one "School master to teach the Children Eng. and Morality, and to give them a true Notion of the Supreme God."[116]

A few years earlier, negotiations between Virginia leaders and Cherokee representatives had led to the enrollment of a small group of Cherokee students. After two of these youth fled, Governor Dinwiddie wrote of their disaffection to Old Hop and other Cherokee sachems:

> If you sh'd think proper to send any, they sh'd not exceed the Age
> of 8 Years. . . . If any come hereafter, about the above Age, I will
> cause proper care to be taken of them.[117]

Two decades later, with the beginning of the American Revolution, the school in the Brafferton still retained some Indian students; but in 1776 its finances were cut off, and it was forced to close shortly thereafter. In 1778, when Governor Thomas Jefferson reorganized the College of William and Mary, naming Brafferton as one of six schools, there was no mention of Indians. After the revolution, the Boyle fund was diverted to the instruction of Negroes in the British West Indies. Jefferson mentioned the Indian School in 1785, suggesting that "the purposes of the Brafferton would be better answered by maintaining a perpetual mission among the Indian tribes." He foresaw the proposed mission as one that would combine teaching Christianity to the tribes with the recording of their cultures. The colonial institution of the Brafferton, however, was not restored.[118]

Thus, the most enduring colonial school for Indian youth came to a close. Through seven and a half decades it had offered a variety of incentives for both colonials and Indians. For the English, it had served as a bargaining tool for negotiations with Indian groups. It had also provided a significant source of income for the College of William and Mary, and the college made good use of additions financed by the Boyle fund: the Brafferton building and the library it housed. Finally, the school fulfilled, to some degree, the educational intent of providing an exposure to English education for the dozens of enrolled Indian boys.

For the Indians, the school may also have served as a bargaining tool enabling groups to negotiate with the colonials to gain alliances or trade advantages. The eagerness of the colonials to enroll their youth provided Indian groups with reverse leverage.[119] For individual Indian students, the impact of the experience at William and Mary was wide ranging. Although their studies differed from those of other students, the everyday lives of the Indian boys at the college—especially those who lived at the Brafferton from the 1720s forward—were cast in a pattern not altogether different from that of their white counterparts. The Indian youths dressed like the white students, ate the same food, and were taught in English.[120] They studied reading, writing, and

arithmetic, and possibly Latin and Greek. Their Indian schoolmaster instructed them in the catechism and in the basic tenets of
the Church of England.

In accordance with the initial instructions of the Boyle fund,
and later reinforced by the statutes of the 1730s, the Indian students were, in theory, to be trained until they were "thought
sufficient to be sent abroad to preach and convert the Indians."[121]
If this remained the theoretical goal of the Indian school, it proved
more illusory than real. None of these Indian students became
missionaries. Some, however, may have become cultural brokers.
John Montour, a student in the mid-1750s and of mixed Indian–
French Canadian ancestry, was bilingual and later participated in
the American Revolution.[122] Still other Indian students saw the
schooling as detrimental to their lives. In addition to youth whose
health was affected adversely by the changes in physical environment, there were others whose years at William and Mary cost
them dearly in lost training for maturity in their native environment. At the Lancaster treaty conference in 1744, the colonial
negotiators offered the Iroquois delegates an opportunity to send
their boys to William and Mary. In his reply, Canassatego, an
Onondaga, told the colonial delegates from Pennsylvania, Maryland, and Virginia that "the Indians are not inclined to give their
Children Learning." (The word "Learning" was interpreter Conrad Weiser's translation for the Iroquois description of English
education; that is, classroom schooling with books.) "We allow it
[Learning] to be good," Canassatego continued, "but our Customs
differing from yours, you will be so good as to excuse us."[123] Some
years later, Benjamin Franklin added further details to this official
transcription, observing that the Iroquois response reflected their
own recollection of what had happened to their youth who had
once "been educated in that college." "[F]or a long time after they
returned to their friends," the Iroquois recalled, these youth "were
absolutely good for nothing being neither acquainted with the
true methods for killing deer, catching Beaver or surprizing an
enemy." According to Franklin, the Iroquois then offered the ultimate response to English "Learning": "if the English Gentlemen
would send a dozen or two of their children to Onondago, "the
great Council would take care of their Education, bring them up in
really what was the best manner and make men of them."[124]

Captain John Smith's Map of Virginia. (© Copyright the Trustees of the British Museum)

RGINIA

The Saſquej ahanaus
are a Gyant like peo ple thus
atyred thus a Sweredres

POWHATAN

CK BAY

Blande

Brooces forest

Harbour

TOCKE
WOGHS

WA.
OKS

and halfe

ATOV

AXACO

HVKES

Graven and Diſcribed by Captayne John Smith 1606
Graven by William Hole

THE PORTRAICTUER OF CAPTAYNE IOHN SMITH / ADMIRALL OF NEW ENGLAND.

Æta 37
A⁰ 1616

These are the Lines that shew thy Face; but those
That shew thy Grace and Glory, brighter bee:
Thy Faire-Discoueries and Fowle-Overthrowes
Of Salvages, much Civilliz'd by thee
Best shew thy Spirit; and to it Glory Wyn;
So, thou art Braße without, but Golde within.

Engraving of Captain John Smith by Simon van de Passe. Poem by John Davies of Hereford. Engraving appeared in Captain John Smith's Map of New England. (© Copyright the Trustees of the British Museum)

81

Commissary James Blair, First President of the College of William and Mary in Virginia. By John Hargrave. (Courtesy of the Muscarelle Museum of Art; College of William and Mary. Gift of Mary M. Peachy 1829.001)

College of William and Mary, Williamsburg, Virginia, 1839. *Left*, The Brafferton; *center*, The Sir Christopher Wren Building; *right*, The President's House. (no credit)

Alexander Spotswood by Charles Bridges. (The Library of Virginia)

The Brafferton, College of William and Mary, 1725. Photograph by Thomas L. Williams. (Courtesy of Colonial Williamsburg Foundation)

The charter granted by Chalres I in 1629 authorized the Massachusetts Bay Colony to use a seal,
and the impression of an Indian (above) was the
one adopted. It was used until the charter was
annulled (1691). (Courtesy Massachusetts Archives)

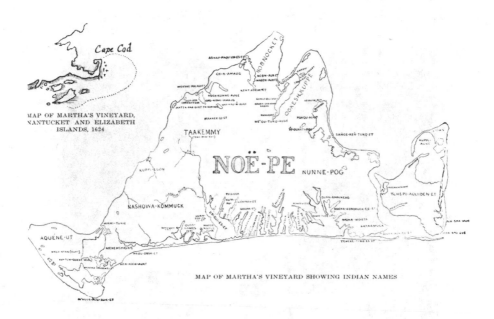

MAP OF MARTHA'S VINEYARD,
NANTUCKET AND ELIZABETH
ISLANDS, 1624

MAP OF MARTHA'S VINEYARD SHOWING INDIAN NAMES

84

MAMUSSE
WUNNEETUPANATAMWE
UP-BIBLUM GOD
NANEESWE
NUKKONE TESTAMENT
KAH WONK
WUSKU TESTAMENT.

Ne quoſhk'innumuk naſhpe Wuttinneumoh *CHRIST*
noh aſooweſit

JOHN ELIOT.

CAMBRIDGE:
Printeuoop naſhpe *Samuel Green* kah *Marmaduke John,*
1 6 6 3.

Title page to the *Indian Bible.*
(Courtesy of the Boston Athenaeum)

"A Prospect of the Colledges in Cambridge in New England, 1726," by William Burgis.
(Courtesy of the Massachusetts Historical Society)

Francis Le Jau, D.D. (1665–1717). Portrait attributed to Henrietta Johnston, wife of Commissary Gideon Johnston.

Engraving of John Wesley, by J. Faber after J. Williams. (© Copyright the Trustees of the British Museum)

Portrait of James Edward Oglethorpe.

Audience given by the Trustees of the Colony of Georgia in America to Tomochichi, Mico of Yamacraw and the Indians, July 3, 1734. Painted by Edmund Dyer. Copy of the original by William Verelst. Given to the State of Georgia in 1926. (Courtesy of the Georgia Archives. Image #LRV213)

"The Holy Club in Session." Engraving by S. Bellin after Marshall Claxton. At the head of the table, John Wesley (standing). Seated at the table with the open book, Benjamin Ingham. To Ingham's right, Charles Wesley. (Courtesy of the Methodist Archives and History Center, Drew University)

"The Rev. John Wesley Preaching to the North American Indians." (Courtesy of the Methodist Archives and History Center, Drew University)

Augustus Gottlieb Spangenberg   David Nitschmann

Portrait of Tomochichi and Toonahowi by William Verelst. (Courtesy of the National Anthropological Archives, Smithsonian Institution. Negative # 1129-b-1)

Judge Samuel Sewall (1652–1730) by John Smibert (1688–1751). Oil on canvas. Painted in 1729. (Photograph © 2007 Museum of Fine Arts, Boston)

Cotton Mather (1663–1728). Engraved by Peter Pelham (1697–1751). (Courtesy of the American Antiquarian Society)

Portrait of Jonathan Edwards. (Courtesy of
the Library of Congress)

Stockbridge Mission House, Stockbridge, Massachusetts. Built by John Sergeant in 1739.

David Zeisberger. By John Valentine Haidt. (Courtesy of the Moravian Archives)

Haddam, Connecticut. The birthplace of David and John Brainerd.

Portrait of Eleazar Wheelock. Painted at
the direction of the trustees of Dartmouth
College by Joseph Steward. (Commissioned by the Trustees of Dartmouth College, Hanover, New Hampshire)

Moor's Charity School. Columbia, Connecticut, formerly a part of Lebanon, Connecticut.
(Courtesy of Dartmouth College Library)

The Reverend Samson Occom (1723–92), painted by Nathaniel Smibert (1735–56). (Bowdoin College Museum of Art, Brunswick, Maine. Bequest of the Honorable James Bowdoin III)

Portrait of Nathaniel Whitaker by Mason Chamberlin. (Hood Museum of Art, Dartmouth College, Hanover, New Hampshire. Gift of the Hon. John S. Whitaker, Class of 1869H)

The Reverend Samson Occom (1723–92). Mezzotint by J. Spilsbury from an oil by Mason Chamberlin. Original painting is lost. (Courtesy of Dartmouth College Library)

Joseph Brant (Thayendanegea, 1743–1807), 1776.
Painted by George Romeny. (Courtesy of the National
Gallery of Canada, Ottawa)

Portrait of William Johnson. A copy after a lost por-
trait painted by Thomas McIlworth at Johnson Hall,
May, 1763. (Courtesy of the Collection of the New
York Historical Society. Negative #6871, accession
#1896.2)

Engraving of Samuel Kirkland by D. C. Hinman. (Courtesy of Hamilton College Library)

Engraving of William, Second Earl of Dartmouth, by R. B. Parkes from a portrait by Sir Joshua Reynolds. (Courtesy of Dartmouth College Library)

Moor's Charity School located at Dartmouth College. Later became Chandler School, an undergraduate department of the college. (Courtesy of Dartmouth College Library)

Founding of Dartmouth College. Wood engraving by Samuel E. Brown, 1839. (Courtesy of Dartmouth College Library)

4 | PURITANS AND INDIANS: NEW ENGLAND IN THE SEVENTEENTH CENTURY

The New England Puritans who settled the Massachusetts Bay Colony in the 1630s were endowed with a sense of mission. During their first decade of settlement, however, the colony devoted a singular lack of attention to the conversion of their new neighbors, the Massachusetts Indians. By the late 1630s the English had already met the Algonquian on the battlefield, but they had not taken any official action to uphold the promises of their charter or of their colony seal, imprinted with the image of an Indian expressing the Macedonian cry: "Come over and help us."

Revisionist scholars writing on the seventeenth-century New England missionaries have been quick to point out the failure of Massachusetts Bay to take immediate steps toward converting the Algonquian.[1] Neal Salisbury suggests that by the early 1640s "the great barriers—linguistic, religious, cultural—between the two peoples, blithely overlooked from England in the earlier instance, were now magnified to insurmountable obstacles."[2] Both Salisbury and Francis Jennings argue convincingly that economic motivations were the most powerful influence guiding the leaders of Massachusetts Bay toward a sudden upsurge of interest in the conversion of Indians.[3] But the economic depression that Massachusetts faced in the early 1640s was compounded by the impact of several tracts, published in England, attacking the colony for its lack of concern for the Indians; and together, these factors provided the colony's leaders with an incentive for action.

Between 1641 and 1649 the battle to secure funds for convert-

Seventeenth Century New England

□ Indian Settlements
● Colonial Towns

ing the Indians, whose financial needs often appeared to be synonymous with those of the colony, progressed on three fronts, the first of which was official action taken by the colony itself. In 1641, Massachusetts Bay sent two agents, the Reverends Thomas Weld and Hugh Peter, to England on a "begging mission" on behalf of the colony. The Weld–Peter mission used the Indian cause as a rationale for the colony's needs. In addition to securing funds, the most prominent result of this mission was the publication of the famous tract "New England's First Fruits" (London, 1643).[4] This promotion pamphlet was designed to obtain financial support for the fledgling Harvard College, founded in 1636 "to advance Learning and perpetuate it to prosperity"; and to revitalize the emigation movement to New England. The colony also passed several internal legislative measures affecting the Massachusett Indians. In 1644, Indians were encouraged to attend religious instruction on Sundays; in 1646, the General Court authorized the purchase of lands "for the incuragment of the Indians to live in an orderly way amongst us," and provided for two ministers to be chosen to preach to the Indians.[5]

At the same time, a second front in the conversion effort was launched by individuals working directly with the Algonquian. Ministers were in the forefront of this effort to remold the Indian. Their most prominent representative was the Reverend John Eliot, the Cambridge-educated pastor at Roxbury, who had come from England in 1631. At this time Eliot began his long and famous career with the "Praying Indians" of Massachusetts. Less well-known was his contemporary, the Reverend Thomas Mayhew, Jr., the first missionary of the island of Martha's Vineyard. Mayhew's conversion of Hiacoomes, a Pawkunnakut or Wampanoag of the Vineyard, marked the first accomplishment of a missionary family that endured in the field until the early 1800s.

While Mayhew's efforts went virtually unrecognized for the first few years, almost every hour Eliot spent with the nearby Massachusett was recorded. This information, in conjunction with Eliot's own letters, was hurried to England, where it provided the substance for further propaganda pamphlets and the beginning of the third front. By 1649, three of these tracts had been published, but it was the third one, *The Glorious Progress of the Gospel, Amongst the Indians in New England*, which enabled its author, Edward Winslow, to secure passage of a bill in the Long

Parliament that guaranteed financial aid to New England's missionary efforts.

As successor to Weld and Peter, Winslow achieved through his parliamentary success of 1649 the goal that New England had been seeking for eight years. The act provided for "a corporation in England . . . by the name of the President and society for propagation of the Gospel in New England."[6] This corporation soon came to be known as the New England Company.

From 1649 to the end of the seventeenth century, the New England Company served as the major source of funds for missionaries in Massachusetts Bay, Plymouth, Connecticut, and New Haven (until it was swallowed by Connecticut in 1665). Thus, the history of the New England Company provides a political and financial framework for Indian education in seventeenth-century New England. Although other companies appeared at the turn of the eighteenth century—including the prominent Society for the Propagation of the Gospel in Foreign Parts (SPG, 1701) and the Society in Scotland for Propagating Christian Knowledge (SSPCK, 1709)—the New England Company had greater longevity and remains today the oldest Protestant missionary organization.

The act that established the New England Company provided for the mechanics of running a complex business organization. The company was composed of sixteen people responsible for the acquisition and investment of funds gathered on behalf of the Indian cause. The initial fund-raising campaign spread throughout England and Wales. Donations came from within the London parishes, from the breadth of the rural countryside, and from the Puritan army, which gave generously. The success of this campaign was phenomenal: in the first five years it gathered £4,582; and by 1660, with the Restoration, the total support raised for the New England missionaries had reached the sum of £15,367.[7]

The directors of the New England Company, a dedicated group of London merchants and men of affairs, found frequent meetings necessary. Their burden was twofold: They were responsible for the recently collected funds, which they invested in "Lands, Tenements, or Hereditaments in England or Wales";[8] and their other main item of business was the allocation of goods and/or money to New England. The New England counterparts to the London directors were the commissioners for the United Colonies of New England, whose organization had been in existence since 1643.

Organized primarily as a military, defensive structure against the Indians, the United Colonies of New England was a strange choice to distribute missionary funds. Its single advantage was that it was the only organization extant that represented most of the New England colonies (ignoring Rhode Island, however). But the commissioners' newly acquired missionary work thrust them into an awkward position, since, as William Kellaway observes, "one of their prime functions was to protect the United Colonies against the Indians."[9] During its four decades of existence, the United Colonies' organization was fraught with dissension, which found its way into the missionary work through the unrelenting domination of Massachusetts Bay.

Despite these difficulties, the commissioners and the company directors persevered. For over three decades, from 1649 to 1684, these two groups managed the investments and directed the funding for almost all of the Protestant Indian educational work in New England.

Missionary work required an enduring commitment. Even among "the good people of New England," few accepted the challenge.[10] This scarcity of workers led the directors of the New England Company, in 1655, to complain "that none labour in the word and doctrine amongst the Indians but Mr. Eliot and Mr. Mayhew."[11] Two years later, the commissioners in New England concurred that there was "indeed much want of pious and meet Instruments to carry on that worke."[12]

In order to alleviate this problem, the commissioners sought to encourage others to train for the Indian work. Between the early 1650s and the mid-1670s, additional ministers and several educators shared in the income made available by the New England Company. Moreover, a number of Indians were employed, for the most part by the Eliot and Mayhew families. Missionary work tended to be family oriented, a pattern true not only for the Eliots and Mayhews but for the missionaries in Plymouth Colony as well. The Reverend Richard Bourne was the first of a missionary family associated for several generations with the Mashpee (Pawkunnakut) of Cape Cod.[13] From 1666 to 1698, the Reverend John

Cotton, Jr., served in Plymouth, where he and his sons worked with the Pawkunnakut.[14] Several missionary families not connected with the New England Company also served in Plymouth. These included Thomas Tupper and his descendants; Samuel Treat; and Richard, Ezra, and Joseph Brown.[15]

Throughout this period, the monetary pie was sliced into uneven portions. When the portion of the income paid solely to missionaries was divided, the Eliots and Mayhews received three-fourths, while the other four missionaries located in Plymouth and Connecticut received one-fourth. When the total income from the New England Company for this period was apportioned, Massachusetts Bay proved to be the primary recipient, receiving 80 percent of the total funding. The colonies of Plymouth, Connecticut, and New Haven had to settle for only 20 percent.[16] Reimbursement for Indian schoolmasters and interpreters was on a par with the colonies outside Massachusetts Bay. Indian salaries, considerably less than those paid to the missionaries, ranged from £3½ per annum to £10 per annum. While the New England Company paid colonial schoolmasters less than it paid the missionaries—an inexperienced teacher received as little as £10 per annum—it generally acknowledged their worth with a salary of £25 to £30, which was at least double that of the Indian schoolmasters. The greatest discrepancy between Indian and colonist, therefore, was the gap separating missionary and Indian. The Indian paid £10 received one-fifth of Eliot's £50 salary; the Indian paid £3½ received one-tenth. The resulting imbalance between colonist and Indian, on the one hand, and between Massachusetts Bay and the other colonies, on the other hand, was largely a reflection of the powerful influence of John Eliot, his family, and all who benefited from his largesse.

Most of the Puritan missionaries believed that Algonquian culture was totally devoid of "civilization." Puritan divines—in contrast to Roger Williams or their Catholic contemporaries to the north, who expressed considerable interest in native cultures—dismissed the Indian cultures as "barbarous."[17] "[T]hese poor Indians," John Eliot wrote, "have no principles of their own nor yet wisdome of their own."[18] In hazarding a guess as to their origin, the Reverend Cotton Mather speculated "that probably the devil decoyed [them] hither, in hopes that the gospel . . . would never come here to destroy or disturb his *absolute empire* over them."[19] Because Eliot, Thomas Mayhew, Jr., and their contemporaries judged these Indians solely through their Puritan vision, they were unable and unwilling to give stature to the Indians' interwoven, albeit partially shattered culture. As Roy Harvey Pearce concludes, the Puritan defined "the primitive in terms of the civilized, the Indians in terms of the Puritan."[20]

Still others saw these Indians differently, and gradually, through the collected accounts of less-biased contemporary observers as well as anthropological research, we have been able to piece together a more coherent picture of the New England Algonquian. They lived east of the Alleghenies, with their villages lying by the Quinnebaug, Blackstone, Neponset, and Charles rivers, and their wigwams bordering the shores of Cape Cod, Martha's Vineyard (Noepe), Long Island, and Narraganset Bay. During the millenium and a half prior to European contact, their culture had evolved from a hunting economy to that of an agricultural and hunting-gathering pattern.[21] Shifting alliances that were common among Indian groups also affected their political relations with one another. Thus, when the Pilgrims and Puritans settled among them in the 1620s and 1630s, the English presence created further shifts in the uneasy balance of power among the Massachusett, Pawkunnakut (or Wampanoag), Narragansett, and Pequot.

Indian groups involved with the colonists in their seventeenth-century educational experiments included the Massachusett, Pawkunnakut, Nipmuc, and Montauk. The Penacook, the Mohegan, the Niantic, and the Narragansett played only a peripheral role in the seventeenth-century educational ventures sponsored by the New England Company. The Narragansett regarded Roger Williams as their only reliable teacher during this period. The Quinnipiac, who lived near Branford in New Haven colony, were instructed by the Reverend Abraham Pierson in the 1650s and early 1660s. Pierson's catechism in the Quinnipiac dialect, published in 1658, was a singular effort, but it proved to be a dismal failure.[22] The Mohegan and Pequot, who lived near the communities of New London and Pequot, were taught in the early 1660s by William Thompson and, later, by James Fitch. But several decades later, when Cotton Mather pressed for the Christianization of the Mohegan he complained that they remained pagans.[23]

Thus, with the exception of Pierson, Thompson, and Fitch, the New England Company concentrated on the Massachusett, Pawkunnakut, Nipmuc, and Montauk.

When the Pilgrims and Puritans met the Algonquian, the strength of these native groups had already been broken. Only the earlier visitors—the occasional explorer and the persistent fishermen who pulled in their harvest off the banks of Newfoundland—had an opportunity to meet these people before they were decimated by the plague of 1616–17. Daniel Gookin, Indian superintendent in seventeenth-century Massachusetts, estimated that the warrior population for this area had shrunk from 18,000 men in 1600 to between 8,000 and 9,000 men in 1674.[24] With the addition of 3 or 4 dependents per warrior, this meant that the native population had declined from about 72,000 people to perhaps 8,500 people. Prior to 1674, with the exception of the Pequot War, the greatest cause for this drastic population reduction was disease, an unwitting European form of conquest that had taken much of its toll before colonization.

In contemporary accounts written by explorers and others who were not concerned with Puritan concepts of Christianization and "civilization," these eastern Algonquian emerge as an admirable people. As W. Vernon Kinietz once pointed out, "In considering all of their characterizations of the Indians, it should be borne in mind that most of the Europeans wanted something . . . and to those who got what they desired, the Indians are sensible, brave and upright people."[25] Thus, when explorer Giovanni de Verrazano was treated well by the natives, he responded in kind. A Florentine and the first European to describe these Algonquian at any length, Verrazano was quite taken with the physical appearance of the natives and with the beauty of their land bordering Narragansett Bay, where he rested his ship for two weeks in 1524. "This is the goodliest people," Verrazano exulted, "and of the fairest conditions, that wee have found in our voyage." Later, sailing by the coast of Maine, where his ship was showered by arrows from some Abenaki, his report was less glowing.[26]

Over a century later, William Wood and Roger Williams echoed Verrazano's praise, lauding the natives' generosity and kindness. "If a tree may be judged by his fruits," he wrote of the Massachusett, "and dispositions calculated by exteriour actions; then may it be concluded, that these Indians are of affable, courteous, and well disposed natures, ready to communicate the best of their wealth to the mutuall good of one another."[27] Williams's lengthy experience among the Narragansett led him to conclude "that a man shall generally finde more free entertainment and refreshing amongst these *Barbarians*, then amongst thousands who call themselves Christians."[28]

Wood concluded that in the planting of corn the Massachusett women "exceede our *English* husband men," and in the trapping of beaver and otter the Massachusett men are highly successful, while "these beasts are too cunning for the *English*, who seldom or never catch any of them."[29] In the complex native economy, the Algonquian had developed a broad network of skills in raising fields of maize, beans and squash; in gathering and storing wild roots, berries, fish and shellfish; and in ensuring plentiful hunting. Family hunting groups controlled specific, inherited lands divided from others by definite boundaries. Each group carefully regulated the resources in its area to provide a continuing harvest for its children or grandchildren.[30] Through selective burning, these groups created "ideal habitats for a host of wildlife species." Despite these accomplishments, however, colonial writers generally failed to acknowledge the merits of the Algonquian economic system. William Cronin has argued persuasively that their myopia was largely a reflection of their own attitudes toward resources. In contrast to the Algonquian, the New England colonists viewed natural resources as commodities, to be exchanged in the market for profit, and from this perspective they could not comprehend why the Indians used the abundant resources only to meet the needs of their families or bands.[31]

If these Algonquian were so well adapted to their environment, then we must account for the attraction of European culture. By the 1620s and 1630s the coastal Algonquian had already reaped a bitter harvest from their contact with Europeans. Neal Salisbury suggests that the "propensities of English visitors . . . toward violence and kidnapping, and their refusal to enter into and maintain reciprocal relationships, finally succeeded in arousing the hostility of most coastal Indians from the Penobscot to Cape Cod." "Then," he concludes, "the epidemic so reduced the coastal peoples in numbers and strength that their ability to maintain autonomy and, thus, real reciprocity with outsiders was largely lost."[32] After the plague of 1616–17, some coastal groups were permanently disabled, both physically and psychologically. The Massachusett shrank from a total population of about 9,000 to 12,000 to a mere 900 to 1,200 people, and the Pawkunnakut (with the exception of those living on Martha's Vineyard) suffered an equivalent loss. By depopulating much of the Plymouth–Boston area, this catastrophe enabled the Pilgrims and Puritans to achieve a solid toehold in the coastal region, and they were not hesitant about penetrating inland. The first to feel the immediate impact of Puritan expansion were the remnants of the Massachusett and Pawkunnakut. The overwhelming Puritan success in the Pequot War of 1637 underlined the seriousness of the colonists' long-range intentions: They would brook no opposition from these already weakened natives; and it was this unstable environment that eased the way for the missionary. As Salisbury has concluded, John Eliot's endeavors achieved the greatest success when directed toward "those Indians most weakened by the English migration."[33]

If we acknowledge the internal difficulties faced by these native groups, we might reconsider those Indians who responded to the English option for an education. True, the new way was not the way of their elders; but evidently there was some uncertainty about the future of their traditional life. An unknown evil had destroyed many of their people during the last generation; perhaps the English way offered a better alternative. John Eliot described this trend in seventeenth-century terminology, writing of "the Spirit of God working mightily upon the heartes of these Natives . . . they being but a remnant . . . for there be but a few that are left alive from the Plague and Pox."[34]

The educational efforts sponsored by the New England Company during these decades of Puritan hegemony were, of necessity, limited in their goals. While optimistic reports prior to King Philip's War suggest that perhaps 3,500 Indians had come under Christianity, this was probably an exaggeration.[35] Moreover, only a small percentage of this total received any schooling. These statistics as well as the paucity of records dictate the nature of the story of seventeenth-century Indian education in New England. This story must be an account of individuals rather than of numbers, and therefore, it must deal with the small group of Algonquian who left sufficient records for posterity: a few interpreters and translators, a few schoolmasters, and the few students who attended Harvard Indian School.

By the late 1630s, the waves of the Pequot War had stranded a young Indian in the colony of Massachusetts, where he remained a hapless victim of Puritan fury against the remnants of the Pequot. Known as Cockenoe, this young man was neither Pequot nor Massachusett; he came from Long Island, where he belonged to the predominant Algonquian group there—the Montauk. While engaged in a foray which had taken him across Long Island Sound to the mainland, Cockenoe was captured during the war and taken to Dorchester, Massachusetts, where he was placed as a "servant" in the home of Richard Callicott.[36] Dorchester was not far from the community of Roxbury, where Eliot was pastor, and within a short time Eliot heard about Cockenoe's presence. For a person of Eliot's nature, the coincidence was too obvious to be ignored. Eliot's successes already reflected a well-established pattern of seizing upon every opportunity as it appeared. In this case, the opportunity provided the entree for his missionary career.

John Eliot was one of the most remarkable leaders of seventeenth-century New England. Viewed initially as a mythic hero in biographies such as Cotton Mather's "Life of Eliot" (in *Magnalia Christi Americana*, vol. 1, 1702) and Ola Winslow's *John Eliot, Apostle to the Indians* (1968), he has been reevaluated in recent years by authors such as Roy Harvey Pearce, Francis Jennings, Neal Salisbury, William S. Simmons, Henry W. Bowden, and James P. Ronda. No one, however, has denied his will power, persistence, political acumen, and ability as a fund raiser. Once he had introduced his Indian education programs, he suffered few setbacks until King Philip's War. Between 1651 and 1674, he founded fourteen praying villages radiating outward from Boston toward western Massachusetts and Connecticut, whose populations in 1674, according to Indian superintendent Daniel Gookin, totaled 1,111 Indians. Eliot established tight social and political control in each of these villages, with each one supporting a school, generally taught by an Indian schoolmaster. During these decades Eliot also succeeded in publishing his *Indian Bible* and a number of other works in the Massachusett language. Throughout his missionary career, however, he remained indebted to Cockenoe.[37]

From Eliot's perspective, the inadvertent capture of Cockenoe served to initiate his growing interest in the nearby natives. Despite the fact that Cockenoe was not a Massachusett, his language was similar enough to suit Eliot's purposes,[38] and during his captivity, Cockenoe acquired Massachusett expressions. Here, then, was Eliot's opportunity to learn the native tongue.

To suggest that the relationship between Eliot and Cockenoe was a one-sided experiment would be to ignore Cockenoe's own linguistic abilities, ingenuity, and willpower. The relationship proved to be one of mutual benefit. Even in Eliot's often harsh judgment, Cockenoe earned surprisingly generous praise from the missionary, who wrote, "this Indian is ingenious; can read; and I taught him to write, which he quickly learnt."[39]

In the long run, Eliot evidently failed to allow for Cockenoe's self-motivation, which was matched by his desire to return to his people. After ten years of instruction and services as a translator, Cockenoe was no longer the young man captured in the war at the age of perhaps eighteen or twenty years. Eliot's teaching had equipped him with a trade; and after he left Eliot sometime in the late 1640s, he pursued an unusual career, one well-suited to his Montauk name, which translates variously as " 'he marks, observes, takes knowledge, instructs, or imitates.' "[40]

Between the 1640s and the 1680s, the Indians in southern New England gradually became bilingual; but for much of this period, especially in the decades prior to King Philip's War, Cockenoe's services were in demand. The rapidly expanding colonial population led to a need for his skills as interpreter in settling land agreements between Indian and white in Connecticut and Massachusetts and among his own people on Long Island. Local residents, the commissioners of the United Colonies of New England, and the governor of New York all required his skills during this period.

The type of payment he received for these services provided him with some support, but his remuneration was in keeping with the barter economy of seventeenth-century New England. In 1658, when he acted as interpreter, witness, and boundary marker for the inhabitants of Huntington, a small Long Island community, he was paid " 'one coat, foure pounds of poudar, six pounds of led, one dutch hatchet, as also seventeen shillings of wampum.' "[41] Cockenoe also employed his linguistic skills on behalf of his own people, successfully defending Montauk ownership of Manhansick (Shelter) Island against claims by colonists.[42]

Although the contribution of this Montauk interpreter may have been forgotten, his name remains on the land. In Long Island

Sound, near the mouth of the Saugatuck River, an island bears the name of "Cockenoe Island," perhaps an unwitting tribute to the role he played in furthering the communication between natives and colonists.

Eliot, however, never quite forgave the young Montauk for leaving.[43] Despite Eliot's dissatisfaction, however, Cockenoe had served his purpose. Less than ten years after their language exchange began, Eliot delivered his first sermon in Massachusett, thus opening his missionary career.

During his preliminary contacts with the nearby Massachusett, he convinced two young Indians to be trained in English homes. On November 11, 1646, Job Nesuton, a young Massachusett, joined the group of Indians who gathered at Nonantum to hear Eliot preach during what was probably his third meeting with the Indians.[44] Shortly after this gathering, Nesuton and one other young man volunteered to serve the English. Since Nesuton's offer came late in 1646, it probably occurred shortly before Cockenoe's departure, thus assuring Eliot an unbroken line of Indian assistants.

Nesuton studied his lessons well. Within three years he had learned to read and write in English, and by the summer of 1650 he had probably already succeeded Cockenoe as chief interpreter and translator. He may not have been as quick-witted as Cockenoe, but he was more faithful. Eliot's first assessment of Nesuton is more reserved than his earlier praise for the young Montauk. In August 1650, he wrote: "I have one already who can write, so that I can read his writing well and he (with some paines and teaching) can read mine." With a trace of anxiety, Eliot added, "I hope the Lord will both enlarge his understanding, and others also to do as he doth."[45]

Eliot's fears for Nesuton's improvement proved to be unwarranted. By the following spring he was so encouraged with the young man's progress that he reported in an almost exultant tone: "It has pleased God this winter much to enlarge the ability of him [Nesuton] whose help I use in translating the Scripture."[46] Already Nesuton had begun the translating effort that became his lasting contribution. When Eliot was in the early stages of establishing both praying villages and the schools, Nesuton assisted him as schoolmaster, in 1651, in Natick, the first village. Within a few months, Nesuton was shifted to translator, and the role of schoolmaster was assumed by Montequassum, also a Massachu-sett.[47]

Montequassum may have been the young Indian who accompanied Nesuton when he offered himself for training in 1646. By this time, he too would have been prepared to teach. When the Rev. John Wilson visited the Natick school in the fall of 1651, he was favorably impressed, concluding that Montequassum "doth read and spell very well himself, and teacheth them to doe the like."[48] The impact of European diseases, however, soon shortened Montequassum's career. In the summer of 1652, his wife and child died of "the sicknesse"—which may have been consumption—and the last record of his teaching was in 1656.[49]

Spared the mortal effects of this wasting disease, Nesuton was able to pursue his own career for about twenty-five years, a lengthy time by seventeenth-century standards. From the year 1650 to King Philip's War, he served as interpreter and translator for Eliot. Throughout most of this period, the New England Company paid him £10 per annum, which was about one-fifth of Eliot's salary; but it was equal to and sometimes greater than the amount paid to other Indians, especially those who served as schoolmasters on Martha's Vineyard.[50]

By modern standards, this may not have been just compensation for Nesuton's contribution to the extensive number of translations that relied heavily on his skills. During these years Eliot was to publish the vast majority of his works in the Massachusett language. But as late as 1651, after a ten-year assistantship by Cockenoe and significant progress by Nesuton, he still expressed serious doubts about the possibilities of publication in the native language. In April of that year, he wrote to the corporation in London: "I have no hope to see the Bible translated, much less printed in my days."[51] Yet a mere ten years later he had completed the New Testament. Entitled *Mamusse Wunneetupana-tamwe Up-Biblum God*, it was not only the first Bible to appear in an Indian language, but also the first Bible published in North America.[52] In the dedication to Charles II, the commissioners assured the king that this offering from New England was far better than Spanish gold: "the souls of men are worth more than the whole world."[53]

How does one account for this remarkable progress whereby Eliot moved in a single decade from despair to actual publication? Scholars generally have tended to credit Eliot alone for these singular accomplishments, and indeed, only his name appears on the title page of the Indian Bible. But Eliot himself admitted the challenge was so great that it demanded a collaborator. In 1661, Eliot was not certain that Nesuton would become this partner. Neal Salisbury, one of the first to acknowledge Eliot's dependency on Nesuton and others, has suggested that "the Indian assistants, rather than Eliot himself, did the actual translating."[54] Without Nesuton and the others, the Indian Bible, The Indian Primer (1664), The Logick Primer (1672), Richard Baxter's A Call to the Unconverted (1664) and other lesser-known works might never have appeared in Massachusett. For too many years this Indian contribution to the publications has been ignored, which is due in part to the sources. The correspondence and published works of Eliot and his colonial contemporaries are the only extant documents available on the period; but even within these materials, there is sufficient evidence to justify enlargement of the Indian contribution.

Just before Eliot and Nesuton completed the New Testament, another young Indian joined them in the publishing venture. This time, however, it was not as a replacement but as an auxiliary. Publishing in the Massachusett language was a demanding task, and it is likely that both Eliot and the Cambridge printer Samuel Green welcomed the assistance of this young Indian whom the colonists had dubbed "James."

About forty miles southwest of Boston and just east of the Nipmuc River was a Nipmuc community known as Hassenamesitt (Groton).[55] Established as either the third or fourth praying village, it had become one of the strongest Indian settlements.[56] Just before King Philip's War it boasted a population of about sixty Indian residents. The young Nipmuc later known as James was born into the leading family in this community around 1640. Probably the youngest child of this prestigious family, he was given the name of "Wowaus." Wowaus's family were close allies of the English, and his older brother as well as his father, Naoas, became leaders under the political, economic, and educational system for the praying villages.[57] In the early 1670s, Wowaus's eldest brother, Anaweekit, was civil ruler of Hassenamesitt, and two other older brothers, Tappokkoowillin—described by Gookin as "a good man"—and Job, were teachers: Tappokkoowillin at

Hassenamesitt and Job at Okommekemesitt, which was perhaps fifteen miles north. Because of the English orientation of this family, they determined that the youngest brother, Wowaus, should receive an English education.

At the age of five years Wowaus was probably taken up to Cambridge to serve in an English home. During the years 1645–46, Henry Dunster, president of the struggling Harvard College (from 1640 to 1654), boarded two young Indians. Samuel Eliot Morison has suggested that it was Eliot who "dumped" the pair of " 'hopeful young plants' " on President Dunster, in response to the president's suggestion that " 'what the Indians wanted was a Harvard education.' "[58] It is likely that Wowaus or James (if this is the same James mentioned in President Dunster's expense account for this period) probably became one of the first Indians to enroll in Master Elijah Corlet's Cambridge Grammar School. If this James did attend the school in 1645–46, there is no further evidence to support his presence in Cambridge during the following thirteen years, or until his next documented appearance in 1659. Nonetheless, George Parker Winship in The Cambridge Press concluded that it is "probable" that the James born Wowaus was the same James who boarded with President Dunster.[59] In 1659, when James reappeared, he and another young Indian were described as follows: "Two of the Indian youthes formerly brought up to Reed and writ are put apprentice; the one to a Carpenter, the other to Mr. Green the printer."[60]

By 1659, Wowaus, or James, had received his basic English schooling, probably with Master Corlet, and he had been apprenticed as a "printer's devil," a position made famous in the eighteenth century by Benjamin Franklin.[61]

Since James's apprenticeship coincided with the publication of the Indian Bible, one suspects that it may well have been arranged through an agreement among John Eliot, Samuel Green, and probably even Nesuton. As Eliot's sole Indian assistant, Nesuton may have welcomed another Indian in this translating and publishing venture. If James's apprenticeship was indeed an arranged event, his studies with Master Corlet probably had been of sufficient quality to attract some attention. Moreover, Eliot was perhaps already acquainted with James's family in Hassenamesitt and had had his eye on James.

In the mid-1600s, the colonists were almost totally dependent on English printing. James's master, Samuel Green, was only the second printer to establish himself in the colonies. Successor to Matthew Day, Green had become director of the printing shop at Harvard College shortly after Day's death in 1649. Initially inexperienced in the craft, Green gained increasing skill during the decade before he signed a probable apprenticeship contract with James.[62] During Green's many decades in the business, he taught the trade to a number of his nineteen children, whose descendents made the family name a printing dynasty in colonial America.

One of the most remarkable aspects of Green's long and successful career was his association with James. By teaching this young Nipmuc the skills of the craft, he ensured Indian involvement in one of the most crucial aspects of the Massachusett publishing venture. Thus, Indians participated from start to finish: Nesuton in the translation and James in the printing. One historian of printing argued that James was the "keystone of this fragile arch"; a more accurate assessment would have included Nesuton.[63]

James had to learn quickly, for the work of printing the *Indian Bible* began almost immediately.[64] Within a few months after his arrival, the commissioners noted that James and the other Indian youth apprenticed to a carpenter "take theire trades and follow their Business very well."[65] Between 1660 and 1663, Samuel Green and Marmaduke Johnson, the newly hired printer sent from London by the corporation to assist in this task, and James Printer worked upwards of twelve to fourteen hours a day to complete the New and Old Testaments.[66]

With the publication of the *Indian Bible*, printing projects shifted to less demanding works. During the next twelve years James's role as a printer's apprentice is a little unclear.[67] As soon as the Bible was completed, Marmaduke Johnson left for England. But he was back within a year, and shortly thereafter he established a separate printing business in Cambridge. The bitter personal dispute between Johnson and Green that had disrupted their earlier relationship was apparently resolved, but the business rivalry continued, even though the two printers formed a brief partnership between 1668 and 1671.[68] During this period, most of the Indian works published bore the mark of Marmaduke Johnson, printer; but the intertwined nature of the Johnson and

Green printing venture make it difficult to assess James's role in typesetting the Indian publications.

The 1670s saw the decline of Indian publishing sponsored by the New England Company. Marmaduke Johnson's death in 1674, which occurred shortly after he had been permitted to establish a printing office in Boston, ended the business rivalry of Johnson versus Green; but the outbreak of King Philip's War not only brought the publishing of Indian translations to a sudden halt, it also led to a wrenching break in the Anglicized life that James had adopted.

When the war broke out in the summer of 1675, James was perhaps thirty-five years old. He had been working in Green's printing office for about sixteen years, so it is doubtful that he was still an apprentice. An average apprentice served only seven years and received no wages.[69] But he probably had some obligation to Green.[70] James, like many other Nipmuc in this civil war, chose to side with King Philip, or Metacomet. But he could not have done so without some reservation, for it meant that he was turning his back on Green and his other Cambridge associates. Ironically, his colleague Nesuton chose the opposite path, maintaining his loyalty to the British.

A year later, when the war was over, James returned, casting his lot once again with the people who had shaped his education. Taking advantage of the Boston council's declaration of mercy, he joined other Nipmuc on his return. Increase Mather and Samuel Sewall both recorded the event, with Mather noting that " 'James, an Indian, who could not only read and write but had learned the art of printing, notwithstanding his apostasy, did venture himself upon the mercy and truth of the English declaration."[71]

This decision enabled James to participate in the final chapter of seventeenth-century publishing in Massachusett. The destruction of *Indian Bibles* during the war compelled the aged Eliot to attempt to reprint the 1663 edition. Once again, James was on hand to set the type. Nesuton, however, had been killed in the war while fighting for the English. Upon hearing the news of his death, Daniel Gookin lamented "the loss of such a useful and trusty man."[72]

Between 1680 and 1685, the long and agonizing process of reprinting the Bible relied heavily on James's skills. In a letter to Robert Boyle, governor of the New England Company and benefactor of this publishing project, the seventy-eight-year-old Eliot wrote of James's contribution: "I desire to see it [the Old Testament] done before I die . . . besides, we have but one man (viz., the Indian printer) that is able to compose the sheets and connect the press, with understanding."[73]

James probably worked on two lesser Indian reprints in the late 1680s.[74] These were the last translations published before Eliot's death in 1690. James's former master, Samuel Green, was also aging, and in the early 1690s his son, Bartholomew Green, managed the Cambridge Press for a short while on his father's retirement. James probably remained with the Cambridge Press until Bartholomew returned to Boston, where he reestablished a printing office, which became, in the early 1700s, one of several competitors with James Franklin.[75] Although James was teaching Indian families at Hassenamesitt at the end of the decade, this does not preclude the possibility of his having joined Bartholomew Green in Boston.[76]

The publication of the *Massachusetts Psalter* in 1707 provides the only evidence that James became an acknowledged printer. Its appearance cemented his reputation as "[t]he first native printer in America."[77] The *Massachusetts Psalter*, which was translated by Experience Mayhew (the grandson of Thomas Mayhew, Jr.), contained Pawkunnakut and English versions of the Psalms and the Gospel of John, and was printed in Boston "by B. Green and J. Printer."[78] At this time, James Printer was probably in his late sixties and had finally reached the apogee of his long career.[79] "He had become," as Frank Speck points out, "an intermediator between the spheres of advanced European and native culture."[80]

The contributions of Cockenoe, Nesuton, and James Printer made a long-term impact on the Indians of New England. Their skills and their commitment matched those of Eliot, Samuel Green, Marmaduke Johnson, and others, and made possible the printing of the *Indian Bible* and a number of other works in the Massachusett and related Algonquian dialects; and this publishing venture, perhaps more than any other event in the middle of the seventeenth century, encouraged cultural exchange among the New England Algonquian. Speck suggested some years ago that these publications in the Indian tongue stimulated "acculturation of the natives with a rapidity and to an extent which no ethnologist has recognized." Their appearance, Speck added, provided "the turning point in native economy, religion and government throughout the southern New England area."[81] By the end of the seventeenth century, therefore, these Indians had acquired something unknown to any other native groups in the British colonies—a written language which transmitted the culture of the colonists.

On Martha's Vineyard, just south of Cape Cod, the Pawkunnakut (or Wampanoag) counterpart of the prominent mainland Indians appeared shortly after John Eliot began working with his first assistant, Cockenoe. This young Pawkunnakut, known as Hiacoomes, was a contemporary of Cockenoe; both were born around 1620. Hiacoomes was probably a little older than Cockenoe when he came under the guidance of the island's first missionary, Thomas Mayhew, Jr., whose work established the Mayhew dynasty.

Five generations of Mayhews dominated Indian life on the Vineyard from the middle of the 1600s to the early 1800s.[82] The son of a rather unsuccessful businessman who had come to New England in 1631–32 as a factor for a London merchant, Thomas Mayhew, Jr., studied Latin, Greek, and Hebrew under the direction of private tutors. Less than a decade after the family had settled in Massachusetts, Thomas Mayhew, Sr., made an investment that would change the course of his life: he purchased the Elizabeth Islands, Nantucket, and Martha's Vineyard. Thomas, Jr., was perhaps twenty years old at the time of the purchase; but his father must have considered him a mature young man, for a year later, in 1642, he sent him with a small party of colonists to settle the Vineyard.[83] When the settlers founded their church in the newly formed town of Great Harbor (now Edgartown), Thomas, Jr., became the first pastor.

In 1642, Great Harbor was the sole English settlement on the island, which was known to its native inhabitants as "Noepe" ("amid the waters").[84] Food was traditionally plentiful on this cluster of islands, and fish, shellfish, and eels, supplemented by game, corn, beans, roots, and berries, supported a fairly large native population.[85] Moreover, isolation from the mainland prevented the disastrous population loss experienced elsewhere in the 1616–17 plague. When the Mayhews arrived, the combined population of the islands numbered approximately 4,500 Indians.[86]

During the first months of his residence, Thomas Mayhew, Jr., grew progressively more aware of the Indians living nearby. One Indian who visited the English settlement attracted Mayhew's attention. He was "a man of sad and a sober spirit," Mayhew recalled, who "came to visit our habitation and publike meetings."[87] "I-a-coomes" was later described by Experience Mayhew as one whose "descent was mean, his speech slow and his countance unpromising."[88] Although Hiacoomes had little stature among the Pawkunnakut, his genuine interest and persistence soon led Mayhew to "discourse with him, inviting him to my house every Lord's day at night."[89] During the year 1643, Hiacoomes was converted.

Hiacoomes's neighbors were less easily convinced of the merit of a religion that obviously contradicted the authority of their powwows, whose power for sorcery and curing had never been seriously questioned. The conversion of the powwows and sachems (or political leaders) was to be a joint effort, and in the struggle, Hiacoomes became Mayhew's indispensable ally. In boldly confronting the Indian opposition, on one occasion he told a powwow "that he did put all the Pawwaws under his heel, pointing unto it; which answers did presently silence the Pawwaws devilish spirit . . . "[90] The natives suffered from widespread sickness during these years, but Mayhew and Hiacoomes had the remarkable good fortune of preserving good health among all those who converted. Moreover, Mayhew himself experienced occasional success in curing the natives, proving that "his God could awe in a situation where the shamans had no power."[91] Mayhew's success in Christianizing these Indians was unparalleled on the mainland, but like the mainland missionaries, he relied on the assistance of an Indian to initiate the process.

When Hiacoomes was paid by the New England Company, usually a sum of £10 per annum, he was generally acknowledged as an interpreter, but he remained more of a preacher than a teacher or interpreter. For many years this "grave and serious Christian" was limited to lay preaching;[92] but in 1679, when the Reverends Eliot and John Cotton came to the Vineyard for the ceremonial gathering of the first Indian church, Hiacoomes was named minister. He remained a strong religious leader for his people until his death around 1690.[93]

For the Mayhews, the initial importance of Hiacoomes was his role as a catalyst, with his early commitment and continuing support making it possible for Mayhew to convince others. But the relationship between Hiacoomes, Mayhew, and the other island Indians differed sharply from similar relationships between Eliot, his assistants, and the mainland Indians. Eliot sought to remold the entire fabric of Indian society; Mayhew adopted a more gradual approach.[94] Eliot required the Indians to settle in the tightly structured praying villages, to "have visible civility, before they can rightly enjoy visible sanctitie in ecclesiastical communion."[95] Mayhew, on the other hand, was most concerned that the Indians "have professed themselves to be worshippers of the great and everliving God,"[96] and in the long run, this low-key effort was more successful.

Mayhew was eager to establish schools, and by the fall of 1652, a decade after settling on the Vineyard, he had enrolled thirty children in the island's one-year-old school for Indian pupils. Even the parents came to class on "Lecture dayes," which Mayhew held each fortnight, for, as James Ronda states, "a potent attraction to the gospel was the offer of literacy."[97] By 1654, the commissioners had promised Mayhew that he should have £10 apiece for a "Scoolmaster and one or two persons . . . to teach the rest."[98]

In 1656, Mayhew persuaded his friend and neighbor, Peter Folger, to assist him by teaching English to the Indian children. Folger, whose posterity was later assured through the fame of his grandson, Benjamin Franklin, had lived on the island for a number of years, perhaps as long as Mayhew, and he was a contemporary of both Mayhew and Hiacoomes. Like Mayhew, he had learned the dialect of the Pawkunnakut and was familiar with their ways.[99] Moreover, he had already taught the colonists' children at the school house built by the settlers.

Folger's employment as schoolmaster to the Indian children lasted only six years before he moved his wife and family to Nantucket; but during much of this brief period, his knowledge and leadership were crucial to the missionary effort. In 1657, when Thomas Mayhew, Jr., was en route to England, his ship was lost at sea.[100] This event left the Vineyard program without leadership; and the commissioners called the loss as "irrepararable."[101] However, Folger remained on the island for several years, sharing the responsibility for the Indians with Thomas Mayhew, Sr., who was then sixty-four years of age.

In 1658, when the loss of his father's ship was confirmed, Matthew, the oldest son of Thomas, Jr., and Jane Paine Mayhew, was ten years of age. In response to the widow Mayhew's request, the commissioners wrote from Boston that they would pay for Matthew's education in order that he might be fit for "service amongst the Indians," but they refused to educate any more of the widow's remaining five children because of their extreme youth. "[T]he charge wilbe great before they bee fitt for imployment," the commissioners explained, "and then uncertaine how theire minds may bee adicted or their harts inclined to this worke."[102] The commissioners' pecuniary prudence was borne out even with Matthew himself, for after they had spent over one hundred pounds on his education,[103] they learned "that the ministry was not his sphere."[104] Fortunately for the sake of the family's continuity in the missionary field, Matthew's brother John inherited the missionary mantle; and as John took over the Indian work, Matthew followed his interests by assuming management of the family's business affairs.[105] Thus, when Thomas Mayhew, Sr., died in 1682, he was assured of many decades of Mayhew hegemony on the islands.

Like Thomas Mayhew, Sr., Hiacoomes also sought to perpetuate his family's posterity by educating his children. One of Hiacoomes's children, named for the Biblical Joel, showed an aptitude for learning. In the early 1650s, when Joel was perhaps eight or ten years of age, he probably attended the Indian school which Mayhew had opened in November 1651; and most likely, Peter Folger assisted in his education. Even though Folger was not paid a salary by the New England Company for another five years, his proximity, his knowledge of Pawkunnakut, and his teaching of the English children suggest that he was already involved in educating those Indian children who showed some interest in English.

One of Joel's friends, Caleb Cheeshahteaumauk, probably began his studies at about the same time.[106] Caleb came from a ruling family; his father, a petty sachem of a typical Algonquian "localized family band,"[107] held sway over a quarter-section of an area known as Chickemmoo. This territory, located along the north shore of the Vineyard,[108] and later deeded by Cheese-chamuk to Thomas Mayhew, Sr., is known only by its English name of Holmes Hole.

Caleb and Joel progressed rapidly with their education. Under Folger's guidance, they probably studied not only basic reading and writing, subjects which were prerequisite to grammar school. Their work probably also included the grammar school curriculum itself. The New England grammar school prepared its pupils for college, even though less than half of its graduates actually attended college.[109] College entrance requirements were rigorous; those established for Harvard College in 1655 stipulated that " 'when any Scholler is able to read and understand Tully Virgil or any such ordinary Classicall Authors, and can reaily make and speake or write true Latin in prose and hath Skill in making verse, and is Competently grounded in the Greeke language . . . hee shall be capab[le] of his admission into the Colledge."[110]

In the spring or summer of 1658, less than a year after his son's death, Thomas Mayhew asked the commissioners to permit Joel and Caleb (and possibly others) to enter Cambridge Grammar School. The commissioners sent a conservative reply: "wee desire they should bee well entered that is fitt for theire accidence before they come hither; wee advise they may not be sent until the Spring."[111] The brief nature of this postponement indicated that the two young men (Joel was probably sixteen or eighteen years old, and Caleb's age at the time is unknown) had already acquired sound scholarly training. Further proof came two years later. Joel and Caleb probably enrolled in Cambridge Grammar School in the spring of 1659, but by the fall of 1661 they were already members of the freshman class at Harvard College, having completed the usual seven-year grammar school course in two years.[112]

When Peter Folger sent them to the mainland to enroll with Master Elijah Corlet in Cambridge, he had prepared them well for their two years of study with one of New England's most famous grammar school educators. Like his contemporary, Ezekial Cheever, renowned master of the Boston Latin School, Corlet taught until the day of his death. Cheever completed seventy years without missing a day and died at the age of ninety-eight. Although Cambridge Latin never boasted a large enrollment—in 1680 it had only nine "scholars"—Corlet's fame attracted the finest students.[113] Cambridge was " 'the school and everybody came from all parts to it to be perfected for the College.' "[114] From 1672 to the end of the century, Cambridge Grammar School sent more graduates to Harvard than any other school,[115] and Corlet and Cheever's commitment was etched in history in the verse of Cotton Mather:

> 'Tis Corlet's pains and Cheever's, we must own
> That thou, New England are not Scythia grown[116]

When Master Corlet enrolled Joel and Caleb from the Vineyard, the New England Company was already promoting higher education for Indian students—one of its most ambitious experiments, and one which ran like an uneven thread through the prewar decades of the company's history. While it was seldom impressive in terms of quantity, the program's persistent support was remarkable. Although a much larger number of Indian youth were taught to read and write under the direction of Indian schoolmasters during this twenty-five year period, the record keepers understandably focused their attention upon students who studied Latin, Greek, and Hebrew and who seemed to prove that the experiment was worthwhile.

Schools for children within Indian communities did not open until 1650–51. These elementary-level schools, which were limited to instruction in reading and writing, had been in existence only two years when, in 1653, the commissioners agreed to a request from the corporation to provide for the training of "about six hopfull Indians . . . in the collidg."[117] The corporation's introduction of this measure was clearly an act of faith. In 1653, the handful of Indians who had received any schooling still lacked the prerequisites for grammar school. At this time, Eliot did send John Sassamon, a converted Massachusett, to Harvard for one or two terms, but Sassamon was not a candidate for a degree and he was otherwise an exception.[118]

The Indian College building was probably not completed until 1656, and for another five years, until 1661, it served no purpose except to house English pupils, such as the sons of interpreter Thomas Stanton.[119] In the meantime, the faith and, perhaps more importantly, the underlying financial support of the English backers led to the expansion of the Indian community schools taught by Indian schoolmasters in the praying villages and on the Vineyard as well as, somewhat later, among the Mashpee on Cape

Cod.[120] Indian pupils also began to be enrolled at the grammar schools in Roxbury and Cambridge.

It is only logical that the proximity of John Eliot in Roxbury would mandate the inclusion of Indian youth at the Roxbury Grammar School. Daniel Weld, Master Corlet's counterpart at Roxbury, enrolled his first Indian pupils in 1656, possibly a full two years before Corlet. The older brother of Thomas Weld, one of the first two agents sent by the colony to England, Daniel was evidently not a college graduate. He was, however, an experienced teacher, and like Corlet and Cheever, he taught until his death at the age of eighty years.[121] In his final decade of teaching, he began to work with Indian pupils. Evidently, he experienced some difficulty in helping them to achieve the levels of Latin and Greek required for Harvard. In 1657, for example, the commissioners advised that Roxbury Indian pupils judged "capable of further improvement" be removed to Cambridge, presumably to study with Corlet.[122]

In the 1650s and 1660s, therefore, three teachers—Peter Folger, Daniel Weld, and Elijah Corlet—were preparing Indian pupils for Harvard. It is virtually impossible to assess with any accuracy the total number of pupils enrolled in their schools. The maximum number taught by Corlet and Weld in a given year was ten pupils each,[123] and among these, only one girl's name appears. Described as "Joane the Indian," this young woman studied with Master Weld at Roxbury for perhaps two years. She was then placed, probably as a servant, with John Endecott, the Massachusetts governor.[124] At this point she disappears from history.

Disease and death were common events in the lives of these Indians. Like their ancestors in 1616–17, they showed little resistance to European diseases, and Indian superintendent Gookin suggested that they were unable to adjust to "the great change . . . in respect to their diet, lodgings, apparel, studies; so much different from what they were insured to among their own countrymen."[125] Among perhaps forty Indians who attended grammar school from 1656 to 1672, four enrolled at Harvard; and of these four, one died of consumption, one stayed only one year, one died of unknown causes, and one was killed by Indians.

Those concerned with Indian higher education placed their hope in Joel and Caleb. In June 1659, when they were still with Corlet, they performed at the public commencement. By successfully translating part of *Buchanans Translation of David's Psalms* into Latin, Master Corlet and Harvard President Charles Chauncy reported, they "gave good satisfaction unto ourselves."[126] Chauncy was largely responsible for their education during their years at Harvard. In their final year, he wrote with some pride that through his instruction in "Arts and languages," they were "in some good measure fit to preach to the Indians."[127] Within a year after Chauncy's words, Joel Hiacoomes was dead, killed by natives on his return to Harvard from a trip to the Vineyard, and Caleb Cheeshahteaumauk was mortally ill with consumption.[128] The only Indian student awarded an A.B. degree by Harvard in the seventeenth century, Caleb had taken his first position at Charlestown, where he died shortly afterward.

Between 1665 and 1700, only two other Indians enrolled in Harvard. The first of these was Wampas, a Nipmuc from Hassenamesitt who remained for only one school year, 1665–66. The second, a young man known only as Eleazar, would have been in the class of 1679, but he died before graduation.[129]

By 1680, then, the experiment in higher education had apparently come to an end. Moreover, by the early 1690s the Cambridge Press had closed. By 1698 the Indian College building, which had witnessed over four decades of New England Company largesse, was torn to the ground, and the physical evidence of the epitome of Indian education in the seventeenth century no longer remained to mock the failures. During the same period, the more modest schools established in the praying villages between 1651 and 1674 suffered a similar decline. The only schools seemingly unaffected by these traumas were those on Martha's Vineyard, which still relied on the same isolation that had protected it during the plague and later in the years of King Philip's War.

A number of conditions combined to sap the strength of the impulse for Indian education in seventeenth-century New England. The most obvious difficulties stemmed from the students' lack of resistance to European disease and the shattering effects of King Philip's War. The war resulted not only in death and slavery for many Algonquian but also extensive loss of land and the forced migration of many family bands, who saw the defeat as a death blow to their people.[130]

Given the vast differences separating English and Algonquian cultures at this time, the adaptability of such individuals as Cockenoe, Nesuton, James the Printer, Hiacoomes, Joel, and Caleb is remarkable, for they all moved between two worlds with amazing ease. In the Carolinas and in Georgia, few Creek or Yamasee counterparts to these Indian cultural brokers appeared in the eighteenth century. There, Indian schooling efforts presented a sharp contrast to those in seventeenth-century New England.

5

THE SOUTHEAST: CAROLINA TRADERS VERSUS SPG SCHOOLING

The Southeast was one of the most complex arenas of colonial Indian education. In the Carolinas and Georgia, the Indian and the colonial encountered conditions found nowhere else in the colonies.[1] The amount of education available to colonial youth in the Southeast offers one clue to the sparseness of Indian schooling. These three border colonies provided less schooling to their European and Afro-American populations than any other region. The fate of Indian schooling itself, however, was dictated by more crucial considerations. The two chapters that follow will look at the cultures of both the native people and the settlers of the Carolinas and Georgia; and more importantly, they will trace the intertwined fortunes of imperial rivalry in the Southeast, the highly competitive trade in deer hides and Indian slaves, and the pervasive warfare that influenced the lives of everyone in the region. Focusing on this strange combination of pressures is essential for understanding Indian schooling in the Southeast, for only then will the struggles and limitations of the SPG missionaries and schoolmasters become clear.

The people who settled these south Atlantic colonies were prompted by motivations different from those of the Puritans who sailed to New England in the 1630s. Successive waves of colonists populated the Carolinas and Georgia, and the earliest settlers were Virginians who moved south into the region of Albemarle Sound to form the nucleus of what eventually became

North Carolina. As early as the 1650s, Virginia officials began granting land to hunters and trappers, Indian traders, former soldiers, explorers, and farmers in search of better land. Within a decade, the population of this region swelled to over five hundred residents.[2]

The area that eventually became the colony of South Carolina did not attract settlers as rapidly as the Albemarle Sound region. Despite eager promotion by the proprietors, the colonists who responded never approached the vast number anticipated during the proprietary period of 1663–1719. The earliest Carolina settlers emigrated from the overcrowded British Island of Barbados; these immigrants became plantation owners settling in the vicinity of what was to become Charles Town. In time, South Carolina's climate and soil would prove to be ideal for two of its important exports, rice and indigo, crops that filled the stomachs of the English and dyed the uniforms of the British army. These Caribbean immigrants also fostered the rapid growth of slave labor from Africa, an institution already familiar to the Barbadians. But in spite of the growth of these economic mainstays, another force challenged the expansion of the plantation economy.

From the late 1680s to the mid-1700s, many English and Scots engaged in the hide or skin trade. Deer skins provided the only export for South Carolina before the cultivation of rice and indigo, and even after the plantation economy began to thrive, as late as the 1750s, deer-skin shipments continued to be important.[3] Between 1699 and 1715, South Carolina annually exported to England almost 54,000 cured buckskins. Colonial Charles Town was, in Verner W. Crane's words, "the metropolis of the whole southern Indian country," and even Georgia's efforts to share in the profits of the hide trade failed to dislodge the preeminence of this port town.[4]

Charles Town teemed with activity each spring as pack trains, loaded with the winter's catch of hides and furs, found their way down broad streets to the bay, where the merchants' warehouses lined the wharves. The jingling sound of the horses' bells during their annual visit to this southern port was but an echo, a sensory reminder of the vast stretches of forested lands adopted by the traders of the Southeast. Charles Town, then, was the pivotal point, the focus of exchange between the Indian hunter and trapper and the awaiting market in England.

From this unique port, the frontier traders moved inland along Indian paths, pushing deeply into the interior of the continent. The traders traveled in one of two directions: northwest along the Savannah River to the mountain country of the Cherokee, where they forded the headwaters of the Savannah and the western streams of the Tennessee River system; or south of the Appalachians along the overland paths that led to the villages of the Lower Creek, who lived for awhile along Ocheese (Ochise) Creek, or Ocmulgee River, and then on the Chattahoochee River. From there, the traders traveled to the Upper Creek villages, along the Alabama, the Coosa, and the Tallapoosa rivers, and then westward to the Tombigbee and Pearl rivers, where they traded with the Choctaw, the Chickasaw, and other groups.[5]

The Carolina traders were favored by the geography of the land, which enabled them to penetrate south of the great mountain range that served as an obstacle for the rest of the British colonies. In addition, they benefited from the quality of British trade goods and the natives' capacious appetite for rum. Above all, they relied on their own adventurous nature. Despite the less salutary aspects of their behavior, they deserved Verner Crane's characterization as "pioneers of English enterprise, matching in audacity the Canadian *coureur de bois*."[6]

The traders constituted the single, most significant force of the British Empire in the southeastern portion of the continent. The hide trade dictated the nature and extent of British influence on Indian groups and tribes in an area stretching from the Savannah to the Mississippi; and the success of this trade provided much of the British strength in the southeastern imperial rivalry waged by England, Spain, and France. In addition, South Carolina's hide trade dictated the status of the internal relationship between South Carolinians and the native peoples living in this colony.

Like their counterparts in seventeenth-century New England and Virginia, the natives of the Southeast awakened the concern of English missionary groups. By the closing decade of the seventeenth century, the motivation that had led the Puritans to found the New England Company in 1649 had also become a compelling interest for influential leaders in the Anglican Church. Foremost among these men was Dr. Thomas Bray (1656–1730), a clergyman of the Church of England.[7] Bray's strong leadership in philanthropic measures and social reform reflected the various dimensions of his social concerns. In the decades between the 1690s and the 1720s, Bray provided the impetus for the birth of several influential church organizations; and the first of these, the Society for Promoting Christian Knowledge, founded in 1698, quickly became engrossed with domestic issues, to the detriment of colonial needs. Already concerned with the health of Anglicanism in the colonies, Bray's anxiety intensified during a brief appointment as commissary for the Church of England in Maryland, where he drafted a provincial bill for the establishment of Maryland's Anglican Church. On his return, Bray petitioned William III for a charter to incorporate an organization that would address the need for a learned Anglican clergy in the colonies, and in 1701 his efforts culminated in the founding of the Society for the Propagation of the Gospel in Foreign Parts. From this date forward, the Venerable Society, or the SPG, has continually engaged in what John Calam aptly described as "its overseas educational adventure."[8]

Although it is difficult to gauge the success of any missionary organization, it is only fair to suggest that the SPG's impact in the American colonies was profound. Between 1701 and 1783 the society appointed more than three hundred missionaries to these colonies. While many priests lived under considerable hardship, "a few found plump living in congenial surroundings." The latter included the Rev. Jonathan Boucher, who became tutor to George Washington's stepson.[9]

The SPG charter directed the Society to minister to the needs of the colonists and to seek the conversion of the heathen. For eight decades these two goals remained intertwined, but contemporary observers as well as historians of the SPG concur that the Society's priests were far more willing and certainly more successful in their work with the colonists. Evarts B. Greene once explained the weakness of Anglicans as missionaries to the Indians by comparing them with the Jesuits. Greene suggests that "it was hard to find men in the English Church at all comparable to the self-sacrificing and adventurous French Jesuits." "Perhaps," he noted wryly, "the practical temper of the missionary was repelled by the slightness of the results in proportion to the energy expended." Most Anglican missionaries believed "that their first duty was to their own misguided countrymen."[10] One priest concluded that "the 'children must first be satisfied and the lost sheep recovered who have gone astray among hereticks and Quakers.'"[11] Perhaps, however, the priest's explanation merely provided an excuse for his unwillingness to change his own ways. A "successful missionary to the Indian," Carson I. A. Ritchie suggests, "was required to live like an Indian himself," which was not "an easy task for anyone, least of all an eighteenth-century gentleman, who liked washing and putting on a clean shirt."[12] Indeed, as the Rev. Thomas Barton reported from Cumberland County, Pennsylvania, the Indians' "customs and manner of living are so opposite to the genius and constitution of our people, that they could never become familiar with them."[13]

Despite the general failures of the SPG in this single strand of its twofold endeavor, it did have some influence, which will be noted later. Moreover, the Venerable Society, in its total ministry, established an innovative means for educational and religious reform. In the words of Lawrence A. Cremin, the Society's "purpose and structure were unprecedented, combining as they did imperial evangelism with philanthropic benevolence and the power of a royal charter with the force of private initiative."[14]

The most persistent efforts of SPG missionaries to the Indians involved the Iroquois. The New England Company and the Society in Scotland for Propagating Christian Knowledge led the missionary endeavors among the Indians in New England, and the efforts of these two groups overlapped into neighboring New Jersey, New York, and Pennsylvania. In the Pennsylvania colony, however, the Moravians became the foremost missionaries to the Indians; and efforts in Maryland to convert the Piscataway, Choptank, and other native groups were dominated by the Jesuits. Other than its work among the Iroquois, SPG missionaries to the Indians were attracted only to the Carolinas and Georgia, where they shared the spotlight temporarily with the Moravians.

When the Carolinians began to settle the southern Tidewater, they encountered a wide variety of native peoples who mostly shared common roots with the widespread Mississippian culture. In Georgia, South Carolina, and western North Carolina, the native people developed a local Woodlands culture, which they modified by borrowing from the Mississippian cultures to the west; and the blend of these two cultures came to be known as the South Appalachian Mississippi. Although the Mississippian culture grew diversified as it spread to the south and to the east, some

common features provided a link among these peoples. Most
Southeast villages included the flat-topped pyramidal mounds
that were used as foundations for temples, mortuaries, or houses
of chiefs. Southeastern Indians combined the intensive cultivation of corn, beans, and squash with hunting and gathering; and
in locating their settlements in river-bottom areas, they added
defensive measures, such as a water-filled moat or a wooden
palisade surrounding their villages.

Although the belief systems of these Mississippian cultures
remained diverse before European contact, archaeologists and
early European visitors have suggested that "substantial cultural similarities" developed in late precontact and early contact
times;[15] in the seventeenth and eighteenth centuries, cultural
blending was encouraged by warfare and other disruptions.

The Carolinians first encountered Tidewater groups that included the Cusabo, a group of small bands who lived between the
site of Charles Town and the Savannah River and whose total
population in 1715 was estimated to be 535. Some of the Cusabo
may have remained in the area permanently; and John R. Swanton has suggested that mixed-blood groups still live in the old
Cusabo country.[16] South and west of the Cusabo in the area of
Spanish influence lived the Yamasee, a group whose population
in 1675 was estimated by the Spanish to be about 1,200.[17] First
visited by Hernando de Soto in 1540, the Yamasee had lived
within the Spanish provinces of Apalachee—northwest Florida,
along the Gulf—and Guale for some decades before the Carolinians arrived. In the 1680s, a group of Yamasee moved to the
frontier of South Carolina, where they settled in some ten or
twelve towns along the west side of the Savannah River. Yet
another inland group, the Catawba (or "Esaw"), had probably
migrated into the region from the northwest. The Catawba, the
largest of the eastern Siouan tribes, had settled in an inland region
up the Savannah River and east of the Cherokee, where some
4,600 of them lived in the early 1680s. Throughout the colonial
period, they remained firm allies of the English, but today they
are scattered, with some living among the Oklahoma Cherokee
and Choctaw, while others remain in their ancestral land in South
Carolina.[18]

The powerful Cherokee, neighbors to the Catawba, traded with
the Carolinians and later found themselves located within the

borders of Tennessee, Georgia, and both Carolinas. Because their relatively remote location discouraged missionary or schooling efforts by the SPG, they were largely ignored prior to the revolution; but in the late eighteenth and nineteenth centuries, they became the focus of intensive missionary endeavors. Not until the 1760s, however, did a Presbyterian foray out of Virginia make a brief and unsuccessful attempt to Christianize some of them.[19]

The most influential Southeast Indians of the Carolinas and Georgia region were the Creek people of the Chattahoochee, Alabama, Cousa, and Talapoosa Rivers. Largely Muskogean speakers, the Creek dominated the interior regions that lay directly in the path of the expanding southern frontier during the postrevolutionary decades. With a population estimated to be about 9,200 in 1738, the combined villages of Lower and Upper Creek provided a home for a constantly expanding people; and like the Iroquois, they incorporated into their confederacy many remnants of other native groups.[20]

With the exception of several small coastal groups in North Carolina—the Pamlico, Roanoke, and Croatoan—the other major group to encounter the Carolinians during the colonial period was the Tuscarora. This Iroquoian-speaking group had a population of some 6,400 people living along the Roanoke, Neuse, Tar, and Pamlico rivers.[21]

In the 1650s, a small but powerful group of Indians migrated south into the Carolina country. Settling along the Westo River— about a week's ride westward from the site of Savannah—these Indians, known as the Westo, were probably an eastern band of the Yuchi, who had moved away from their homeland in Tennessee. After acquiring weapons, the Yuchi or Westo band in Carolina became notorious warriors, and word of their terrorizing of Cusabo coastal towns quickly spread south to the Spanish, who dubbed these warriors "Chichumecos."[22]

Carolinians soon saw evidence of Westo raids as well as learning of their attacks on powerful inland groups such as the Creek. Within a few years, however, the advantages of trading with the new settlers combined with the diplomacy of explorer and adventurer Henry Woodward to persuade the Westo to make an alliance with the Carolinians. By 1680, the Carolinians had forged yet another alliance with several bands of Shawnee who had migrated recently into the area claimed by the Westo. Although they remained in the region for only about three decades, the Shawnee changed the course of Carolina history, not only joining with the English to defeat the Westo, but leaving their name on the land through the Carolinian adoption of Savanno (Shawnee) for the Savannah River (formerly the Westo River). By 1683 allegedly fewer than fifty Westo remained, and those who did survive settled as a town among the Lower Creek.[23]

The destruction of the Westo and the departure of the Shawnee failed to ensure a lasting peace in Carolina. During the Tuscarora uprising of 1711–13, South Carolina sent two successful expeditions into the area, defeating the Tuscarora and forcing their exodus north. Two years later, the southeastern Indians began the Yamasee War, for which the Charles Town traders were largely responsible. For more than two and a half decades these traders abused the Indians of the region, with their treatment of the native people ranging from outright brutality and widespread enslavement to a reliance on cheating weights to ensure a handsome profit. When southeastern Indians raised the war hatchet in revenge, the Lower Creek were joined by the Yamasee, Choctaw, Apalachee, Catawba, possibly a Shawnee remnant, and the smaller tribes of the Piedmont and coastal plains. Rev. Francis Le Jau, the remarkable Frenchman who served as SPG missionary in Goose Creek parish from 1706 until his death in 1717, described the Indian alliance shortly after the war began: "It appears this Misfortune has been long since Designed by the General Conspiracy of the Indians that Surround us—from the borders of St. Augustin to Cape fear, we have not one Nation for us."[24]

The first blows fell on Good Friday, April 15, 1715, when the Yamasee killed a number of Indian traders, including Thomas Nairne, South Carolina Indian agent. Once the news spread, Carolinians fled in terror to the safety of Charles Town. In May, following a battle in which a number of his parishioners were killed, Le Jau and his family joined other refugees, escaping to the parsonage near Charles Town. Still a refugee, he wrote in late August, "Our Assembly is now Sitting and Contriving means for the preservation of this province."[25]

The intervention of the Cherokee on behalf of the English was a decisive event in the war, but Carolinians continued for some time to be exposed to isolated attack by bands of hostile Indians. As late as November 1716, ten months after the Cherokee had attacked the Creek in the Tugaloo massacre, Le Jau wrote: "As for our Indian warr, it is not ended, on the Contrary the barbarous enemy in small parteys of 3 or 5 or 6 make Incursions every week or fourth night upon our outward Settlements." The return by Le Jau and his family to their home in the previous December had not allayed their fears: "we Expect every hour to be alarmed out of our houses and forced to fly away."[26] In the following January, Le Jau's fellow minister, Rev. William Tredwell Bull, noted that at his parish of St. Paul's "we are still in a very unsettled condition . . . so that several of ye Inhabitants are not yet returned to their former Habitations."[27] Three months later, Le Jau expected the war to end soon: "It is said that Crick Indians Sue for peace for 32 of their towns, if our Government agrees with them the Warr will be pretty near at an End."[28]

The war was waged at a terrible cost. Le Jau estimated that one thousand Carolinians were killed during the hostilities.[29] Although this figure was well above the later estimate of South Carolina Governor Robert Johnson, who calculated about four hundred deaths, it still bore testimony to the intense emotional anxiety suffered by contemporary Carolinians. In addition to the deaths, uncounted numbers of settlers had fled the colony during the war, and among those who stayed, many abandoned their farms to seek refuge in Charles Town in 1715 and 1716. In 1717, Carolinians endured a severe food shortage, with one settler suggesting that Charles Town residents were "ready to Eat up one another for Want of provisions."[30]

In Goose Creek parish, Le Jau wrote that "we live very hard upon Indian corn we buy at 10 sh a bushell with little or no meat."[31] The war cost South Carolina not only a decisive financial setback and a change in government from proprietary to royal colony (from 1719 to 1729); it also led to a hiatus in the fur trade and in missionary work.

Although SPG missionaries declared that the war had crippled their work among the Indians,[32] the ministers had been outspokenly critical of the traders long before the war began. As early as 1708, Le Jau had written:

> I perceive daily more and more that our manner of giving Liberty to some very idle and dissolute men to go and Trade in the Indian Settlements 600 or 800 Miles from us where they commit many Enormities & Injustices is a great Obstruction to our best designs.[33]

Throughout the war the missionaries maintained that if higher ethical standards between Carolinians and Indians had prevailed, the hostilities might have been avoided. By the 1720s, when Carolinians were attempting to regain what they had lost in the war, few Indians remained in the proximity of settlements where schooling might have been available for their children. Between the 1660s and the 1720s, the Westo had been destroyed or dispersed; the Yamasee had fled to Florida; the Lower Creek had returned to the Chatahoochee; the Tuscarora were emigrating to Iroquois country; and other tribes had been vastly reduced in numbers. The Creek and the Cherokee—the only major groups remaining within the boundaries of the Carolinas—lived some distance west of the settlements, where they saw only the traders who resumed their annual treks.

The first SPG missionary to Carolina was the Rev. Samuel Thomas, who arrived in Charles Town on Christmas Day, 1702, one year after the SPG charter had been signed. Thomas's initial assignment was to serve as missionary to the Yamasee. Indeed, at the time of his appointment the SPG voted £10 "to be laid out in stuffs for the use of the wild Indians."[34] For Thomas, however, the task appeared to offer too great a risk.

Shortly after Thomas's arrival, Queen Anne's War began. Soon rumors forecast Spanish reprisals against the Yamasee for their support of the English. Fearful of a Spanish invasion, the Yamasee, according to Thomas, were "not at leisure to attend instruction." Moreover, it was deemed to be dangerous "to venture among them."[35] As an alternative, Thomas justified ministering to those whose needs were equally great and who lived in areas already settled by Carolinians. Thomas argued convincingly that the number of both Negro and Indian slaves living in the Copper River district outnumbered the total Yamasee population, declaring that these slaves were deemed "capable" of receiving instruction. After settling in the Copper River district, where he remained until his death four years later (1706), Thomas accumulated a record of faithful service to the Carolinian slaves as well as to the settlers. The settlers appeared to be in drastic need of assistance, for as Thomas concluded, they "were making near approach to that heathenism which is to be found among Negroes and Indians."[36]

Thomas's brief ministry set the pattern for SPG service in the Southeast. Like Thomas, most SPG missionaries preferred to remain in the more settled areas of these colonies. In deliberately avoiding martyrdom, they attempted to preserve some sense of normality in their lives, in the form of marriage, rearing a family, and communicating with like-minded Christians. Thus, while they were sympathetic to the needs of both Negroes and Indians, they concluded that those needs could best be met under circumstances that were favorable to their personal priorities. This is not to suggest that these men were selfish, for their lives, as Le Jau illustrates, were difficult at best. They were tested by unrelenting hardship, but as a rule, they did not desert their families to live in areas they would have described as "wilderness," and the Indians they instructed had to come to them. Both Thomas and Le Jau, for example, responded willingly to Indians living in areas settled by Europeans, and in their writings, both men referred to their work with Indian slaves as well as making occasional references to Indians who voluntarily chose to live near the settlers.

In the early eighteenth century, slaves living in South Carolina already outnumbered other residents. By 1708 the number of Indian slaves in the colony totaled about 1,400 men, women, and children in a total population of 9,580. While Indian slaves made up a much smaller proportion of the population than the Negroes, who totaled 4,100, theirs was nonetheless a significant portion of the populace, and the Indian slave trade in South Carolina provided the most important source of Indian chattel labor for other British colonies.[37]

In addition to the Christianizing efforts of SPG missionaries during the decade preceding the Yamasee War, a few Carolinian settlers attempted to instruct neighboring Indians. In 1711, John Norris, a Carolina planter living only twenty miles from the Yamasee towns, expressed hope that his son might improve his knowledge of the Yamasee language in order to teach English to their youth. If this project proved to be successful, Norris proposed that his son continue as general schoolmaster to the Yamasee. "And if it please God to prosper these endeavours with good Success," he concluded, "I hope that hereafter from the Society may be sent a supply of Books for learning and Instruction to them as may be necessary therein."[38] Norris also wrote to the Society concerning his neighbor, Ross Reynolds. Describing Rey-

nolds as "Schoolmaster in the English tongue," Norris noted that
he had "encouraged and undertaken to Instruct gratis these young
Indians that wou'd frequent his School." Although Norris ap-
plauded Reynolds's effort, he predicted that "the distance of his
School from their habitations will prove a discouragement."[39]
Shortly thereafter, Norris's pleasure with the Indian response
to Reynolds's school led him to urge Carolina governor Robert
Gibbes, Commissary Gideon Johnston, and the SPG parish missionary to consider the plan. As far as the Yamasee were concerned, Norris reported, "I find they seem generally well pleased
& Admire that We make Paper speak (as they term it) and are very
sensible and apprehensive of what they are Instructed in."[40]

In response to the requests by Norris and others, the Society
sent schoolmasters to South Carolina to teach the youth. But the
number of Indians involved in this instruction was evidently
modest, and probably included only Indian youth who happened
to live near a school. Francis Le Jau urged the Society to send a
schoolmaster to Goose Creek Parish, and in 1711 the Society
complied. In September of that year, Le Jau wrote that the parish
had responded thankfully by endeavoring "to raise a fund to
build a house and a School upon a piece of land of 24 Acres
contiguous to my Glebe land."[41] Although it would appear that
the primary role of Benjamin Dennis, the new schoolmaster in
Goose Creek Parish, was to attend to the needs of the children of
the parish, Frank Klingberg states that Dennis was also in charge
of the Indians in the parish.[42] His role, therefore, was evidently
twofold, like that of the missionaries.

In the first month after his arrival, Dennis suffered through a
period of such travail that he may have wished that he had never
left Clerkenwell Parish in England. Although the Goose Creek
settlers had initially appeared eager to welcome him, they made
little progress in their school building project. As Le Jau lamented, "He has [not] met yet the Encouragement he Justly de-
serves, his settlmt is neglected by the People, just as my own and
the Building of our Church." To complicate matters, Dennis sus-
tained a broken thigh when he fell from a horse sometime in
December.[43] For most of a year he was also separated from his
wife and two children, who were in Virginia. In May 1712, when
his family was sailing to South Carolina "in a Sloop Loaden with
corn from Maryland," their vessel "fell unfortunately into the

hands of a Privateer near the Capes." When the pirates found no fortune in the sloop, "they rob'd the Passengers of all their goods and sent them back to Virginia."[44] Mrs. Dennis and the children finally arrived in August 1712, but in the meantime, the schoolmaster had contracted the malarial fever that struck so many colonists.[45]

Finally, at the end of a full year, Dennis's situation began to improve in the fall of 1712. He continued to serve as schoolmaster for the parish until the spring of 1716, but during the last twelve months of his service his difficulties increased considerably with the outbreak of the Yamasee War. While attempting to serve as both soldier and schoolmaster, he had been, as Le Jau put it, "reduced to Low Circumstances by this miserable warr."[46] Dennis soon discovered that teaching and soldiering did not mix, and after being confined to a garrison and required to stand watch half of every night, he asked the SPG to recall him.[47]

During his four and a half years of teaching, Dennis had enrolled a small number of Indian youth. In the first three years two Indians had been in his class annually; in the last year he had taught "two mustees, or half Indians." Despite their disproportionately small number, the Indian pupils must have held a singular appeal to the young schoolmaster. In one of his last communications before he becomes lost to history, he wrote to the SPG that he was teaching a Cherokee boy.

These modest experiments in the schooling of Indians in colonial Carolina by schoolmaster Benjamin Dennis and others have received scant attention from historians; hence, no one has considered their impact. How would this type of instruction have affected the handful of Indians involved?

If Dennis and other Carolina schoolmasters with Indian pupils followed the pattern of contemporary eighteenth-century colonial schoolmasters, it is likely that they taught the rudiments of a reading school curriculum. They would have instructed the young Indians in the English language, in reading and writing (probably by means of a New England Primer), and perhaps in ciphering. These Indians probably attended the instruction by day, returning to their families each evening; or perhaps they boarded for short periods of time. As a result, their schooling was probably less an intrusion in their lives than it was a supplement. Since their lessons did not totally obviate their own cultural moorings, they may have applied what they learned with some ease.

This informal schooling probably occurred to a greater extent in the American colonies than has been previously recognized. Wherever Indian youth lived in proximity to areas settled by colonials, it was possible for local schooling to include some Indian children. But since few records are available to document this type of spontaneous cross-cultural instruction, one can only speculate about its prevalence.[48] Regardless of the extent of such schooling, wherever it occurred it offered one clear advantage for the Indian: it allowed for gradual rather than forced acculturation.

Such haphazard and largely undocumented local opportunities for instruction contrast sharply with highly publicized incidents that purportedly transformed the Indian youth from "savage" to "civilized." Incidents of cultural "transformations"—an Indian suddenly becoming like a white—punctuate the history of Indian–white contact from Don Luis, or Opechancanough, of the late sixteenth and early seventeenth-century Powhatan to Charles Eastman, or Ohiyesa, of the late nineteenth and early twentieth-century Santee Sioux. Although the story of Pocahontas is probably the best known incident in colonial Indian history, another southeastern Indian shared the stage briefly in the early eighteenth century.

This young Indian comes down to us through history with the singular name of the "Yamasee Prince." And while his fame is clearly a half-step below that of Pocahontas, virtually every account of early eighteenth-century Carolina mentions this chief's son who voyaged to England to be Christianized and educated.[49]

One of the pivotal figures in the tale of the Yamasee Prince was the commissary for the Church of England in South Carolina. Upon the commissary's shoulders rested the hierarchy of leadership for the Church of England in the colonies. Since the Church failed to appoint a bishop throughout the entire colonial period, the commissary retained ecclesiastical jurisdiction for the given colony. Appointed by the Bishop of London, he served as the bishop's representative. Thomas Bray had held this position in Maryland during the 1690s. In the same decade, James Blair held the position in Virginia. In 1707, Henry Compton, then Bishop of

London, appointed an Irishman by the name of Gideon Johnston to the commissary position in South Carolina.

By early 1708, Commissary Johnston had settled himself and his family in Charles Town and had begun to work toward his aim of strengthening the Church in South Carolina. During the ensuing years, Johnston was plagued by ill health and constant debt, the result of the insurmountable difficulty in supporting his family on the meager financial allowance allotted by the Venerable Society. In 1711, his wife voyaged to England to make a partially successful plea for further financial support. By the following year, Johnston himself had determined to go home for the "air of England." Perhaps a stay in England, he reasoned, would enable him to recover his health, overcome his debts, and resolve some of the difficulties that faced the Church in South Carolina.[50]

One of Johnston's policy concerns focused on the general failure of the Church to Christianize the free Indians as well as both Negro and Indian slaves. In order to exert more ministerial influence over the Indian hide and slave trade, he sought in vain to be appointed as a commissioner to the Indian trade. About this time, shortly before his departure for England, another opportunity to Christianize the Indians of South Carolina presented itself.

In 1713, Commissary Johnston reached an agreement with a "chief" of the Yamasee living in the vicinity of Port Royal and the Savannah and Combabee rivers. According to this mutual understanding, the Yamasee chief permitted Johnston to assume the "civilization" of his son, instructing the young man in "the Christian religion and the manners of the English nation."[51] One wonders how the seventeen-year-old Yamasee youth responded to the decision. Regardless of who initiated the arrangement, it was a significant coup for the commissary: For the first time in the troubled history of the young colony, an Indian would be educated in England and might therefore become the first active missionary to his own people.

The plan engineered by Johnston and the Yamasee chief began on a note of optimism. Since Johnston already intended to return to England, he could add this experiment to his business; and with his own two sons already there to further their education, Johnston must have looked forward to the visit. In March 1713, the commissary and his charge sailed out of Charles Town; and sometime in January, shortly after their arrival, they made an appearance before the Society to plead their cause. Perhaps unaccustomed to such a novel request for support, the executive body demurred by appointing a committee to determine whether the request was in accordance with the Society's charter. Johnston, and perhaps his Yamasee charge as well, was undoubtedly cheered by the committee's favorable decision to provide the Society's support to the project. Under the committee's interpretation of the charter, it was agreed that the Yamasee youth might "be maintained, put to school and instructed at the charge of the Society."[52] Six weeks later, he began his lessons with Mr. Noblet, the tutor who also instructed one of Johnston's sons.

What were the thoughts of this young man as he walked the streets of the huge, squalid city that was the capital of the British empire? Did he sense the confinement experienced by the young Pocahontas, who had survived only one winter in London nearly a full century before his arrival? Both of these southeastern Indians—one Yamasee and the other Powhatan—had been reared in closely knit towns with complex ceremonial structures; both came from farming people, although the Powhatan economy depended more heavily on seafood; and both were accustomed to the warm southeastern climate. London, with its fog, rain, strange noises, and city odors, must have seemed an alien environment to each of these Indians training to become cultural brokers.

Neither remained for a lengthy period. Pocahontas, or Lady Rebecca, survived for ten months. The Yamasee or Prince George, as he came to be known, remained for two years. Under the instruction of three consecutive tutors, he progressed sufficiently to be baptized by Bishop Compton and to meet the first Hanoverian, George I. But once he had "Learn'd Writing reading Arithmetick & was instructed in the principls of ye Christian Religion," Prince George was more than ready to return to South Carolina.[53]

A full year earlier, in the summer of 1714, he had asked Johnston if he might return home, and Johnston was forced to use all of his wiles to persuade him to remain three more months. He promised the young man that they would return to South Carolina and that he would arrange an audience with the king, and he also complied with the youth's request that a small gift be sent to his father. Thereupon, the Society purchased a pair of stockings and a gun, and sent them on the next ship that sailed to Carolina.[54]

The three months stretched into nine, and not until June 1715 did Johnston and his Yamasee pupil board a ship for Charles Town. The Yamasee youth had reached nineteen years of age, and he probably looked forward to a reunion with his father, to whom he would have many stories to tell of the great adventure arranged for him two years earlier. But the late summer of 1715 was an unfortunate time to return to South Carolina. Since spring the Yamasee had been the enemy of the Carolinians. Following the April attack, they had gone into hiding, had fled to Florida, or had been taken prisoner.

Father and son despaired of seeing each other again. The older man was living near St. Augustine when the son returned; and neither dared risk the dangers of travel as long as the entire area was disrupted by war. While Prince George was waiting, he wrote a polite thank-you note to the society.

> I humble thank the good Society for all their Favours which I never forget. I got into Charles Town the 30 September. I have hard noos that my Father as gone in Santaugustena and all my Friends. I hope he will come to Charles Town. I am with Mr. Commissary Johnston house. I learn by Commissary Johnston as Lady. I read every Day and night and Mr. Commissary Johnston he as well kind to be alwas. I hope I learn better than when I was in School. Sir, I humble thank the good Society for all their Favours.[55]

Johnston, who had taken the youth into his home, noted that he was "Extremely Sunk and dejected at the present war."[56]

By the following spring, and a few months after the massacre at Tugaloo, the father had been captured and sold as a slave in Charles Town, where the son was living with Johnston and family. No record exists of a reunion between father and son before the former was enslaved; and no sooner had Johnston reported this melancholy news to the SPG than he himself was drowned. Johnston left a widow, two daughters, and a niece in Charles Town; his two sons in England; and his Yamasee charge Prince George.[57]

Thus, the experiment that began with such optimism ended in despair. Prince George, no longer connected with the SPG, simply dropped out of sight. Even the indefatigable correspondent Le Jau failed to mention him after Johnston's death. It is possible that he returned to Florida to join the majority of his surviving people, who eventually became a part of the Seminole,[58] among whom his descendants may live today.

Why has this solitary incident received so much attention? Part of the answer may lie in this tragic story's illustration of the expectation level of missionaries and isolated settlers during the 1704–1715 period. Had Indian and white warfare not destroyed this climate of expectation, further episodes of cultural "transformation" might have occurred. Thus, the Prince remains unique. For proponents of cultural change, he serves as a symbol for what might have been. In addition, his story illustrates the Anglican view of success in native education. Somehow, the Indian who traveled to England, changed his garb, learned to read and write, adopted some English customs, and seemingly became an Anglican symbolized a great deal more than his lesser known counterparts who were tutored by colonial schoolmasters but retained their own goals, their own spiritual outlook, and a sense of community. Perhaps "success," in this instance, was equated with the eighteenth-century ethnocentric notion of the need for total assimilation, a view which presumed that only those Indians who appeared to renounce their own culture offered clear-cut proof of the "natural superiority" of English civilization. Hence, as objects of intense curiosity, visibly acculturated Indians were subjected to sharp scrutiny by the contemporary world. They held the spotlight at center stage—everyone had heard of them because only they were worthy of notice. This contemporary focus on their lives also fed the myth that surrounds them in history. Thus, each new generation of scholars repeats the story of the Yamasee Prince. While ignoring the more obscure efforts by schoolmasters or missionaries to instruct Indians in Carolina, historians continue to relate the same bare facts about Prince George, implying that his was the only significant event in Carolina Indian schooling.

One of the many ironies in the story of eighteenth-century Indian education in the Carolinas emerges in the efforts of Thomas Nairne. A leading planter who had settled in the southwestern (Colletin-Granville) border of the colony, Nairne was an early spokesperson not only for Indian trade reform but also for the

Christianization of the Indian through the SPG. In 1703, well before he became South Carolina Indian agent, he urged that missionaries be sent to the Yamasee. At about the same time, the SPG missionary Samuel Thomas concluded that missionary work among the Yamasee was too dangerous. Almost as if in response to Thomas, Nairne wrote that "the Missionaries they send must not be a nice delicate sort of People but such who are willing to bear some hardship & Troubles."[59]

Nairne offered a canny proposal to finance this missionary effort. He recommended that a portion of the necessary funds come from Queen Anne, "out of her Dues in this province." Remaining funds, however, were to be derived from a tax on the Indian traders. "These Sparkes," he noted, "make little of drinking £15 or £16 at one Bout in Towne, they may spare so much from the Punch keepers for this end, and they are no poorer at the years end." Therefore, he concluded that it was only reasonable that they contribute "towards converting and civilizing a People among whom they have got good Estates, and to whom they have hitherto shown none of the best Examples."[60]

Unfortunately for Nairne and for all of South Carolina, the measure for regulation of the Indian trade enacted in 1707 proved to be largely ineffectual. When unscrupulous traders forced the Yamasee to go into debt and then extracted payment by enslaving Yamasee women and children, the Yamasee revolted. Thomas Nairne was among those most severely punished. It was reported that he was "burned at the stake 'a petit feu,' a refinement of torture which was protracted several days."[61] This proponent of Christianization and education was seen by the Yamasee as the antithesis of the reformer of Indian policy that he had attempted to become. In April 1715, Nairne was destroyed, along with all hope for Indian education in South Carolina.

Two decades later, in the new colony of Georgia, another small group of missionaries from the SPG, in cooperation with their Moravian counterparts, would once again bring hope and optimism to the prospects for Indian education in a border colony.

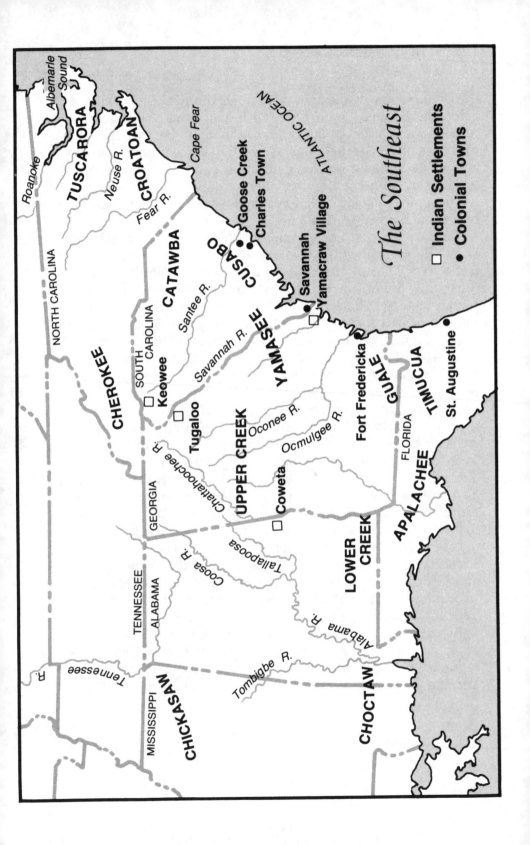

6

THE SOUTHEAST: METHODISTS AND MORAVIANS MEET THE YAMACRAW

South Carolinians and Georgians were hardly cut from the same cloth, especially during Georgia's proprietary period from 1732 to 1752. As a symbol of the philanthropic mood that characterized late seventeenth and early eighteenth-century England, Georgia under James Oglethorpe and his immediate successors was curtailed by a restrictive code and supervised by a benevolent Board of Trustees reminiscent of those who directed the New England Company. Envisioned as a utopian colony for debtors incarcerated in London's Newgate Prison, Georgia under the trusteeship was equally bound to exclude several institutions commonly accepted by her northern neighbor, including alcohol (rum), slavery, and plantations larger than fifty acres.

As was the case in the Carolinas, the opening of Georgia appealed to a mixture of Europeans, some of whom were looking for available land, some for profit, and others for a haven from persecution. Ironically, few debtors settled in Georgia, although the trustees did sponsor some village tradesmen and artisans as members of the "worthy poor." In addition to French Huguenots, Georgia also attracted English Anglicans, Scottish Presbyterians, Dutch, Portuguese, Italians, some Jews, and two groups from central Europe—a band of Lutherans from Salzburg and one of the various Moravian settlements emanating from Germany and Bohemia.

The founding of Georgia was motivated by more than philanthropy. If the southern Atlantic were to remain under English control, the Hanoverian monarchy needed to demonstrate its strength south of the Savannah River, a goal partially responsible for the establishment of the thirteenth British colony. Georgia, then, served as protection against Spanish Florida, ensuring that Spain's previous efforts to occupy this controversial section—formerly known as Spanish Guale—would not be repeated. In addition, Georgia served as an eastern bulwark against French encroachment from the Mississippi. Thus, considerations of defense set the tone for this colony during its early years. Fears of Spanish attack or of Spanish-incited Indian attacks preyed on the minds of those who settled in Frederica or Savannah. This imperial rivalry also affected the relations between the settlers and the Indians.

As the last of the American colonies, Georgia was the only one of the thirteen that experienced the benefit of SPG ministers from its earliest years. In 1732, the Society claimed three decades of experience, and so it did not hesitate to accept the offer of the Rev. Henry Herbert, who volunteered his services during the settling of the new colony. Herbert sailed aboard the *Anne*, which left Gravesend in November 1732, carrying among its 114 passengers James Oglethorpe, a prominent member of the Board of Trustees and the first leader of the colony.[1] After serving only a few months, Herbert died on the return voyage to England. His successor also chose to return after a brief stay in Georgia. In a period of less than three years, then, the small settlement had gained and lost two SPG ministers; and the man who was to serve as the third did not significantly improve the record of longevity.

On October 14, 1735, the Rev. John Wesley, who would shortly be appointed as SPG missionary to Georgia, wrote in his journal:

> Mr. Benjamin Ingham, of Queens College, Oxford, Mr. Charles Delamotte, son of a merchant in London, . . . my brother Charles Wesley, and myself, took boat for Gravesend, in order to embark for Georgia. Our end in leaving our native country was not to avoid want . . . nor to gain the dung or dross of riches or honor; but singly this,—to save our souls, to live wholly to the glory of God. In the afternoon we found the *Simmonds* off Gravesend, and immediately went on board.[2]

Thus, with this rather inglorious note, John Wesley began one of the earliest and most controversial adventures of his lengthy life.

John Wesley did not go to Georgia alone, and even though he dominated the colony through the force of his intellect and personality, the religious endeavor there was viewed as a multifaceted enterprise. Like a complex scene from a play, the Anglican and Moravian ministry to the Indians in Georgia during the mid-1730s involved intense emotions, personality clashes, religious soul-searching, and even temptation. The interplay of characters was dramatized against a backdrop of unique New World conditions. The English saw themselves as the bearers of "civilization." The few Indians—occasional delegations of Creek and Cherokee, Choctaw and Chickasaw, but primarily a remnant group of mixed Creek–Yamasee—reacted with caution, but they were not naive. As a people they had confronted various Europeans for almost two centuries, beginning with the fruitless trek of Hernando de Soto in 1540. More recently, they had been well treated by James Oglethorpe, but they would wait to evaluate the education and religion offered by the English and German missionaries.

The missionaries involved in this brief drama were of two faiths. The Anglicans included the Rev. John Wesley, SPG missionary; the Rev. Charles Wesley, secretary to Oglethorpe and minister in Frederica (the southern defense post established to guard against potential attack by Spain); and the Rev. Benjamin Ingham, schoolmaster and student of the Creek language. The fourth member of this unusual group, Charles Delamotte, served as schoolmaster in Savannah. Like his compatriots, Delamotte believed he had been called to Georgia for a holy purpose. Ingham recalled that when Delamotte joined the Wesleys, he "had a mind to leave the world and give himself up entirely to God."[3] During his months in Georgia, Delamotte played an important role, serving as a foil for John Wesley and Ingham when conditions demanded that they make difficult decisions.

The Wesley brothers and Ingham brought to Georgia a common bond forged during their years at Oxford. Although John Wesley was four years older than Charles and eight years the elder of Ingham, all three had been active in a series of groups known as the Oxford Methodists, gatherings which attracted an impressive assemblage of men (and one woman, a Miss Potter, who led a group in town) whose positions at Oxford in the 1720s and 1730s ranged from undergraduate to tutor. The groups included the Wesleys, Ingham, George Whitefield, and others. The Oxford Methodists were able and talented figures who went on to make distinguished careers, and their participation in the groups served as a viable expression of their dedication to the faith. Luke Tyerman described them as "sincere and earnest inquirers after truth."[4]

No one exemplified the sincerity of their quest more ably than John Wesley. In his late twenties and early thirties during this period at Oxford, he was already a Master of Arts, a lecturer in Greek, a Fellow of Lincoln, and an ordained priest. John and Charles were reared with their older brother Samuel, Jr., and seven sisters in the stimulating and rigorous household of the Rev. Samuel Wesley, rector at Epworth, and his remarkable wife, Susanna.[5] Both John and Charles Wesley and Benjamin Ingham, who as an eighteen-year-old grammar school graduate had entered Queen's College in 1730, reflected the moral code and religious tone of their family backgrounds. As Tyerman concluded, "they were studious, devout, self-denying, charitable."[6] Such admirable qualities, honed to a fine point by the self-willed perseverance of the young clergymen, were soon put to the test among settlers and Indians along the Tidewater of the southeastern Atlantic shore of North America.

During the voyage to Georgia, Ingham, Delamotte, and the Wesleys became acquainted with a group of twenty-five Moravian colonists from Saxony. These German-speaking settlers were religious refugees, members of the group that sought to revive the ancient religious order known as the *Unitas Fratrum*, which traced its origins to John Huss. Founded in 1457, the group emphasized an evangelical Christianity. At the time of the Reformation, it was highly respected by reform leaders in Germany and Switzerland; but during the remainder of the sixteenth and throughout the seventeenth century, the *Unitas Fratrum* suffered devastating persecution. Only the efforts of a few leaders saved it from total destruction. In the early eighteenth century one of these men made arrangements with Nicholas Ludwig, the Count von Zinzendorf and a Lutheran inclined toward pietism, for some of the Moravian Brethren from Bohemia and Moravia to reside at

Herrnhut, his estate in Saxony. From this refuge, the Moravians initiated a missionary impulse which led them to Georgia and Pennsylvania. Count Zinzendorf became a Moravian bishop in 1737, and provided leadership for the Moravians in Europe and America until his death in 1760.[7]

Those who voyaged on the *Symond* with the young Anglicans would serve as reinforcements for the pioneering group of ten Moravians who had arrived in April 1735 in Savannah, then a settlement of about six hundred people. According to the original agreement with the Board of Trustees, the Moravians promised to settle on a five-hundred-acre tract granted to Count Zinzendorf by the Georgia trustees. Zinzendorf himself had instructed the first company:

> Your one aim will be to establish a little place near the heathen where you may gather together the dispersed in Israel, patiently win back the wayward, and instruct the heathen tribes.[8]

Although their goal appeared to be settlement, the Moravians themselves viewed it as but a means to the greater end of missionary work.

During the winter voyage of 1735–36, the Anglican ministers and Moravian colonists opened their hearts to each other. The trip was recorded in the journals of four of the passengers— Moravian Bishop David Nitschmann and his fellow Moravian John Andrew Dober, a potter by trade; John Wesley and Ingham.[9] Some of their accounts refer to lengthy discussions of religion that would continue during the ensuing months in Savannah. The admiration and affection that John Wesley and Ingham expressed toward the Moravians was generated on board the *Symond*. During the voyage, Ingham found himself amazed at the behavior of the Moravians. While observing them "harmoniously singing the Praises of the Great Creator, which they constantly do in Public twice a Day wherever they are," he commented, "their Example was very edifying." The young minister likened the Moravians to "Primitive Christians" because they had retained "the Faith, Practice, and Discipline delivered by the Apostles." He praised their manner of living for its "perfect Love and Peace." His concluding assessment of these people reflects the admiration of a young man who had himself struggled to meet the high standards set by the Oxford Methodists. He observed:

They are more ready to serve their neighbors than themselves. In their Business they are diligent and Industrious: in all their Dealings strictly just and conscientious. In everything they behave themselves with great meekness, Sweetness and Humility.[10]

Such a positive assessment was not restricted to Ingham's observations of the Moravians during the voyage. Later, as the Moravians continued to reinforce this image, their behavior led Ingham to propose a cooperative Anglican–Moravian venture among the Yamacraw Indians.

Despite the obvious differences of cultural background, language, and religion, the Anglicans in Savannah—John Wesley, Ingham, and Delamotte—and the Moravians—all of whom settled in Savannah—shared much in common. First, they were young: the three Moravians best known to the Anglicans were twenty-year-old David Nitschmann, the bishop who voyaged with them to Georgia and remained there about six weeks; Anton Seifert, a deacon and a linen weaver by trade; and John Toltschig, a young man in his twenties. Toltschig was described as Zinzendorf's flower gardener, an appellation probably bestowed on him to satisfy the requirement that settlers be provided for the court's land grant, for his interest in the *Unitas Fratrum* far outweighed his concern with gardening;[11] and after the second group of Moravians arrived, Toltschig was elected manager of the body. Of their Anglican counterparts, John Wesley, at thirty-two years of age, was the eldest of the group.

The Moravians' failure to achieve their goal—to remain in Georgia as missionaries to the Indians—must be attributed largely to the misunderstanding that arose about their exemption from military service. As warfare between England and Spain grew increasingly likely, their pacifism became a barrier to continued residence in the colony, and when they saw no future in Georgia, they removed themselves reluctantly, shifting the focus of their work among the Indians to the Pennsylvania frontier. The Wesley brothers, on the other hand, displayed a degree of poor judgment attributable to their age, their lack of experience, and the level of maturity of their faith. Augustus Spangenberg, the prominent Moravian who met the Wesleys in Georgia, described the older brother with favor: "He told me how it was with him and I saw that true Grace dwelt in and governed him." He depicted Charles, however, as "an awakened but flighty man."[12] Frank Baker, the author of numerous studies on the Wesleys and Methodism, has suggested that during the Georgia interlude both John and Charles faced a crisis in their own identity. Both were "seeking the perfect life of religion by ever-increasing self-discipline in devotional practices, in denying themselves most bodily comforts, in service to the needy." At the same time, while others "accounted [them] saints [they] knew that their own religion lacked something vital." Neither of them found what was missing until the return to England, and not until then did they attain their place in history as the founders of Methodism.[13]

The second major bond shared by these Anglicans and Moravians was their goal of serving the Indians. Wesley had expressed his own intense commitment during his heroic efforts to convince Ingham to join the holy crusade. Ingham recalled, in a letter written to his mother from Georgia, that John Wesley had sent a note to him from Oxford about six weeks before departure, urging him to join their party. Wesley had advised Ingham: "Fast and pray; and then send me word whether you dare to go with me to the Indians." In Wesley's mind, the desirable field of endeavor was not the settlers but the natives. Ingham demurred, believing that he could not go to Georgia "without being called." When the Wesley brothers and one other member of the party visited him in London, Ingham was anxious to understand more and inquired of their rationale. "They answered," he wrote, "they thought they could be better Christians, alleging particular Advantages which they might reasonably expect would further their spiritual Progress by going amongst the Indians."[14]

Even in the speculation on Georgia, then, the Wesleys revealed an ambivalence in their interest in Christianizing the Indians. John, especially, wove together a selfless desire to teach the Indians with a selfish desire to improve the state of his own spiritual progress. John Wesley's wavering dedication to the Indians was further complicated by his appointment to the colony, confirmed by the SPG in January 1736 as "Missionary at Georgia."[15] According to established SPG procedure, Society missionaries shared the dual responsibility of serving both colonists and "the heathen"; in reality, however, the Society missionary was restricted by the immediate conditions in the colony itself. In John Wesley's case, this meant that his desire to be among the Indians became secondary to his primary duty to the colonists, as perceived by Oglethorpe. In the long run, Oglethorpe deemed the spiritual needs of the colonists more important than those of the Indians.

When the *Symond* and its sister ship *The London Merchant* reached the mouth of the Savannah River early in February 1736, those on board were eager to begin the adventure. Benjamin Ingham may have summed up their attitude when he wrote: "I was struck with a deep Religious Awe considering the greatness and Importance of the Work I came upon."[16]

Shortly afterward, the eager missionaries welcomed aboard ship the first representatives of the native people—between five and ten Lower Creek–Yamasee from the Yamacraw community located a few miles upriver from Savannah. This small Yamacraw group represented a village of perhaps two hundred, including forty or fifty hunters.[17]

The story of this remnant group of mixed-heritage Creek–Yamasee addresses the cunning rivalries of diplomacy and warfare that dominated the Southeast during the seventeenth and eighteenth centuries. The place of the Yamacraw in this intricate, complex drama formed a single but typical scene duplicated over and over again among people whose lives were tangled in the morass of shifting Indian and European alliances. Like the Yamasee Prince and his family, the people of Yamacraw reaped the unsettled harvest of this tumultuous period in American history.

The leader of the Yamacraw was a man named Tomochichi. Although his personal background has been the subject of some speculation, probably the most reasonable guess is David Corkran's suggestion that he was the son of a Creek mother and possibly a Yamasee father.[18] How and why these Lower Creek–Yamasee chose to settle at Yamacraw Bluff above the Savannah is essentially a mystery. Swanton, Crane, and Corkran all agree that they had been banished from their own country and were forced to wander for a time near the Carolina frontier. A synthesis of Crane and Corkran's detective work suggests that their banishment occurred in 1728, when the Lower Creek reached an agreement with the British that led to the reopening of trade and ended "ten years of uncertain peace" following the Yamasee War. At this time, the Lower Creek were divided between those who supported the British and those who remained loyal to the Spanish and their allies, the Yamasee, the Coweta, and the Pallachacola (Appalachicola). So the Lower Creek probably banished the Yamasee supporters, including Tomochichi and his followers. As part-Yamasee, Tomochichi was attracted to the Yamacraw Bluff because it was an ancient burial site of his ancestors.[19] But the presence of a trading post owned by Mary Musgrove, a half-Creek woman, and her husband John was an added incentive.

Of all the characters involved in this drama in early Georgia, none is more intriguing than this woman known to posterity as Queen of the Creeks. Mary Musgrove played a vital role in the early development of the colony and in the short-term educational endeavor of the Anglicans and Moravians. Her significance resulted from her unique position as arbiter in the frontier demarcation line. During the brief period of Oglethorpe's leadership in the 1730s, this woman with a pugnacious personality was simply in the right place at the right time.

As half-Creek, she could not have selected more influential native relatives. Born circa 1700, and known as a child by the name Cousaponnakeesa, she was the niece of Brims, the *mico* (or chief) of the Lower Town of Coweta. Old Brims was the architect of Creek diplomacy during the decade after the Yamasee War. His family provided leadership among the Creek for the better part of a century, between 1670 and 1763. Her heritage enabled Cousaponnakeesa to retain a degree of power among the Lower Creek through most of her life. This was due in part to her own mixed blood. Her father was a white trader, rumored to be Henry Woodward, of South Carolina. As a child, Cousaponnakeesa was sent to PonPon (Ponpon), South Carolina, where she was baptized and received a Christian education. When she returned to Creek country after the Yamasee War, she was given in marriage by her Uncle Brims to Johnny Musgrove. Son of Col. John Musgrove, Johnny was also the child of a white father and Indian mother. Henceforth, Cousaponnakeesa came to be known by her Christian given name, Mary, and by the surnames of her successive husbands, of whom Musgrove and Bosomworth are the two remembered in history.[20]

In 1733, when James Oglethorpe met Mary, she and Johnny were running the trading post near Yamacraw Bluff, where Tomochichi had settled nearby. A profitable economic venture, the Musgroves' business reputedly traded twelve hundred pounds

of deerskins to Charles Town in a single year.[21] Like Tomochichi, Oglethorpe was also drawn to Yamacraw Bluff. Having just
reached Georgia with the first group of settlers aboard the sloop
Anne, Oglethorpe was out with a small party searching for a
location for their settlement when they saw the bluff above the
river. Later that spring, the site was described in a letter written to
the Board of Trustees:

> This is a very high bluff, forty feet perpendicular from the high
> water mark. . . . This bluff is distant 10 miles from the mouth of the
> river on the South side . . . and is so situated that you have a
> beautiful prospect. Both up and down the river it's very sandy and
> barren, and consequently a wholesome place for a town or city.[22]

Oglethorpe may have had similar thoughts when the party encountered the Musgrove trading post and the nearby Yamacraw
settlement. Mary Musgrove was one of the first to speak to Oglethorpe, who described her as a woman "in mean and low circumstances being only Cloathed with a Red Stroud Petticoat and
Osnabrig Shift."[23] But the value of Mary and her husband quickly
became apparent to Oglethorpe, when they spoke to him in English and then persuaded Tomochichi and the Yamacraw that
they should permit the English to settle nearby.[24]

   Since South Carolina's agreement with the Creek at the end of
the Yamasee War had forbidden English settlement beyond the
Savannah River, Oglethorpe soon realized the need to negotiate a
new treaty with the Lower Creek, whose villages lay some three
hundred miles to the west. Not only did the English need legal
title to their land; Oglethorpe also saw the necessity of establishing trade relations with the Creek. He sent invitations to the *micos*
in the Lower Creek towns to come to Savannah, and by the middle
of May, Creek leaders had arrived from the Chatahoochee country
to enjoy the festivities and ceremony and to affix their marks to a
document providing ample land for British use and establishing
trade agreements. The treaty read, in part:

> We are glad that their People [the English] are come here and
> though this Land belongs to us, the Lower Creeks, we that we [sic]
> may be instructed by them do consent and agree that they shall
> make use of and possess all those Lands which our Nation hath not
> occasion for us to use.[25]

Through this treaty, Oglethorpe scored a significant victory for the future of the young colony. Georgia would benefit from not repeating the errors of the Carolinians, and Oglethorpe's efforts reflected a pattern of diplomacy that earned the respect of the Indians. As a negotiator and overseer of Indian relations, he was at his best.[26] One of the first to respond to Oglethorpe's diplomacy was the *mico* at Yamacraw, Tomochichi, with whom Oglethorpe established a respectful relationship on the day that he landed at Yamacraw Bluff; and through Tomochichi's aid, the plans for the treaty negotiations moved forward. During the negotiation speeches in Savannah, Tomochichi declared:

> The Chief men of all our Nation are here, to thank you for us, and before them, I declare your Goodness. . . . We all love your People so well, that with them we will live and die.[27]

In response to the warm bond of affection that had grown between them, Oglethorpe invited Tomochichi to voyage to England to attend the formal ratification of the treaty. In the following spring of 1734, Oglethorpe embarked on the trip, accompanied by the party of nine Indians. The group included Tomochichi's wife, Senaukey; his great nephew and successor, Toonahowi, whom Oglethorpe had already begun to educate; four other Creek men; and Johnny Musgrove, who served as interpreter. The visit lasted from June 19 to October 31, and was an unqualified success. The Indians had an audience with George II; they were entertained and clothed, and they met with the Board of Trustees; Tomochichi and Toonahowi posed for their portrait by the artist Verelst; they were introduced to the Archbishop of Canterbury; and they visited with the Earl of Egmont, a member of the Board of Trustees, at his estate known as "Charlton." "I entertained with dancing, & musick," he noted, and "walk'd them in the wood, which much delighted them as it put them in mind of their own Country." As they parted, Tomochichi commented to the Earl that "he hoped we would take care to make their children Christian."[28]

In the fall of 1734, Oglethorpe was still searching for a missionary to respond to Tomochichi's request. His correspondence with the Rev. Samuel Wesley, who was informally assisting him in the search, is revealing. Shortly after the Creek returned to Georgia,

Oglethorpe wrote to Wesley of his assessment of these people and their response to Christianity:

> With respect to the Indians they are People of an Excellent Temper and will hear with great Joy the glad Tidings of Salvation. They will not only hear with patience but with Pleasure the Doctrine preached to them: but they will Sift everything that is alledged with great penetration. They will ask very shrewd Questions and will argue with great Strength and Solidity and always give up their Opinion to Reason. They are greedy of Knowledge and having plenty of all things merely necessary, and desiring nothing more, their Genius's, not being pressed by Poverty, nor clogged by Luxury, exert themselves with Great Lustre: their Expressions are high and lofty and their Sentiments noble.[29]

It was one of those strange coincidences in history that Samuel Wesley's own son John was eventually called upon to respond to Oglethorpe's assessment. By the time John Wesley and his companions had arrived in Georgia, in February 1736, Tomochichi and the Yamacraw had been waiting for a missionary for three years. Eager to meet the man who was to fulfill Oglethorpe's promise of 1733, Tomochichi, Sinaukey, Toonahowi, and several other Creek visited the Anglicans aboard ship on Saturday, February 14. "Sinaukey brought us a jar of milk and another of honey," Wesley noted, soon learning that these were symbolic gifts. "She said she hoped when we spoke to them we would feed them with milk, for they were but children, and be as sweet as honey towards them."[30] Tomochichi reminded the missionaries of the lengthy wait: "When I was in England, I desired that some might speak the Great Word to me." He lamented the troubles that had occurred with the Spanish, French, and British during the intervening months, and promised to "assemble the great men of our Nation . . . to compose our Differences; for without their consent, . . . I cannot heer the Great Word." Only Ingham, the future schoolmaster to the Yamacraw children, noted Tomochichi's request, "I would have you teach our Children." The old *mico*, however, added a qualifier. "We would not have them made Christians as the Spaniards make Christians; for they baptize without Instruction, [but], we would hear be well instructed, and then be baptized when we understood."

Again, only the schoolmaster Ingham took note of the precise arrangements for language instruction, which were prerequisite to teaching the Creek children. Unlike Wesley, Ingham had already turned his thoughts in this direction. During the voyage, Wesley had busied himself learning German in order to hold discussions with the Moravians; Ingham, on the other hand, "began to write out the English Dictionary in order to learn the Indian [Creek] Tongue." Despite his feelings of inadequacy—expressed in the plaintive query, "O! Who is sufficient for these things"—he persevered: "We generally spent the Evenings [aboard ship] in Conversation with Mr. Oglethorpe, from whom we learnt many Particulars concerning the Indians." Nehemiah Curnock has suggested that Ingham also acquired some knowledge of Muskogean through these conversations with Oglethorpe.[31] Thus, during the initial visit with the Yamacraw aboard ship, Ingham noted Mary Musgrove's uniqueness. "She can read and write," he commented, "and is a well civilized woman. She is likewise to teach us the Indian tongue."[32] From the earliest contact with the Yamacraw and the able Mary Musgrove, then, the arrangements for language instruction and eventual schooling for the Yamacraw youth focused on Benjamin Ingham rather than on Wesley. Wesley, indeed, "had not come to America simply and solely to save either Indians or colonists, but 'to save my own soul.'"[33]

Had Ingham been independent, he probably would have begun his task of learning the Creek language immediately. Unfortunately, both he and the Wesleys learned quickly that their personal wishes in Georgia remained subservient to the general needs of the colony; and it was Oglethorpe who determined the colony's health and where it needed attention. Whenever Ingham and John Wesley sought to put the needs of the Indians before those of the settlers, they were firmly denied. Despite Oglethorpe's enlightened Indian policy, which had led to their appointments, in practice his sense of priorities made it very difficult for them to introduce education and Christianization to the Indians.

Upon his arrival in Georgia, Ingham abruptly encountered this mandate. Two days after the visit by the Indians, Oglethorpe directed him to accompany the party traveling south along the coast to the Altamaha River, where they were to establish the defensive town of Frederica. From February 16 until the end of March, Ingham found himself confined to the tedious task of

dealing with quarrelsome settlers a significant distance from Savannah and the Yamacraw village, and he was not free to return
until Oglethorpe dismissed him. During his absence, however,
John Wesley and the Moravians, Nitschmann, Spangenberg and
Dober, had made several day trips to visit Mary Musgrove and the
Yamacraw. With the guidance of Mary and Tomochichi, they
selected a site for the missionary house that Oglethorpe had
promised to build for them. Wesley pointed out that the "chief
merit of the site was its nearness to Mrs. Musgrove and to the
Creek Indians."[34] At this time, he did not reveal whether he
hoped to live there.

No sooner did Ingham return to Savannah than John Wesley
and Delamotte left for Frederica, where they assisted Oglethorpe
and Charles Wesley in the difficulties of founding the new town.
In their absence, Ingham found it necessary to assume their responsibilities, which included Wesley's church and the school
that Delamotte had begun; and his new duties meant that the
Indian task was again set aside. Shortly before Easter, however,
John Wesley and Delamotte returned, and Ingham and Wesley
determined to begin their language project. The intervening two
months had provided little more than frustration.

In the final week of April, the two missionaries launched a boat,
especially purchased for the trip, and despite strong tides the
force of their determination gave them the strength to row up-
stream to Mary Musgrove's place, which they all referred to as the
"Cowpen." The name came from Mary herself, who had once
described the business as a "very good cow-pen and plantation."
Indeed, during the colony's early years she and Johnny owned the
"broadest acres" in Georgia, feeding hungry colonists with supplies from her storehouse, with not only meat and bread, "but also
with liquor and other necessities.[35] Language teacher and cultural broker Mary Musgrove held a singular attraction for the two
Anglicans, the Moravians, and even Miss Sophie Hopkins, the
young woman whose life was intertwined with John Wesley during these months. Contemporary accounts of Georgia in the 1730s
lend credence to the fact that Mary Musgrove retained a great deal
of power in her hands at this time, and Oglethorpe himself acknowledged her importance. Her power continued to expand
with the growth of Savannah as the key city of the region.

Thus, on that day in April, when she met with Ingham and John

Wesley to inaugurate the language program, she was merely acting out one of her many roles as a figure of prominence in early
Georgia. (Unfortunately, this role disintegrated after Oglethorpe
departed permanently, and her later career took on a shrill note
missing from this period.) It is likely that shortly after Easter—
1736, by the Christian calendar—the little missionary house had
been completed, whose first resident missionary and student of
the Muskogee language was to be—not John Wesley—but Benjamin Ingham. John Wesley returned to Savannah from the Cow-
pen after the agreement with Mary Musgrove was concluded,
while Ingham evidently remained to begin his great adventure. In
his record of the negotiation with Mary Musgrove, he noted that
he "agreed to teach her children to read, and to make her whatever
recompense she would require more for her trouble." Moreover,
he agreed "to spend three or four days a week with her, and the
rest in Savannah." In the town of Savannah he would communicate what he had learned to Wesley "because he [Wesley] intends,
as yet wholly to reside there." Throughout his stay in Georgia,
Wesley continued to express his wish to serve as missionary to
the Indians. As Curnock put it, his "call to missionary work
among the Indians never wavered." But at this point he transferred responsibility for the Yamacraw to Ingham, who would
have to assume the role Wesley had once envisioned for himself.[36]

The knowledge of the Muskogean language was not to be limited to Ingham and his student Wesley. Soon, the Moravians expressed an "interest," and by June they had selected three of their
number—Seifert, George Neisser and John Bohner—to study
with Ingham when he was instructing Wesley. Since the Yamacraw visited Savannah often, the Moravians received an opportunity to practice their Muskogean on their visitors. From their
earliest days in Georgia, they had offered hospitality to the Indians.[37] Two unexplained dimensions of the language instruction
arrangement have emerged, however. First, one wonders why
Peter and Catherine Rose, who later taught with Ingham at Yamacraw, were not among those selected by the Moravians to learn
Muskogee. Second, despite a careful recording of all minutiae in
his life, ranging from the reading of Greek to the study of Spanish
and German, John Wesley never once mentioned studying Muskogee with Ingham. He often recorded Ingham's arrival and de-

parture, as Ingham traveled to and from Yamacraw, but the instruction plan either failed to materialize or simply was not noted. For a man who kept an intimate record of his life, such an omission by Wesley is out of character.

Indeed, the reading of the accounts kept by the Wesley brothers provides an intensive leap into the minds of these two remarkable eighteenth-century Englishmen. The description of an experience that they shared with Charles Delamotte illustrates their style. One morning early in July 1736, the brothers took their customary early morning bath with Delamotte in the Savannah River. Charles wrote:

> Between four and five this morning, Mr. Delamotte and I went into the Savannah. We chose this hour for bathing both for the coolness and because the alligators were not stirring so soon. We heard them, indeed, snoring all around us; and one very early riser swam by within a few yards of us. On Friday morning we had hardly left our usual place of swimming when we saw an alligator in possession of it. Once afterwards Mr. Delamotte was in great danger, for an alligator rose just behind him, and pursued him to the land, whither he narrowly escaped.[38]

To his lessons in Muskogee from Mary Musgrove, Ingham soon added another task. At about the time that the instruction began, he approached Tomochichi and Senaukey to discuss his tutoring of Toonahowi, or "the young prince," as Ingham described him. "They consented," he reported, "desiring me to check and keep him in, but not to strike him."

As a perceptive observer, and perhaps aided by the conversations with Oglethorpe, Ingham had already learned that these people "never strike their children, neither will they suffer anyone to do it." Despite Ingham's unconcealed pleasure with this agreement, he was also troubled by the assignment, an ambivalence partly due to his own modesty: "I told them I would do my best as far as gentleness and good advice would go. How I shall manage God alone can direct me." But he was also reacting to the generally debauched state of Toonahowi and the Creek. "The Youth," Ingham lamented, "is sadly corrupted and addicted to Drunkenness, which he has learnt of our Christian Heathen." Ingham then expanded his indictment to include the "Whole

Creek Nation," which "is now generally given to this Brutal Sin, whereto they were utter Strangers before Christians came among them." In viewing the task that lay ahead, Ingham noted, "O! What a Work have We before us! Who is sufficient for these things?"[39]

From the end of April to the month of July, Ingham studied Muskogee and, at least in theory, extended the fruits of his lessons to his friends in Savannah. In June, a large group of Lower Creek led by Chigelley, Brims's brother and successor or "First Man" of the Lower Creek, arrived in Savannah to confer with Oglethorpe, with Mary Musgrove, Chigelley's niece, serving as translator during the meetings. Wesley noted that during the visit Ingham spoke with the Creek of their alphabet, which he had been studying for some time.[40] Until the summer equinox had passed, Ingham maintained the singular role of language student and instructor to Toonahowi; but from that point forward, the Moravians began to act on their missionary impulse. In July, they sent two of their members, Peter and Catherine Rose, to live with the Yamacraw. The Roses began to study Muskogee and, as much as possible, taught the Creek the precepts of their Christian faith. It may have been their project that affected Ingham, or Ingham may have been influenced by other events that occurred in July. During the first week of that month some twenty Chickasaw had spent several days in Savannah, and their visit must have reminded both Wesley and Ingham of the potential for missionary work. But this time it was not Oglethorpe who turned them down; it was the Chickasaw themselves. When Wesley asked if they wanted to be taught from the Bible—"We have a book that tells us many things of the beloved ones above; would you be glad to know them?"—they replied, "We have no time now but to fight. If we should ever be at peace, we should be glad to know."[41]

By July, then, these English had been denied almost every opportunity to serve as missionaries to the Cherokee, the Lower Creek on the Chatahoochee, and the Chickasaw. Now, the potential for schooling at Yamacraw gained greater significance in their eyes. Moreover, the departure of Charles Wesley, who sailed from Charles Town near the end of July, meant that his brother John would become even more indispensable to Oglethorpe and the settlers. If the great dream to teach the Indians were to be realized,

Ingham would have to act, and with over three months of language study behind him, he was better equipped than he had been in April.

At some point in August, Ingham broached his plan to the Moravians. He explained that Oglethorpe had promised to build a schoolhouse for the Yamacraw children, and if it were near the village, it could provide basic instruction for the children and Christian teaching for the adults. They could share the building in a joint project, with one room for Moravian missionaries, one for Ingham, and one for the school itself. Would the Moravians be interested in constructing the building? The trustees' fund would cover the costs of their labor. The Moravians, who liked Ingham, considered his offer. Toltsby, a close friend, described him as "a very young man, about 24 or 25 years of age, who has many good impulses in his soul, and is much awakened."[42] They agreed to Ingham's proposal and "out of their zeal for the work undertook the building at a low price."[43] Toward the end of September, the schoolhouse known as "Irene" was completed and ready for its new occupants—Peter and Catherine Rose, Ingham, and the Yamacraw children who were to come each day to learn reading and writing.

During the weeks of construction, Ingham wrote a description of the site. The "almost built" schoolhouse, he noted with pride, is "60 foot long and 15 wide. It will be divided into three rooms, one at each end consisting of 15 foot square, and the school room in the middle as large as both the others." The Moravian builders had dug a cellar under one of the end rooms, and the building itself stood "on a little hill which we call Irene, by a brook side, about half a quarter of a mile above Tomochichi's town, where the River Savannah divided itself into three streams."[44] The existence of the hill was a puzzle to the Europeans. Ingham guessed that it was about one hundred years old and had been made "perhaps to perpetuate the memory of some illustrious hero or famous action." In the twentieth century, however, archaeologists have proven that it was a political or ceremonial center dating from the South Appalachian Mississippian culture, like the mounds located in Ocmulgee National Park in Macon, Georgia. Ingham's comment on the cellar suggests that it might have been a burial mound. When the Moravians dug the cellar, he noted, "they found abundance of oyster shells and some bones and buck horns." Moreover, when Ingham chose the site, the Yamacraw asked him if he were "afraid to live upon a hill." His negative reply led them to admit that they were afraid "because they believed that fairies haunted hills," a response in keeping with Southeastern Indian beliefs in the persistence of the spirit after death.[45]

In September 1736, Ingham's spirits were high. Not only was he optimistic about the school at Irene, which he estimated would "have a good number of scholars"; he was also pleased by the favorable response to schooling expressed by Chigelley when he visited Delamotte's school in Savannah. Ingham recalled that Chigelley "was well pleased when he saw the children say their lessons" and had even suggested that "perhaps the time is now come when all our children are to be taught learning." Malatchi, his dissolute nephew, added that "if he had 20 children, he would have all of them taught."[46] Ingham's optimism led him to suggest the need for reinforcements. "What I wish for at present," he wrote, "is one or more of my dear Oxford friends to come over and help me." He acknowledged the presence of the Moravians, but he implied that working with them would not be quite as familiar or as comfortable as a venture undertaken with some of the Oxford Methodists. "I cannot indeed say that I am alone," he admitted, "because the Moravian brethren join heartily with me, and from such helpers one may expect good success." Nonetheless, Moravian brethren were not Oxford Methodists.[47]

Tomochichi had been one of Ingham's strongest supporters. Thus, the old *mico*'s serious illness early in July had aroused grave anxiety on the part of Ingham, John Wesley, and Oglethorpe. When John Wesley and Oglethorpe went upriver to Yamacraw to visit the ailing Tomochichi, the *mico* was apparently close to death. Wesley wrote, "Oglethorpe was ill with grief."[48] All were relieved when he recovered. At this stage in the summer of 1736, his continued health dictated, at least in part, the success of Georgia's Indian relations and the fate of Ingham's imminent proposal to begin instruction among the Yamacraw. The appreciation that Ingham expressed in September reveals that Tomochichi's support did continue. In writing of the *mico*'s recovery, Ingham noted: "He has been very earnest to promote the school." The *mico* himself was said to have commented that the "children of his tribe would now have a place where they would hear the good

Word." Thus, with the schoolhouse almost completed, Ingham forecast cautiously: "I have three boys that I think will be able to read and write their language as soon as I shall be able to speak it." He did not yet feel confident in Muskogee, but he knew the Yamacraw villagers well enough to estimate the scholarly aptitude of the youth.[49]

Despite Ingham's initial optimism, the school had a short life span. It opened around the first of October 1736, with Ingham remaining there for a period of about five months until late February 1737, when he sailed for England. After Ingham's departure, Peter and Catherine Rose decided to remain, and Count Zinzendorf endorsed their commitment by writing from Herrnhut to Tomochichi and "commanding his interest in their message." The Yamacraw donated five acres of land for a garden, which Peter Rose cleared and planted. Nonetheless, forces beyond their control began to intervene. Late in 1736 and early in 1737, the actions of the Spanish led the Georgians to believe that Spain would try to regain all of the Florida territory that it had once held. In response to these fears, Oglethorpe had left for England in November 1736, determined to acquire financial and military aid for the colony. His departure, incidentally, inspired Wesley to lament: "Mr. Oglethorpe sailed for England leaving Mr. Ingham, Mr. Delamotte, and me at Savannah, but with less prospect of preaching to the Indians then we had on the first day."[50] At this point, however, only Wesley despaired, since Ingham was well engaged in his task. At any rate, Oglethorpe's departure, which was compounded by rumors, led to a rising fear in both Georgia and South Carolina that a Spanish expedition had sailed from Havana for Florida. At the Yamacraw School at Irene, Peter and Catherine Rose were among the first to be directly affected when the Yamacraw began to leave to fight against the alleged Spanish attack. By late summer the fears of war with Spain had declined, but by then it was too late for the school, for the Moravians in Savannah recalled Peter and Catherine Rose sometime in the spring. Thus, with the exception of some additional sporadic efforts by the Moravians, the instruction of the Yamacraw came to an end.[51]

One of the deepest puzzles about the school for the Yamacraw pertains to Ingham's departure and his failure to return. Wesley described the contemporary rationale in his journal entry for February 24, 1737: "We agreed that Mr. Ingham should set out for

England; chiefly that he might confer with our friends there, and endeavor to bring some of them over to help us." Ingham sailed for England two days after this entry, and eight months later, while in England he wrote to Charles Wesley: "I have no other thoughts but of returning to America. My heart's desire is that the Indians may hear the gospell. For this I pray both night and day."[52] By this date, October 1737, Ingham had returned to his family home in Ossett, Yorkshire, where he had already begun to demonstrate his power at preaching.[53] In spite of his affirmation to Charles Wesley, Georgia and the Yamacraw pupils may already have grown dim in his thoughts. But the event which probably clarified and perhaps eased his decision not to return to Savannah was the sudden departure of John Wesley, only six and a half weeks after Ingham had written to Charles. John Wesley found himself forced to flee Savannah when the legal recriminations against his imprudent church decisions became too difficult for him to deal with. His poignant but disastrous romance with "Miss Sophy" Hopkey had become the catalyst that sent him away. No one has described Wesley's departure as dramatically as he:

> Dec. 3, Friday. . . .
> I saw clearly the hour had come for [me to fly for my life] . . . and as soon as evening prayers were over, about eight o'clock, the tide then serving, I shook off the dust of my feet, and left Georgia, after having preached the gospel there . . . not as I thought, but as I was able, for one year and nearly nine months.[54]

Nor did anyone lament the Georgia experience as much as John Wesley. Pressured to remain among the colonists—first by Oglethorpe and then by his infatuation with "Miss Sophy"—he had never reached out toward his goal of converting the Indians, nor had he improved the state of his own soul. Shortly before his ship sighted England, he recorded his anguish:

> I went to America to convert the Indians: but oh, who shall convert me! Who, what is he who shall convert me from this evil heart of unbelief? I have a fair summer religion.[55]

Upon arriving in England, he added: "I, who went to America to convert others, was never myself converted to God."[56]

John Wesley's return to England in late February 1738 probably facilitated Ingham's determination not to return to Georgia. Even though the Moravians were to remain there for a short while longer, until the war with Spain forced them to move north to Pennsylvania, the Moravians alone could not have drawn him back to the Yamacraw.

What had Ingham accomplished as the single most influential schoolmaster to this Creek–Yamasee village? His knowledge of the language, aided by the teaching of Peter and Catherine Rose, suggests that he may have been successful in instructing the three boys he singled out. It is likely that he taught them basic reading and perhaps a little writing—the alphabet, if nothing more. Perhaps these youth, in turn, became interpreters for their people. Their lives were soon to change, for after Tomochichi's death in October 1739, the war against Spain again altered the settlement location of the Yamacraw.[57] In 1753, Tomochichi's successor, Toonahowi, was killed in a skirmish against the Spanish near Fort Augustine; and sometime later, the people of the Yamacraw village moved back to rejoin the Lower Creek.[58] In the middle and late 1700s, the Creek would find themselves increasingly dependent on interpreters as the colonists drew inexorably closer to their traditional lands.

In addition to his instruction, Ingham also contributed a linguistic record. Beginning perhaps as early as the voyage from England to Georgia, Ingham attempted to compile a dictionary or vocabulary of words in both English and Muskogee. Luke Tyerman, Ingham's biographer, suggests that the end result of this endeavor was a list of "about one half of the words in the Indian language."[59] Unfortunately, Tyerman did not reveal the source for this statement. Other secondary accounts repeating the gist of this statement rely on Thaddeus Mason Harris's early nineteenth-century description of Ingham. Harris stated that during Ingham's stay among the Lower Creek he "employed himself in making a vocabulary of their language, and composing a grammar."[60] The difficulty with these nineteenth-century sources lies in their lack of evidence. Ingham's grammar has never been found. If it were, it might well rank with the seventeenth-century efforts of Cockenoe, Nesuton, John Eliot, and James Printer among the Massachusett; Father White in Maryland; and David Zeisberger.

Schooling for Georgia's southeastern Indians in the eighteenth century was intensive, narrowly focused, and extraordinarily brief, with all of it taking place in a single decade. Ingham and the

Moravians Peter and Catherine Rose made only a slight impact on one village of lower Creek–Yamasee. In South Carolina, Ross Reynolds and Benjamin Dennis instructed a handful of Yamasee and other Indian groups in the colony. In North Carolina, fleeting references suggest a similar degree of individual instruction. Finally, Commissary Gideon Johnston changed the life of the Yamasee Prince. In the long run, therefore, schooling efforts among Indians of the Southeast probably achieved but a single dimension of success. These few attempts may have encouraged a small number of Indians to become cultural brokers, dealing in that cultural frontier dividing the Indian from the colonial; but the records in this area are scanty and unrewarding, making it difficult to assess the impact of these few, partially schooled Indians. Yet if the colonial experience of Indian cultural brokers elsewhere may serve as an example, it is likely that they wielded some influence among their people. Here, then, is the legacy of Indian schooling in the southern Atlantic colonies of the British empire.

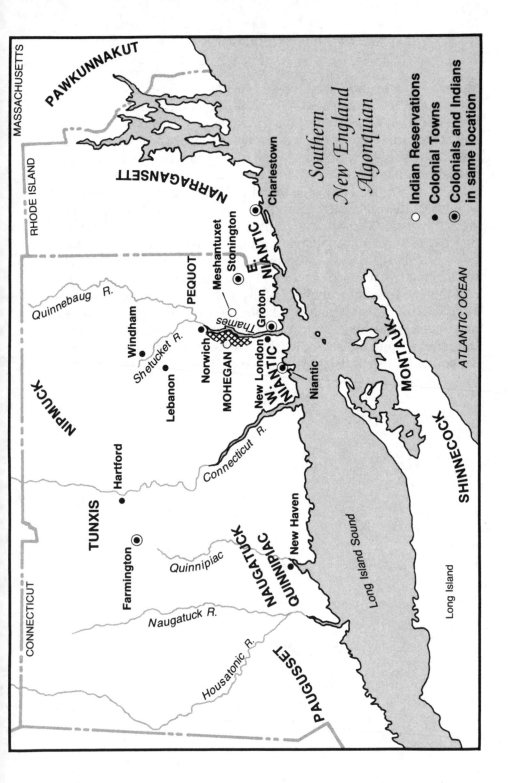

Southern
New England
Algonquian

Indian Reservations ○
Colonial Towns ●
Colonials and Indians ◉
in same location

MASSACHUSETTS

PAWKUNNAKUT

RHODE ISLAND

NARRAGANSETT

Charlestown

Stonington

Meshantuxet

E. NIANTIC

Quinnebaug R.

PEQUOT

Groton

Windham

Shetucket R.

Thames

Norwich

New London

MOHEGAN

W. NIANTIC

NIPMUCK

Lebanon

Niantic

Hartford

Connecticut R.

MONTAUK

TUNXIS

SHINNECOCK

ATLANTIC OCEAN

Farmington

New Haven

NAUGATUCK

QUINNIPIAC

Quinnipiac

Long Island Sound

Naugatuck R.

Long Island

CONNECTICUT

Housatonic R.

PAUGUSSET

7

SCHOOLING FOR THE SOUTHERN NEW ENGLAND ALGONQUIAN, FROM THE 1690s TO THE 1730s

Several decades separated Indian schooling in seventeenth-century New England from its eighteenth-century counterpart. The turn-of-the-century years marked a time of transition, when missionaries and laymen forged links with Indian groups in building the foundation for some of the schooling efforts spawned by the Great Awakening.

The period of King Philip's War served as a rough dividing line between two eras in New England Indian schooling. Despite its destructive impact, the war did not end the possibilities of further Indian education. In the years immediately following the war, the estrangement between Indian and white was softened by Boston's general pardon, which permitted men such as James Printer to return to their former positions in the English world and, equally important, enabled them to move once more between the two worlds. Probably the single major educational accomplishment in this period was the second printing of the *Indian Bible*, a joint effort by Eliot and James Printer.

The *Indian Bible* and other bilingual books had been printed by the College Press, in its headquarters in Harvard's Indian College building; and when the press closed, the task of printing these works simply moved to Boston, where Bartholomew Green, the son of printer Samuel Green, and others continued to produce the bilingual publications used in the colony's various Indian com-

munities. In addition, the Indians James Printer and Neesnummin had rejoined the publishing process.

The death of John Eliot marked the end of an era that had begun
six decades earlier, in the 1630s. By the middle of the nineties
almost every Englishman and Indian who had been prominent in
this era were also gone. The aged and highly respected Hiacoomes died about the same time as Eliot. His old friend Thomas
Mayhew, Sr., had succumbed to old age several years earlier.
Others included Daniel Gookin, the superintendent for the praying villages, and Richard Bourne and John Cotton, the missionaries who had served the Indians of Cape Cod. The end of the era
was further symbolized by the death of Robert Boyle, the able
governor of the New England Company.

When Boyle died, he left a will that provided a financial incentive for the future education of Indians in New England and in
Virginia. Those other individuals who died at this time left a
legacy for Indian schooling. In most areas where there had been
some Indian schooling, new missionaries and schoolmasters,
both Algonquian and white, assumed the responsibilities held by
their predecessors. In a number of cases, the newcomers were
descendants of the old guard. From 1708 forward, the names of
Indians dot the Receipt Book kept by Judge Samuel Sewall, secretary treasurer for the Boston commissioners. A few of those listed
by Sewall had a record of service that dated back perhaps a
decade or more. Some of these Algonquian served as schoolmasters or as preachers, and others held positions not clearly defined.
Among the Indian names were those of James Printer, schoolmaster of Hassenamesitt; John Hiacoomes, preacher and teacher of
the Vineyard; Thomas Waban of Natick; Jonas Nummack, teacher
at Mashpee; Thomas Sampson, teacher at the Elizabeth Islands;
William Simonds, preacher and teacher at Dartmouth; John Neesnummin, preacher and translator; Ephraim Wampom, teacher at
Yarmouth; and Joseph Wanno, preacher at Manomet Ponds, Plymouth.[1] Many of the English names in Sewall's receipt book belonged to missionary-schoolmaster families in the area. In addition to the Mayhews, the most famous of these were the Tupper
family of Sandwich; the Bourne family of Cape Cod (Mashpee);
John Cotton and his sons at Plymouth; the Rawson family (Grindal was at Mendon); the Gookin family at Natick; and the Treat
family of Plymouth.

Even the destruction of Harvard's brick Indian College building did not necessarily close Harvard's doors to Indian students, for the Robert Boyle Fund created new opportunities. However, inept administration of the income from the Brafferton estate prevented Harvard College from receiving any direct payments until 1711. The initial agreement provided that half of the funds would go to "two ministers as their salary for instruction [of] the natives 'in or near his Majesty's colonies in New England in the Christian knowledge,' " while the other half was intended for the president and fellows of Harvard, who were to use it to pay the salaries of two ministers who taught "Indians in or near the College."[2] This agreement, which was based on a rental figure of £90, was modified in 1698 to allow for the residue of the rent monies (after the payment to Harvard) to provide for the care and education of Indian children at the College of William and Mary. Between that year and the first decade of the eighteenth century, Harvard waited in vain for its annual £45. In 1710, when the New England Company received a letter of inquiry from Harvard, Sir William Ashurst, who was then treasurer, offered the hope of future payments of Harvard's share of £45. Ashurst suggested that past payments would be impossible to make up since the commissioners had used the funds for ministers's salaries instead of paying them to the college, as the company had requested.[3] In spite of this disclaimer, the first payment to Harvard recorded by Sewall was for the grand sum of £136, and in the ensuing years through 1718, the payments fluctuated annually but never fell below £90.[4] Most likely, the company was attempting to make up for the earlier losses.

At least one Indian student, Benjamin Larnell, attended Harvard in the early years of the eighteenth century. Larnell, whose first teacher was the Rev. Grindal Rawson, pastor at Mendon and missionary for the New England Company, exhibited such promise that Rawson enrolled him in school—probably a grammar school—where he prepared for college. In 1712, Larnell entered Harvard, where he was described as "An Acute Grammarian, an Extraordinary Latin Poet, and a good Greek one." Cotton Mather, a man not easily impressed, sent a poem written by Larnell to William Ashurst in London. Larnell, however, like his seventeenth-century predecessors at Harvard, did not survive to teach. In the summer of 1714, he went for a swim one day, took a chill, and died a short while later. A white student, Oliver Peabody, also benefited from the Boyle Fund, enrolling in Harvard a few years after Larnell's death. In his junior year, upon receiving £45 from the Boyle fund, Peabody was advised to plan for the "indian service." In 1721 he began to preach at Natick, the first of the praying villages, where he was ordained in 1729. Supported by the New England Company throughout his tenure, he continued to teach and preach to the small number of Natick Indians until his death in the early 1750s.[5]

Thus, the work begun in the decades before King Philip's War did not come to a complete halt. Although the war damaged beyond repair the status of the praying villages (which declined from a prewar total of fourteen to four or five), both the Algonquian and the English retrieved the remnants of their work and the pace began to quicken again by the end of the 1690s. The decades between 1698 and the 1730s probably did not share the dramatic flavor that characterized both the earlier and the later periods. But the interim period witnessed a continuation of Indian schooling in Massachusetts Bay and its slow expansion into the communities of the southern New England Algonquian living in the Connecticut and Rhode Island colonies.

In these interim decades the thrust came, as it had come earlier, from a small group of men in Massachusetts Bay. By 1698, the changing of the guard had begun to take place.

Just before the turn of the century, the New England Company responded to frequent requests from Boston by appointing six new commissioners to replace those who had died or simply ceased to participate because of infirmities. Two of the most significant among these six appointments were Samuel Sewall and Cotton Mather. In 1697, the Rev. Increase Mather, Cotton Mather's father and one of the few remaining active company commissioners, had written to Ashurst, encouraging the forthcoming appointments and explaining the stagnation in recent years. "Since the death of Mr. Eliot (that American Apostle)," Mather wrote, "there has bin a signal blast of heaven on ye Indian work." Eliot's death, however, was not the only reason for the lack of action; for, as Mather added, there was a paucity of competent people, with "very many of the most pious Indians (both professors & preachers) being dead also, & others of equal worth not appearing to succeed them."[6] Sewall, who was soon to be named secretary treasurer, recorded his own attitude toward the considerable responsibility of the commissioner position: "Seventh-day October 14 [1699]. I meet with the Governour, Lt Govr, Mr. I. Mather, &c about the Indian Affairs, which is the first time. The Lord make me faithful and useful in it."[7] Sewall's humility contrasts with the egoism of Cotton Mather, whose awakened concern for the Indians emerged largely as an extension of his personality. A few months before the first meeting of the Boston commissioners described by Sewall, Mather observed a day of personal resolutions, planning worthy projects yet to be undertaken. One of these concerned Indians. In resolving to commit some of his singular talents to the Indian cause, Mather proposed:

> That I would shortly write a little Book, which my Kinsman shall Translate into the Indian Tongue, to make the Knowledge of Christ, and Christianity, more effectually apprehended among the Indians, and their Children.[8]

The new commissioners strongly supported the work begun under the remnant group that included Increase Mather, and they continued to sponsor the printing of bilingual works for their Indian readers. They relied on the services of three translators, including Grindal Rawson, who had formerly collaborated with John Eliot; Samuel Danforth, the minister at Taunton; and Experience Mayhew, the great grandson of Thomas Mayhew, Sr., and one of the most renowned missionaries to bear the family name. During this period, Cotton Mather, in accordance with his resolution, obligingly submitted several of his works, including An Indian Primer, as well as various sermons; all were translated and then printed. In his own assessment of the Massachusett language, he described it as one "wherein words are of sesquipedalian and unaccountable dimensions."[9] Mather probably was flattered when he became the first colonial divine to have one of his works translated and published in Iroquois. This item, Another Tongue brought in, to Confess the Great Savior of the World, appeared in 1707.[10]

Throughout the early decades of the eighteenth century the commissioners remained divided on a singularly important issue in bilingual printing: whether to publish a third edition of the Indian Bible. By this time the commissioners retained only a few copies of the second edition of 1685, so the issue of reprinting assumed immediate importance. There was no question as to need, for two decades later the Pawkunnakut of the Vineyard were still asking Experience Mayhew for copies of the *Indian Bible* that he could not supply.

New Englanders involved with Indian education at the turn of the century no longer shared the assumptions of the 1650s and 1660s. The decades separating John Eliot's world from that of the commissioners in the early 1700s had brought a shift in attitudes toward bilingualism. Whereas Eliot had seen the necessity of reaching out to the Algonquian in their own tongue, the eighteenth-century commissioners, viewed language as an integral expression of culture, arguing that "the best thing we can do for our Indians is to Anglicize them in all Instances." "They can scarce retain their Language," the commissioners asserted, "Without a Tincture of other Salvage Inclinations, which do but ill suit, either with the Honor or with the design of Christianity."[11] These men bested Eliot at his own game of total assimilation, a feat that underscored the increasing ethnocentrism of the New Englanders, whose plan to "Anglicize" the Indians allowed no room for native ways. Thus, despite the urging to reprint the *Indian Bible* by both London's New England Company and Boston's Samuel Sewall, the local advocate of reprinting, no action was taken and the issue died. And while the commissioners were procrastinating over the issue, they were congratulating themselves on successes achieved among the Indians of Massachusetts and the Vineyard and seeking new groups of Indians to Christianize. "Almost all that remain under the influence of the English, in this Massachusetts province," they observed, "are so far christianized as that they believe there is a God, and that Jesus Christ is the Son of God and the Saviour of the world."[12]

The commissioners based this conclusion on the findings of two ministers employed by the New England Company, Grindal Rawson and Samuel Danforth. Since both of these men were fluent in the Massachusett language, the commissioners requested in 1698 that they visit all of the Indian settlements in the Bay colony and prepare a report. The Rawson–Danforth trip in the summer of 1698 lasted almost a full month, and for several decades it remained the final word on the Indians of the area.[13] While visiting Indian villages on both the islands and the mainland, the two ministers found a substantial survival of the efforts of Eliot, the Mayhews, and other early missionaries. Some of the villages had Indian pastors; others alternated between Indian and English. A number of them employed Indian schoolmasters, such as James Printer, who was teaching at Hasenamesitt at the time. All of these men were paid varying salaries by the company. Rawson and Danforth praised the schoolmasters for their regular catechizing of the children. Beyond catechizing, however, their descriptions of curricula were notably absent, except for their observation that many of those whom they visited could read. Despite this optimism, Rawson and Danforth expressed concern about the survival of these native people, noting: "We have been credibly informed of a great Mortality among the *Indians* within these few years past."[14] Disease continued to take its toll.

Armed with this report on the progress of education among Indians in the Bay colony, the commissioners were eager to expand their reach. The area that beckoned to them included southern Connecticut and Rhode Island. As early as 1705, the commissioners expressed concern about the progress of the southernmost New England Algonquian. They lamented their past failures with the Mohegan, the Pequot remnant, the Niantic, and the Narragansett. The Mohegan had been "Obstinate in their Paganism," the commissioners declared, "and their Obstinacy has put a stop at present unto our Endeavours." However, some hope flickered for the Narragansett, who had benefited from the ministrations of "a most exemplary *Indian Minister* named Japhet. A Christianized Pawkunnakut, Japhet was pastor at the Indian Church in Chilmark on Martha's Vineyard. Samuel Sewall had first met him on a trip to the Vineyard in 1702, where he recalled having enjoyed "much discourse" with Japhet and other Indian pastors. One of the pastors, however, had professed to be an "Anabaptist," which Sewall found very disconcerting.[15] Pleased with Japhet's visits to Rhode Island, the commissioners resolved to give the Indian preacher "all possible encouragement," since, in their estimation, "God has Crown'd his Endeavours with considerable Success."[16]

In the following year, the Boston commissioners determined to appeal to the Connecticut government for assistance with their plans. Thus, they wrote directly to John Winthrop, who was then governor:

It is well known to you that you have a body of Indians within the very bowels of your Colony, who to this day ly perishing in horrid ignorance and wickedness, devoted vessels of Satan, unhappy strangers to the only Saviour.[17]

The commissioners suggested that the Connecticut ministers meet in order to select one among them to preach to the Indians. Evidently, those in Massachusetts Bay were far more serious about converting Indians than their counterparts in Connecticut, for the commissioners were disappointed with the lack of results.[18] But the historical dimension of missionary work may clarify the reason for this uneasy relationship between Connecticut and the Bay colony. No missionary work could proceed without funds, and for well over half a century, especially during Eliot's years of power, the bulk of New England Company funding had been distributed within Massachusetts Bay. After the Boston commissioners wrote to Connecticut in 1706, the commissioners there applied to Cotton Mather for funds "for ye xtionizing their Indians," and when William Ashurst, company treasurer, received this request, he recalled that Connecticut's previous "endeavours of that nature had been baffled." Ashurst evidently left the financial decision (the funding for Connecticut) to the Boston commissioners. The continued paucity of schoolmasters or missionaries in Connecticut at this time would suggest that Winthrop's colony may not have offered to the Boston commissioners sufficient proof of their willingness to plunge into a program for Christianization of the Indians.

Cotton Mather, however, was not deterred. A few years later, he recorded a note in his diary indicating that the matter was still uppermost in his mind. As the temperamental gadfly for the Boston commissioners, he implied that most of their commendable actions were the direct result of his urging. In 1711, he wrote that he planned to ask them to "send a couple of Missionaries unto the Mohegin Indians, and their Neighbours . . . which, unto the Shame of us all, continue still in Paganism."[19] A year later, he wrote to William Ashurst that he was still "pressing" the cause of Christianizing the Mohegans, who remained "obstinate pagans."[20] Woe unto the Mohegans with Cotton Mather on their trail.

In the following year, the Boston commissioners determined to acquire firsthand information about the southern New England Indians. They chose their envoy carefully, selecting one of the most devoted missionaries in the employ of the company, Experience Mayhew (1673–1758). In 1713, Mayhew had twenty years of missionary work behind him, and over forty remaining ahead of him. Mayhew was as brave as he was devoted. He was so committed to the Christian faith that the very real possibility of facing a group of resentful and openly hostile southern New England Algonquian did not disturb him. As he delivered his "discourses" among the hostile, he debated openly, holding his ground with antagonistic, suspicious leaders such as Ninnigret II, the sachem of the Narraganset. The commissioners made a wise choice, and Mayhew gave them an honest report.[21]

Traveling through Narragansett, Mohegan, and Pequot settlements during two consecutive fall trips in 1713 and 1714, Mayhew visited every group of Indians either willing to listen to him or to discuss Christianity on a one-to-one level.

Occasionally, some Algonquian responded positively to Mayhew. His most optimistic remarks were directed toward the Garretts, a Pequot family of Stonington, Connecticut. Descended from a line of Pequot and Niantic sachems, Joseph and Benjamin Garrett and their sister appeared to hold promise as Christians. It was Joseph, however, who became Mayhew's most frequent companion on these trips; his command of English enabled him to serve as Mayhew's interpreter. Mayhew discovered his own language facility limited, for, as he noted, the dialects of southern New England Algonquian were "very different from ours at Martha's Vineyard."[22] Mayhew wrote highly of Joseph, whose "decent and manly carriage" was exceedingly pleasing to the missionary. After ascertaining that his Pequot interpreter was "a person of good parts, and of very good quality among the Indians," he "took much paine with the young man, seeking to explain Christianity to him."[23] "He seemed to be affected at my Discourse," Mayhew observed during the first visit.[24] A year later, Mayhew discovered with some dismay that Joseph had been "overtaken with drink" on at least one occasion. Nonetheless, Mayhew retained "considerable hopes of him" as he "offered to . . . forsake his drunkenness" and other sins and to serve the only true God. "And," Mayhew added, "he did before I came away, do accordingly."[25]

All three of the Garrett siblings—Joseph, Benjamin, and their sister—had sons. When Mayhew discussed the education of these boys, all of the Garretts said they were "willing to devote [their sons] to Learning if the Honnble Comissioners will be at the charge of it."[26] Benjamin's son, also called Benjamin, was about seven years of age in 1714, and when he too became a father, he sent his daughter, Hannah, to a boarding school in Lebanon, Connecticut, directed by Eleazar Wheelock. Here, as in Massachusetts Bay, the roots for education lay deep in the history of families such as the Garretts.

The Garretts, however, proved to be an exception. More often, Mayhew found it necessary to detail in his journal reasons for opposition to the missionaries in these communities. In the fall of 1714, the Mohegan of Groton were so upset by a recent land grab initiated by the whites that they refused to permit Mayhew to meet with them. Mayhew rationalized: "These things hap'ning just before I came . . . produced in the Indians a greater aversion to the English and their Religion than otherwise they would have had."[27] Others confronted him with arguments that he found difficult to refute. Ninnigret II "demanded" of Mayhew "that he make the English good in the first place for he said many of them were still bad." The shrewd Narragansett sachem also attacked the factionalism in Christianity, pointing to the divisions among the nearby English, "some keeping Saturday, others Sunday, and others not keeping any day." Thus, he declared, "ye Indians could not tell what religion to be of, if they had a mind to be Christians."[28] The Mohegan living in a settlement north of New London might as well have been coached by Ninnigret, for some of their sachems present at the meeting with Mayhew denied the "necessity" of the Christian religion. "Others said they could not see that men were ever the better for being Christians, for the English that were Christians," they declared, "would cheat the Indians of their land and otherwise wrong them." These sachems asserted that even literacy made the English more wicked, for "their knowledge of books made them the more Cunning to Cheat others & so did more hurt than good."

Despite these formidable challenges, Mayhew's convictions remained strong. He concluded his description of the Mohegan sachems by observing, "They sometimes seemed well pleased with the answers I gave unto their objections." However, it is likely that Mayhew's report was not well received in Boston.

Since the journals revealed "the enormous practical difficulties to which missionaries were exposed in Connecticut and elsewhere," William Kellaway notes, "it is not surprising that neither the Commissioners nor the Company published them."[29]

Difficulties merely whetted the appetites of strong-willed individuals like Cotton Mather. Consequently, under Mather's urging, the pressure for Christianizing these Indians continued, and by 1717 the General Assembly of the Connecticut colony had taken some action. In the spring of that year the assembly passed a measure declaring that the Indians falling under their jurisdiction should be gathered into villages, encouraged to farm, and taught Christianity. Husbandry, land ownership, and the gospel were to be reintroduced in an effort to further the "avowed design" of the founders of the colony.[30] At the next session of the assembly, Governor Gurdon Saltonstall, former minister of New London, endorsed these ideas and suggested that upon settling in the villages the Indians be instructed by a schoolmaster.[31]

A few years prior to this action, Saltonstall had met with Experience Mayhew to discuss the purpose of Mayhew's tour. At that time, Saltonstall had promised Mayhew that he and the Rev. Eliphalet Adams, who had succeeded the governor as minister in New London, would "spend one more day among these Indians [after Mayhew's departure] & endeavour to persuade them to embrace the good offers [Mayhew] made to them."[32] Thus, the governor's cooperation with the assembly was in accordance with his earlier position.

The measures enacted at this time suggest the absence of any earlier Christianization and education among the Connecticut Indians. While this is not quite true, the missionaries of seventeenth-century Connecticut were certainly fewer in number than their counterparts in the Bay colony. The fact that John Eliot had controlled the purse strings for the colonial end of the New England Company contributed to this condition. In situations where Eliot could extend his personal control over the Connecticut Indians, he saw fit to lessen Massachusetts Bay's stranglehold on the financial operation. Such was the case when the praying villages began to expand southwest into Nipmuc country. The seven "new towns" founded shortly before King Philip's War were all located within the territory of the Nipmuck, whose lands straddled the border of Connecticut and Massachusetts Bay. In this way, the influence of company funding extended to some Connecticut Indians through the expansion of the praying villages.

Aside from this network of Eliot's direct influence over the praying villages, only a few missionaries had labored in Connecticut. Other than the Rev. Abraham Pierson, who worked with the Quinnipiac, and William Thompson, who taught the Mohegan–Pequot for a few years, the only missionary in Connecticut during the seventeenth century was James Fitch.

Educated by the Rev. Thomas Hooker, Fitch emigrated from Essex to New England during the Great Migration. By the 1640s he had moved to Connecticut, and in 1660 he settled in Norwich, where he remained until his death in 1702.[33] Situated to the west of the Quinebaug River, Norwich lay at the northeastern edge of the Mohegan country and along the northern boundary of the old Pequot territory. Within perhaps thirty miles of the town were a number of scattered Indian settlements, and several of these were Pequot—Stonington, Groton, and Meshantuxet—all of which lay east of the Thames River. The closest Mohegan community was located west of the river, between the towns of Norwich and New London. During the 1660s and early 1670s, however, residents of Norwich complained that the Indians resided within the town itself. About a decade after his arrival and shortly before King Philip's War, Fitch became missionary to the Mohegans, and by winning the crucial support of Eliot, he was guaranteed some funding. Eliot wrote of Fitch to the commissioners: "I desire that [Fitch's] work may be countenanced and supported in that end of the country."[34]

After learning the Algonquian tongue of the Mohegan living in and near Norwich, Fitch worked hard to convert them. Although he admitted to making little headway with Uncas and other sachems, he did persuade the "poorer, gentler, and more scattered families, particularly among the tributaries and those adopted from other tribes." These he gathered into a village reminiscent of the praying villages, and like Eliot, Fitch himself "taught and trained" those who served as "instructors and guardians" in the small community. King Philip's War interrupted Fitch's endeavors, and while he continued to serve the Mohegan during and after the conflict, little is known of these postwar years.[35]

When Experience Mayhew met with the Mohegans in 1714, a

little over a decade after Fitch's death, they recalled the difficult adjustment required by the Christianity that Fitch had preached. Mayhew recorded their complaint in his journal: "Their fathers they said had made some tryal in Mr Fitches time, and had found Religion too hard for them, and had therefore quitted it."[36]

It is evident that Fitch's efforts were engraved in the memories of these Mohegans. Perhaps he even instructed a few of them in reading. It is less likely, however, that the Quinnipiac or the Mohegan–Pequot whom Thompson ministered to retained significant memories of their missionaries. Thus, the assembly's action of 1717–18 suggests that these eighteenth-century colonials had finally determined to make up for lost time; for they and their forbears had been settled in the colony for over seven decades, and they had still failed to bring Christianity and schooling to the Indians.

Some of the Mohegan of the New London area cast a different view on the matter. Reflecting on their fathers' tribulations with Mr. Fitch's religion, they told Mayhew that "they thought themselves no better able to endure the hardships of it than they [their fathers] were."[37]

On several occasions, Mayhew asked the Indians to clarify various aspects of religion. In a typical question, Mayhew inquired, "what kind of being god was?" When an Indian responded, "Indians could not know that, because they could not read," he provided Mayhew with the entrée he sought. Mayhew then recalled that he "further labored to show him how needful it was for them to learn to read . . . so they might come to the knowledge of those things that tend to their happiness."[38]

Missionary and schooling efforts during the next two decades laid the groundwork for the impact that the Great Awakening would have on the Indians in the 1740s. During the years between 1718 and 1750, schooling efforts in Connecticut focused largely on two centers: one was among the Mohegan–Pequot–Niantic living in the southeast along the Thames River and its tributaries, the Shetucket and the Quinebaug. The other was among the Tunxis and Connecticut River Valley bands in the community of Farmington, in the north-central region, west of the Connecticut River and along the upper Quinnipiac River.

The Indian community of Mohegan, which lay between New London and Norwich, hosted a flurry of Christianization and

schooling efforts during these decades. In the mid-1720s, Eliphalet Adams, Saltonstall's successor as minister in New London,
began to preach to neighboring Indians,[39] and by the end of the
decade he had taken Ben Uncas III into his home. Destined to
become the future sachem of the Mohegan, the youth was the
grandson of the Uncas who had been a thorn in James Fitch's side.
Shortly after Adams extended his ministry to the Mohegan, Captain John Mason obtained Mohegan permission to open a school
there; and with the backing of Eliphalet Adams and Connecticut
Governor Joseph Talcott, Mason carried his proposal to the Boston commissioners, who approved it. The Connecticut colony
built the Mohegan schoolhouse, a modest structure measuring
twenty-two feet by sixteen feet; and the Mohegan school was in
session by the end of 1726.[40]

Mason probably owed his success with the Boston commissioners to his thorough planning and his rather aggressive attitude. As Kellaway has noted, Mason "was not retiring in
character." His careful preparation, combined with a forceful
personality, evidently overpowered the commissioners. The list
of requirements that he submitted to them suggests that he intended to reach out to several Indian communities for potential
pupils. He requested three "Stroud Blankets for the Sachems of
the 3 tribes, vizt the Mohegin Pequot & Nianticks." Here, Mason
revealed not only his shrewdness, but also a familiarity with the
Indian trade. The stroud blanket was the most valuable item of
European clothing in the entire colonial Indian trade, and in the
middle 1700s its purchase price was the equivalent of £9, or
about thirty dollars. Hence, Mason chose well.[41]

His intention to board some of the students was also a knowl-
edgeable decision, for it indicated that he understood the appeal
that "free board and room" held for Indian parents, who were
themselves on the edge of destitution. The success of Mason's
presentation to the commissioners can be gauged, in part, by the
fact that his budget item of £2 for "the hire of a House 1 year for
the School" was superseded by their counteroffer to construct a
schoolhouse at the expense of the Connecticut colony. Although
Mason's planning was exemplary, local conditions intervened to
shorten the life of this endeavor.

Under Mason's direction, the Mohegan–Pequot–Niantic

schoolhouse lasted just under a decade. In the early years of that decade, those who observed Mason's instruction were impressed. Eliphalet Adams, who had a personal stake in the progress of the pupils, reported that after only six months of instruction the Mohegan boys "could Spell very prettily in their primmers & . . . rehearsed the Lord's Prayer, the Creed, & the ten Commandments in English very Expertly." Moreover, Mason had assured him that the youth "begin to take in the meaning of the Things . . . They seem to delight in their Learning & Value themselves pretty considerably upon it."[42]

Unfortunately for Mason, a bitter land dispute between the Mohegan and the Connecticut colony disrupted the school. By 1735, unable to resolve the disagreement, he closed the school and took his grievances to England, where further misfortune awaited him. Despite his pleas, he was unable to resolve the case before he died.[43] The school was then run briefly by Jonathan Barber, yet another missionary sent to the Mohegan by the Boston commissioners; but Barber's fortunes with the Mohegan were tied to Mason's failures concerning the land dispute, and he remained only a few years. However, Barber did succeed in converting Ben Uncas II, the father of the youth who had boarded with Eliphalet Adams. As a reward for this momentous event, the Connecticut General Assembly gave the sachem a hat and coat, "English style," and provided his wife with a "gown," all at public expense.[44] Like Mason, the assembly, knew the value of gifts in dealing with Indians.

Changes parallel to those at Mohegan occurred at Farmington, the second center for Christianizing and educating the Connecticut Indians. Indians living in the Farmington vicinity at this time were taught by the Rev. Samuel Whitman. Arriving in 1732, Whitman saw schooling as one of his first priorities. Although he chose a route that differed from Mason's, his method of achieving his goal was equally successful. Whitman took his schooling proposal directly to Connecticut Governor Talcott, asking him to intervene on his behalf with the Boston commissioners. Instead of asking the commissioners for an Indian school and schoolmaster, Whitman asked them to pay for the Indian pupils who attended the community's English school. The simplicity of his plan may have appealed to the Boston administrators; or they may have appreciated the opportunity that English schooling afforded for the further assimilation of the Indian pupils. At any rate, they agreed.

Whitman, like Eliphalet Adams, boarded an Indian youth in his own home. The tribal background of this young man, known as John Mettawan (or Mattawan), has not been identified, but he was probably a Tunxis. As the "brightest" of the Indian students enrolled at the English school, Mettawan was perhaps eighteen or nineteen years old when Whitman arrived, and his interest in Christianity probably served as a tremendous stimulant for Whitman. Indicating to Whitman that he wanted to become a minister to his people, probably the Tunxis, and perhaps the Connecticut Valley bands, Mettawan received instruction in theology for several years.

By 1737 Mettawan was ready to instruct his own people. Seeing that they might have one of their own as a schoolmaster, and supported by Whitman who provided the funds out of his own pocket, the Indians built a schoolhouse. After the school was built, Whitman continued to teach Mettawan, expressing an almost fatherly pride in his pupil's accomplishments. To exemplify Mettawan's skills, Whitman sent the Boston commissioners a letter that Mettawan had written in English and translated into Latin. In summarizing his student's progress, Whitman said, "I take him to be a christian indeed."[45] Up in Boston, however, the commissioners took a more prosaic approach to gauging the youth's progress. If he were inclined "to be bro't up to Grammar, and even Colledge Learning, with a resolution to become a Minister to the Indians," they declared that they would foot the bill for his instruction. Moreover, they would also pay for a "Homespun Coat, Jacket, and Breeches, two shirts, stockings, shoes and Hat, after the English fashion." But the commissioners made it clear that this offer of English clothing applied only if Mettawan persisted in striving toward his worthy goal. Therefore, they cautioned Whitman, "If the Indian Youth does not desire to be bro't up to Learning and be a Minister, he is not then to be Clothed in the English Fashion, but only to have the largest Blanket."

After such preparation and progress, the energies exerted by Mettawan and Whitman and the financial assistance provided by the commissioners all went for naught. After 1738, Mettawan's name fails to appear in the records. Evidently he, like so many of his contemporaries, died at a young age, probably from consumption or another disease carried by Europeans across the Atlantic. Whitman must have been saddened by Mettawan's death, but he continued his work with the Tunxis and other Farmington Indians until his own death in 1751.

The perseverance of these missionaries—including Whitman in Farmington; the Rev. Jacob Johnson, who instructed the Groton Pequot with the assistance of an Indian schoolmaster; and their counterparts at Mohegan, Adams, Mason, Barber, and the Rev. David Jewitt, who began preaching there after Barber left—suggests that, in accordance with the spirit of the general assembly's measures of 1717–18, they were making an honest attempt to Christianize and educate the Indians of Connecticut,[46] and in retrospect, their goals remain fairly clear.

The Indian response to these goals is more clouded. Not surprisingly, few sources remain to reveal this side of the story. These Indians were more likely than any of their contemporaries to have kept records because they represented the small number of natives who were literate during the colonial period. But their life expectancy was so brief that only a few lived long enough to compile any record of their experiences. Thus, Samson Occom, one who did write of his life at this time, was a rare individual. The catalyst for Occom's schooling was the Great Awakening.

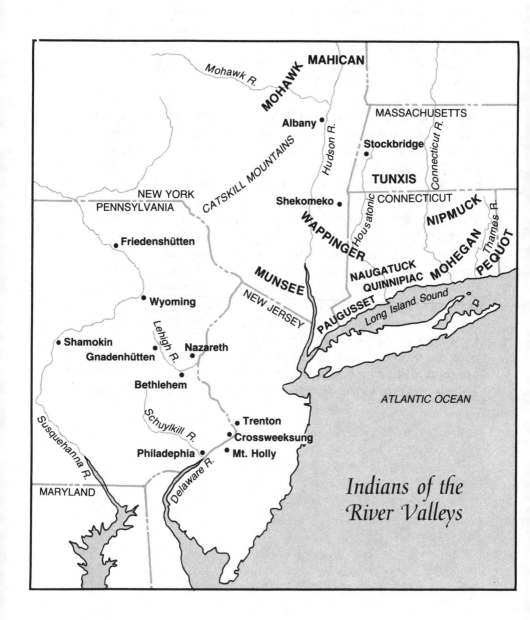

Mohawk R.

MOHAWK

MAHICAN

Albany

MASSACHUSETTS

Hudson R.

Stockbridge

Connecticut R.

CATSKILL MOUNTAINS

TUNXIS

NEW YORK

PENNSYLVANIA

Shekomeko

CONNECTICUT

WAPPINGER

NIPMUCK

Housatonic

Friedenshütten

Thames R.

NAUGATUCK

MOHEGAN

MUNSEE

QUINNIPIAC

PEQUOT

Wyoming

NEW JERSEY

PAUGUSSET

Long Island Sound

Lehigh R.

Shamokin

Nazareth

Gnadenhütten

Bethlehem

ATLANTIC OCEAN

Schuylkill R.

Trenton

Susquehanna R.

Crossweeksung

Philadephia

Mt. Holly

MARYLAND

Delaware R.

Indians of the
River Valleys

190

8

THE GREAT AWAKENING AND INDIAN SCHOOLING

The Enlightenment and the Great Awakening were the two great movements that molded American life and thought in the eighteenth century. One appealed to the mind or the reason, while the other tugged at the heart; or as Edwin Scott Gaustad puts it, one was anthropocentric, the other theocentric.[1] The friction between these two poles of consciousness pulled and twisted the colonials as they sought to reinterpret their world in terms of their own lives, the relationship of the colonies to England, and their comprehension of the universe. Through this friction, the colonials acquired a dynamic energy that was realized through endeavors they might not have even considered otherwise. One of the most significant endeavors fueled by this energy was the impetus for Indian schooling.

From the 1730s through the 1760s, New England and the Middle Colonies witnessed a flurry of experiments in schooling for Indian youth. Indian schools of one kind or another opened their doors in the colonies of Pennsylvania, New Jersey, Rhode Island, Connecticut, New York, Massachusetts, and offshore islands such as Martha's Vineyard. Some of the most renowned missionaries of eighteenth-century America became involved in the process: eminent divines such as Cotton Mather, Experience Mayhew, Eleazar Wheelock, Samson Occom, David and John Brainerd, Jonathan Edwards, Gideon Hawley, John Sergeant, Benjamin Colman, and David Zeisberger.

In the summer of 1724, Cotton Mather—who had not forsaken his vigilant watch over the Algonquian of southern Connecticut and Rhode Island, and the Mohegan especially—wrote a letter to Gurdon Saltonstall, congratulating him on his recent appointment as Governor of the Boston commissioners. In the letter, Mather also revealed his own "Despondencies" about the "Gospelizing of our Indians," and expressed his hope that Saltonstall's appointment "will not only procure something more Effectual than what has yet been done for your *Mohegins*, but will also inspire a New Vigour into all our Motions."[2]

Had Mather lived perhaps two or three decades longer—he died in February 1728—he would have witnessed the Christianization and education of the most remarkable Mohegan in colonial America. Samson Occom was born in 1723, just a short time before Mather wrote the letter to Saltonstall. Given Mather's long-term interest in converting the Mohegan, it is perhaps unfortunate that these two ministers never met; on the other hand, Occom would undoubtedly have received a more genuine welcome from Samuel Sewall, who did not appear to share his compatriot's disdain for the Indian as a fellow human being.[3]

Like Cotton Mather, Occom was descended from respected families in his culture. His paternal grandfather, "Tomockham alias Ashneon," had lived for some time in the region between the Shetucket and Quinebaug Rivers before moving south to join the families living at Uncas Hill, later known as Mohegan. It was fitting that Tomockham became known as a supporter of the sachem Uncas, for his grandson Samson Occom was reputedly descended from Uncas on his maternal side. Tomockham's wife bore him at least three sons, and one named Joshua, who was known as "a great hunter," was Occom's father. Samson Occom later wrote that his parents, Joshua and Sarah, "led a wandering Life up and down in the wilderness." In qualifying the term *wandering* for his English readers, he explained that "they Chiefly Depended upon Hunting, Fishing, & Fowling for their Living." At some point during this seasonal cycle, in 1723, Samson Occom (or Aukum) was born.[4]

Occom recalled his childhood in a memoir that paralleled the years of Eliphalet Adams and Jonathan Barber.

> Once in a fortnight in ye summer Season, a Minister from New London used to Come up and the Indians to attend; not that they

regarded the Christian Religion, but they had Blankets given to them by the Fall of the Year and for these things, they would attend.

Occom remembered that gifts rather than religion had attracted the Mohegan to Adams's preaching. He also acknowledged the painful memory of schooling, with Barber as schoolmaster:

> And when I was about 10 Years of age there was a man who went about among the Indian wigwams, and wherever he Could find the Indian children, would make them read; but the Children used to take care to keep out of his Way:—and he used to Catch me Some times and make me Say over my Letters; and I believe I Learnt Some of them.[5]

In the later 1730s, when the Rev. David Jewitt arrived in the vicinity of Mohegan, the revivals that led to the Great Awakening were already taking place in the Connecticut River Valley among the parishioners of the Rev. Solomon Stoddard and his grandson, the Rev. Jonathan Edwards. Ordained in 1739, Jewitt had been preaching for only a short time when revivals suddenly began to spread across the land.[6]

In September 1740, the Rev. George Whitefield preached his first sermon in New England. The Great Awakening was but a small flame when this famous evangelist made his first whirlwind tour of the New England colonies. Coming at a "time of extraordinary dullness in religion,"[7] Whitefield fanned the flame into a lively blaze.

New London, already "the seat of his Majesty's custom-house and so the port of greatest note in the colony" was in the heartland of this emotional swelling.[8] Close on the heels of Whitefield's visit, and in response to a request from the great evangelist himself, the Rev. Gilbert Tennent toured New England in the winter of 1740–41. Arriving in New London in March, at the end of his itinerant swing through the colonies, the Presbyterian Tennent paused there briefly before returning home to Pennsylvania. In following the pattern of preaching adopted by the itinerant revival ministers, Tennent delivered seven sermons in two days, including three at night.[9]

In March 1743, two years after Tennent's visit, one of the most erratic itinerants, James Davenport, visited New London. Davenport was a graduate of Yale and Congregational minister at Southold, Long Island (Long Island had long been a cultural outpost of

Connecticut); but he had already been vigorously condemned by
the New England clergy for his prolonged attack upon them, and
many churches had closed their doors to his itinerant preaching.
His visit to New London in the spring of 1743 marked the climax
of his notoriety. There, he convinced a considerable following to
engage in two days of book-burning as well as in the burning of an
assortment of material possessions representing the "world," including "wigs, cloaks and breeches, Hoods, Gowns, Rings, Jewels
and Necklaces."[10] This outrageous episode not only shocked New
Londoners, it also marked the demise of Davenport's already
dampened popularity. After the bonfire episode, Davenport is-
sued a public apology that he delivered at the urging of some
ministerial advisors, including his brother-in-law, the Rev. Eleazar Wheelock.[11] Wheelock, married to Davenport's sister, was
also a well-known but more moderate itinerant preacher whose
congregation was in Lebanon, Connecticut, a small town northwest of New London.

During this dramatic period, the Indians of Rhode Island and
Connecticut, and particularly those living in the New London
area, found themselves caught up in the revival's emotional intensity. Samson Occom's mother, Sarah, was among the Mohegan
converted through David Jewitt's preaching. Occom's own description of the Great Awakening remains a unique commentary:

> When I was 16 years of age, we heard a Strange Rumor among the
> English, that there were Extraordinary Ministers Preaching from
> Place to Place and a Strange Concern among the White People: this
> was in the Spring of the Year. But we Saw nothing of these things,
> till Some Time in the Summer, when some Ministers began to visit
> us and Preach the Word of God; and Common People also Came
> frequently, and exhorted as to the things of God.

Occom recalled that he had been very convinced of the truth of
what the Indians were being taught. He noted the "conviction and
Saving Conversion of a Number of us," adding, "amongst whom, I
was one that was Impresst with the things we had heard."[12]

The emotional intensity that characterized the revival reached
out to Occom, and the clarity of his recollection, written many
years later in the late 1760s, suggests that this moment in his life
stood out in stark contrast with the years that preceded it. Occom's personal awakening and eventual conversion provided a

brief interlude of hope, while the remainder of his life would be filled with much disillusion, depression, and despair.

The conversion provided the springboard for his choice of direction, with literacy serving as the first tool to take him in that direction. In Occom's words,

> After I was awakened & converted I went to all the meetings I could come at; & continued under Trouble of mind about 6 Months; at which time I began to Learn the English letters; got me a Primer & used to go to my English Neighbors frequently for Assistance in Reading, but went to no School. . . . Thus I continued till I was in my 19th year; by this time I could Read a bit in the Bible.[13]

By age nineteen Occom had experienced the frustration of teaching himself without systematic instruction, and he foresaw the need for a tutor to provide some coherence in his studies. In the early 1740s, the signs seemed to point in the direction of Lebanon, where Eleazar Wheelock, still one of the most popular itinerant New England preachers, was pastor of the North Society.

When Samson Occom and his mother turned their attention to Wheelock, he had served his Lebanon parishioners for nearly eight years. Wheelock's great grandfather, Ralph Wheelock, had arrived in Massachusetts during the Great Migration. His own parents had resided in Windham, Connecticut, near the headwaters of the Shetucket, but his mother was from Norwich, where she had been a contemporary of James Fitch during his ministry to the Mohegan. As a student at Yale, Wheelock was described by his biographer as "pious, ponderous, and studious." The first two epithets aptly characterize his career as minister and educator, while the last was eventually discarded because the frenetic pace of his life as pastor, administrator, and fund raiser for his charity boarding school for Indians and whites as well as farmer, husband, and father permitted little time in which to pursue scholarly endeavors. He remained a pious Congregationalist, but the nature of his multifaceted interests, especially the direction of an Indian school, dictated a practical rather than a philosophical outlook on life.[14]

As with Occom, the Great Awakening was the turning point in Wheelock's life. As an itinerant preacher, he was "Connecticut's most energetic supporter of the movement," and as a native son called to his own pulpit, he was not subjected to the criticism leveled at outsiders such as Whitefield, Tennent, and Daven-port.[15] He traveled widely. In one of his more extensive journeys he preached about forty-five sermons in a twenty-five day trip through Rhode Island en route to Boston.[16] Attracting the attention of notable figures in the ministry, he came in touch with men such as Jonathan Edwards, who asked him to preach in North-ampton. Wheelock, as Gaustad says, was "a popular and perva-sive preacher,"[17] but as the revival began to wane, he searched for new outlets for the enormous energy generated by his itinerant tours.

The year 1743 was an important year in the lives of Wheelock and Occom, and it would have a strong impact upon many other lives influenced by the two men during the decades that fol-lowed. Many years later, Occom described his introduction to the minister.

> At this time my Poor mother was going to Lebanon and having had some Knowledge of Mr. Wheelock and hearing he had a Number of English youth under his Tuition, I had a great Inclination to go to him and to be with him a week or a Fortnight, and Desired my Mother to ask Mr. Wheelock, Whether he would take me a little while to Instruct me in Reading. Mother did so: and when She came Back, She Said Mr. Wheelock wanted to See me, as Soon as possible.

Occom thought his stay with the minister would be brief. "So I went up," he wrote, "thinking I should be back again in a few Days." But the visit stretched into weeks, months, and finally years. "When I got up there, he received me With kindness and Compassion and instead of Staying a Fortnight or 3 Weeks, I Spent 4 years with him."[18]

Occom arrived at the minister's home on December 6, 1743. Although only twenty years old, he had already assumed the duties of Councillor for his people. That spring, he had signed a Mohegan memorial to the Connecticut General Assembly con-cerning the still unresolved Mohegan land dispute with Con-necticut, which came to be known as the Mason case.[19] In the mid-1700s, responsible young men had grown increasingly im-portant to the Mohegan as their numbers declined; although esti-mates vary, the Mohegan population in the 1730s may have num-bered only around four hundred.[20] Occom's prominent heritage, combined with his interest in becoming literate, thrust him to the forefront among the Mohegan. He served directly under the leadership of the sachem Ben Uncas II and his son, Ben Uncas III; the latter was Occom's contemporary and had become schoolmaster at Mohegan in 1739, a post that he held for over a decade.

Such responsibility probably matured Occom. At age twenty, Occom was only twelve years younger than his mentor, who was thirty-two; and he was a willing and able pupil. During the years of his schooling, from 1743 to 1747 or 1748, he studied with Wheelock and other instructors in the area. His lessons included English, Latin, Greek, and Hebrew. Although he may not have been proficient in Hebrew, he did purchase *A Grammar of the Hebrew Tongue* during a trip to Boston and Natick, and his Hebrew Bible showed evidence of use. By the age of twenty-five, as his biographer Harold Blodgett suggests, Occom "was probably no more poorly educated than many a preacher of his day, and in eloquence, earnestness and simplicity, superior to not a few."[21]

During these years of preparation for the ministry, Occom did not remain isolated in Lebanon. Not only was his place of instruction shifted, depending on Wheelock's availability to teach; Occom himself also traveled. Thus Occom established the pattern that he would follow in future decades by becoming an itinerant preacher to Indian people. Throughout his own course of instruction, he served informally as minister for the Indian communities of southern Connecticut and environs. He interrupted his studies frequently to travel to nearby communities with sizable Indian populations—the Pequot of Groton, the Niantic near Long Island Sound, his own people at Mohegan, and the Montauk on Long Island. In August 1745, when Whitefield visited New London for five days, Occom may have stood among the crowd gathered around the great evangelist. One of those listening was Joshua Hempstead, a resident of New London. In this midsummer week, while Hempstead was busy stacking hay and hauling barley and wheat to be ground at the mill, he still found time for several visits to hear Whitefield. On the eleventh, Hempstead noted that Whitefield spoke "und ye oak Tree," with those attending forming "a great assembly, phaps twice So many as could possably Sitt in ye meetinghouse." Hempstead described Whitefield as "an excellent precher."[22]

When Samson Occom spoke to his own people, he too was an

excellent preacher. Finally ordained as a Presbyterian minister in 1759, Occom found his true voice, his calling, when he preached to the Indians. Occom was well known to the Rev. Samuel Buell, another itinerant pastor of the Great Awakening, whose preaching in Northampton had moved Jonathan Edwards to tears. While delivering the sermon at Occom's ordination, Buell pointed out the emergence of Occom's unique skills when he addressed Indians. "[W]hen he preaches to the Indians," Buell observed, "[he] is vastly more natural and free and eloquent." "As an Instructor of the Indians," Buell concluded, "he makes frequent Use of apt and significant Similtudes, to convey and illustrate Truth."[23]

Occom also maintained his concern for the affairs of the Mohegan, and their land case in particular, which continued to plague him for many years.[24] The idea of caring for his own people as well as for the area's other Indian communities must have been forming in his mind at this time. During a trip to Boston in 1747, he visited Natick, the first of the praying villages. Natick had been the beacon for Indian conversion. In 1747, it symbolized not only the decline but the virtual demise of the Massachusett Indians who had lived there during the decades of promise before King Philip's War. Did this experience, as W. DeLoss Love has suggested, form the seed in Occom's mind that later bore fruit in the idea of Brothertown, the community for southern New England Algonquian established during the period of the American Revolution?[25] Did Occom view the proximity of Natick to Boston as a warning to his own people and their Indian neighbors of southern Connecticut? It is a likely thesis, but a difficult one to prove. What is certain is that he did initiate his pastoral care for his people during this period.

Occom also had to provide for his own future, however, and this was a continuing challenge to him from the late 1740s forward. His studies were forced to come to an end at this point because of eyestrain, which remained so severe that it postponed indefinitely any possibility of attending Yale to prepare further for the ministry. He began then to seek employment as a schoolmaster in nearby Indian communities, but prospects were not encouraging. Each Indian community he visited either had a schoolmaster, as was the case with the Niantic, or like the Narragansett, they demonstrated little interest in hiring one. At about this time, he decided to go with some of his friends on a fishing trip to Long Island. Once there, however, instead of fishing he began to address the Montauk, as was his custom, by gathering them together and preaching; and he was so successful that they asked him to be their schoolmaster. Following Wheelock's advice, he accepted the position, thus procuring his first employment at the age of twenty-six.

In a letter addressed to "Dear child," Wheelock recommended that Occom take the teaching assignment "for half a year," cautioning his former student that "if you do it with this proviso yt if your health shod be restord you may be at Liberty to Obey any order you Shall have from the Honle Commssrs."[26] But the six months stretched into years, and Occom was to retain the Montauk position for a total of some twelve years before leaving; and in the interim, he married Mary Fowler, a young Montauk woman who bore him six children. Economically, the Montauk years proved very difficult for Occom and his growing family. The Montauk themselves were "so poor and So much in Debt" that he could "Expect little or nothing from them" in the form of remuneration.[27] The Boston commissioners, who had been willing to support his schooling with Wheelock, were hesitant to provide further funds when he interrupted his studies, even though his dual role at Montauk, as schoolmaster and preacher, strongly influenced the Christianization of the remnant families residing there.[28] For at least two years, he taught without any salary; later, due to the pleas of Wheelock and other supporters, he was granted a sparse compensation which remained significantly less than whites employed in the same work. As he noted, "They gave me 180 Pounds for 12 years Service, which they gave for one years Service in another mission."[29] This kind of financial arrangement was eventually to become one of several sources for the bitterness that Occom bore in his later years.

While Wheelock's first student was encountering the realities of competing with whites in their own domain, the minister—schoolmaster himself was in the throes of launching his great experiment. The single, most important contribution that Occom made to Wheelock's life was his own excellence as a student. As a firsthand witness to Occom's astounding progress in the 1740s, Wheelock developed a growing conviction that all Indian youth could achieve a level of education sufficient to employ them as instructors to other Indian youth.

But Occom's achievements extended beyond the realm of the intellect, and for Wheelock's purposes, the Mohegan's perseverance was equally important. By his dogged persistence, Occom belied the colonial stereotype of the Indian. If Occom met his standards, Wheelock reasoned, then so would other Indian students. While promoting his Indian school in 1763, Wheelock wrote of his success with Occom: "He was several Years ago ordained to the sacred Miistry . . . and has done well . . . after seeing the Success of this Attempt, I was more encouraged to hope that such a Method might be very successful."[30]

Occom's impact was reinforced by the timing of his influence on Wheelock. In the mid-1740s, he offered Wheelock a potentially new avenue for his energies. Occom's example illustrated that only a short step separated one of the most popular itinerant preachers of the New England revival from the foremost Indian educator of eighteenth-century colonial America. Wheelock took the step with characteristic forcefulness.[31]

The charity boarding school for Indian and white youth established by Wheelock in 1754 is described in chapters 9 and 10. Here, Moor's Indian Charity School is viewed in a broader context. During the period when it was located in Lebanon, from 1754 to 1759, Moor's School and its director served as a hub or, at the very least, as a focal point for most of those Indian schools established in the region during the period of the Great Awakening. Wheelock's school may have been one of the most active; certainly, it was one of the most highly publicized Indian schools that opened during the mid-1700s. In addition to the Connecticut Indian schools, New England and the Middle colonies witnessed three experiments in Indian education during this period. These were orchestrated by the Rev. John Sergeant (later succeeded by Jonathan Edwards) in Stockbridge, Massachusetts; the Moravians, who ranged across the Pennsylvania frontier and later into Ohio; and David and John Brainerd, who began along the Delaware River and continued their missionary work in New Jersey.

By the mid-1700s the Indians who became the focus of these missionaries were living on the frontiers of New England and the Middle Colonies. In the 1730s, the settlement line was pushing west into their lands, and as it moved the missionaries moved with it. At this stage of British colonial expansion, settler and missionary faced several Indian groups residing in this area. They encountered the Mohawk and Oneida west of the Hudson, and along the Delaware and its tributaries, they met refugee bands of Delaware, or Lenni Lenape, many of whom bore the scars of previous encounters with expanding settlements. Between the Hudson and the Housatonic rivers, they found the Mahican or River Indians; and among the Mahican living near the Berkshire Mountains, they encountered Indians who had migrated there from the lower Housatonic and Naugatuck valleys of western Connecticut.

These Indians were no strangers to colonial expansion. The Mohawk and River Indians had found themselves directly in the path of fur trade and settlement, and had experienced the sporadic missionary efforts of the Dutch Reformed Church during the years of Dutch hegemony. From the early 1700s forward, missionaries for the SPG had struggled to convert and school the Mohawk, and before them the Jesuits had attempted to do the same. The Delaware had been spared heavy doses of Christianization, but they suffered damaging encounters with land-hungry frontiersmen and their inevitable commodity of alcohol.

In the 1730s and 1740s, three denominations sent missionaries into this newly opened frontier. The Boston commissioners for the New England Company provided funding for the Stockbridge mission in the Housatonic Valley. The Society in Scotland for Propagating Christian Knowledge, or the SSPCK (1707), supported David and John Brainerd (with John also receiving funds from the Presbyterian synod of New York). The Moravians provided internal support for their Indian missions and schools; and they also raised funds through the Society for the Furtherance of the Gospel, which existed from 1745 to 1764 and was supported both internally and externally.[32]

These three groups shared some similarities. All three were affected by the Great Awakening, which spread from New England into the Middle Colonies, through Moravians and Presbyterians alike, and eventually reaching the Delaware and other Indians. But the bonds between the Congregational and the Presbyterian—the New England Company and the Scottish Society— were far stronger than those linking these two denominations with the Moravians. The two groups dissenting from the Church of England knew of the missionary work of the *Unitas Fratrum*, but their vast network of missionary fund-raising on both sides of the Atlantic generally did not include contact with the Moravians.

When the Moravians moved into the missionary field in New York and Pennsylvania, they struck out largely on their own, remaining separate, by and large, from other denominations during the extent of their endeavors in this region. Suspicion of the *Unitas Fratrum* abounded in the colonies where they settled. As Paul A. W. Wallace points out, "they found themselves hated and feared like the Jesuits . . . though, like the Jesuits, in the end they confounded their detractors by the single-hearted devotion of their missionary work among the Indians.[33] Even in the "religious melting pot" of Pennsylvania, they succeeded in alienating themselves from every other group represented: the Lutherans, Mennonites, Dunkers, Presbyterians, Reformed, and Separatists, to mention only a few. Although during the Great Awakening, Zinzendorf may have been to the Germans "what Whitefield was to the English," he was also a man who made many enemies, including Gilbert Tennent.[34] Thus, Zinzendorf's efforts in 1742 to unite Pennsylvania's Protestants "had the opposite effect," leading not to ecumenicism but to a more stubborn denominational consciousness.[35]

The pacifism of the Moravians also led to trouble. Undaunted by their experience in Georgia, they maintained their pacifist stance in the middle colonies, where they encountered fierce opposition from the Scotch-Irish and other belligerent frontiersmen, especially in Pennsylvania. Five years after they founded their first mission, Shekomeko (in Dutchess County, New York), the colony of New York ordered them to abandon it because of the erroneous conviction that they were trying to persuade the Mahican to support the French.[36] Finally, the general dislike or distrust of the Moravians was exacerbated by the fact that they spoke a different language. While this had been merely a challenge to a man such as John Wesley, it proved a barrier for many of the non-German-speaking colonials of the middle colonies.

Although these difficulties encumbered the Moravians, they refused to be deterred from their missionary goals. By the early 1740s they had begun their missions along the Delaware River, working with the Lenni Lenape and other remnant groups to found the missions at Bethlehem and Nazareth.[37] Spreading west, they established missions at Gnadenhutten, at the confluence of the Mahoning and Lehigh, and on the Susquehanna. Despite Indian attacks on the Susquehanna settlement at Shamokin as well as at Gnadenhutten, they remained in the area throughout the French and Indian War and Pontiac's Rebellion. The negotiation of the Treaty of Fort Stanwix in 1768, however, threw them into an utenable position. By this agreement, William Johnson, longtime friend of the Mohawk and superintendent of Indian affairs for the Northern District, persuaded the Iroquois to cede a large portion of their land, including the Moravian Indian settlements on the Susquehanna. As a result, some of the brethren sensed the inevitable: the Moravians would have to follow the main body of non-Christian Delaware who had already been forced west.

Foremost among those anticipating the move was David Zeisberger, Jr. The son of a Hernhutter, Zeisberger had fled his home and sailed to Georgia in 1737, at the age of seventeen; he would become one of the most famous Moravian missionaries to the Indians.[38] From 1767, when he crossed the Alleghenies to found a new Moravian mission settlement, until 1792, when he led the Christian Delaware north from the Ohio to form their settlement along the Thames River in Ontario (where they live today), David Zeisberger was a close friend and confidante of these migrant people. Zeisberger worked not only with the Delaware; he also served the Mahican, Shawnee, Wyandot, Chippewa, Ottawa, Seneca, Cayuga, and Onondaga during a missionary career that spanned sixty-two years.[39]

Throughout this period, from 1740 until the postrevolutionary decades and beyond, the Moravians pursued their missionary goals. In some respects, their approach shared the philosophy of John Eliot. They believed in what Richard Henry Pratt was later to call "total immersion." Conversion to Christianity was not sufficient; the Moravians also asked the Indians to change every aspect of their culture. Reminiscent of Eliot's praying villages, the Moravian Indian settlements fostered a Euroamerican cultural system. Upon baptism, all Indians acquired a Christian name. They were taught to respect the sanctity of monogamous marriage; they learned not to labor on the Sabbath; they were to shun any rum or strong drink and to avoid "heathenish" dances or festivals; and they were to be "obedient" to their "teachers and helpers." The "teachers" were the missionaries themselves; their "helpers" were Indian converts with multiple duties: they visited the "brethren," cared for the sick, settled quarrels, and were responsible for the observation of the civil and religious ordinances in the mission village.[40]

A significant contribution to cultural change occurred through the establishment of schools, for every Moravian Indian settlement included a school. Marie Kohnova has described the founding of the Moravian Indian settlements: "in each case the church was built first, next the school, and the houses last."[41] Beginning in the 1740s, with the Mahican settlement at Shekomeko in New York, and continuing across the Alleghenies, the Moravians taught Indian children to read so they would have access to the Bible and other pious works. The schools continued even during the French and Indian War, when some of the Moravian Christian Indians sought protection in Philadelphia and were held in barracks. Bishop Spangenberg, who had met the Wesleys and Ingham in Georgia, was active in providing translations of his own sermons for Delaware youth; but David Zeisberger, who was fluent in several Indian languages, led the missionaries in translating. Zeisberger provided works for Delaware schoolchildren in their own language, and also translated the Bible, a selection of hymns, and a grammar into Onondaga.[42] Zeisberger had been reared among a people who loved both voice and instrument, for music always played an important role in Moravian life. These people wrote the first Protestant hymn book, which appeared in 1501; and the translation of hymnals was one means of extending their love of music to the Indians. Like David Brainerd among the Mahican, Wheelock's Indian schoolmasters among the Iroquois, and Benjamin Ingham among the Yamacraw, the Moravian missionaries and teachers evoked a unique response when they turned to music.

But the translations, the schools, the music, and the cultural immersion did not suffice, for the Moravians faced opposition by both frontiersmen and a succession of wars. From the Anglo–Spanish hostilities in Georgia through the French and Indian War, the American Revolution, and as late as the War of 1812, these pacifists found themselves pushed continually to new frontiers. Kohnova suggests that "other whites, Americans, prevented the Moravians from achieving better results,"[43] but the story of these many Indian groups and the Moravian missionaries is an intriguing one that remains to be told.

While the Moravians were struggling on the edge of the frontier, from the Delaware westward and beyond the Alleghenies, their Congregational and Presbyterian counterparts were duplicating their efforts in closer proximity to settled areas.

For some time the Connecticut River Valley had served as the western frontier for the Massachusetts Bay Colony. Although it was well settled in towns that lay along the river, it was still subject to Indian raids, as exemplified in the repeated attacks on the town of Deerfield. For several decades the valley had lain under the spell of the Rev. Solomon Stoddard, minister at Northampton. As Gaustad notes, Stoddard's ministry "had exercised a profound influence not only over his own frontier congregation but throughout Massachusetts and Connecticut colonies."[44] Stoddard's death in 1729 did not mark the end of his family's influence, for his position was promptly filled by his grandson Jonathan Edwards, the preeminent theological mind of eighteenth-century America.

In the late 1720s, one of the ministers of the valley, the Rev. Samuel Hopkins of West Springfield, became interested in the Indians living west of the Connecticut Valley and beyond the Berkshire Mountains.

The River Indians of Hopkins's awakened concern had adopted the Housatonic Valley as their home only in recent times. Largely Mahican, they were known as the Muh-ha-ka-ne-ok, or "the people of the continually flowing waters." A once powerful tribe, the Mahican had wrestled with their traditional enemy, the Mohawk, for control of the lands surrounding the Hudson River. Driven east by the Iroquois and Dutch during the seventeenth century, a group of them gradually settled along the Housatonic, a region that had formerly served only as their hunting grounds; while a smaller group of Indians migrated north to the valley from the Naugatuck and lower Housatonic. These two groups of Indians chose as their homeland one of the richest and most scenic valleys of New England.[45]

Samuel Hopkins' interest in them sprang from his Congregational missionary impulse. His curiosity was piqued when he discovered, first, that one of their influential leaders wanted to

become a Christian; and second, that French influence did not
extend into the domain of these River Indians. Thus, he reasoned
that a Congregational missionary might live among them and
instruct "not only the men but also their Families: their Children
might be taught to read and write and be led into a knowledge of
the principles of Christianity."[46]

Hopkins was a man of some influence in the valley. Not only
was he a respected minister, he had also married one of Jonathan
Edwards's sisters. In the early 1730s Hopkins sent two fellow
ministers, the Rev. Stephen Williams of Longmeadow and Nehemiah Bull of Westfield, to the Housatonic Valley, where they
conferred with the Indians and reached an agreement about the
missionary proposal. Before leaving, Williams gave the River
Indians a small belt of wampum "as a Confirmation of what had
passed between them and as a Sort of Record thereof."[47] Williams
and Bull then submitted the mission proposal to the Boston commissioners, who approved it in August 1734 and delegated them
to select a missionary.

Thus, in the summer of 1734, the Indians of the Housatonic
Valley had sealed their fate by accepting the belt of wampum. For
the next five decades, they and their descendants would remain
in the valley, but the whites who moved in gradually squeezed the
Indians onto smaller and smaller parcels of land. In the early
years, when John Sergeant was alive, the Indians and whites were
partners. Sergeant's successor, Jonathan Edwards, attempted to
maintain this relationship, but he was outpressured and outnumbered by other whites, and the Indians began to be reduced to an
inferior status. After Edwards's departure, the Muhhakaneok became a living anachronism, outcasts relegated to rapidly disappearing lands where they lived in poverty. During the revolutionary era, when John Sergeant, Jr., became their missionary, they
joined the migration led by Samson Occom and other southern
New England Algonquian to establish a new home on a portion of
the land remaining to the Oneida. Following the Peace of Paris, in
1784, fifty years after accepting the belt of wampum, the Muhhakaneok or Stockbridge Indians emigrated to the new lands in
upstate New York; but unbeknownst to them, they had still further migrations to make: most moved to Wisconsin in the early
1800s, while others eventually migrated farther west. Throughout these years, they had lost their lands, their homes, and their

river, the Housatonic, but they retained in varying degrees the Christianity first taught to them by John Sergeant in 1734.

A young tutor at Yale, John Sergeant was twenty-four years old when Williams and Bull asked him to serve among the Housatonic Valley Indians. Born in 1710, Sergeant had lost his father while very young and had been educated by his stepfather. Because he had also lost the use of his left hand through a boyhood accident with a scythe, he chose a less physically active career.[48] As a student at Yale, Sergeant expressed an interest in ministering to the Indians. Hopkins recalled that Sergeant "had rather be employed as a missionary to the Natives, if a Door should open for it, than accept a Call any English Parish might give him." When word of Sergeant's interest in the Indian reached the Connecticut Valley, Williams and Bull offered him the position.[49]

Sergeant began his service among the Muhhakaneok in the fall of 1734. HIs journal of the trip described his arrival in the valley. On the day before, Sergeant and Nehemiah Bull, who accompanied him from the Connecticut Valley, planned to spend the night "at a House about 15 m. onwards upon the road," the only shelter between Bull's town of Westfield and the Housatonic. Before they reached the house, however, darkness overtook them and, as Sergeant recalled, they were "forced to lodge in the Woods without Fire or Shelter." "The next Day," Sergeant continued, "we got to the Housatunnuk, a little before Night, thro' a most doleful Wilderness & the worst Road, perhaps, that ever was rid."[50]

John Sergeant had grown up in New Jersey and had lived in New Haven for nine years. Thus, in his initial encounter with what he termed the "doleful Wilderness," his background as an individual accustomed to living in settled areas was surmounted by a commitment and faith in the worthiness of his task that carried him through the difficulties of the early years. "I was sensible I must not only lose a great many agreeable amusements of life, especially in leaving my business at College," he wrote, "but also expose myself to many fatigues and hardships. . . . Indeed, I should be ashamed to own myself a Christian, or even a man," he admitted, "and yet utterly refuse doing what lay in my power to cultivate humanity, and so promote the salvation of souls."[51]

Sergeant represented the eighteenth-century New England colonialist. He preached with rigorous conviction the attributes of the long-held New England virtues of education and pious living. His own labors among the Muhhakaneok exemplified the piety that he sought to teach these Indians. By and large, he found himself unable to attribute any value to their customs, for he could not comprehend the positive features of their culture when he compared them with his own.

The integrity of Mahican culture, therefore, went largely unrecognized during these five decades of coexistence. As northeastern Algonquian, the Mahican represented traditions that had evolved over centuries. The women raised "Indian corn, beans, and little squashes," and probably sunflowers as well. In the fall, the men hunted for "deer, beaver, otter, racoon, fisher, martin, for their clothing and drying meat for the ensuing season." In the early spring, they hunted "for moose on the Green Mountains, where these animal keep for winter quarters." They also tapped the sugar from the maple trees. Later in the spring, the men fished for herring and shad, and through the summer they gathered freshwater mussels, which were dried and smoked for winter. Their families were important to them, and they instructed their children carefully. They acknowledged a supreme being, whom they knew as "Waun-theet" or the "Great Good Spirit."

The Mahican had also prospered. Their fathers had told them that, at one time, the Muhhakaneok Nation could raise about one thousand warriors. More recent estimates suggest that in the early 1600s, according to Dutch records, the Mahican numbered 1,600 warriors or a total population of 4,000 or 4,500. Then came defeat by the Iroquois and the Dutch occupation of the fertile lands along the Hudson. These events, combined with European diseases had reduced their numbers and their vitality. By 1700 the tribal population had shrunk to about 500. When Sergeant arrived in the Housatonic Valley, the local Muhhakaneok, under the leadership of Konkapot and his lieutenant Umpachenee, numbered between 50 and 90.[52]

Sergeant's goals for these people bore some resemblance to those of John Eliot for the Massachusett. Although Sergeant went about his task in a more gentle fashion, he was determined that the Muhhakaneok change their ways, which meant instruction through sermons and schooling and the adoption of farming as a single source of economic support. In short, Sergeant wanted the Muhhakaneok to relinquish their custom of moving with the season and remain in one location throughout the year, where he could teach them new ways. In turn, he vowed to learn their language.

Within five years he had not only gained mastery of the language, but was so fluent that the Indians said of him: "Our minister speaks our language better than we ourselves do." He also translated several works for the Muhhakaneok, including part of the Bible, some prayers, and Isaac Watts's shorter catechism.[53]

These early years of the mission were rewarding for both Sergeant and the Muhhakaneok. Konkapot and Umpachenee quickly agreed to baptism, and others followed suit. The Indians were attentive observers at Sergeant's ordination in Deerfield in August 1735. A year later, the General Court of Massachusetts laid out a six-square-mile township for the Muhhakaneok. In reality, they were granting to the Indians a portion of their own land, but the township of Stockbridge was viewed as a status symbol like the praying villages of a century earlier. Even its name, the copy of a town in Hampshire, England, implied that these Mahican were select and well on the road to civilization. In the newly built church–schoolhouse, Sergeant preached to the Muhhakaneok in their own language, and he also began teaching their children.

Within a short time, twenty Indian children were enrolled in school. In the first months of the mission, Samuel Hopkins procured a schoolmaster to assist Sergeant. The new instructor, Timothy Woodbridge, proved to be a gifted teacher. Moving in with Konkapot, he directed affairs at the mission during the six to seven months when Sergeant returned to Yale to complete his studies. Woodbridge taught the Muhhakaneok as well as some Mohawk children whose families had been encouraged to move to the valley. During his stay at Yale, Sergeant wrote to the Indians. Addressing them as "my good friends and Brethren," he advised that "knowledge is certainly good: It is to the mind what light is to the eye. . . . Truth is more precious than the light of the snow."[54]

The first five years also marked the arrival of the first settlers in the valley. In 1737, four families were encouraged to locate there by the General Court and the Connecticut River Valley ministry responsible for the mission. Foremost among these first families was the one headed by Ephraim Williams. Throughout the years that followed, Williams contributed to eventual white control by inveigling the Muhhakaneok out of their lands. Within two years after his arrival, the relationship between Williams and the missionary had been cemented by Sergeant's marriage to Ephraim's seventeen-year-old daughter Abigail. The youngest of John and Abigail's three children, John, Jr., was born in 1747; he would follow in his father's path by becoming missionary to the Stockbridge Indians in 1775.[55]

In the second year of the mission, Sergeant received an abundant offer of financial aid from the Rev. Isaac Hollis, a Baptist minister living in London. The Housatonic mission had quickly become a fashionable English charity. Through a complex ministerial network extending from Sergeant through the Rev. Benjamin Colman in Boston and then by way of Isaac Watts in England, Hollis had learned of the mission, and in his eagerness to contribute part of his ample fortune, he offered to maintain "twenty scholars" per annum.

Due to a series of difficulties, the Hollis schooling project never became a great success. Hollis's financial backing encouraged Sergeant to propose a more grandiose scheme, whereby additional funding from the colony itself and further private donors in England would support a local charity boarding school for Indian youth. In a slim volume entitled *A Letter from the Rev. Mr. Sergeant of Stockbridge, to Dr. Colman of Boston . . .* (1743), Benjamin Colman publicized Sergeant's idea, but the response was negligible, sufficient only for him to continue to urge construction of a school building. Only the Hollis funding proved dependable, and by 1748 Sergeant sent the first group of twelve boys to Newington, Connecticut, where they were placed under the care of Capt. Martin Kellog. In the meantime, Sergeant continued to seek funding for a local boarding school; but in 1749 this and other projects were cut short by his death.[56]

Sergeant's death at age 39 came as a severe blow to the cause to which he had given all of his energies. He had won the esteem of the Muhhakaneok by his caring attention; he had allied himself with the Williams faction by marrying into the family; he was on the verge of founding the Indian boarding school; and he had established a firm partnership with schoolmaster Timothy Woodbridge, whose concern for the Muhhakaneok matched Sergeant's own commitment.

After Sergeant's death, the factionalism that had threatened the welfare of the Indians erupted into fierce internal warfare. The leaders of the two sides solidified, with Ephraim Williams leading the faction later dubbed the "Indian Ring," which baldly asserted white control over the town and the valley lands; and Woodbridge leading the Indians and their few allies. For two years the mission awaited the appointment of a new minister. The position reputedly was offered to the Rev. Samuel Hopkins, nephew of the minister who had introduced the initial plan in the early 1730s; but he turned it down, urging the appointment of his former mentor, Jonathan Edwards.[57] The Rev. Ezra Stiles, who later became president of Yale, gave the position far more serious consideration. As Edmund Morgan points out, Stiles retreated largely because of the threat to his own rather unorthodox theological reputation, which was subject to potential damage in the continuing debate between Old Lights and New Lights.[58] The impasse following Stiles's rejection of the position was resolved when Edwards accepted the offer.

Two years after Sergeant's death, in July 1752, Edwards and his wife Sarah moved their large family to the valley and settled in the former Sergeant home. They had left chaos in Northampton, where the family suffered a series of calamitous events, beginning with the death of the Rev. David Brainerd, the young missionary whose life was recounted in Edwards's *An Account of the Life of the Late Reverend Mr David Brainerd* (1749). A close friend of the family as well as Edwards's student, Brainerd had died of consumption at the Edwards home and in the presence of his fiancee Jerusha, the Edwards's second daughter, who also died shortly thereafter. The decisive blow came with the eruption of the controversy between Edwards and his parishioners, which resulted in his dismissal from the church. In moving to Stockbridge, the Edwards family unwittingly stepped from one conflict into another. Edwards had looked forward to leaving Northampton and its troubles, but he was not yet aware that he would again encounter a branch of the Williams family who had driven him out of the Connecticut Valley. Thus, he wrote benignly seven months after his arrival, "my wife & children are well pleased with our present situation. They like the place far better than they expected." "Here, at present," he added with a note of caution, "we live in peace; which has of long time been an unusual thing with us."[59]

The peace was soon shattered. The rift that had widened with

Sergeant's death now became a chasm. Edwards found it justifiable to ally himself with the Indian supporters, consisting of Timothy Woodbridge; the Indians (the Muhhakaneok, the Mohawk, and some Oneida); and Gideon Hawley, the newly appointed schoolmaster who was to direct the local boarding school that would supersede Capt. Kellog's Connecticut Valley school. The opposition consisted of Ephraim Williams, his daughter Abigail, Sergeant's widow, and their supporters. One supporter, who had rapidly shifted to side with the "Indian Ring," was Abigail's new husband, Brigadier General Joseph Dwight, a former admirer of Edwards who had moved into the valley after Sergeant's death. One of the goals of the Williams–Dwight group was to control the entire mission budget through the funding for the Indian schools. They insisted that Kellog or one of their supporters become director of the boarding school, which had an enrollment of sixty pupils, largely Iroquois. To this end they harrassed Hawley, and when Edwards came to his defense they simply burned the school building itself, although no one could prove their guilt. The Iroquois supported Hawley, but when the situation became too unpleasant they moved back to their own lands. The other aspect of the Williams venture into education involved Abigail Sergeant Dwight, with Dwight urging that Abigail be made schoolmistress for the proposed school for Indian girls.

Edwards's reaction to these measures was initially couched in an almost defensive framework demonstrating the unhealed wounds from the Northampton feud. In response to attacks by Dwight, he wrote in 1752 that Dwight's representation of him as a man of "very stiff temper may have made some impression," adding, "that I am inflexible, I well know was abundantly said of me at Northampton." But he regretted that Dwight's alliance with the Williamses had led him to concur with the assessment "which my enemies have cast upon me."[60] Edwards moved quickly from defense to attack when the situation became intolerable. Within five months he described the altered milieu: "there is a very dark cloud that at present attends the affairs, relating to the Indians at Stockbridge, occasioned by . . . measures very contrary to the measures of the Commissioners of the Society in London."[61]

As the French and Indian War became a greater issue along the frontier, the Boston commissioners leaned toward those who retained the support of the Housatonic Indians—Edwards, Woodbridge, and their followers. Although Gideon Hawley had left by 1753, the Iroquois whose children attended the boarding school had also moved. Thus, the plan by the Williams-Dwight faction to control the boarding school failed to materialize.[62] The proposed school for Indian girls also apparently fell through. Timothy Woodbridge, however, continued in his post at the day school, remaining there until his death in 1775.

Edwards's impact on the Indians at Housatonic was not equal to that of his predecessor. Although he wrote a treatise on the lan- gauge of the Muhhakaneok, he never delivered a sermon to them or to the Iroquois in their own tongue, and much was lost in the translation. But he did take his assignment seriously, preaching to the Indians so frequently that he aroused the ire of Dwight, who specifically objected to Edwards preaching to the Mohawk. At least one of Edwards' sermons to the Indian youth—"To the In- dian Children at Stockbridge"—has been preserved, as well as others directed to a wider Indian audience.[63] Moreover, Edwards also assisted his former schoolmaster Gideon Hawley in Hawley's struggle to begin a mission in Iroquoia.[64] In considering the fact that it was during this brief tenure at Stockbridge that Edwards completed some of his most remarkable treatises, particularly *Freedom of the Will* (1754), it is a testimonial to his perseverance that he found time for the Indian cause.

In 1757, Edwards was called to the presidency of Princeton, where he was to succeed his son-in-law Aaron Burr, and by early 1758 he had made the move. Within a few weeks after his arrival, a smallpox inoculation led to his death, which shocked the En- glish-speaking world. His years at Stockbridge had witnessed not only the flowering of his thought; they had also seen the demise of the "Indian Ring." Edwards had finally triumphed over part of the Williams family. Nonetheless, the number of settlers who began to pour into the Housatonic Valley at the end of the French and Indian War spelled the end of the Muhhakaneok residency among the Berkshires and by the "continually flowing waters."

During the years when Sergeant ran the mission, David Brain- erd occasionally rode over to the Housatonic Valley from the site of his first missionary endeavor. Brainerd had entered the mis- sionary field by serving at Kaunaumeek, located about midway between Albany and Stockbridge. Through an arrangement with the society in Scotland, he had agreed to minister to a group of

Mahican living in the valley. There, the young Presbyterian began his brief labors, initiating the methods he would use in other locations. He preached and prayed, studied the language, translated some works, and taught the children through singing and general instruction.[65]

On his visits to Stockbridge, a ride of about twenty miles from Kaunaumeek, he studied the language of the local Mahican with the aid of Sergeant, who was already a master of the tongue. Brainerd also taught the Housatonic Indians to sing the prayers and psalms he had arranged in metrical form for the Mahican at Kaunaumeek.[66]

A year after he had begun his work, the Scottish Society requested that Brainerd shift locations from Kaunaumeek to the forks of the Delaware. At Brainerd's suggestion, the Mahican to whom he had ministered moved east to the Stockbridge mission, while he shifted to the Delaware, or Lenni Lenape, who lived at the forks. Here, Brainerd encountered the nucleus of the people he would serve both at the forks and later in New Jersey. Brainerd's death came three years later, when he was twenty-nine years of age.[67]

The young missionary had attended Yale during the height of the Great Awakening, and he was a strong supporter of the revival. At the head of his class, he suffered a severe setback during his senior year of 1742–43, when an offhand remark about a member of the faculty led to his expulsion.[68] During this period of emotional strain, David's younger brother John was in his first year at the college. Undeterred by the harsh censure of his older brother, John continued his studies for the ministry, graduating in 1746, and less than a year later, a few months before his brother's death, he began to serve in David's place. Ordained by the Presbytery of New York and endorsed by the Scottish Society, John Brainerd began a lengthy missionary service among the remnant Lenni Lenape, who remained in New Jersey until the end of the eighteenth century.

David Brainerd's endeavors as missionary and educator for the Indians lasted only four years. By contrast, John Brainerd served the Delaware for the thirty-four years that remained in his life. These remarkable brothers were reared in a family of nine children, and they shared a great deal of affection for each other. Nonetheless, John was identified throughout his life as the brother of David Brainerd. In 1764, when John protested George White-field's suggestion that he travel to England to raise funds for the Indian school which eventually became Dartmouth College, Whitefield argued that he consider the offer because, among other reasons, he "was Mr. David Brainerd's brother." As late as the 1770s, in the last decade of John's life, a Methodist missionary to the colonies described their meeting in the following words: "here I met with Mr. John Brainerd, brother and successor to that great and good man Mr. David Brainerd, missionary to the In-dians."[69]

Considering the fact that one of these missionary brothers served only four years and the other thirty-four, why did the older brother overshadow the younger? David may have been more brilliant, perhaps more daring, and some said more spiritual, but his perseverance and commitment to the Indian cause did not overshadow the same aspects in his brother's character. Nonethe-less, David was the pioneer of the two. He sought out the Dela-ware at the forks, preached to them, and then persuaded them to move to Crossweeksung, New Jersey. They were already estab-lished there in a small community when John arrived as David's successor. More important, Edwards's publication of David's jour-nal and later his biography meant that David's unstinting devo-tion to the Indians was on the lips of every clergyman in the eighteenth-century British colonial world, with his example also serving as an inspiration for other missionaries. In 1753, when Gideon Hawley, the former Stockbridge schoolmaster, traveled to Onohoghgwage to serve the Iroquois, he wrote: "I read my Bible and Mr. Brainerds Life the only Books I bro't with me, and from them have a little support."[70] Through a combination of Ed-wards's publicity and his own early death, David Brainerd be-came in essence a martyr. Edwards's endorsement of "my dear and Reverend Brother Brainerd" assured the missionary a fame not only for the eighteenth century but for posterity as well.

It was fortunate for his younger brother that modesty prevented him from seeking glory, since it was not to be John Brainerd's lot. Of the two brothers, however, it was John, by virtue of his longev-ity in the field, who served as a pivotal figure in the Indian schooling network that sprang from the Great Awakening and the focal point established by Wheelock in Lebanon. By the time Wheelock had completed the tutoring of Samson Occom and had begun to formulate his plans for an Indian charity school, John Brainerd had gained several years of experience with the Delaware community. John Brainerd preempted Wheelock's Indian schooling, in part because of his access to the Delaware community. No Indians lived in Lebanon itself, which certainly accounted for a portion of Wheelock's stress on the advantages of a boarding school. Wheelock reasoned like some of the SPG missionaries in the Carolinas: if he were unwilling to go to the Indians, then the Indians would have to come to him. John Brainerd, as a virtual itinerant to both Indian and white—especially after these Delaware were forced to move from Crossweeksung, or Bethel, to a new site known as Brotherton—either lived near the Indians or attended them closely via his constant rounds on horseback.

When John Brainerd arrived at Crossweeksung, he found the school begun by his brother. After four years, the community had grown to include forty families, and the school numbered at most fifty children. "The children in general seem as apt to learn as English children," he wrote to a friend in England. "Not less than twenty . . . are able to read pretty distinctly in the Bible and repeat most of the Assembly's Short Catechism . . . and some of them can write a decent legible hand."[71] The school maintained an uneven existence during these decades, and disrupted by the move to Brotherton, it suffered from budgetary limitations as well as from Brainerd's difficulty in retaining a schoolmaster. But Brainerd was a dogged individual, and he continued to request schooling funds from his various sources of support: the New Jersey Board of Correspondents for the Scottish Society, the Presbytery of New York, and the College of New Jersey, later known as Princeton.

As early as 1751, Brainerd's encouragement had led to the enrollment of one Delaware youth in the College of New Jersey. A year later, he described this youth, who was supported by the Scottish Society in his training for the ministry: "he is a very promising young man, makes good proficiency in his learning, and is, I hope, truly pious." Brainerd added, with typical eighteenth-century piety, "may the Lord continue his life, and make him a rich blessing to his pagan brethren."[72] After another year had passed, this young Delaware had died of "a quick consumption," and in lamenting the loss, Brainerd declared that the young man had been "much beloved by his classmates and the other scholars."[73]

The next Delaware who attended the college did not acquit himself as honorably. Jacob Wooley was one of the first two Delaware youth sent by Brainerd to Wheelock in 1754 to attend the newly founded Moor's Indian Charity School. A few years later, Wheelock sent Wooley to the college, but the experiment was a failure. Brainerd noted cryptically: "little Jacob was not fit to enter college, but the commissioners, however, took him under their pay."[74]

By 1754, Brainerd had been appointed a trustee to the college, and he probably found Wooley an embarrassment. Wooley's irresponsibility was but one of many disappointments for Brainerd among those Delaware youth he selected for further education. However, at least one other Delaware youth recommended by Brainerd did attend the college during the colonial period. Bartholemew S. Calvin, brother of Hezekiah Calvin, was enrolled at Princeton in 1770, remaining there until the Revolutionary War cut off his financial support from the SSPCK; and Calvin later became a schoolmaster. Under Brainerd's encouragement, six Delaware youth were sent to Moor's School and at least three enrolled in Princeton during the decades between 1750 and the American Revolution. All six had benefited to some degree from Brainerd's perseverance, for he did not have a large population to draw from within the Delaware community.

After Brainerd's death in 1781, neither the Scottish Society nor the Presbyterian Synod continued to support the Delaware congregation at Brotherton, which had shrunk to a small number. In 1802, the estimated sixty to eighty-five Delaware remaining moved to join the Brothertown–Stockbridge communities located on land granted by the Oneida, and in the 1820s they joined these remnant groups when they moved west to Wisconsin.[75]

John Brainerd's Delaware had proved to be an important source for Wheelock's school. Brainerd provided not only the first students; he also sent one Delaware girl, who participated in one of the few coeducational Indian schools in the colonial period.

9

INDIAN WOMEN BETWEEN TWO WORLDS: MOOR'S SCHOOL AND COEDUCATION IN THE 1760s

In a small hand-hewn booklet, Eleazar Wheelock carefully jotted down the record of one of his female pupils: "one pair of shoes, . . . 5 yards and ½ of corse osnaberg . . . 9 yards and ¼ of salt sacking." He listed several more items and concluded with a measure of muslin for an apron.[1] Schoolmasters during this period seldom taught Indian boys in their classrooms, and instruction for Indian girls was even more rare. Hence, this memo—a clothing ration for an Algonquian girl who attended Moor's Indian Charity School in the 1760s—is a unique colonial document. It attests to the unusual nature of this coeducational school for Indian and white charity students in eighteenth-century Connecticut.

Eleazar Wheelock was the pivotal figure in this educational effort. He founded Moor's School, supervised its sixteen-year life span in Lebanon, and engineered its metamorphosis and relocation to Hanover, New Hampshire, where it formed the nucleus for Dartmouth College.[2] Wheelock also kept most of the school's records. But some instinct—perhaps a sense of history—led him to preserve not only his personal writing but frequently the words of the Indian students as well. As a result, the story of Moor's School moves well beyond the ethnocentric focus of its director. The survival of both male and female Indian correspondence affords a rare glimpse into the attitudes of a small group of partially educated Iroquois and southern New England Algonquian.

Encouraged by the scholarly successes of Samson Occom, Wheelock grew determined to begin a charity boarding school for Indian and white youth.[3] Six years after Occom had left the Wheelock home, the minister's dream took shape. In December 1754, the first pupils—John Pumshire, a fourteen-year-old Delaware, and Jacob Woolley, an eleven-year-old Delaware—enrolled in Moor's Indian Charity School. Both Pumshire and Woolley were sent by John Brainerd. A visible testimony to Brainerd's faith in Wheelock's dream, the two Delaware boys served as the initial successors to Samson Occom. By the end of the decade, Wheelock decided to add Indian girls to his all-male school, and his first female pupils—Amy Johnson, a Mohegan, and Miriam Storrs, an eleven-year-old Delaware—arrived in 1761.

Launching Moor's School had not been an easy task. In the early stage, before Wheelock had considered the advantages of coeducation, the school remained small. In 1755, Wheelock received "about 2 Acres of Pasturing, a small House and Shop" from Colonel Joshua More, a farmer in nearby Mansfield, for whom the school was named; but the minister–schoolmaster still enrolled fewer than ten pupils, all of them recruited from nearby Algonquian communities.[4] The institution increased its enrollment, adding not only female Algonquian, but both male and female Iroquois pupils as well because of Wheelock's skills as director and promoter. He assessed his needs in a practical fashion and then set about to meet them. First, he needed a source of income that would stretch his meager minister's salary and the miscellaneous landholdings that supported his growing family. A larger school would require extensive financial aid, which would involve the creation of a convincing rationale and a widespread promotional campaign. Like John Eliot, his illustrious predecessor, Wheelock never underestimated the need for political pressure to secure economic assistance, and his efforts in this direction earned him the sobriquet of "religious politician."[5]

The rationale for "the great Design"—Wheelock's grandiose title for his experiment in Indian education—was an appealing one. The minister–schoolmaster began by reminding New Englanders of their "great obligations" as "God's Covenant-People," and chastising them for their "neglect of the previous Souls of our Fellow Creatures, who are perishing for lack of Vision."[6] He projected his plan, which was initiated during the French and Indian

War, as a remedy to appease the constant fear of frontier attack. The money spent on education, he argued, would serve New England as a better defense against Indian assaults than expensive forts.[7] Sounding a theme that would become familiar in the nineteenth century, he suggested that if the Indians were "brought up in a Christian manner . . . , instructed in Agriculture, and taught to get their Living by their Labour," they would no longer "make such Depradations on our Frontiers."[8] In a modified echo of John Eliot and the Mayhew family, he also recommended that Indians, rather than whites, be trained as preachers and teachers "for carrying the Gospel into the wilds of America."[9] Here, he appealed to the supporters' pocketbook: "an Indian may be supported with less than half the Expense that will be necessary to support an Englishman."[10] Moreover, "the Influence of their own Sons among them will likely be much greater than of any Englishman whatever."[11] There is little indication that Wheelock initially made the addition of girls to Moor's School a strong selling point, but when he did add them, he justified the action to his supporters with similar arguments.

With this rationale for "The great Design" in hand, Wheelock began to garner his support, and although he experienced uneven success, he established an extensive network of contacts. Individuals and organizations in England and the colonies came to the aid of the growing number of male and female charity scholars. In the colonies, Wheelock received funds from the general assemblies of Masachusetts and New Hampshire, and Connecticut twice authorized the reading of briefs in the churches, which led to subscriptions for the school's benefit. In Britain, two organizations aided Wheelock's experiments: the Society in Scotland for Propagating Christian Knowledge (SSPCK) and the New England Company. The SSPCK was represented by four colonial boards located in Massachusetts, New Jersey, New York, and Connecticut. Wheelock became a virtual dictator of the Connecticut board, approved by the SSPCK in 1764.[12] Funds from the New England Company came through its Boston board. Wheelock also benefited from private donations, especially from the Countess of Huntingdon and the Marquis of Lothian.

For Wheelock, however, fund-raising was an unending task. Even when the school was well established, financial pressure constantly drained his energies. In the two and a half decades that the minister–schoolmaster devoted to Indian education, from 1754 to his death in 1779, he constantly appealed for support. In addition, between 1763 and 1775 he published nine separate *Narratives*, which served as a continuing promotional effort for Moor's School and, eventually, for Dartmouth College.[13]

Once a measure of financial support was guaranteed, Wheelock introduced one of the most interesting and least publicized aspects of his experiment—schooling for Indian girls. The notion of educating Indian girls had been a subject of some concern for New England missionaries during the Great Awakening and afterward. In the 1740s, the Rev. John Sergeant, missionary at Stockbridge, and Rev. Dr. Benjamin Colman of Boston had stressed the role played by Indian women in "the Care of the Souls of Children in Families . . . for the first 7 or 8 Years."[14] John Brainerd expressed similar concern about the need of education for the Delaware women in his community.[15] These women, Brainerd believed, were "much better inclined in all respects than the men." Not only did they have better morals; they were more industrious. Since they were unable to support themselves except by making baskets and brooms, Brainerd suggested to his Scottish financial supporters, the SSPCK, that he establish a "female school" where the young women could be taught to spin and knit.[16] This dream, like so many others Brainerd held, never materialized.

While Wheelock was in communication with these men, he also wrote to colonial school teachers scattered among the small Algonquian communities and to the more prestigious Sir William Johnson, ally of the Iroquois and superintendent of Indian affairs for the northern colonies. In the late 1750s, when Wheelock decided that Moor's School was financially able to include girls, he turned to these men for potential students.

Between 1761 and 1769, Wheelock enrolled some sixteen Indian girls at Moor's School. Their attendance provided perhaps a fourth of the total Indian enrollment.[17] Some of the girls stayed only a few months; five, possibly seven, were there for at least two years; two of them remained for five years, and one for six years. They came from nearby groups, including the Narragansett, Mohegan, Niantic, and Pequot; from the Delaware; and from two Iroquois groups, the Mohawk and Oneida. Of these tribes, most of the Algonquian groups had been in contact with Europeans since the early 1600s. Of the Iroquois, the Mohawk, who were Sir William Johnson's neighbors, had been most exposed to European culture. Thus, Wheelock dealt with girls who were familiar with the rudiments of Christianity, were accustomed to European trade goods, spoke some English and may have had some schooling; were almost all very poor, and whose material cultures had changed radically from precontact days.

A practical schoolmaster, Wheelock based his plan for the education of Indian girls on two considerations: the fact that they were female and his conviction that their education should not be a financial burden to the school. Wheelock believed that their schooling should be similar to that of young colonial women, whose intellectual skills were summarized in a gently ironic couplet borrowed from Abigail Adams:

> The little learning I have gained
> Is all from simple nature Drained.[18]

New Englanders knew that women were fit for home and hearth; therefore, girls should receive the rudiments of a formal education—reading and writing—but most of their training should be for the home. While parents apprenticed colonial girls to another home for training in housekeeping, more often they learned such skills in their own family.

Here lay a fundamental difference between colonial daughters and the Indian girls at Moor's School. Whereas the former were usually trained at home, Wheelock settled the latter in nearby community homes where they were treated as servants, possibly even as slaves.[19] Wheelock argued that he did not have space to board the girls in his own home, and for this reason, he "Hired women in this neighborhood to instruct [them] in all the arts of good House wifery."[20] Nonetheless, Wheelock did provide for their clothing, and he also assumed responsibility for their moral instruction and their basic educational skills.

For both Indian and white girls, instruction was limited to a relatively few hours. Schooling for colonial girls often occurred only in the early morning or late afternoon, when boys were not using the schoolroom. Indian girls received instruction only one day a week. But Wheelock did require homework, assigning them to "write four lines on each Day they are Absent."[21] This limitation on their formal schooling was imposed in order to minimize financial expense. Wheelock reasoned that he could afford to maintain the girls as pupils if they cost him only one day's schooling and dinner per week. On the one day the girls attended school, they "were to be instructed in writing &c, till they should be fit for an Apprenticeship, to be taught Men's and Women's Apparel."[22] Like their white counterparts, their education trained them to serve their husbands' needs. Woman's relation to man, wrote a New Englander in 1761, is to be "an Help to him."[23] The education of these Indian girls, Wheelock explained in 1763, is "in order to accompany these [Indian] Boys, when they shall have Occasion for such Assistance in the Business of their Mission."[24]

The boys, on the other hand, were directly under Wheelock's thumb and were subjected to a rigorous, daily routine. Like all schoolmasters of the period, Wheelock adhered to the maxim: "Idleness in youth is scarcely healed without a scar in age."[25] At Moor's School, the day began before sunrise. Following early morning prayer and catechism, the boys remained in the classroom until noon, where they received a classical training in Latin and Greek, and sometimes Hebrew. After a two-hour break, they returned to work until 5:00 P.M. Just before dark, they attended evening prayers and public worship, and then studied until bedtime. This schedule was altered only on Sunday, when they spent the day in meetings and catechism classes.

Sometimes, however, this educational environment was more illusory than real. Despite Wheelock's protests to the contrary, drunkenness, misbehavior, and running away were also a part of daily life. In a note of realism, Wheelock suggested that the girls be added "for the purpose that these Boy[s] may not be under absolute necessity to turn Savage in this manner of living for want of those who can do the female part for them when they shall be aboard on the business of their Missions and out of reach of the English."[26] The inclusion of girls, however, may have merely increased Wheelock's chronic discipline problems at the school. A confession by Hannah Nonesuch, written on her first day in Lebanon, was typical of those pleas for forgiveness that Wheelock kept in his files.

> I Hannah Nonesuch do with shamefacedness acknowledge that on the evening of the 8th Inst I was . . . guilty of being at the tavern and tarrying there with a commpany of Indian boys & girls for . . . a frolick . . . I am heartily sorry, & desire to lie low in the dust & do

now beg forgiveness of God, the Revd & worthy Doctor Wheelock, his family & school, and all whom I have hereby offended.

March 1768[27]

The story of three of Hannah's companions—Miriam Storrs (a Delaware student from 1761 to 1767), Hannah Garrett (a Pequot student from 1763 to 1766), and Mary Secutor (a Narragansett student from 1763 to 1768)—illustrates the problems that plagued Wheelock's "great Design."

Miriam Storrs, the second girl to enroll in Moor's School, grew up in the small Delaware community served by John Brainerd.[28] Miriam came from one of the more religious families in this community, and her mother was a member of Brainerd's church, where Miriam was baptized as an infant. She was the only girl among the six young Delaware sent by Brainerd to Moor's School.[29] She had started on the trip to New London, Connecticut, with Elizabeth Quela, but Elizabeth's recurring illness had forced her to turn back before the ship left. As the two girls were departing, Brainerd had written to Wheelock:

> I feel tenderly concerned for these little girls, & as it is a very considerable thing for them to go so far away from their parents, I hope they will meet with the kindest & best treatment.[30]

Upon Miriam's arrival in Lebanon, Wheelock described her as "an amiable little black savage Christian."[31] During the next six years, she changed from an eleven-year-old girl to a young woman.

Wheelock provided for Miriam's physical needs, purchasing material for her clothing and finding her a place to live.[32] Shortly after she arrived, he hired a "proper Gentlewoman" to train her and her companions in "all parts of good Housewifery. Tending a Dary, Spining, the use of their needle."[33] A few years later, when more girls had arrived, he sought to hire a tailoress to equip them with more advanced skills.[34] When Miriam came to Wheelock's home once a week for her lessons, his "Masters" taught her the minimum reading and writing skills. Wheelock himself assumed responsibility for the condition of her soul.

Miriam's housekeeping duties probably prevented her from participating in daily worship at the school, but she and the other pupils attended church on Sunday, where she sat at the rear and on the side reserved for the community's women. She probably attended the catechism classes held between Sunday meetings, receiving there a solid grounding in Calvinist religion. "Every *Grace* enters into the Soul through the *Understanding*," Cotton Mather had written in 1704, and understanding could come about only through a knowledge of the Scriptures and intense introspection.[35]

The religious state of his pupils greatly concerned Wheelock. Shortly after Miriam turned thirteen, he noted her progress. "[Miriam] has of late," he wrote, "had such discoveries of the truth, Reality, and Greatness of things revealed, as were more than Nature could sustain; she fainted under them."[36] Here was the spiritual enthusiasm that Wheelock had elicited during the Great Awakening; yet here too was one of the most difficult aspects of boarding-school life for both Indian girls and boys. As one of Miriam's companions wrote, "I have no peace of conscience."[37]

In late 1767 or early 1768, when Miriam was sixteen or seventeen years old, she left the school. Had she been reared in a traditional Delaware community, she would already have been married and raising a family. Had she achieved the goal established by Wheelock—becoming a housewife, schoolmistress, or tailoress—she might have been able to adjust, but she had not reached that goal and now found herself ill prepared to cope with colonial society. When she left school, she headed south through Connecticut to New York City, where, after several jobs, she wrote a letter of bitter disappointment to her former mentor. Composing the message required effort, and although the grammar was poor and the script almost illegible, the meaning was clear. "Sir I have heard but one prayer since I went from Norwich," she lamented. "Since I went from thy house instead of prayers [I hear] filthy talk. . . . I have been under many trials . . . which caused me soo to weep nights." However, she retained her faith: "I found no rest until I put my whole trust in God."[38]

Miriam soon tired of New York, and within a year she returned to her Delaware community. "Her poor old parents were overjoyed to see her," Brainerd wrote, and "I wish she might be a blessing to them."[39] Miriam, however, did not progress as Brainerd and Wheelock had expected. Brainerd tried to apprentice her to a tailor so as to "perfect her trade" as a seamstress, but he reported no success. The only occupation she could pursue was housework, the basic skill she had learned in Lebanon. In the ensuing years, Brainerd reported on her occasionally, each time with an edge of despair in his words. "Miriam Store is not the thing I want her to be, by any means," he wrote in June 1769. "There is too much truth in that common saying, 'Indians will be Indians.' "[40] Three and a half years later, when only twenty-three, Miriam was suffering from severe rheumatism and had "but poor use of her hands." There is no further mention of her name.[41]

By Brainerd and Wheelock's standards, Miriam's contemporary Hannah Garrett came much closer to success. Hannah was a descendant of the Pequot, a tribe almost decimated in the Pequot War of 1636. When the remaining Pequot warriors were divided among the Mohegan, Narragansett, and Niantic tribes, Hannah's ancestors were among those sent to Narragansett territory in Rhode Island.[42] Many decades later, in 1713–14, her grandfather, Joseph Garrett, had met Experience Mayhew and earned high praise from him. By the 1750s, when Hannah was growing up, the Narragansett had established their own Protestant church under the guidance of a well-known Indian preacher. The elementary school in Charlestown, which Hannah may have attended, was the first school for several of Wheelock's Narragansett pupils;[43] and in 1764, there were four girls at the school: Miriam, Hannah, Amy Johnson, and Mary Secutor.

Within a year of her arrival, Hannah was being courted by Joseph Woolley, an eighteen- or nineteen-year-old Delaware who had studied with Wheelock for seven years. Woolley had just begun to court Hannah when Wheelock sent him to Onohoghgwage to serve as a schoolmaster to the Mohawk children. En route, Woolley wrote to Wheelock asking him to advise Hannah's father of the marriage proposal. Although Hannah, a dutiful daughter, refused to take any further steps without her father's permission, Woolley feared a possible change of heart by Hannah: "I can't take it well f[ro]m her, if Just at the End, she should turn the Contrary." But he and Hannah never saw each other again, for consumption soon cut his life short.[44]

Another scholar then began to court Hannah. David Fowler, a Montauk, and the younger brother of Mary Fowler Occom, Samsom Occom's wife, commenced his studies with Wheelock when he was twenty-four, and by the time the fourteen- or fifteen-year-old Hannah arrived in Lebanon, he was already twenty-eight. During Hannah's third year in Lebanon, Wheelock sent David Fowler to Canowaroghere to teach the Oneida children. David had no illusions about living in the wilderness without a wife. On the eve of his departure, he planned to marry Amy Johnson, a former pupil at Wheelock School.[45] This relationship soon cooled, however, and by the following spring David had determined to marry Hannah Poquiantup, a Niantic. "I find it very hard to live here without the other Rib," he wrote to Wheelock from Canajoharie.[46] Fearing that Hannah Poquiantup might break the bargain they had made, he wrote again to Wheelock, "If she won't let her bones be joined with mine, I shall pick out my Rib from your House."[47] David's fears of Hannah Poquiantup's refusal were realized, and he returned to Lebanon, going directly to Wheelock's school with a determination born from two failures and one lonely winter. Evidently, it was not too difficult for this frantic thirty-one-year-old bachelor to convince the seventeen- or eighteen-year-old Hannah Garrett to marry him. Their courtship was noted drily by Wheelock in an exchange between the minister and Fowler: "how you & Hannah ha' Spent yr prec. Hours yesterday & t'day I know not—Or how yo will live or wn you will serve togr I know not."[48]

Wheelock had wearied of David Fowler's romances, and probably with some relief, he sent Hannah and David back to the Iroquois country. He and David continued to correspond, but if Hannah learned how to write at school, no evidence of it has survived. By David's account, however, she proved to be the wife he had hoped for. "I find very great Profit by having the other Rib join'd to my Body for it hath taken away all my House work from me," he wrote to Wheelock during the first winter following the marriage.[49] In June of the following year, Hannah bore their first child, a boy they named David.

Shortly after the birth of their son, Hannah and David returned to Montauk, where David taught school. Following the revolution, they moved with their six children to Brothertown, an Algonquian settlement on Oneida land established by David, his brother-in-law Samson Occom, and several other Indian leaders.[50] Here, they settled among their own people for the remainder of their lives. Hannah outlived her husband by four years and died in 1811.

Of the sixteen girls who attended Moor's School, Hannah Garrett was the only one who achieved the goal of marriage established by Wheelock. There is no record of any courtship for

Miriam Storrs, and the brief account of the third girl in this trilogy, Mary Secutor, is underlined by disappointment. Like Hannah Garrett, Mary Secutor had grown up on the Narragansett reservation. She, too, probably attended the school in Charlestown before going to study with Wheelock in December 1763. Following her arrival at the age of perhaps thirteen or fourteen, she matured sufficiently during the next three or four years for Wheelock to describe her as "well accomplished and very likely."[51] Up to this point, Mary appears to have been a model student. Upon her arrival, she had met a young Delaware by the name of Hezekiah Calvin. Mary and Hezekiah were together for a year and a half before Wheelock sent seventeen-year-old Hezekiah to keep school for Mohawk children. During the next two winters, Hezekiah taught school near Fort Hunter, but his mind was not on his teaching; he was preoccupied with the Narragansett girl back at Moor's School. As he later confessed to Wheelock, "nothing was in my thoughts but being married."[52] When he returned to Lebanon after the second winter among the Iroquois, he wrote to Mary's father, asking him for permission to marry her. "It may be no small thing I have to acquaint you with," he began, "the design that lay between your daughter Moley and me, Pardon me if I blush to Name it, that is *Matrimony* but I shall not attempt it without yr Consent & approbation." John Secutor opposed the marriage, and with no explanation he wrote to Wheelock to urge him to use his "reasonable powers to Dissuade my Daughter from such design."[53] There is no record of Mary's feelings at this time, but in later correspondence she stated, "I have had more regards for Calvin than ever I had for anny Indian in my life."[54] Without the approval of Mary's father, however, the two young people were in a quandary. A few months later, both Mary and Hezekiah apologized in written confessions for "gross sins"; they had been involved in drinking and other "vile" behavior. In the spring they wrote second confessions, and by the following summer they had left school.[55]

Hezekiah and Mary returned to their own people, but the appropriate moment for their proposed marriage seems to have passed. When Mary's father finally gave his permission, she found herself plagued with uncertainty. "I love him well enough," she wrote to Wheelock, "but what to do I know not. . . . I hope I shall be Derected to do what is rite."[56]

From Wheelock's point of view, his eight-year experiment with women's education must have been a keen disappointment. It was yet another aggravation to add to his bitter feelings of failure regarding the young Indian men he had trained to serve as schoolmasters among the Iroquois, no more than half of whom, he wrote in 1771, had "preserved their characters."[57] Only six of the girls who enrolled at Moor's School stayed longer than two years, and they had come from the more assimilated Algonquian communities. Of these six, Hannah Garrett was the only one who lived an exemplary life. Miriam Storrs disappointed both Brainerd and Wheelock; Mary Secutor's last letter dwelt on her indecision in marriage; Amy Johnson was consumptive; Sarah Wyog was remembered only as the instigator of a "frolick"; and Sarah Simon's last letter, which was filled with Calvinist angst, was a recital of woe.[58]

Wheelock provided these girls with a practical skill, minimum reading and writing ability, and a Calvinist view of life, but he had failed to convince them that they should adopt the cultural traits of his own people. Wheelock and his contemporaries needed certain values in order to achieve individual success in the fluid and expanding economy and society of eighteenth-century America. Few New Englanders would have disputed the maxims so well epitomized in the sayings of Poor Richard: "A penny saved is a penny earned"; "Early to bed, early to rise, makes a man healthy, wealthy and wise"; "Light purse, heavy heart"; "God helps them that help themselves." Benjamin Franklin popularized these phrases, but his New England neighbors lived the precepts. When John Adams wrote to his wife Abigail concerning their children's education, he summarized the prevailing attitude:

> The Education of our Children is never out of my Mind. Train them to Virtue, habituate them to industry, activity, and Spirit.[59]

Industry, diligence, frugality, and temperance were all aspects of Wheelock's character as well. By adding piety, which he possessed in great abundance, his framework for success was complete. It was ironic, then, that the cultural values that served Wheelock so well were the very qualities he was least able to transmit to his pupils. His failure may have been due in part to their retention of native values, which ran counter to those of the contemporary New Englander.

It is generally accepted that the material culture of these girls' tribes had changed radically since the early 1600s. Less recognized, however, is the possibility that their cultural values may have persisted, perhaps to a far greater extent than Wheelock and his contemporaries cared to admit. Wheelock had theorized some years earlier that the boarding school would remove Indian children from "the pernicious influence of *Indian* examples," but for Miriam and her contemporaries, the learning acquired at Moor's School was merely superimposed on their earlier education.[60] Despite a century and a half of contact, these Indian groups continued to live cooperatively with nature. The scarcity of game had made hunting increasingly difficult, but they still fished and clung to their patches of corn and beans.[61] They were a people who balanced *being* with *doing*, in contrast to the colonialist bound to his code of industry and diligence. They lived by seasonal, or in effect, natural time, unpunctuated by the colonial hourglass, calendar, or the notion of "wasting time."[62] Their group orientation persisted: the family and community were of greater importance than any single member, and without this support the individual felt that he was unable to cope with the world.[63]

Wheelock's emphasis on Puritan values did not destroy the family and community orientation of these Indian girls, nor did it prepare them adequately for the heterogeneous morality of colonial society beyond the small New England community. Miriam Storrs was witness to this cultural shock during her search for a place in the colonial world. Even had Wheelock's influence succeeded, one additional factor would have continued to dissuade these Indian girls from participating in colonial society: the insidious strength of racial prejudice. Prejudice was a fact of life for the Indian in colonial America. These girls met it in Lebanon homes; in church, where they were seated *behind* the women of the community; in school, from a mentor who had described one of them as a "black savage Christian" and was accused by another pupil of treating the girls as "slaves";[64] and in the postschool society, where it was commonly accepted that "ye Indians are dispized by ye English."[65] For many colonists, the Indians "were mere tools used by grasping and uneasy men to obtain their own

selfish ends."[66] For some Indian girls, racial prejudice was probably the blow that sent them back to their own people. Hannah
Garrett, the most successful girl, never confronted white colonial
society because she and her husband chose to live among communities composed of Indian people who had rejected many of
the colonial values.

Rejection of colonial society did not necessarily mean that it
was easy for the girls to return to their people. They may have felt
a dissatisfaction with their lives at this stage. Moor's School and
their experiences in Lebanon had given them a taste of colonial
living. They would no longer be totally content with the traditional values of their people, nor could they be comfortable in
colonial society. Their frustrations bespoke the uncertainty of
imbalance. An Indian woman with a veneer of New England
culture and facing both prejudice in colonial society and uneasiness in her native society confronted an enduring dilemma.

Even when Wheelock admitted disillusion with the earlier
phase of "the great Design," and moved his school to Dartmouth,
he still failed to comprehend the dimensions of the choice he had
imposed on his students, female as well as male. "It grieves &
breaks my heart," he wrote in 1768, "that while I am wearing my
life out to do good to the poor Indians, they themselves have no
more Desire to help forward the great Design of their Happiness . . . but [there] are so many of them . . . pulling the other way
& as fast as they can undoing all I have done."[67] Perhaps he would
have understood if he had walked in their path, but cultural
myopia dimmed Wheelock's comprehension. To his death, he
remained convinced of the righteousness of his cause.

Iroquois and Southern New England Algonquian in the 18th Century

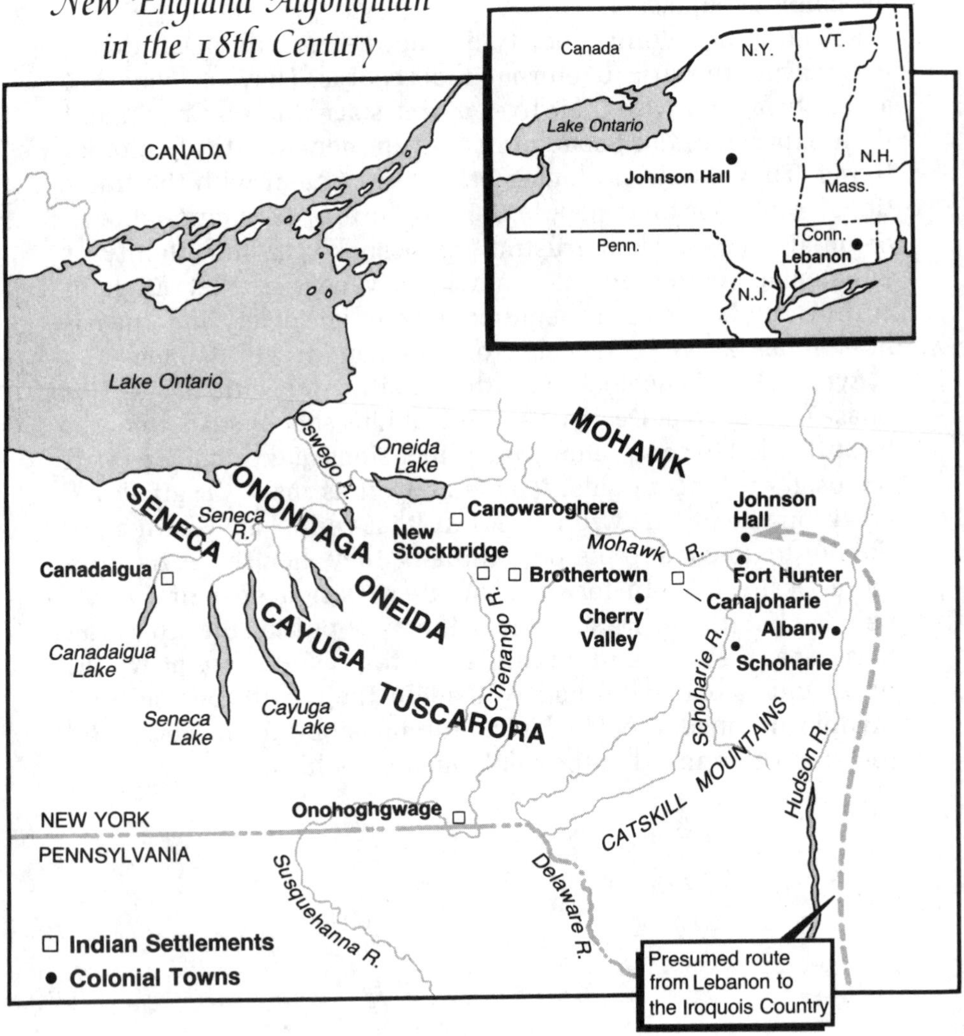
Canada
N.Y.
VT.
Lake Ontario
Johnson Hall
N.H.
Mass.
Penn.
Conn.
Lebanon
N.J.
CANADA
Lake Ontario
Oswego R.
Oneida Lake
MOHAWK
SENECA
ONONDAGA
Seneca R.
Canowaroghere
Johnson Hall
New Stockbridge
Mohawk R.
Canadaigua
Brothertown
Fort Hunter
ONEIDA
Canajoharie
Cherry Valley
Albany
CAYUGA
Chenango R.
Schoharie R.
Schoharie
Canadaigua Lake
Seneca Lake
Cayuga Lake
TUSCARORA
CATSKILL MOUNTAINS
Hudson R.
Onohoghgwage
NEW YORK
PENNSYLVANIA
Susquehanna R.
Delaware R.
Indian Settlements
Colonial Towns
Presumed route from Lebanon to the Iroquois Country

10

INDIAN SCHOOLMASTERS TO THE IROQUOIS, FROM THE 1760s TO THE 1770s

At about the same time that Wheelock decided to add female students to his school, he determined to expand his educational experiment in other directions. Bearing in mind two prerequisites for expansion—a new tribal source for Indian students and a potential future site for Moor's School—he began to eye the Great Lakes region and the Iroquois Confederacy.

In the first of his publicity broadsides, the *Narrative* of 1763, Wheelock's analysis of the potential for schooling among the Iroquois revealed that he had already given the subject much serious consideration. Even at this early date, he argued that there were only two places where schools might "be maintained to some good Purpose" among the Six Nations: namely, among the Oneida at Onohoghgwage, "where there have been heretofore several faithful missionaries," and among the Mohawk, "where Mr. Ogilvie and other Episcopal Missionaries have bestowed such Labour." As an experienced educator of partially assimilated Algonquian, Wheelock recognized the distinct advantage of tilling soil that already had been turned by others. "But even in these Places," he cautioned, "we may find it more difficult than we imagine before the Trial be made."[1]

During his first decade as director of Moor's School, Wheelock had heard numerous tales about the failure of English schoolmasters to interest Algonquian parents in schooling for their children. After citing the dissatisfaction of the Mohegan and Stockbridge

233

schoolmasters, he concluded: "such is the savage Temper of many [Algonquian], their want of due Esteem for Learning . . . and especially their want of Government, that their Schoolmasters, tho' skilful and faithful men, constantly complain they can't keep the Children in any Measure constant at School."[2]

Such repeatedly negative reports on Algonquian day schools served only to reinforce Wheelock's conviction in the superiority of the boarding school as an institution. Throughout his career, Wheelock remained convinced that community schools could not compete with an educational environment in which children "are taken out of the reach of their Parents, and out of the way of Indian examples, and are kept to School under good Government and constant Instruction."[3] Over a century later, Richard Henry Pratt would take a page from Wheelock's argument in founding Carlisle Boarding School.

While basing his design for Iroquois schooling on the negative example of the Algonquian community schools, Wheelock believed that a boarding school among the Six Nations would provide the most effective type of education for their youth. As the school's director, he would appoint former Indian students from Moor's School as schoolmasters and schoolmistresses. In this way, he would provide an opportunity for his Indian students to embark on careers as teachers to the "children of savages."[4] Moreover, if the school materialized, it would establish an enduring niche for Wheelock in the annals of Indian education.

By 1763, Wheelock had already demonstrated his willingness to stake his future on the potential for this school. The year before he had written to William Johnson, influential friend of the Mohawk, asking, "could not your Hon^r. make way for the Setting up of this School & the Settlement of three or four Towns of the better Sort of our people round about it; Somewhere near Susquaana River or in Some other Place more convenient for it? If Such a Door was opened with a prospect of extensive usefulness of it among the Indians, I would gladly remove with it."[5]

Despite Wheelock's perseverance, Johnson remained evasive. Forced to compromise, Wheelock reasoned that the door might be opened eventually if he could ease his way into Iroquoia through a temporary introduction of community day schools. This would enable him to salvage part of the boarding school plan: he could send his missionaries and schoolmasters among the Six Nations, and if they succeeded his influence would be assured.

Wheelock was convinced that Indian missionaries or school-masters would have significant advantages over their white counterparts. "The Influence of their own Sons among them," he argued, "will likely be much greater than of any Englishman whatever." As proof, he cited his first pupil, Samson Occom: "This is quite evident in the Case of Mr. *Occom*, whose Influence among the *Indians*, even of his own Tribe, is much greater than any other man's." Acknowledging the difficulty of the language barrier, Wheelock noted that an Indian who speaks their language "would be at least four times as serviceable among them." He also made allowance for frontier living conditions: "abundant Experience has taught us that such a change of Diet, and manner of Living as missionaries generally come into, will not consist with the Health of many *Englishmen*." As a practical aside, then, he suggested that "an *Indian* Missionary may be supported with less than half the Expence, that will be necessary to support an *Englishman*, who can't conform to their Manner of Living."[6]

These arguments may have persuaded Wheelock's English donors, but during the life span of the Iroquois experiment in community schooling, they proved to be fallacious. While the difficulties that Wheelock foresaw for his English missionaries were indeed a detriment, he failed to anticipate the possibility that they would also plague his Indian schoolmasters.

After sending several ill-timed and short-lived missionary ventures during the hostilities of the early 1760s, Wheelock finally succeeded by the middle of the decade in launching the modified plan for community schooling. In the fall of 1764 and during the following spring and summer, he sent a total of three white missionaries and eight Indian schoolmasters to Iroquoia; but the reaction of William Johnson to the boarding school concept continued to disappoint Wheelock. Of the Indian schoolmasters who arrived in the summer of 1765, Johnson wrote: "I am pleased with the Proficiency the Boys have made, and they are now distributed amongst the Indian towns as School-Masters." But in his response to tentative location suggestions for the boarding school, Johnson spelled out his opposition to a site within Iroquoia, recommending that Wheelock select "any place to the Eastward of *Hudson's River*."[7]

Thus, as early as 1765 it was clear that the modified school plan would never have the opportunity to expand into a boarding school with adjacent towns. The next year, Johnson was elected to membership in the SPG, and from that point on his interest in the establishment of SPG Indian schools took precedence over his willingness to aid in providing Dissenter education for Indians.[8] By 1769, Wheelock recognized the futility of pursuing any further plans for Iroquois schooling and transferred his attention to New Hampshire.[9] The community school experiment survived for eight years, with its existence contingent on the goodwill of Johnson and the tribes involved. In the eight-year period between 1764 and 1772, Moor's School was represented in Iroquoia by a total of twenty-two students, who were located among five of the six tribes (excluding only the Cayuga). Eight of these graduates were white missionaries, while the remaining fourteen were Indians (thirteen males and one female) who were almost equally divided between the Algonquian and Iroquois. While the majority of the Algonquian had attended Moor's School for a period ranging from four to eight years, none of the Iroquois had been enrolled longer than three and a half years. Even though the Algonquian had received more formal schooling, when the schoolmasters arrived in the Great Lakes country, the Iroquois enjoyed a distinct advantage. They were returning to their homeland, to their own people, and to their native language. In the ensuing years, as the community school experiment faltered, the commonality that the Iroquois schoolmasters shared with their people acquired further importance. Eventually, this distinction between Iroquois and Algonquian marked the cutting edge between success and failure, and the Algonquian returned to their own people.

In 1772, at the end of the eight-year period, only one of the white missionaries, Samuel Kirkland, decided to stay, and he and Wheelock had already suffered a bitter parting of the ways.[10] Not surprisingly, the Iroquois schoolmasters had chosen to remain, and while Mundius, an Oneida, was reportedly the only one of them still teaching among his people, several of his compatriots continued to serve as interpreters.[11] The last Algonquian schoolmaster fled the Six Nations in the summer of 1768.

Because the vast wilderness empire of the Iroquois would serve as the proving ground for Wheelock's educational experiment, he could well have benefited from some acquaintance with these people. But the frenetic pace of his life during this period—as director and fund-raiser for the school, minister in Lebanon,

farmer and landowner, and husband and father of a large family—
prevented him from making even a perfunctory visit to the Mohawk, the keepers of the eastern fire and the most assimilated of
the tribes. Wheelock's acquaintance with the Six Nations, was
limited to the two-dozen Iroquois pupils enrolled in Moor's
School, half of whom remained less than a year, and his correspondence with Johnson, who became superintendent of Indian
affairs for the Northern District of North America in 1756.[12] Sir
William's "[u]nderstanding and Influence in Indian Affairs, is, I
suppose, greater than any other Man's," Wheelock had once observed.[13] The minister profited from his relationship with Johnson, but the Wheelock–Johnson correspondence was no substitute for firsthand experience with the Iroquois in their own
environment. Thus, from the limited perspective of his Connecticut Indian charity school, Wheelock assumed that a common
bond of Indianness would enable his Algonquian schoolmasters
to live compatibly in the Iroquois communities.

But the Iroquois of the mid-eighteenth century bore little resemblance to the New England Algonquian. When the Algonquian schoolmasters encountered the Six Nations, they described
them with the same phrases employed by the English missionaries: one schoolmaster called them "savages," while another
dubbed them "perishing pagans."[14] In the eyes of these young
Algonquian, the Iroquois were a foreign people.

The responsibility for such a peculiar dichotomy lay less with
the schoolmasters than with Wheelock himself. As organizer,
fund-raiser, and administrator, Wheelock demonstrated a great
deal of political acumen. He obtained thousands of English
pounds from various sources in England and Scotland without
ever crossing the ocean. But his woeful inexperience in dealing
with the Six Nations left him and his students unprepared for
their educational experiment among the Six Nations.

Wheelock was the most vocal representative of the noncon-
formist ministers who sought to convert the Iroquois during this
period. These Presbyterians and Congregationalists were late-
comers to the Six Nations, arriving in the middle of the eighteenth
century; by that time the Iroquois had been dealing with Europeans and their colonial counterparts for over two hundred years.
However, if the nonconformists were among the last of the Christian missionaries to reach the Iroquois, the missionaries of the

Church of England could hardly claim to be the first. The Venerable Society sent eight missionaries to serve the Mohawk between 1700 and the American Revolution. When the first of these men, the Rev. William Andrews, reached the Mohawk Valley in 1704, he had been preempted by the indomitable Jesuits, who had been in the area since the middle 1600s. But Jesuit strength, reaching south from French Canada, was most pronounced among the most western tribes. Thus, in the early 1700s, the Anglicans had already made significant inroads among the Mohawk, and by the time William Johnson had settled in the Mohawk Valley the Mohawk were "nominally Christian."[15]

In 1756, when Wheelock initiated his correspondence with Johnson, the transplanted Irishman had been settled among the Mohawk for almost three decades, and his expertise was invaluable for Wheelock's schoolmasters and missionaries.[16] Nonetheless, Johnson remained an Anglican and a Loyalist. Thus, his favorable attitude toward Wheelock's experiment was threatened from the beginning, and it was only the delayed timing of his upsurge of interest in SPG schooling for the Indians that postponed his rupture with Wheelock. Had his concern with Anglican schooling been awakened earlier, it is likely that Wheelock's students would have found it difficult to establish a foothold among the Iroquois. During his brief years of support, however, Johnson provided these young men with physical respite, sage advice, and a diplomatic entrée to the various communities where they would serve.

In November 1764, Johnson welcomed the first contingent from Moor's School to his palatial mansion in the Mohawk Valley. Johnson Hall reflected the expansive congeniality of its host.[17] Moreover, it was a haven in the wilderness for southern New Englanders unaccustomed to the harsh winters of the Iroquois country. The earliest of Wheelock's students to arrive were Joseph Wooley and Samuel Kirkland. Wooley, the first Algonquian schoolmaster to teach the Iroquois, was a Delaware from New Jersey who had studied at Moor's School for seven years. Probably about eighteen years old, he had been away from home since the age of eleven. His companion, Samuel Kirkland, formerly a white charity student at the school, had studied for missionary service at the College of New Jersey. With Johnson's assistance, Wooley and Kirkland made the difficult journeys to their respective communities, with Wooley going south to the Oneida and Tuscarora, near Onohoghgwage; and Kirkland traveling to the Seneca, the westernmost and probably least assimilated of the Six Nations.

By the following spring, reinforcements had arrived. In March 1765, the Connecticut Board of Correspondents for the Society in Scotland for Propagating Christian Knowledge (SSPCK), one of Wheelock's key funding sources, met to consider the qualifications of a number of missionaries and schoolmasters.[18] The meeting was interrupted by the arrival of "Good" Peter (Gwedelhes Agwerondongwes), an Oneida sent by his people on the three-hundred-mile trek to ask for a minister.[19] "And so remarkable was the Providence of God," Wheelock said, in describing the events, "that an Interpreter came in at the same Instant, who had lived with these *Indians* for ten Years, by whose Assistance we were able to understand them and they us."[20] The board, undoubtedly impressed by such a fortuitous coincidence, approved for service two white missionaries—Titus Smith, who was sent to the Oneida at Onohoghgwage, and Theophilus Chamberlain—and nine Indian schoolmasters and assistants (called "ushers"). The schoolmasters included Joseph Wooley, approved in his absence; David Fowler, a Montauk; and Hezekiah Calvin, a Delaware. The assistants were Jacob Fowler, David's brother, and five Mohawk—Moses, Johannes, Abraham Primus, Abraham Secundus, and Peter.[21] Wheelock defended the premature return of the Mohawk youth, explaining that their parents were eager to see them and that they were "well qualified for School Masters" and might "preserve and perfect themselves in their own tongue" during their stay. But when he informed George Whitefield that they were "to return to this School in the Fall," he probably knew that such an event was unlikely.[22]

David Fowler was the most promising Algonquian schoolmaster. Described by Wheelock as "serious, active, a good Scholar, and well acquainted with Farming," Fowler and his brother Jacob exemplified the importance of familial ties at Moor's School.[23] The link that had attracted David and Jacob Fowler to Wheelock's school was their sister Mary, who had married Samson Occom. Occom, in turn, had been the Fowlers' schoolmaster in the Long Island community of Montauk. Since Samson Occom was only about twelve years older than David Fowler, he was probably like an older brother, for when Occom arrived in Montauk, Fowler was about fourteen years old, an impressionable age. Another decade elapsed before Moor's School was fully launched and Fowler enrolled, at the age of twenty-four.

The strength of the relationship between these brothers-in-law encouraged Wheelock to send Fowler with Occom on the first recruiting trip to the Six Nations. When the Boston Board of the SSPCK promised Wheelock a gift of twenty pounds to support several Iroquois students—"A Number of Indian Boys, not exceeding three, to be put under Mr. Wheelock's Care and Instruction"—Wheelock wasted little time in procuring the students. On the ensuing trip to the Oneida and Mohawk, Fowler and Occom recruited three Mohawk youth, one of whom would become the school's most prominent Iroquois student, Joseph Brant. The brother-in-law of William Johnson, Brant was already familiar with the culturally mixed milieu of the superintendent's baronial establishment along the Mohawk River. His experiences at Moor's School, however, broadened his knowledge of English colonial culture and contributed to the stance he later assumed as a cultural broker.[24] For Occom and Fowler, this initial tour was only the first of many experiences in Iroquois country. Both of them returned to the Six Nations in the summer of 1762: Occom traveled as a missionary, and Fowler recruited three more Mohawk students.

Three years later, on April 29, 1765, David Fowler again headed west on the three-hundred-mile journey from Lebanon to the Mohawk Valley. This was his third trip to Iroquoia, but this time he planned to stay indefinitely. He brought with him a letter of recommendation to William Johnson, who had helped him procure the Mohawk students. The letter attested to the fact that Fowler was "a youth of good Abilities [who] . . . comes with design if he meets with proper Encouragement to Settle down among the Onoyadas . . . in the Capacity of a School Master."[25] In acknowledgement of Johnson's pivotal role in this experiment, Wheelock also appealed for his guidance: "And as the life and Success of the whole under God very much depends upon your Excellency's Countenance, I have advised him [David] to submit the whole to your Direction and Conduct."[26]

The long-term commitment that Wheelock designed for David Fowler lasted two years.[27] Fowler was thirty years old when he began his stint in 1765, so he was sufficiently mature for the position of schoolmaster. His decision to leave Oneida grew initially from his own background. Like the other Algonquian sent among the Iroquois, Fowler came from a Christianized, well-settled, and relatively stable Indian community; and he was appalled by the deprivation that characterized the Oneida's daily life. In the drought years of the late 1760s, they lived a literally hand-to-mouth existence. Food supplies accumulated from the women's harvest of corn, squash, and beans, along with the game procured by the men in the fall hunt, failed to carry them through the lean months of famine in late spring. During Fowler's first weeks among the Oneida, he wrote, "I live like a Dog here, my Folks are poor & nasty, I eat with Dogs, for, they eat & drink out of the same as I do."

The meager diet of the Iroquois had a direct effect on the schools opened by Fowler and his compatriots. The Algonquian schoolmasters learned quickly that a food supply that failed to include adequate reserves had to be replenished frequently. Early in his first summer of teaching, Fowler discovered a direct relationship between diet and attendance. When the students' families needed to procure food, the students were not in school. "It is ten thousand Pities they cante keep together," he wrote to Wheelock in Late June. "They are often always going about to get their Provisions." But the need was all too real: "My Father one of the Chiefs at whose House I keep told me he beleived some of the Indians would starve to Death this Summer; some of them have almost consum'd all their Corn already."[28]

As a student at Moor's School, Fowler was undoubtedly influenced by the colonial conviction that deemed agriculture as the highest attainment of civilization. Like others concerned with the Indian cause, Wheelock also grasped this theme as central to Indian change, believing that tribes must be "civilized, Christianized, and Husbandry introduced among them."[29] Moreover, he forecast an early demise for those tribes who failed to adopt more intensive agriculture. Of the Iroquois, he wrote: "their idleness and universal aversion to cultivate their lands . . . must unavoidably hasten their destruction."[30]

Most of Wheelock's Indian pupils had shown little enthusiasm for the "Affairs of Husbandry"; the only exceptions were Fowler and Joseph Wooley. "These Lads will likely make good Farmers,"

Wheelock admitted, and of the two he singled out Fowler as more likely "than all the rest."[31]

With Wheelock's blessing as well as some limited farming experience, Fowler needed only a firsthand encounter with scarce provisions to become a firm advocate of the need for more sophisticated farming among the Iroquois. His first weeks among the Oneida sealed his conviction. Echoing his benefactor, he predicted that improved agriculture among the Iroquois would be "the only thing that will kept them together."[32] Eager to teach his students the skills of husbandry learned at Moor's School, Fowler wrote to Wheelock during the first autumn that he would "come down next year after I have planted Corn and my Garden things come, so that I may be able to tell my Chldren how they must manage the Garden in my Absence."[33]

But Fowler's plans for teaching husbandry did not materialize. With other challenges looming, he discovered that he had little time for teaching colonial farming techniques to the Oneida. He was hard-pressed to survive his first winter. Thrown from the stable environment of Moor's School, where all of his economic needs were provided for, into one in which he depended on the already hard-pressed Oneida for food and shelter, he found himself forced to rely more and more on his own ingenuity. The new challenge of survival caused him "much Warry and Fatigue," as well as a "hungry Belly."[34]

Training for economic self-sufficiency had not been included in the curriculum at Moor's School. No one there had anticipated the need to teach these Algonquian students the essentials of survival. Therefore, whatever economic skills they had acquired in their own native communities prior to boarding school had been largely recast by Wheelock's curriculum, which was divided between academic studies and farm chores.[35] Under Wheelock's tutelage, the Indian students were totally dependent on the school for their basic needs, and they acquired a taste for luxury items in the colonial economy, such as tea and coffee; thus, they discovered that their training bore little relation to their calling once they had settled among the Iroquois. They had adopted all of the material trappings of colonial culture, but they had learned none of the skills for dealing with Iroquois culture or for living on the land.

From this perspective, then, the Algonquian schoolmasters

were removed from their Iroquois brethren by a time and cultural span of at least two generations. Their own grandparents and great-grandparents of the seventeenth and early eighteenth century would have shared a commonality with these mid-eighteenth-century Iroquois. They too were self-sufficient and knew survival skills; and despite their encounters with the colonists, they held a native view of the world that reflected centuries of accommodation with their own peculiar environment. Thus, while the grandparents could not have taught Latin, Greek, or Biblical passages to the Algonquian schoolmasters, they might have served as skillful instructors in native culture(s) and economic survival, areas of expertise that were not shared by Wheelock or his tutors at Moor's School.

The schoolmasters' lack of preparation for the Iroquois environment soon became apparent. Inadequate food, poor shelter, and worn clothing detracted from their efforts to teach, and rang as a dull refrain throughout their letters. The long winters saw them separated from the source of supply—their benefactor—by over three hundred miles of difficult trails and poor roads.[36] After eight months of Canowaroghere, Fowler lamented to Wheelock: "Sir I am almost Necked, my Cloathes are coming all to pieces."[37] The following summer, Hezekiah Calvin wrote from Fort Hunter: "Please Sir to send up some Stokins . . . a pair of shoes."[38] Earlier, Joseph Wooley had sent a similar plea from Onohoghgwage, "My shirts are most wore out, by wearing them so long without washing."[39]

The ability of the schoolmasters to remain dedicated to their main task of teaching varied with the severity of their living conditions and their individual levels of maturity. Fowler himself did not admit defeat until the second winter, and even then his difficulties did not wholly dampen his enthusiasm for teaching. When he initiated his classes, he was bursting with optimism; and on the twelfth day after he opened his school, he wrote: "I have put eight of my Scholars into third Page of the Spelling book: some almost got down to the Bottom of the same third:—I never saw Children exceed these in learing."[40]

Teaching at this elementary level may have reminded Fowler of his earlier studies with Occom at Montauk, for the small Iroquois day schools offered only the rudiments of education, with their level of achievement generally comparable to that of the New

England Dame school. The lengthy studies of Latin and Greek that had challenged these young men at Moor's School served little purpose in an Iroquois setting. Where they had once pondered over recitations of Horace or Cicero, their pupils struggled to master spelling books, occasionally progressing to the New Testament.

Despite Wheelock's failure to provide appropriate training for much of this unique assignment, he did equip Fowler with some textbooks. The number of volumes was not insignificant, but like other supplies, the book inventory also proved inadequate within a few months. On his first trip, Fowler was burdened with a considerable load, consisting of twenty spelling books, ten Bibles, two Catechisms, and several other volumes. For his own perusal, he carried a copy of the *School Masters Assistant*, but it was of dubious value for teaching students who spoke only Oneida.[41]

Like the other Algonquian schoolmasters, Fowler was immediately stymied by the difficulty in communicating with students who understood neither English nor his native Montauk. Although Fowler worked hard to increase his knowledge of Oneida, in the first months he was "miserably of[f] for an Interpreter."[42] This may have been why he turned to music, or perhaps he recalled the singing of psalms at Moor's School. Anxious to succeed as schoolmaster, he adopted singing as a communitywide means of instruction that could be enjoyed by everyone, regardless of language barriers. The frequency with which Fowler wrote of his "Singing School" suggests that it may have been one of the highlights of his stay. In declaring that "both Old and Young" in the community "take great Pleasure in learning to sing," Fowler may well have enjoyed this aspect of teaching as much as the Oneida. In his first weeks he boasted to Wheelock, "We can already carry Three Parts of several Tunes."[43] At Canajoharie the next year, Fowler's brother Jacob described a similar accomplishment: "we have got the Indians so that we can sing good many Tunes with all three Parts."[44]

Eager to please his benefactor, Fowler undoubtedly glossed over some of the initial difficulties he encountered in teaching. During the first summer, Joseph Wooley wrote to Wheelock from Johnson Hall of rumored criticism of his Montauk compatriot: "I have heard of Fowler . . . he begins to beat his Schollers . . . makes their Hands to swell very much which the Indians dont like very well." The Oneida, Wooley reported, counseled patience: "They say, he ought to have suppressed it longer, & not begin so soon."[45] Fowler may have gained greater rapport with his students, or perhaps others failed to report his punishment practices, for there is no further evidence that he continued to beat his "Schollers." His injudicious use of discipline, however, tends to reinforce the assessment of his temperament made by David Avery, one of the white missionaries, who said of Fowler: "His natural Temper is well known to be violent and sometimes his Passion blinds his reason."[46]

By the spring of 1766, Fowler had managed to weather the first year's challenges. He had survived; he had learned some Oneida; his students were progressing; and in midwinter he was still able to write, "I am pursuing my Business with all Courage and Resolution that lies in my Power of Capacity."[47] But Fowler, at age thirty-one, had determined not to pass another winter among the Oneida without a wife. Just prior to his departure in the spring of 1765, Fowler had planned to marry Amy Johnson, a Mohegan, but her poor health forced him to change his plans.[48] After less than a month in Iroquois country, he wrote a letter to his benefactor that supported Wheelock's argument for training his female students "to render them fit" to accompany the young Indian men as "housewives, School-mistresses, Tayloresses, &c."[49] In acknowledging the importance of the "other Rib," Fowler complained: "without the other Boon, I am oblidg'd to wash, mend my Clothes, cook all my Victuals and wash all the things I use, which is exceeding hard."[50] By the following September, Fowler had traveled to Lebanon, wooed and won a bride, and returned with her to Oneida country.[51] The winter was to prove trying for Fowler and his new wife, Hannah Garrett, the young and able Pequot student from Moor's School. Fowler had no quarrel with the advantages of marriage, including his newly acquired freedom from the chores of "housework," but he was increasingly dissatisfied with the relationship between himself and another member of the household, the Rev. Samuel Kirkland.

After eighteen turbulent months with the Seneca, Kirkland had left in May 1766, returning to Lebanon for two months' rest. There, he was ordained and commissioned by the Connecticut Board of Correspondents as a missionary to the Indians. No longer committed to the remote Seneca, he turned to the more

accessible Oneida, beginning his missionary endeavors among
them just a few weeks before the Fowlers arrived. The 12' x 12'
log cabin built by Kirkland at Canowaroghere was soon filled to
capacity. In addition to the Fowlers, Joseph Johnson (a Mohegan),
Amy's fifteen-year-old brother, was also to spend the winter. "It is
thought fit by Mr. Kirkland," Johnson wrote to Wheelock from
Oneida, "that I should tarry here this winter to git knowledge of
Davids Art in teaching the Natives and to know how to keep
School in every Article."[52]

Several years earlier, Wheelock had theorized that an idyllic
relationship would develop between the Indian and English graduates sent to the frontier. "INDIAN Missionaries," he wrote, "will
not disdain to own English ones who shall be Associates with
them . . . as elder Brethren; nor [shall these Indians] scorn to be
advised or reproved, counselled or conducted by them."[53]

Wheelock's theory received its first blow at Oneida. Had Kirkland's log cabin been twice as spacious, it would not have been
large enough to accommodate the tension that developed between the white missionary and the Algonquian schoolmaster.
Fowler's fragile ego had been boosted considerably by his appointment as schoolmaster that previous year. "O that my Heart
would melt with Gratitude both to God and Man," he wrote to
Wheelock, "for he has distinguished me from many of my poor
Brethren, in setting me up to be their Instructor."[54] As a figure of
authority among his Oneida students, Fowler sought to maintain
this position at home, but here he was forced to deal with Kirkland. At the age of thirty-one, Fowler was not only six years older
than the missionary; he was also the oldest of the four residents. It
is likely, then, that he saw himself as the rightful head of the
household. But Kirkland did not share this view, nor did Wheelock.[55]

Fowler's tenuous confidence was no match for Kirkland's self-
esteem. Despite his youth, the missionary was both imperious
and self-righteous. Having suffered extensive privation during
his traumatic stay with the Seneca, he had little patience with
these Algonquian schoolmasters, who complained for lack of
food, clothing, and even luxuries. A year earlier, he had chided
Joseph Wooley at Onohoghgwage: "You write me for Bokes tea
coffee and powder. I should advise you to make use of those teas
which nature had provided us in the wilderness such as pine

buds, sassafras blows & the bark of the root *spice wood.*" He had even advised Wooley to consider adopting Indian clothing. "Pray what would you think of getting a *leather shirt* and Indian breeches while you reside among them," he asked. "It will be no disgrace to your characters and colour."[56]

The irony of Kirkland's attitude was not lost on these Algonquian. While the youthful Joseph Johnson may not have questioned the missionary's authority that winter, Fowler complained bitterly to Wheelock. "[H]e can't order me," Fowler fumed, "nor no missionary that shall come into these parts. As I am an instructor I am able to act for myself, without having a master over me, &c."[57]

Late in the winter of 1766–67, Fowler became so distressed with Kirkland's arrogance that he reached the decision to depart which he was later to regret.[58] It is important to note, however, that the crisis that forced Fowler's hand was not precipitated by his teaching. Had teaching been the issue, he probably would have remained among the Oneida, for even in his most despairing moments he continued to express pleasure with his students. Thus, in a single letter to Wheelock he lambasted his benefactor for forgetting him—the "one who has done most"—and praised his scholars. "Some of them," he boasted, "have got to the twenty fourth chapter of Matthew."[59]

Fowler's decision was based on the growing pressures of internal dissension and heavy household responsibilities. The burden of supporting the four-member household weighed heavily. "[I]t is too hard for me to carry farming for two Families in a New Country," he wrote to Wheelock.[60] Moreover, Hannah was pregnant. In despair, he recalled the Montauk position offered to him when he left for Oneida.[61] Occom had left this position and was in the British Isles on a fund-raising tour for Wheelock's proposed Indian school in New Hampshire. His brother Jacob, who had been at Canajoharie all winter, was too young for the job. In addition, his "aged" parents needed care.[62] By May, Fowler determined to leave Oneida and take his family to Montauk. A month later, young David Fowler was born, and by September the Fowlers had returned to the people they knew.

Fowler's departure from Oneida country left sixteen-year-old Joseph Johnson in charge of the school at Old Oneida. That fall, Johnson was joined by Nathan Clap, who was either Mashpee or

Nausett, from Cape Cod. Johnson and Clap were the last Algonquian teachers to remain among the Iroquois before the American Revolution. Joseph Wooley, who had arrived in 1764, had died of consumption a year later, at the age of perhaps nineteen years.[63] Jacob Fowler had left the Mohawk at Canajoharie, returning to teach among the Pequot in southern Connecticut. Samuel Ashpo, a Mohegan, had completed two brief stints of teaching at Chenango, and did not return. The only other Algonquian who had remained among the Iroquois for the better part of two years was Hezekiah Calvin.

Hezekiah Calvin's teaching career among the Mohawk at Fort Hunter had paralleled David Fowler's among the Oneida. But Calvin's youth and inexperience had made his adjustment more difficult than Fowler's. While Fowler had the advantage of being in his early thirties, Calvin, at sixteen or seventeen years, was roughly Joseph Johnson's age. Moreover, he did not share Johnson's advantage of training for a year with an older schoolmaster such as Fowler. Despite some missionary supervision, Calvin faced his first Mohawk students on his own; and after spending a winter with his people, whose wandering habits and frequent bouts with alcohol made for an uncertain existence, he was all too ready to return to Lebanon shortly before spring.

Thus, it is surprising that Calvin agreed to return to the Mohawk for a second winter. Despite his traumatic experiences during the previous year, when his life was threatened during the Mohawks' "Drunken frolics," Calvin responded obediently, albeit somewhat uneasily, to Wheelock's authority.[64] But Calvin's heart was clearly torn between the Mohawk and his own people, the Delaware. Before he returned to Fort Hunter, he wrote: "I think I shall never try to see that Country no more if I could but only See my Parents this time. . . , But I Leave the Matter with Mr. Wheelock."[65] Although these young Algonquian frequently expressed their distress to Wheelock, he turned a deaf ear to their entreaties.

Calvin's second winter at Fort Hunter was his last.[66] Like his compatriots, he found that he had less in common with the Iroquois than with his friends at Moor's School. At school, all the students spoke the same language, English; they came from similar backgrounds; and they were engaged in a common enterprise. Among the Iroquois, however, their commonality vanished. Calvin spoke for most of his fellow schoolmasters when he reflected that among the Mohawk he had felt "as a dumb stump that has no tongue to use."[67] Unlike Fowler, however, Calvin made little effort to learn the new language. According to the Mohawk, "Calvin would come into their Houses and go out with out saying how do you do."[68] For Calvin, the flaw of the Iroquois was that they had not been assimilated. Thus, he concluded, "I should be very glad to see my Brethren [the Mohawk] become christians and live like Christians."[69] For the Mohawk, on the other hand, the flaw in an Algonquian schoolmaster like Calvin was that he had become too assimilated. He took "but little Note of them at any time and Shewd great business said he wanted to go Home," one of the missionaries observed. When the Mohawk learned that Calvin was gone, the missionary added, "they did not seem to lament his departure."[70]

At Oneida, Joseph Johnson and his friend Clap held out for one more year. Johnson's students progressed in the usual erratic fashion, attending school for a few weeks, disappearing for the fall hunt, and returning only to leave again when provisions were low. Nonetheless, like Fowler, Johnson remained enthusiastic about teaching throughout the winter. In February, he reported that his fourteen "Scholars" "all learned very fast both Singing and reading." Taking a cue from Fowler's success, Johnson also gathered the Oneida for a "Singing School every Evening" and reported "very full meetings."[71]

The problem of provisions remained as serious as it had been the previous winter. Living "Intirely upon the affare of the Indians," Johnson reported that he was "Sometimes glutted to the full at other times half Stearved." The diet was "never Steady"; in moments of plenty, the Oneida added eel, fish, or deer meat to meals, but much of the time their food contained little protein. Thus, it was a happy occasion when the young schoolmaster wrote: "they now begin to cook Some good dried guts of Dear . . . to Season the corn; Likewise some rotten fish which they have kept Since last fall to Season their Samps, rottener the better they Say as it will Season more broth."[72]

In late March or early April, when the fifteen-year-old Johnson had been teaching for about six months, he made a trip to Lebanon, where he may have celebrated his sixteenth birthday. When he reopened the school shortly after his return, he found only five "Scholars" in attendance, and he wrote to Wheelock, it "is hardly worth staying for." In addition to his own depression, Johnson also sensed a discontent among the Indians, which was partly due to the recent visit of Ralph Wheelock, Eleazar's oldest son. Ralph Wheelock's undiplomatic visit with the nearby Onondaga served as one of the early episodes (climaxed in the disastrous Fort Stanwix treaty negotiations in the fall) leading to a break between the Iroquois and his father.[73] At these meetings, the Onondaga attacked Wheelock's treatment of Iroquois children; " 'brother, do you think we are altogether ignorant of your methods of instruction?' " they asked. " 'Why, brother, you are deceiving yourself! We understand not only your speech, but your *manner* of teaching Indians. . . . You have spoke *exceeding* well, even to our surprise, . . . that our children should become *wise in all things*, by your instructions, & treated as *children* at your house, & not *servants.*' "[74]

But education was not all that was on the minds of the Onondaga. "They hear," Joseph Johnson wrote to Wheelock, "that they must not get drunk if they embrace the Gosple which your son offered to them; which goes against their deep rooted Appetites."[75] Johnson's criticism of the Onondaga's fondness for alcohol was probably an admission of his own weakness, for after his return from Lebanon he and Clap had also sought temporary relief in alcohol. Thus, early in his seventeenth year, Johnson's youth and immaturity finally caught up with him and led to a spree of wild behavior that Kirkland would condemn as "diabolical Conduct."[76] Well aware of their sins, Johnson wrote to Wheelock in May that due to "the state of things at present" Clap was being sent back to Lebanon, where Wheelock might deal with "his defect and Uncapableness of carring on the business which he is intrusted with." Johnson's own feelings of attrition were summarized in his contrite pleas to Wheelock: "I Seem to be intirely content to be disposed of as seems best in your sight."[77]

Sometime during the summer, after recovering from wounds suffered in "Combat" with several drunken Oneida, Johnson returned to Connecticut.[78] Although Kirkland severely chastised Johnson, claiming that the young schoolmaster had been "actually in ye Devils service," Wheelock greeted Johnson's lapse with remorse rather than scorn. "Oh! my dear Sir," Wheelock wrote to Kirkland in the fall, "how shooking it is that one after another turns out so. It looks as though the whole of them excepting a small remnant were nigh unto cursing."[79]

Wheelock's lament for Johnson was premature, for the young Mohegan had yet to make his mark. While Clap disappeared into obscurity, Johnson required only three or four years to recover his balance. After a few months of "always roaving about," unable to approach Wheelock because of his shame for his "own wickedness," he finally went to sea for about a year and a half, returning to Mohegan early in 1771.[80] Here, at the age of twenty-one, with his wanderings behind him, he began to fulfill the calling that Wheelock had once expected of his Indian students.

Less than a year after Johnson and Clap had left Oneida, Wheelock wrote to George Whitefield of the demise of his schoolmaster experiment: "I am fully convinced yt God dos not design, yt Indians shall have ye lead in ye affair."[81] But the Algonquian summarily dismissed by Wheelock had drawn their own conclusions about the experiment. By living among the Iroquois, the schoolmasters had learned that they could not influence these people directly because the disparity between their cultures was too great. Their sojourn also taught them a deeper appreciation for their own cultures. When they returned to New England, they chose to live not among the colonists, but among their own people, and they brought to these communities the sifted experiences of Moor's School and Iroquoia.[82]

Joseph Johnson epitomized the unique blend of individual influenced by these mixed environments. The member of a prominent Mohegan family and son of an Indian warrior who had died fighting for the British in the French and Indian War, Johnson entered Wheelock's school in his seventh year.[83] Thus, while he spent his early childhood among the Mohegan, even as a youngster he knew of his father's commitment to the British military cause. During the most impressionable years he lived at Moor's School, immersed in the milieu of New Light Calvinism and grammar school curriculum, and amid a group of Algonquian students from communities across southern New England. Thus, he was already learning to look beyond the narrow boundaries of his own village and his Mohegan people.

At the age of fifteen, he was shifted to the Iroquois, where he was urged to transmit his newly acquired education to the children of a people who evidently cared little about white schools. Johnson's confusion at the age of seventeen reflected the strange amalgam of cultures thrust upon him; and his recovery was remarkable. By the early 1770s, he knew who he was and where he wanted to live. At Oneida, he had signed a letter to Wheelock: "So I remain your Ignorant Pupil & good for nothing Black Indian."[84] By this time Wheelock had stripped him of his self-esteem as well as his pride in his Indianness; but when he began teaching the Tunxis as Farmington, Connecticut, he had retrieved both.[85] In 1772, he wrote, "I am, kind friend, an Indian of the Mohegan tribe . . . I keep a School at Farmington amongst my Indian brethren. An it is to be hoped that I maintain a Good Character both among the English; and also among my brethren."[86]

Johnson's newly sharpened focus on the world gave him a clear vision of his people's needs. It was time, he reasoned, for his brethren to "leave the English," who had made his brethren "very poor" and "striped" their forefathers of their land. It was the English who had "as it were cut off their right hands," and now his brethren must move their homelands and "Seek a place . . . to settle down together in peace."[87] Johnson's concept of a new homeland for the New England Algonquian did not originate with him, however. Although he was to play a pivotal role in the emigration, he did not become embroiled in the cause until several years after the introduction of the idea, which probably came from Wheelock originally. In 1769, when Johnson was in the midst of his wanderings, Wheelock wrote to Occom and the Fowler brothers, urging them to consider the idea. Wheelock's proposal, which envisioned "the Settlement of a Town of our Christian Indians," bore an uncanny resemblance to his 1763 proposal for the establishment of a boarding school and towns among the Six Nations.[88] By 1769, however, Wheelock's schooling prospects in Iroquoia were bleak. Sir William Johnson's growing involvement with Indian schooling proposals by the SPG, the Stanwix fiasco, and the abrupt request by the Oneida that their youth be withdrawn from Moor's School all contributed to wielding the death blow to Wheelock's Iroquois experiment.[89] Wheelock's acknowledgement of this failure had already committed him to the founding of a college in New Hampshire. Nonetheless, a community of Christian Algonquian, all of whom were indebted in one way or another to him and to his school, would provide means by which he might maintain a modicum of influence among the Iroquois. Thus, he asked the most stalwart of his former pupils—Occom and the Fowler brothers—if they might not "open a door" for the proposed community.

None of them accepted the challenge. David Fowler still carried a grudge against his former master. Convinced that Wheelock owed him a sum of money for his labors, he probably felt even less charitable toward Wheelock after he lost his teaching job at Montauk in 1770.[90] Heavily in debt, Fowler had to resort to farming and fishing to support his growing family;[91] and probably for mixed reasons, he chose not to respond favorably to Wheelock's request.[92] Nor was there any known response from Jacob, his younger brother, who had secured the schoolmaster position at Groton, Connecticut, where he was teaching the local Pequot children.

Occom, the most logical choice, was at the low point of his career. Shortly after his return from Britain in 1768, he was beset with problems that would plague him for some time. The decades-old Mohegan land case (brought against Connecticut), which had occupied part of his attention in England, split the Mohegan tribe into bitter factions, with Occom and the supporters of the Mohegan claim lined up against the descendants of former sachem Ben Uncas and supporters of Connecticut (and the Mason family heirs).[93] Poverty, coupled with ill-health, virtually prohibited Occom from making any plans. The little money he had received from the English tour disappeared quickly, and the failure of the Boston commissioners to reimburse him for his frequent preaching to the Mohegan and other Algonquian meant that he had no means other than farming to support his family.[94] He also suffered from a brief bout with alcohol, which led him to send a formal apology to the Connecticut Board of Correspondents.[95]

Finally, this period witnessed a rupture in the once warm relationship between Occom and his former mentor. Occom had embarked on the English tour in good faith, convinced that he was raising funds for the cause of Indian education. What he heard about Dartmouth on his return—"that the Indian was converted into an English school & that the English had crowded out the Indian youths"—depressed his spirits.[96] At about the same time, he was distressed to learn of the cleavage between Wheelock and the Iroquois, a division partially created by the disastrous diplomatic failures of Ralph Wheelock.[97] The cumulative effect of these events led Occom to rebuff Wheelock's offer. How could he, a poor and lame Indian, undertake such a venture when he had borne the burdens of so many other troubles, including his mentor's betrayal of the Indian cause?[98]

For the next four years, from 1769 through 1772, Wheelock's entreaties drew only negative responses. Wheelock could no longer command performances as the puppeteer who guided the movements of his Indian pupils. Most of his former pupils had either broken with their mentor, or they had settled for an uneasy truce. The Brothertown movement was therefore suspended until Joseph Johnson returned from his long sea voyage to the West Indies.

When Johnson arrived in Mohegan in 1771, two decades had passed since the death of Samuel Whitman, the Farmington minister who had trained John Mettawan. During the ministry of Whitman's successor, the Rev. Timothy Pitkin, Indian youth continued to attend the English school, but the missionary interest in the Indians had declined. Yet Whitman had laid a foundation, and the seeds would soon bear fruit. Johnson's Uncle Zachary put his nephew to work tending his farm lands; and Amy, who had attended Wheelock's school with her brother, also returned. Thus, after many years of separation, Joseph Johnson was ensconced once more in the close-knit ambience of family and tribe. During the first year of his return—1771–72—Johnson's relatives and friends at Mohegan were led by Occom in a local Indian revival; and caught up in the midst of the enthusiasm, Johnson was converted. At this point, the local family and cultural influences mixed with the outside influences of Moor's School, the Oneida experience, and Christianity, combined to strike a responsive chord in his being and to turn him and, consequently, his people in a new direction.

Johnson's eagerness led the Brothertown movement to pick up momentum. From late 1772 until the first years of the revolution, Johnson plunged ahead with plans, making up for the years he had lost. As Wheelock noted, he was "Abundant and unwearied in his Labours."[99] In March 1773, the seven communities of southern New England Algonquian held their first meeting to discuss emigration and the purchase of a tract of land, possibly from the Iroquois.[100] The representatives who gathered at the central town of Mohegan came from six additional communities: Montauk, Charlestown (Narragansett), Stonington (Pequot), Groton (Pequot), Farmington (Tunxis), and Niantic. (See Map 6, pg. 172) Negotiations between delegates from this body—primarily Joseph Johnson, Elijah Wampy (of Farmington), Occom, and the Fowler brothers—and the Oneida and Sir William Johnson were held in a series of gatherings over the next year and a half.[101] While somehow managing to squeeze in his marriage to Samson Occom's daughter Tabitha (in 1773), his often-interrupted teaching duties at Farmington, his licensing as a preacher of the gospel to the Indians (held at Dartmouth in August 1774), and sidetrips to secure desperately needed funding, Johnson joined David Fowler and Occom at Oneida in the fall of 1774. There, they secured the tract of land promised by the Oneida.[102] Less than six months later, in March 1775, the first group of emigrants, led by Johnson, David Fowler, and Elijah Wampy, left for their Oneida lands.

Feeling some responsibility for the initiation of this venture, Wheelock saw the emigration as one of the first genuinely hopeful results of his decades of commitment to Indian education. They will "settle in a Body," he wrote of the Brothertown Indians, "as a Civilized and Christian People," and they will "support all Divine Ordinances and Schools among them, and invite their Savage Brethren to an imitation of them."[103] Thus, Wheelock's hope for influencing the Iroquois revived briefly with the Brothertown emigration.

Aside from obvious financial difficulties and the inherent problems of organizing a widespread group of people, the greatest barrier faced by the Brothertown emigrants was the timing of their venture. Less than a month after the first settlers departed, the shots fired at Lexington and Concord marked the beginning of drastic changes in the lives of American colonialists and the Algonquian emigrants. Unrest and dissension within the Six Nations soon forced these first settlers to join their brethren at Stockbridge, where they remained for the duration of the war.

Joseph Johnson, however, remained on the move. Eager to acquire funding and other support from the provincial assemblies and to assist the colonies as well, he traveled to New York and to New Hampshire, and finally, in the spring of 1776, he met with General George Washington. General Washington secured Johnson's services as the bearer of a conciliatory message from the American colonies to the Six Nations, urging the Iroquois not to "take up the hatchet except they chuse it."[104] Johnson left New England with the message that summer, but at some point during the trip he disappeared. There are no known records of the circumstances or time of his death.

But the heritage of his commitment and leadership emerged in the second emigration movement, which began directly after the war. By 1785, even Samson Occom, at sixty-one years of age, had determined to pull up roots and share the fate of the Brothertown Indians. On the evening of November 7, 1785, Occom recorded in his journal:

> now we proceeded to form into a Body Politick. We Named our Town by the Name of Brotherton, in Indian Eeyamquittoowsuconnuck . . . [We] Concluded to have a Centre near David Fowlers House . . . [We] Concluded to live in Peace, and in Friendship . . . They desired me to be a teacher amongst them, I Consented to Spend Some of my remaining [days] with them, and make this Town my Home and Center—[105]

The Iroquois experience had taught the leaders of Brothertown the need for their own community. But if Wheelock's experiment was indirectly responsible for the founding of Brothertown, it was simultaneously a failure in terms of its own goals. It did not provide an entree for the boarding school and surrounding towns; it did not offer substantial employment for his Indian students; and it did not enable Wheelock to establish himself as an influential figure in Iroquois education.

In his lengthy war on behalf of Indian education, Wheelock's defeat in the battle for Iroquoia was the result of a complex set of causes. In this instance, Wheelock was largely his own enemy: the defeat was due, at least in part, to his own miscalculations. His unwillingness to acquire firsthand knowledge about the Six Nations contributed to his inability to assess the degree of assimilation of his Algonquian schoolmasters in relation to their Iroquois students. The training he provided equipped his pupils to teach among their own people, but it had little bearing on their survival as schoolmasters among the Six Nations. There, they faced almost certain defeat in their struggle with foreign languages, with different customs, with economic uncertainty and starvation, and with their own fragile and uncertain concept of themselves as human beings.

In the ten-year-old fight for Iroquoia, Wheelock's errors were compounded by the challenges that faced him there. In 1772, when the Iroquois cut the final cord, severing their relations with Wheelock, they chose this course for several reasons. They had retained their vivid memory of the hostile encounters with Ralph Wheelock. Their respect for Sir William led them to honor his pressure against nonconformists, particularly when they were personified by Wheelock. Furthermore, they continued to harbor their own suspicions about Wheelock's schooling. "Father, possess your mind in peace," the Oneida counseled David Avery, representing Wheelock in February 1772. "We do not consent to your proposal of our childn returning to you—we rather choose to make forther trial of them under our own Eye that we may observe their conduct."[106]

In the long run, Wheelock himself might have forecast the failure of the Iroquois experiment, for in his view any community school plan held little potential for success. Thus, the results among the Six Nations bore witness to his own apprehensions about community schooling. In 1772, however, Wheelock chose to attribute the failure to the Iroquois themselves. "They have long been and still are pining away in their wickedness," he concluded, "and there is much reason to fear, 'they are nigh unto cursing.' "[107]

The "door" Wheelock tried to open among the Six Nations failed to materialize, and later, at Dartmouth, he turned his attention to other tribes, primarily Canadian (some of whom were emigrants from the Iroquois). Only in the founding of Brothertown was he able to find some solace for the disturbing demise of the Iroquois experiment. Despite the failure, the community schools among the Iroquois led almost inadvertently to the formation of the Brothertown community, thus helping to provide both an identity and a raison d'être for a small remnant of New England Algonquian who began life there anew after the American Revolution.

11

CONCLUSION

Views on Indian schooling in colonial America have changed in the last few decades. Until recently, those addressing the subject have gauged their evaluations through an ethnocentric framework, thus limiting their criteria for assessment to mainstream concepts of success and failure. By these standards, success has been equated with the endurance of schools, quantity of Indian students, and the degree of assimilation in these students. Reliance on such criteria revealed that Indian schooling in colonial America was, with few exceptions, a failure. Either schools did not materialize at all, as was the case with the College at Henrico and the East India School, or they achieved little permanence, such as the school at Irene. Even the few so-called accomplishments are subject to question. John Eliot's achievements could be considered as tarnished, since the praying villages were virtually destroyed by King Philip's War. And even Wheelock's credibility becomes dubious.

Wheelock was stymied in his long-held dream to establish a school in Iroquoia. When he proposed a college to be devoted primarily to Indian students, he was able to persuade Samson Occom to raise funds in England. Soon afterward, however, Occom and other disillusioned critics withdrew their support, having concluded that Dartmouth would never fulfill their expectations as a place for Indians to receive a college education. At the College of William and Mary, a modest Indian enrollment was maintained throughout much of the eighteenth century, but its Indian students shared only a tangential connection to the college course, with their instruction confined to a very elementary level.

Assessments of Indian schooling from a contemporary perspective were made from a variety of angles. While Indian students, parents, and tribes might reflect a wide number of views, these were further complicated by colonial missionaries, schoolmasters, and their financial supporters, who added to the confusion by contributing additional opinions on Indian schooling.

Colonial schoolmasters and missionaries viewed their efforts to educate the Indians through the perspectives of their own regions. Thus, the concepts of education that framed their own thinking provided the basis for their schooling of Indian youth. When these individuals worked with Indian students, their goal was to graft their views of education onto the educational background that the students had already received through their own families and communities. To the degree that the missionaries and schoolmasters achieved this goal, they may have congratulated themselves on their accomplishment; but in so doing, they may also have taken into account the influence of the student's native culture on the entire process.

In many cases, the degree to which the Indian youth was affected by colonial schooling was in direct proportion to the extent of disruption experienced by that student's native culture. The Massachusett who responded favorably to John Eliot's perception of Christianization and civilization had suffered severe trauma from the devastating effect of the 1616–17 plague. By contrast, the powerful Powhatan Algonquian saw their culture as superior to the colonial culture. As a result, Virginians encountered overwhelming difficulty in attempting to persuade native families to educate their children through residence in European homes. Moreover, the acculturation of the Indian community also affected the student's response to schooling. Southern New England Algonquian who sent their children to school in the 1700s, placing them under the tutelage of men such as Ben Uncas or Samuel Whitman, had lived side by side with Euroamericans for a full century. Over the decades, they had adopted many of the manifest trappings of contemporary New England culture. David Fowler was strongly influenced by his Mohegan brother-in-law Samson Occom, who bore the markings of such cultural contact.

Hannah Garrett (Fowler) carried a lengthy heritage of interaction with New England educational ideas dating back to her grandfather's dialogue with Experience Mayhew. Tomochichi had sailed to England himself, while his people had experienced many decades of contact with Europeans. When Tomochichi welcomed the Wesley brothers and Benjamin Ingham, he knew well what he considered as the advantages of Christianization and civilization.

In each of these instances, the talents of the missionary–schoolmaster carried no greater weight than the peculiar condition of the student's own culture. For this reason, one of the missionary–schoolmaster's greatest handicaps proved to be his inability to comprehend the native culture. Since most colonials were not aware of the complexity and sophistication of Indian cultures of the eastern seaboard, let alone the integrated means by which they educated their children, it is not surprising that those who taught Indians in school shared this general naivete. They were themselves simply the product of the ethnocentrism that shaped the views of colonial Americans. Those involved with Indian schooling were unable to account for the persistence of native cultures because they saw no merit in a way of life which, from their perspective, was the antithesis of civilization. Eleazar Wheelock's continued failure to understand the tenacity of his students' native values exemplifies this attitude, but John Brainerd and others were equally bewildered. Despite their decades of work with Indian youth, they were unable to understand why their own goals were stymied by native cultural persistence. It never occurred to them to give any credit to the cultures themselves.

Other conditions also contributed to the schooling experience, helping to determine how contemporaries judged that experience. The foreign nature of the school environment proved to be one of the greatest difficulties for the transplanted natives. Much of the daily routine was contrary to their previous upbringing. They spent a considerable portion of their time inside buildings rather than out of doors. Some were required to wear colonial clothing and to change their hair style and general appearance. The omnipresent Christianity was both foreign and difficult to comprehend, and in the case of some of Wheelock's students, it became an onerous burden. To compound matters, the colonial Christians they met appeared not to follow the tenets that they themselves had been taught by the missionaries. Often, the stu-

dents were removed from all previous ties of family and community, which meant a wrenching separation from the very foundations of security. Many of them suffered and died from European
diseases; others succumbed to alcohol. And during most of the
colonial educational efforts, Indian students encountered some
form of overt or subtle prejudice. Regardless of which type they
experienced, however, the message was always clear. Often it
provided the death blow that dissuaded the student from any
previous attraction to Euroamerican society. For some, this provided a powerful incentive to return to their own people and a
familiar milieu where they would not be scorned. While their
schooling might hinder their social reacceptance in some instances, such discomfort did not rank with their treatment by
colonial society.

The other influence that molded Indian schooling came from
the general cultural exchange. The broad dimensions of this exchange, ranging from warfare to the impact of material goods,
retained a powerful pressure on the fragile experiments in Indian
education. In some regions, perhaps most clearly in the Carolinas,
these aspects of the cultural exchange were largely responsible
for the destruction of the tenuous efforts of missionaries and
schoolmasters. Despite the attempts by Le Jau and others, their
schooling experiments did not survive the short-sighted behavior
of the hide and slave traders and the warfare that resulted from
their actions. Thus, the already fragile structure of the schooling
also had to contend with the potentially devastating impact of the
overall cultural situation.

The net results of colonial Indian schooling, were therefore
determined by many interlocking conditions. Those who viewed
the experiments from within saw the interplay of these conditions through their own cultural lenses and evaluated them accordingly. Until recently, some historians have continued to follow this precedent, with their modern assessments reflecting the
values of their own cultures. This dilemma leads us back to where
we started: How should one evaluate these efforts to school the
Indian? To begin with, we might return to an earlier question:
Whose criteria shall we use to determine "success"? Shall it be
that of the Indian student, his family, community or tribe? Or
shall it be determined according to the goals established by the
missionary–schoolmasters; by the colony; by the missionary or-

ganization, which had the legal right to withdraw funds if it deemed the schooling a failure; or by other financial supporters in the colonies, England, and Europe? In each case, the person or group posing the question established different goals and analyzed the success or failure according to their own criteria.

If we choose to adopt colonial Euroamerican standards for judgment, we continue to encounter complications in determining the elusive quality of "success." Here, even the colonial educators disagreed. Some championed the minimal need of literacy for the Indians, and once this had been achieved they were convinced they had reached their goal. Others, such as the New England Company, began to shift their attitudes from acknowledging the merits of elementary schooling to anticipating Indian college graduates who became the symbols of success. On the other hand, one might consider the level of difficulties encountered. In regions such as in the Carolinas, where the colonial school was largely inadequate and other conditions appeared to work against the establishment of Indian schools, the few efforts to educate the Indians might be considered as a greater achievement than that of their counterparts elsewhere.

Yet another criterion for "success" revolved around the nature of the student's achievement. Should plaudits be given to a youth like the Yamassee Prince because his adoption of the accoutrements of civilization was heralded by the English? Or should the term *success* be applied to the less visible youth who was schooled only in reading and writing in a day school located relatively close to family and community? Such students did not bear the trappings of English civilization, but their schooling may have been of greater benefit to their own people. Locally educated Indian youth could serve as interpreters for their communities, while others might be able to read legal documents that could have serious consequences for their people. Again, the determination of success remains relative, firmly rooted in the expectations of the given culture. Thus, for the ethnohistorian, arbitrary pronouncements on "success" or "failure" have little meaning.

Numerous stories of colonial Indian schooling have never entered the pages of recorded history. A colonial who lived in Farmington, Connecticut, in the middle of the eighteenth century recalled that Indian children in the schools were "not much fewer" than white children. In snowballing parties, the Indian children took one side and the whites the other; and "they would be so equally balanced in numbers and prowess as to render the battle a very tough one and the result doubtful."[1] Such instances probably occurred in many sites of colonial American schooling. Whenever a schoolmaster included one or two Indians among his students, he was engaged in an attempt to educate the Indians, but since it seldom occurred to him to record his effort, it has largely escaped our scrutiny.

Among those schooling experiments that were recorded, however, probably the most unusual involved Indian students who went on to become cultural brokers. These Indians should be acknowledged in the annals of colonial history. They met a significant challenge in their lives by achieving a balance between two or more cultures. The remarkable accomplishments of the two Algonquian students at Harvard, Joel Hiacoomes and Caleb Chee-shahteaumauk, were unequaled in colonial America. The Euro-american-schooled Creek, Mary Musgrove, enabled James Oglethorpe and the Georgians to establish peaceful relations with the Creek Nation, and especially with the Yamacraw of Tomochichi's village. Pocahontas provided a symbol that may have led to intensified efforts to educate the youth of her Powhatan people. Cockenoe, James Printer, Nesuton, and other New England Algonquian made possible the printing of the *Indian Bible* and other works, which led to literacy among their people. Joseph Brant's biculturalism encouraged him to become a leader for the Mohawk and other Loyalist Iroquois during the period of the American Revolution. The schooling of Samson Occom, Joseph Johnson, Hannah Garrett, David Fowler, and their contemporaries enabled them to guide their people on new paths. Eventually joined by other Algonquian from Stockbridge and by the Delaware from New Jersey, these groups formed their own communities, where they were to recast their lives in a new mold containing a blend of cultures.

All of these Indians attained the unique position of cultural broker. This liaison role enabled them to serve as intermediaries between their own people and Euroamericans and Afro-Americans. Their noteworthy achievements provide a touchstone for assessing the merits of the many ventures in Indian schooling in colonial America.

ABBREVIATIONS

AA	*American Anthropologist*
AHR	*American Historical Review*
BAE	Bureau of American Ethnology
CA	Connecticut State Archives
CL	Congregational Library
DAP-PTS	David Avery Papers, Princeton Theological Seminary
DCA	Dartmouth College Archives
HCL	Hamilton College Library
JAH	*Journal of American History*
JE-HL-ANTS	Jonathan Edwards Transcripts, Hills Library Andover-Newton Theological School
MA-JRL	Methodist Archives, John Rylands University Library of Manchester
MHS	Massachusetts Historical Society
NEQ	*New England Quarterly*
SKP	Samuel Kirkland Papers
SPG, LC	Records of the Society for the Propagation of the Gospel in Foreign Parts, Manuscript Division, Library of Congress
SSPCK	Society in Scotland for Propagating Christian Knowledge
VMHB	*Virginia Magazine of History and Biography*
WMQ	*William and Mary Quarterly*

NOTES

CHAPTER 1

1. (Chapel Hill, North Carolina).

2. Ronda, "Beyond Thanksgiving: Francis Jennings, *The Invasion of America*," *The Journal of Ethnic Studies* 7 (1979):88.

3. (Chapel Hill, North Carolina).

4. Axtell, "The Ethnohistory of Early America: A Review Essay," *William and Mary Quarterly* 35, 3d ser. (1978):110–44 (hereafter cited as *WMQ*); Axtell, *The European and the Indian: Essays in the Ethnohistory of Colonial North America* (New York and Oxford, 1981); Neal Salisbury, *Manitou and Providence: Indians, Europeans and the Making of New England, 1500–1643* (New York and Oxford, 1982); James P. Ronda, " 'We Are Well as We Are': An Indian Critique of Seventeenth-Century Christian Missions," *WMQ* 34, 3d ser. (January 1977):66–82; Ronda, "Generations of Faith: The Christian Indians of Martha's Vineyard," *WMQ* 38, 3d ser. (July 1981):369–94; Nancy Oestreich Lurie, "Indian Cultural Adjustment to European Civilization," in James Morton Smith, ed., *Seventeenth Century America: Essays in Colonial History* (New York, 1959, 1972), pp. 33–60; Bruce G. Trigger, *The Children of Aataentsic: A History of the Huron People to 1660*, 2 vols. (Montreal, 1976).

5. Axtell, *European and the Indian*, p. 5. For Axtell's most recent work on this subject, see: Axtell, *The Invasion Within: The Contest of Cultures in Colonial North America* (New York and Oxford, 1985); see especially, chap. 5, "The Little Red School."

6. Jennings, *Invasion of America*, p. vii.

7. Trigger, *Children of Aataentsic*, vol. 1, p. 26.

8. Neal Salisbury, review of Jennings, *The Invasion of America*, in *New England Quarterly* 49 (1976):159.

9. (Chapel Hill, North Carolina).

10. Ibid.

11. (New York, 1970).

12. See James Axtell, "The English Colonial Impact on Indian Culture," pp. 245–71, and "The Indian Impact on English Colonial Culture," pp. 272–315, in Axtell, *European and the Indian*.

13. William N. Fenton, "Northern Iroquoian Culture Patterns," in *Handbook of North American Indians, Northeast*, vol. 15, ed. Bruce G. Trigger (Washington, D.C., 1978), p. 314.

14. Alice C. Fletcher and Francis La Flesche, *The Omaha Tribe*, 2 vols. (Lincoln, 1972), vol. 1, p. 117. The Otos also cut a hole in the infant's moccasin.

15. *The Jesuit Relations and Allied Documents*, ed. Reuben Gold Thwaites (Cleveland, 1876), vol. 1, p. 277; vol. 16, p. 68; vol. 57, p. 231 (hereafter cited as *Jesuit Relations*).

16. David H. Corkran, *The Creek Frontier, 1540–1783* (Norman, Okla., 1967), p. 34. Robert Beverly, *The History and Present State of Virginia*, ed. Louis B. Wright (Chapel Hill, 1947 [1705]), p. 170.

17. George A. Pettitt, *Primitive Education in North America* (Berkeley, 1946) (hereafter cited as *Primitive Education*).

18. Alfonso Ortiz, *The Tewa World* (Chicago, 1971), pp. 172–73.

19. Wilfred Pelletier, et al., *For Every North American Indian Who Begins to Disappear I Also Begin to Disappear* (Toronto, 1971), p. 8.

20. Robert K. Thomas, "The Role of the Church in Indian Adjustment," in Pelletier, *For Every North American Indian*, p. 88.

21. Pettitt, *Primitive Education*, pp. 5, 22.

22. Myron Jones, "Indian Education Overview," National Institute of Education (unpublished monograph in author's collection, 1977).

23. Boyce Richardson, *Strangers Devour the Land* (New York, 1976), p. 7.

24. *Jesuit Relations*, vol. 67, 139–41.

25. Peter Whiteley, "Third Mesa Hopi Social Structural Dynamics and Sociocultural Change: The View from Bacavi" (Ph.D. diss., University of New Mexico, 1982), p. 133.

26. William G. McLoughlin, *Cherokee Renascence in the New Republic* (Princeton, N.J., 1986), pp. 14–15; Charles M. Hudson, *The Southeastern Indians* (Knoxville, 1976), pp. 317–19; 336–37; 351–52; 365–75.

27. See Philippe Ariès, *Centuries of Childhood: A Social History of Family Life* (New York, 1962), pp. 96–98.

28. *Jesuit Relations*, vol. 38, 261.

29. Howard A. Norman, trans., *The Wishing Bone Cycle: Narrative Poems from the Swampy Cree Indians* (New York, 1976), p. 4.

30. Pablita Velarde, *Old Father, the Story Teller* (Globe, Ariz., 1960), p. 25.

31. P[ierre] de Charlevoix, *Journal of a Voyage to North-America* (London, 1761), vol. 1, pp. 113–16, as cited in *The Indian Peoples of Eastern America*, ed. James Axtell (New York and Oxford, 1981), p. 34.

32. Allen Quetone (Kiowa), in *Can the Red Man Help the White Man? A Denver Conference with the Indian Elders*, ed. Sylvester M. Morey (New York, 1970), p. 49.

33. Paul Radin, *Crashing Thunder* (New York, 1926), p. 71.

34. Leo W. Simmons, *Sun Chief: The Autobiography of a Hopi Indian* (New Haven, 1971), p. 51.

35. Sherman Sage (Arapaho), as quoted by Sister M. Inez Hilyer in "Arapaho Child Life and Its Cultural Background," *BAE Bulletin*, no. 148 (Washington, D.C., 1952), p. 100.

36. Fletcher and La Flesche, *Omaha Tribe*, vol. 2, p. 333.

37. Victor Barnouw, *Wisconsin Chippewa Myths and Tales and Their Relation to Chippewa Life: Based on Folktales Collected by Victor Barnouw et al.* (Madison, Wisconsin, 1977), p. 4.

38. James P. Spradley, *Guests Never Leave Hungry: The Autobiography of James Sewid, a Kwakiutl Indian* (New Haven, 1969), p. 24.

39. Velarde, *Old Father the Story Teller*, p. 17.

40. See, for example, Frank James Newcomb, *Hosteen Klah, Navajo Medicine Man and*

Sand Painter (Norman, 1964); Simmons, *Sun Chief*; Anthony F. C. Wallace, *The Death and Rebirth of the Seneca* (New York, 1972); and John C. Neihardt, *Black Elk Speaks* (Lincoln, Nebr., 1970).

41. Fletcher and La Flesche, *Omaha Tribe*, vol. 1, p. 115–16.

42. Melville Jacobs, *The Content and Style of an Oral Literature: Clackamas Chinook Myths and Tales* (Chicago, 1959), p. 184.

43. Pettitt mentions that southeastern groups retained both. *Primitive Education*, p. 38. For an observation on initiation of boys among the Delaware and other Pennsylvania groups in the eighteenth century, see John Heckewelder, *History, Manners, and Customs of the Indian Nations Who Once Inhabited Pennsylvania and the Neighboring States* (New York, 1971; 1876), pp. 245–48.

44. Robert Beverly, *The History and Present State of Virginia*, ed. Louis B. Wright (Chapel Hill, 1947; 1705, rev. 1722) p. 207; Elsie Clew Parsons, "The Social Organization of the Tewa of New Mexico," American Anthropological Association, *Memoirs*, no. 36 (Menasha, Wisc., 1929), p. 151; Elsie Clew Parsons, "Taos Pueblo," *General Series in Anthropology*, no. 2 (Menasha, Wisc., 1936), pp. 46–47.

45. Parts of the guardian spirit quest account are based on interviews with Yakima Indians, 1964–1967. Also see Verne F. Ray, "Native Villages and Groupings of the Columbia River Basin," *Pacific Northwest Quarterly* 27 (April 1936):7–8; and Hermann Haeberlin and Erna Gunther, *The Indians of Puget Sound* (Seattle, 1975), first published as University of Washington *Publications in Anthropology*, vol. 4, no. 1 (1930), p. 46. On the Ottawa, see *Jesuit Relations*, vol. 54, pp. 141–43.

46. Hoebel, *The Cheyennes, Indians of the Great Plains* (New York, 1960), p. 59.

47. Edna Kenton, ed., *The Indians of North America*, vol. 1 (New York, 1927), p. 90, as quoted in Wallace, *Death and Rebirth of the Seneca*, p. 38. Also see Pettitt, *Primitive Education*, p. 6; *Jesuit Relations*, vol. 9, pp. 105–6.

48. Hrdlicka, *The Aleutian and Commander Islands and Their Inhabitants* (Philadelphia, 1945), p. 72.

49. William W. Newcomb, Jr., "The Culture and Acculturation of the Delaware Indians," *Anthropological Papers*, no. 10 (Ann Arbor, 1956), p. 34.

50. Thomas Wildcat Alford, as told to Florence Drake, *Civilization* (Norman, 1936), p. 19.

51. Hilda Mortimer, with Chief Dan George, *You Call Me Chief* (Toronto, 1981), p. 76.

52. *Jesuit Relations*, vol. 57, p. 45.

53. Erna Gunther, "Klallam Ethnography," University of Washington *Publications in Anthropology*, vol. 1 (Seattle, 1927), p. 289.

54. Verne F. Ray, "The San Poil and Nespelem: Salishan People of Northeast Washington," University of Washington *Publications in Anthropology*, vol. 5 (Seattle, 1932) p. 131.

55. James Adair, *The History of the American Indians*, ed. Samuel C. Williams (Johnson City, Tenn., 1930), pp. 163–64, as quoted by Arrell Gibson, *The Chickasaws* (Norman, 1976), p. 21.

56. B. H. Quain, "The Iroquois," in *Cooperation and Competition among Primitive Peoples*, ed. Margaret Mead (New York, 1937), p. 272.

57. Hudson, *Southeastern Indians*, p. 324.

58. Hrdlicka, *Aleutian and Commander Islands*, p. 171.

59. Newcomb, "Culture and Acculturation of the Delaware Indians," p. 34.

60. Richard K. Nelson, *Hunters of the Northern Forest: Designs for Survival among the Alaskan Kutchin* (Chicago, 1973), p. 375.

61. Nuligak, *I, Nuligak* (Toronto, 1968), p. 57.

62. *Jesuit Relations*, vol. 67, p. 139.

63. Parsons, "Taos Pueblo," p. 40.

64. Margaret Coel, *Chief Left Hand: Southern Arapaho* (Norman, 1981), pp. 8–9.

65. Hoebel, *Cheyennes*, p. 92.

66. William Wood, "New England's Prospect" (1631), in Samuel Eliot Morison, *The Founding of Harvard College* (Cambridge, 1936), p. 108.

67. Pettitt, *Primitive Education*, p. 19.

68. Goodbird, *Goodbird, The Indian: His Story*, ed. Gilbert L. Wilson (New York, 1914), p. 24.

69. Clark Wissler, "Social Life of the Blackfoot Indians," American Museum of Natural History *Anthropological Papers*, vol. 7 (New York, 1911), p. 24, as quoted in Pettitt, *Primitive Education*, p. 51.

70. On this phenomenon among the Hopi, see Simmons, *Sun Chief*, and Wayne Dennis, *The Hopi Child* (repr., New York, 1967), pp. 65–66.

71. Clark Wissler, *The American Indian* (New York, 1922), as cited in Pettitt, *Primitive Education*, p. 50.

72. John A. Swanton, "Source Material for the Social and Ceremonial life of the Choctaw Indians," *BAE Bulletin*, no. 103 (Washington, D.C., 1931), pp. 198–99.

73. Eastman, *Indian Boyhood* (n.p., 1902), pp. 9–10.

74. Pettitt, *Primitive Education*, p. 48.

75. Leslie Spier and Edward Sapir, "Wishram Ethnography," University of Washington *Publications in Anthropology*, 1929–30, vol. 3 (Seattle, 1931), p. 261.

76. Hugh A. Dempsey, *Red Crow, Warrior Chief* (Lincoln, Nebr., 1980), p. 17.

77. Haeberlin and Gunther, *Indians of Puget Sound*, p. 46. On the Creek and adjacent groups, see Hudson, *Southeastern Indians*, pp. 325–26.

78. "The Autobiography of a Fox Woman," *BAE Annual Report*, no. 40 (Washington, D.C., 1925), p. 299.

79. See, for example: Fletcher and La Flesche, *Omaha Tribe*, pp. 368–70; Haeberlin and Gunther, "Diversions," in *Indians of Puget Sound* pp. 62–66; Dennis, *Hopi Child*, pp. 48–64; Stewart Culin, "Games of the North American Indians," *BAE Annual Report*, no. 24 (Washington, D.C., 1907); Hudson, *Southeastern Indians*, p. 324; Wallace, *Death and Rebirth of the Seneca*, p. 36.

80. "Narrative of a Southern Cheyenne Woman," ed. Truman Michelson, Smithsonian *Miscellaneous Collections*, vol. 87, no. 5 (Washington, D.C., 1932), p. 3.

CHAPTER 2

1. "As You Like It," Act 2, Scene 7, in *Shakespeare, The Complete Works*, ed. G. B. Harrison (New York, 1958), p. 789.

2. Two classic studies which expand on this theme are Bernard Bailyn, *Education in the Forming of American Society* (New York, 1963), and Lawrence A. Cremin, *American Education: The Colonial Experience, 1607–1783* (New York, 1970).

3. Peter Laslett, *The World We Have Lost* (New York, 1965), p. 72.

4. George Parker Winship, *The New England Company of 1649 and John Eliot* (New York, 1960; 1920), pp. 120, 133, and 148.

5. Bailyn, *Education in the Forming of American Society*, p. 91.

6. Laslett, *World We Have Lost*, pp. 11, 19, 21, and 54. For an equally intriguing account of the family in early France, see Philippe Aries, *Centuries of Childhood: A Social History of Family Life* (New York, 1962).

7. Cremin, *American Education*, p. 135. Also see Bailyn, *Education in the Forming of American Society*, pp. 15–18.

8. J. William Frost, *The Quaker Family in Colonial America* (New York, 1973), p. 105.

9. See Kenneth A. Lockridge, *Literacy in Colonial New England* (New York, 1974), pp. 72–101.

10. Cotton Mather, *Cares about the Nurseries* (Boston, 1702), as quoted in Wilson Smith, ed., *Theories of Education in Early America, 1655–1819* (Indianapolis and New York, 1973), pp. 11–12.

11. Jasper Godwin Ridley, *Nicholas Ridley* (London, 1957), p. 109. On literacy and the social impact of schooling in Tudor and Stuart England, see Lawrence Stone, "The Educational Revolution in England, 1560–1640," *Past and Present* 28 (July 1964):43–80.

12. Cremin, *Colonial Experience*, pp. 41–46. Also, see pt. 1, chap. 1, for "The Practice of Piety."

13. *Diary of Samuel Sewall*, 2 vols., ed. M. Halsey Thomas (New York, 1973), vol. 1, p. 249. Fourteen children were born to Hannah and Samuel Sewall, of whom seven lived to maturity.

14. Frost, *Quaker Family in Colonial America*, pp. 75–76.

15. Hunter Dickinson Farish, *Journal and Letters of Philip Vickers Fithian, 1773–1774: A Plantation Tutor of the Old Dominion* (Charlottesville, 1967; 1943), p. 76. For another interesting account by a Virginia plantation tutor, see *The Journal of John Harrower, An Indentured Servant in the Colony of Virginia, 1773–1776,* ed. Edward Miles Riley (Williamsburg and New York, 1963).

16. On Cremin's interpretation of Locke's influence on colonial education, see *Colonial Experience*, pp. 273–78. Locke's philosophy of education is the subject of a cogent analysis by James Axtell, ed., *The Educational Writings of John Locke* (Cambridge, 1968).

17. On Ezra Stiles, see Edmund S. Morgan, *The Gentle Puritan, A Life of Ezra Stiles, 1727–1795* (New Haven, 1972).

18. For Cremin's analysis of the teaching of civility, see *Colonial Experience*, pp. 58–79.

19. Jefferson to Colonel Edward Carrington, January 16, 1787, in *Jefferson's Letters*, arranged by Wilson Whitman (Eau Claire, Wisc., n.d.), p. 60.

20. Carl Bridenbaugh, *The Spirit of '76: The Growth of American Patriotism before Independence* (New York, 1975), pp. 53, 86. On the impact of the press in this period, see Bernard Bailyn, *The Ideological Origins of the American Revolution* (Cambridge, Mass., 1971), chap. 1.

21. Bridenbaugh, *Spirit of '76*, p. 138.

22. Jefferson to Colonel Carrington, January 16, 1787, in *Jefferson's Letters*, p. 61.

23. Cremin, *Colonial Experience*, p. 480. Bernard Bailyn saw the family's role as increasingly threatened; see *Education in the Forming of American Society*, pp. 22–29.

24. Even in New England, which supported the largest number of grammar schools, less than half of the graduates in the seventeenth century went on to college. See Walter Herbert Small, *Early New England Schools* (New York, 1969; 1914), p. 66.

25. These statistics are based on Carl Bridenbaugh, *The Colonial Craftsman* (Chicago, 1961; 1950), pp. 66, 108.

26. Ibid., p. 74.

27. John Demos, *A Little Commonwealth: Family Life in Plymouth Colony* (London, New York, 1971), pp. 71, 75; Frost, *Quaker Family in Colonial America*, pp. 142–146; Edmund S. Morgan, *The Puritan Family* (New York, 1966, 1944), pp. 76–77; Edmund S. Morgan, *Virginians at Home: Family Life in the Eighteenth Century* (Chapel Hill, 1952), pp. 22–25; *Diary of Samuel Sewall*, vol. 1, p. 314.

28. Morgan, *Puritan Family*, p. 67.

29. Thomas Woody, *A History of Women's Education in the United States* (New York, 1929), vol. 1, p. 260.

30. Bridenbaugh, *Colonial Craftsman*, pp. 105–7; Woody, *History of Women's Education*, vol. 1, p. 259.

31. This section relies on Morgan, *Puritan Family*, pp. 67–75; and James Axtell, *The*

School upon a Hill: Education and Society in Colonial New England (New York, 1976; 1974), chap. 3.

32. *Diary of Samuel Sewall*, vol. 1, p. 121, 371, n., 372, n.

33. *Hampshire Gazette*, Northampton, Mass.

34. Rolla Milton Tryon, *Household Manufactures in the United States, 1640–1860* (New York, 1966; 1917), p. 93.

35. See Cremin, *Colonial Experience*, pp. 133, 482–83.

36. This is a major theme of Carl Bridenbaugh's *Cities in Revolt: Urban Life in America, 1743–1776* (London, Oxford, and New York, 1971 [1945]); see especially chaps. 4 and 5.

37. Ibid., p. 76; see also Robert F. Seybolt, *The Evening School in Colonial America* (Urbana, 1925). On apprentice education, see Marcus Wilson Jernegan, *Laboring and Dependent Classes in Colonial America, 1607–1783* (Chicago, 1931), pp. 126–28.

38. *The New England Primer*, edited by Paul Leicester Ford (New York, 1962; 1897).

39. See Morgan, *Puritan Family*, pp. 88–90; and Axtell, *School upon a Hill*, pp. 167–69.

40. Samuel Eliot Morison, *The Intellectual Life of Colonial New England* (Ithaca, N.Y., 1956; 1936), pp. 17–18.

41. See Axtell, *School upon a Hill*, chap. 7; Roy Harvey Pearce, *Savagism and Civilization* (Baltimore, 1965; 1953), pp. 80–85; and Robert Berkhofer, *The White Man's Indian* (New York, 1978), pp. 5–8, 19–35.

42. Small, *Early New England Schools*, p. 395.

43. Ibid., pp. 380 and 385.

44. "Some Special Points Relating to the Education of My Children," in *The Diary of Cotton Mather, 1681–1708*, ed. Worthington Chauncey Ford (New York, 1957), vol. 1, p. 535.

45. Lockridge, *Literacy in Colonial New England*, pp. 13 and 38.

46. Cremin, *Colonial Experience*, pp. 321–30, 505.

47. On schooling for girls, see Woody, *History of Schools*, chaps. 6 and 11.

48. Gary B. Nash points out that in Boston Negroes comprised 10 percent of the population. See Nash, *Red, White, and Black: The Peoples of Early America* (Englewood Cliffs, N.J., 1974), p. 198. See also Lorenzo Johnston Greene, *The Negro in Colonial New England* (New York, 1971; 1942), pp. 237–41.

49. Small, *Early New England Schools*, p. 126.

50. See Frank J. Klingberg, *Anglican Humanitarianism in Colonial New York* (Philadelphia, 1940), chap. 4.

51. William Webb Kemp, *The Support of Schools in Colonial New York by the Society for the Propagation of the Gospel in Foreign Parts* (New York, 1913), see chap. 6. On the SPG in America, see also: John Calam, *Parsons and Pedagogues: The SPG Adventure in American Education* (New York, 1971); C. F. Pascoe, *Two Hundred Years of the S.P.G.: An Historical Account of the Society for the Propagation of the Gospel in Foreign Parts, 1791–1900* (London, 1901); and David Humphreys, *An Historical Account of the Incorporated Society for the Propagation of the Gospel in Foreign Parts* (New York, 1969; 1728).

52. Kemp, *Support of Schools in Colonial New York*, p. 268.

53. James G. Leyburn, *The Scotch-Irish, A Social History* (Chapel Hill, 1962), pp. 56, 72–78.

54. Leonard J. Trinterud, *The Forming of an American Tradition: A Re-examination of Colonial Presbyterianism* (New York, 1970; 1949), p. 201.

55. Lyman H. Butterfield, *John Witherspoon Comes to America* (Princeton, N.J., 1953).

56. Frost, *Quaker Family in Colonial America*, p. 94.

57. See George Brookes, *Friend Anthony Benezet* (Philadelphia, 1937).

58. For a detailed study of Negro education in South Carolina, see Frank J. Klingberg, *An Appraisal of the Negro in Colonial South Carolina* (Washington, D.C., 1941), chap. 5.

59. Davies to Richard Crutenden, March 1755, as cited by George William Pilcher,

Samuel Davies, Apostle of Dissent in Colonial Virginia (Knoxville, 1971), p. 112. For Davies as educator, see chap. 6.

60. Davies to JF, March 2, 1766, as cited in Pilcher, *Samuel Davies*, p. 112.

61. Richard Beale Davis, *Intellectual Life in the Colonial South, 1585–1763*, (Knoxville, 1978), vol. 1, p. 262.

62. Philip Alexander Bruce, *Social Life in Old Virginia*, from the *Institutional History of Virginia in the Seventeenth Century* (New York, 1965; 1940), pt. 2, chap. 5.

63. Ibid., pp. 343–62. See also *A Documentary History of Education in the South before 1860*, ed. Edgar W. Knight (Chapel Hill, 1949), vol. 1, on the Symes–Eaton School, pp. 202–34, and on educational provisions in wills, pp. 296–334.

64. On early dissenter schooling in Virginia, see Sadie Bell, *The Church, The State, and Education in Virginia* (Philadelphia, 1930), pp. 132–46.

65. Bridenbaugh, *Cities in Revolt*, pp. 379–80.

66. *The Prose Works of William Byrd of Westover*, edited by Louis B. Wright (Cambridge, Mass., 1966), pp. 11 and 12.

67. Louis B. Wright, *Culture on the Moving Frontier* (Bloomington, Ind., 1955), p. 26; Wright, *The First Gentlemen of Virginia* (San Marino, Calif., 1936), p. 165.

68. See Knight, *Documentary History of Education*, vol. 1, pp. 553–70.

69. See Axtell, *Educational Writings of John Locke*, chap. 2, pp. 42–46 especially.

70. Woody, *History of Women's Education*, vol. 1, p. 271.

71. Julia Cherry Spruill, *Women's Life and Work in the Southern Colonies* (New York, 1972), p. 187.

CHAPTER 3

1. Henry Steele Commager, ed., *Documents of American History* (New York, 1934), p. 8.

2. See Thomas Hariot, "A Brief and True Report of the New Found Land of Virginia," in *The Roanoke Voyages 1584–1590*, ed. David B. Quinn (London, 1955); *Travels and Works of Captain John Smith*, ed. Edward Arber and A. G. Bradley (Edinburgh, 1910), a more recent edition of which is *The Complete Works of Captain John Smith, 1580–1631*, ed. Philip L. Barbour, 3 vols. (Chapel Hill, 1986); William Strachey, *The Historie of travaile into Virginia Britannia. . . .* , ed. Louis B. Wright and Virginia Freund (London, 1953); Robert Beverly, *The History and Present State of Virginia*, ed. Louis B. Wright (Chapel Hill, 1947; 1705).

3. On the Siouan and Iroquoian Indians of Virginia, see Ben B. McCary, *Indians in Seventeenth-Century Virginia* (Charlottesville, 1970; 1957), pp. 8–10; John Reed Swanton, "The Indians of the Southeastern United States," *BAE Bulletin* 137 (Washington, D.C., 1946), pp. 110–15, 149, 152, 163–64, 178–79, 200–201, and passim; James M. Crawford, "Southeastern Indian Languages," in *Studies in Southeastern Indian Languages*, ed. Crawford (Athens, 1975), pp. 19–23, 49, 57–58; Charles M. Hudson, *The Southeastern Indians* (Knoxville, 1976), pp. 8, 24; James Mooney, "The Siouan Tribes of the East," *BAE Bulletin* 22 (Washington, D.C., 1894), pp. 7–8, 10–11, 23–53; and Nancy Oestreich Lurie, "Indian Cultural Adjustment to European Civilization," in James Morton Smith, ed., *Seventeenth Century America: Essays in Colonial History* (New York, 1972; 1959), p. 43.

4. Powhatan reputedly gave this information to Strachey, but John R. Swanton suggests that Powhatan's statement actually meant "less time." See Strachey, *The Historie of travaile into Virginia Britannia*, ed. R. H. Major (London, 1849), p. 33. Swanton, "Indians of the Southeastern United States," p. 24. On the migration, see also Frank G. Speck, "The Ethnic Position of the Southeastern Algonquian," *American Anthropologist* (hereafter cited as *AA*) 26 (April–June 1924): 190–194.

5. Strachey, *Historie*, ed. Wright and Freund, p. 70; Arber and Bradley, *Travels and Works of Captain John Smith*.

6. Hariot, "Brief and True Report of the New Found Land of Virginia," p. 371.

7. *Travels and Works of Captain John Smith*, vol. 1, p. 65. On Smith's insights into these Algonquian, see the intriguing biography of Philip J. Barbour, *The Three Worlds of Captain John Smith* (Boston, 1964), p. 99.

8. Strachey, *Historie*, ed. Wright and Freund, p. 88. See also *Travels and Works of Captain John Smith*, vol. 1, p. 75.

9. The Powhatan word for corn is in Strachey's *Historie*, ed. Wright and Freund, p. 118. The dates for corn planting are in *Travels and Works of Captain John Smith*, vol. 1, p. 62. For an interesting discussion of foods of the early Indians, see Maurice Monk, "Virginia Ethnology from an Early Relation," *WMQ*, 23, 2d ser. (April 1943):82–84. See also Wesley Frank Craven, *White, Red, and Black: The Seventeenth-Century Virginian* (Charlottesville, 1971), p. 48.

10. *Travels and Works of Captain John Smith*, vol. 1, p. 69.

11. See ibid., pp. 68–69; Strachey, *Historie*, ed. Wright and Freund, p. 80; James Mooney, "The Powhatan Confederacy, Past and Present," *AA* 9 (1907), 147; the quotation on kinship is in Theodore Stern, "Chicahominy: The Changing Culture of a Virginia Indian Community," *American Philosophical Society Proceedings* 96 (1952), 212, 213.

12. Stern, "Chicahominy," 219.

13. Strachey, *Historie*, ed. Wright and Freund, p. 113. This is taken directly from Captain Smith; see *Travels and Works of Captain John Smith*, vol. 1, p. 67. See also "An Account of the Indians in Virginia . . . 1689," an anonymous manuscript edited by Stanley Pargallis, *WMQ* 16, 3d ser. (April 1959), 234; Beverly, *History and Present State of Virginia*, p. 171.

14. See Pargallis, "An Account," 232; *Travels and Works of Captain John Smith*, vol. 1.

15. Strachey, *Historie*, ed. Wright and Freund, p. 113.

16. Strachey, *Historie*, ibid., pp. 113–14; Pargallis, "An Account," p. 234. For further descriptions of the Huskanaw ceremony, see Beverly, *History and Present State of Virginia*, pp. 205–8; McCary, *Indians in Seventeenth-Century Virginia*, pp. 62–65.

17. See William R. Gerard, "Virginia's Indian Contributions to English," *AA*, 9, new ser. (1907): 111–12.

18. *Travels and Works of Captain John Smith*, vol. 1, p. 65. See also Mooney, "Powhatan Confederacy," pp. 130, 132–36.

19. On Mooney's procedure for establishing native population estimates, see Douglas H. Ubelaker, "The Sources and Methodology for Mooney's Estimates of North American Indian Populations," in William M. Denevan, ed., *The Native Population of America in 1492* (Madison, 1962), p. 258. For recent estimates see Christian F. Feest, "Virginia Algonquians," in *Handbook of North American Indians*, vol. 15, ed. Bruce G. Trigger (Washington, D.C., 1978), p. 256; and J. Frederick Fausz, "Opechancahough: Indian Resistance Leader," in *Struggle and Survival in Colonial America*, ed. David G. Sweet and Gary B. Nash (Berkeley, Los Angeles, and London, 1981), p. 22.

20. Strachey, *Historie*, ed. Wright and Freund, p. 104–5.

21. This article appears in Carl Bridenbaugh, *Early Americans* (New York and Oxford, 1981), pp. 5–49. See also: Clifford M. Lewis and Albert J. Loomie, *The Spanish Jesuit Mission in Virginia, 1570–1572* (Chapel Hill, 1953); Lurie, "Indian Cultural Adjustment to European Civilization," pp. 34–36; and J. Frederick Fausz, "The Invasion of Virginia: Indians, Colonialism, and the Conquest of Cant; A Review Essay on Anglo–Indian Relations in the Chesapeake," *Virginia Magazine of History and Biography* (hereafter cited as *VMHB* 96 (April 1987), 146. Increased interest in the Roanoke colony has led to a number of publications: David Stick, *Roanoke Island: The Beginnings of English America* (Chapel

Hill and London, 1983); Karen Ordahl Kupperman, *Roanoke: The Abandoned Colony* (Totowa, N.J., 1984); David Beers Quinn, *Set Fair for Roanoke: Voyages and Colonies, 1584–1606* (Chapel Hill and London, 1985).

22. Mooney, "Powhatan Confederacy," p. 129.

23. Roy Harvey Pearce, *Savagism and Civilization* (Baltimore and London, 1965; 1953), p. 8.

24. Craven, *White, Red and Black*, p. 52.

25. See Bernard W. Sheehan, *Savagism and Civility: Indians and Englishmen in Colonial Virginia* (Cambridge, 1980), p. 124.

26. Susan Myra Kingsbury, ed., *The Records of the Virginia Company of London*, 4 vols. (Washington, D.C., 1906–1935), vol. 3, p. 14. Abbreviations in the text have been written in full.

27. Ibid., p. 27.

28. See Robert Johnson, *The New Life of Virginia* (Rochester, New York, 1897; 1612); and Reverend Alexander Whitaker, *Good News from Virginia* (repr., n.p., n.d. [1613]). These are cited in Robert O. Land, "Henrico and Its College," *WMQ*, 18, 2d ser. (1938), 472–73.

29. Kingsbury, "Records of Virginia Company," vol. 3, pp. 147–48.

30. See Philip L. Barbour, *Pocahontas and Her World* (Boston, 1970), chap. 5; and J. Frederick Fausz, "Middlemen in Peace and War: Virginia's Earliest Interpreters, 1608–1632," *VMHB* 95 (January 1987):41–57. A more general discussion of non-Indians choosing to live with Indians is in James Axtell, "The White Indians of Colonial America," in James Axtell, ed., *European and the Indian* (New York and Oxford, 1981), pp. 168–206.

31. See Edmund S. Morgan, *American Slavery, American Freedom: The Ordeal of Colonial Virginia*, (New York, 1975), pp. 75–91.

32. Strachey, *Historie*, ed. Wright and Freund, p. xxiv.

33. Edward Eggleston, *The Beginners of a Nation* (New York, 1899), p. 26.

34. Morgan, *American Slavery, American Freedom*, pp. 73, 89. Critical of Morgan's assessment, Fausz argues that "the colonists were more pragmatic than Morgan gave them credit for" (Fausz, "The Invasion of Virginia," pp. 148–49).

35. Lurie, "Indian Cultural Adjustment to European Civilization," pp. 39, 44.

36. Strachey, *Historie*, ed. Wright and Freund, p. 57; *Travels and Works of Captain John Smith*, vol. 1, p. 81.

37. Lurie develops this theme in "Indian Cultural Adjustment to European Civilization," pp. 43–44.

38. Strachey, *Historie*, ed. Wright and Freund, p. 113; *Travels and Works of Captain John Smith*, vol. 1, p. 67.

39. Kingsbury, *Records of the Virginia Company*, vol. 3.

40. Ibid., pp. 128–29.

41. Ibid., p. 228.

42. Ibid.

43. W. Stitt Robinson assumes that "Yeardley carried out his proposal," but this is doubtful. See Robinson, "Indian Education and Missions in Colonial Virginia," *Journal of Southern History* 18 (May 1952), 155. On Opechancanough's January 1621/22 agreement to exchange families, see Robinson, "Indian Education", p. 155. Fausz argues that Opechancanough's agreement was duplicitous, designed to lull the English into complacency in order to ensure the success of his plan to annihilate them ("Opechancanough: Indian Resistance Leader," pp. 30–31).

44. Kingsbury, *Records of the Virginia Company*, vol. 3; quotation is on page 71, and for the entire letter, see pp. 70–72.

45. See W. Gordon McCabe, "The First University in America, 1619–1622," *VMHB* 30

(1922): 145–46; Grace Steele Woodward, *Pocahontas* (Norman, Okla., 1969); Barbour, *Pocahontas*, pp. 173–74. Barbour's biography remains the most intriguing portrayal of Pocahontas.

46. For a documented account of the collection procedure, see Peter Walne, "The Collections for Henrico College, 1616–1618," *VMHB* 80 (April, 1972):259–66; the quotation is on p. 260.

47. A detailed description of the portraiture of Pocahontas can be found in Barbour, *Pocahontas*, pp. 178–79, 233–35.

48. *Travels and Works of Captain John Smith*, vol. 2, 534. Smith also wrote to the queen on Pocahontas's behalf; an "abstract" of this "epistle" (as Barbour describes it in *Pocahontas*, pp. 155–56) is found in *Travels and Works*, pp. 530–33.

49. Edgar W. Knight, *A Documentary History of Education in the South before 1860* (Chapel Hill, 1949), vol. 1, pp. 5–6.

50. Kingsbury, *Records of the Virginia Company*, vol. 3, p. 446.

51. Wesley Frank Craven, *The Southern Colonies in the Seventeenth Century* (Baton Rouge, La., 1949), p. 143; Fausz, "Opechancanough: Indian Resistance Leader," p. 31.

52. See, for example, Kingsbury, *Records of the Virginia Company*, vol. 1, pp. 247–48; 421–22 (Raleigh Map), 589; and vol. 3, pp. 575–76. For further discussion of these gifts, see Sadie Bell, "The Church, the State, and Education in Virginia," (Ph.D. diss., University of Pennsylvania, Philadelphia, 1930), pp. 16–21.

53. Land, "Henrico and Its College," p. 490.

54. See Craven, *Southern Colonies in the Seventeenth Century*, pp. 143–44; and Land, "Henrico and Its College," pp. 483, 485–87.

55. Land, "Henrico and Its College," pp. 478, 480; Francis Jennings, *The Invasion of America* (New York, 1976), pp. 53–56; Wilcomb Washburn, "Philanthropy and the American Indian: The Need for a Model," *Ethnohistory* 15 (1968), p. 54.

56. Kingsbury, *Records of the Virginia Company*, Vol. 1, 268.

57. Lurie, "Indian Cultural Adjustment to European Civilization," p. 51. On this theme also see Fausz, "Middlemen in Peace and War: Virginia's Earliest Interpreters, 1608–1632," pp. 54–55.

58. Morgan, *American Slavery, American Freedom*, pp. 99–100.

59. Craven, *White, Red and Black*, p. 65.

60. Joseph A. Le May, *Men of Letters in Colonial Maryland* (Knoxville, Tenn., 1972), pp. 11–14.

61. Christian F. Feest, "Nanticoke and Neighboring Tribes," in *Handbook of North American Indians, Northeast*, vol. XV, edited by Bruce G. Trigger (Washington, D.C., 1978), pp. 240–45; James H. Merrell, "Cultural Continuity among the Piscataway Indians of Colonial Maryland," *WMQ* 36, 3d ser. (October 1979):550–55; Andrew White, "A Briefe Relation of the Voyage Unto Maryland" (1634), in Clayton Colman Hall, *Narratives of Early Maryland* (New York, 1970), p. 40.

62. White, "Briefe Relation."

63. Bernard Ulysses Campbell, "Early Missions among the Indians of Maryland," *Maryland Historical Magazine* 1 (December 1906), 312.

64. Ibid., pp. 307–08; John D. G. Shea, *History of the Catholic Missions among the Indian Tribes of the United States, 1529–1854* (New York, 1969; 1855), p. 491.

65. Campbell, "Early Missions among the Indians of Maryland," pp. 302–3; Le May, *Men of Letters in Colonial Maryland*, p. 25; Merrell, "Cultural Continuity among the Piscataway Indians of Colonial Maryland," p. 557.

66. Le May, *Men of Letters*, p. 352.

67. Frank W. Porter III, "A Century of Accommodation: The Nanticoke Indians in Colonial Maryland," *Maryland Historical Magazine* 74 (June 1979), 179; Merrell, "Cultural Continuity among the Piscataway Indians of Colonial Maryland," pp. 560–61.

68. Clinton Alfred Weslager, *The Nanticoke Indians—Past and Present* (Newark, 1983), pp. 63–64.

69. Ibid., pp. 140–57, 194–202; Feest, "Nanticoke and Neighboring Tribes," pp. 245–48.

70. Sadie Bell, *The Church, the State and Education in Virginia* (Philadelphia, 1930), p. 27.

71. Ibid., pp. 25–26.

72. William W. Hening, *The Statutes at Large; Being a Collection of All the Laws of Virginia, 1619–1792* (Richmond, 1809–1823), vol. 1, p. 326, as quoted in Warren M. Billings, ed., *The Old Dominion in the Seventeenth Century: a Documentary History of Virginia, 1606–1689* (Chapel Hill, 1975), pp. 227–28.

73. Bell, *The Church, the State and Education in Virginia*, p. 25.

74. Hening, *Statutes at Large*, vol. 1, p. 396, as cited in Bell, pp. 26–27.

75. Hening, *Statutes at Large*, vol. 1, pp. 455, 481, as quoted in Bell, pp. 26–27.

76. Hening, *Statutes at Large*, vol. 2, p. 194, as cited in Bell, p. 27.

77. Robert Greene, "Virginia's Laws," in Peter Force, ed., *Tracts and Other Papers* (Washington, D.C., 1836–1846), vol. 3, p. 6.

78. Hening, *Statutes at Large*, vol. 2, p. 56, as quoted in Billings, *Documentary History of Virginia*, p. 378.

79. See Billings, *Documentary History*, pp. 210–11.

80. Virginia population statistics are in W. Stitt Robinson, "Tributary Indians in Colonial Virginia," *VMHB* 67 (January 1959), 57; Craven, *White, Red and Black*, p. 59.

81. John R. Swanton, "The Indian Tribes of North America," *BAE Bulletin* 45 (Washington, D.C., 1952), p. 71.

82. *The History of the College of William and Mary from Its Foundation, 1660 to 1874* (Richmond, 1874), p. 45. On Blair's impact on the founding of the college, see Michael G. Kammen, ed., "Virginia at the Close of the Seventeenth Century: An Appraisal by James Blair and John Locke," *VMHB* 74 (January 1966), 144–45.

83. Edgar Knight, *Documentary History of Education in the South*, vol. 1, p. 1.

84. W. Stitt Robinson, Jr., "Indian Education and Missions in Colonial Virginia," 162. Karen A. Stuart, " 'So Good A Work,' The Brafferton School, 1691–1777" (Master's thesis, College of William and Mary, 1984; hereafter cited as "The Brafferton School").

85. H. L. Ganter, "Some Notes on the Charity of the Honorable Robert Boyle," *William and Mary Quarterly Historical Magazine*, 15, ser. 2 (January 1935), 14, 16.

86. Ibid., pp. 17–18.

87. *History of the College of William and Mary*, p. 40. See also Mary Newton Stanard, *Colonial Virginia, Its People and Customs* (Philadelphia, 1917), p. 284.

88. *History of the College of William and Mary*, p. 46.

89. Stuart, "The Brafferton School," appendix B, pp. 85–86.

90. Spotswood to the Council of Trade, November 11, 1711, in *The Official Letters of Alexander Spotswood*, (Richmond, 1973; 1882–85), vol. 1, pp. 121–22 (hereafter cited as *Spotswood Letters*).

91. Billings, ed., *Old Dominion in the Seventeenth Century*, p. 226. As the Indian population dwindled, so did their ability to pay the tribute. By the end of the century Virginia accepted reduced tributes. See Walter Stitt Robinson, "Tributary Indians in Colonial Virginia," *VMHB* 67 (January 1959), 58–59.

92. Spotswood to the Council of Trade, July 26, 1712, in *Spotswood Letters*, vol. 1, p. 167. On population change for these Indians, see also Beverly, *History and Present State of Virginia*, pp. 232–33; Swanton, "Indians of the Southeastern United States," pp. 175–76.

93. Spotswood to the Council of Trade, November 11, 1711, in *Spotswood Letters*, vol. 1, p. 122.

94. Stuart, "The Brafferton School," p. 17.

95. Spotswood to the Bishop of London, July 26, 1712, in *Spotswood Letters*, vol. 1, pp.

174–75. See also Leonidas Dodson, *Alexander Spotswood, Governor of Colonial Virginia, 1710–1722* (Philadelphia, 1932), pp. 72–73.

96. Spotswood to the Lords Commissioners of Trade, January 27, 1714, (1715), in *Spotswood Letters*, vol. 2, pp. 99–100. See also Dodson, *Alexander Spotswood*, p. 79.

97. W. Neil Franklin, ed., "Act for the Better Regulation of the Indian Trade," *VMHB* 72 (April 1964), 142–43. See also Dodson, *Alexander Spotswood*, p. 83.

98. Hugh T. Lefler and William S. Pavell, *Colonial North Carolina* (New York, 1973), pp. 206–7.

99. Spotswood to the Bishop of London, January 27, 1714, in *Spotswood Letters*, vol. 2, p. 90.

100. William Byrd, "The History of the Dividing Line," in Louis B. Wright, ed., *The Prose Works of William Byrd of Westover* (Cambridge, Mass., 1966), p. 200.

101. Spotswood to the Lords Commissioners of Trade, June 4, 1715, in *Spotswood Letters*, vol. 2, p. 113.

102. Spotswood to Bishop of London, October 26, 1715, in ibid., p. 138.

103. Griffin to Bishop of London, 1716, as quoted in Bell, *The Church, the State, and Education in Virginia*, p. 32.

104. Hugh Jones, *The Present State of Virginia*, ed. Richard L. Morton (Chapel Hill, 1956; 1724), p. 59.

105. Spotswood to Bishop of London, October 26, 1715, in *Spotswood Letters*, vol. 2, p. 138.

106. Spotswood to Lords Commissioners of Trade, February 16, 1716, in ibid., p. 141.

107. Bell, *The Church, the State and Education in Virginia*, p. 32.

108. Byrd, "History of the Dividing Line," in Wright, *Works of William Byrd*, p. 220.

109. Ibid., p. 221; Jones, *Present State of Virginia*, p. 59.

110. Letter of June 24, 1718, in *Spotswood Letters*, vol. 2, p. 282.

111. In addition, Jones suggested that the students also may have lacked "proper necessaries" and "due care." *Present State of Virginia*, p. 114. But Robinson takes issue with this conclusion, in "Indian Education in Virginia," p. 166.

112. Jones, *Present State of Virginia*.

113. Lyon Gardiner Tyler, *Williamsburg, The Old Colonial Capital* (Richmond, 1907), pp. 134–37.

114. Stuart, "The Brafferton School," pp. 85–86.

115. Ibid., pp. 26, 38–40.

116. Dinwiddie to Lords of Trade, February 23, 1756, in *The Official Records of Robert Dinwiddie*, arranged by R. A. Brock, Collections of the Virginia Historical Society (Richmond, 1934), vol. 2, p. 339.

117. "Message of Governor Dinwiddie to the Emperor Old Hop and Other Sachems of the Great Nation of the Cherokees . . . " in ibid., p. 446.

118. Bell, *Church, the State, and Education in Virginia*, p. 34; Thomas Jefferson, *Notes on the State of Virginia* (New York, 1964), p. 45.

119. Stuart suggests that a group of Cherokee who visited Williamsburg in 1751, and who discussed the Indian school during their stay, may have been encouraging the rivalry between Virginia and South Carolina. See Stuart, "The Brafferton School," pp. 56–57.

120. In the earliest years of the Indian School it was suggested that the students "have a careful man of their own country to wait upon them & to serve them & to talk continually with them in their language that they do not forget it whilst they are amongst the English" William Stevens Perry, *Historical Collections Relating to the American Colonial Church* [Hartford, Ct., 1870], vol. 1, pp. 123–24.

121. "The Statutes of the College of William and Mary, Codified in 1736," *WMQ* 22, 1st ser. (1914):281–96. For a discussion of the statutes see Stuart, "The Brafferton School," pp. 30–31.

122. The son of Andrew Montour (Oneida–Huron and French-Canadian), and a trader and interpreter who served the British during the French and Indian War, John Montour supported the British and then the Americans during the American Revolution. On both father and son, see: Paul A. W. Wallace, *Conrad Weiser, Friend of Colonist and Mohawk* (Philadelphia and London, 1945), pp. 143, 179, and passim; Randolph C. Downes, *Council Fires on the Upper Ohio* (Philadelphia and London, 1969; 1940, pp. 239–40, and passim; *The Official Records of Robert Dinwiddie*, vol. 1, p. 17 n. 22, 58, 243–44; vol. 2, p. 35; "A Mystery Resolved: George Washington's Letter to Governor Dinwiddie, June 10, 1754," ed. Peter Walne, in *VMHB* 79 (April 1971), 136, n.9. The author is grateful to Karen A. Stuart for some of these citations.

123. *Indian Treaties Printed by Benjamin Franklin, 1736–1762*, ed. Carl Van Doren (Philadelphia, 1938), p. 76.

124. *The Papers of Benjamin Franklin*, ed. Leonard W. Labaree (New Haven, 1961), vol. 4, p. 483.

CHAPTER 4

1. For recent scholarship on Indian–white relations in seventeenth-century New England, see: Neal Emerson Salisbury, "Conquest of the 'Savage': Puritans, Puritan Missionaries, and Indians, 1620–1680" (Ph.D. diss., University of California, Los Angeles, 1972); Salisbury, "Red Puritans: The 'Praying Indians' of Massachusetts Bay and John Eliot," *WMQ* 31, 3d ser. (1974):27–54; Salisbury, *Manitou and Providence, Indians: Europeans and the Making of New England 1500–1653* (New York and Oxford, 1982); Francis Jennings, *The Invasion of America: Indians, Colonialism, and the Cant of Conquest* (New York, 1976); James P. Ronda, "Generations of Faith: The Christian Indians of Martha's Vineyard," *WMQ* 38, 3d ser. (July 1981):369–94; Ronda, " 'We Are Well as We Are': An Indian Critique of Seventeenth-Century Christian Missions," *WMQ* 34, 3d ser. (January 1977):66–82; Henry W. Bowden and James P. Ronda, *John Eliot's Indian Dialogues: A Study in Cultural Interaction* (Westport, Ct., 1980), pp. 21–56; James Axtell, "The Scholastic Philosophy of the Wilderness," *WMQ* 29, 3d ser. (1971):335–66; William S. Simmons, "Cultural Bias in the New England Puritans' Perception of Indians," *WMQ* 38, 3d ser. (1981):56–72; Simmons, "Conversion from Indian to Puritan," *New England Quarterly* 52 (1979):197–218.

2. Salisbury, "Conquest of the 'Savage,' " p. 124.

3. Ibid., pp. 126–27; Jennings, *Invasion of America*, pp. 233–47.

4. Reprinted in Samuel Eliot Morison, *The Founding of Harvard College* (Cambridge, Mass., 1935), p. 432.

5. Nathaniel E. Shurtleff, ed., *Records of the Governor and Company of the Massachusetts Bay in New England* (Boston, 1853–1854), vol. 2, pp. 166, 178–79; vol. 3, pp. 6–7. Quoted in Salisbury, "Conquest of the 'Savage,' " p. 126.

6. George Parker Winship, *The New England Company of 1649 and John Eliot* (Boston, 1920; rpt., New York, 1967), pp. vi, vii.

7. Ibid., pp. xxxv, xxxvi.

8. Ibid., p. xvi.

9. William Kellaway, *The New England Company, 1649–1776* (London, 1961), pp. 62–63. See also Salisbury, "Conquest of the 'Savage,' " p. 128.

10. Cotton Mather, *Magnalia Christi Americana, or the Ecclesiastical History of New England*, vol. 1 (1702; rpt., Hartford, Conn., 1853), p. 573.

11. Corporation to commissioners, September 15, 1655, in Ebeneezer Hazard, *Historical Collections, Consisting of State Papers*, vol. 2 (Philadelphia, 1794), p. 351.

12. Business of Commissioners, September 12, 1657, in ibid., p. 371.

13. Remember Bourne, granddaughter of Richard Bourne, married Experience Mayhew, grandson of Thomas Mayhew, Jr.

14. Cotton learned Wampanoag on Martha's Vineyard, where he served briefly before moving to Plymouth. Frederick Lewis Weiss, The Colonial Clergy and the Colonial Churches of New England (Lancaster, Mass., 1936), p. 62; Charles Edward Banks, History of Martha's Vineyard, vol. 1 (1911; repr., Edgartown, Mass., 1966), p. 34.

15. Martha Mayhew, daughter of Thomas Mayhew, married the son of Thomas Tupper. Lloyd C. M. Hare, Thomas Mayhew, Patriarch to the Indians (New York, 1932), p. 222.

16. These figures are based on records of the commissioners for 1653–72, in Hazard, Historical Collections, vol. 2, pp. 300–531.

17. See Mayhew to Corporation, October 22, 1652, in John Eliot, "Tears of Repentance: or, a Further Narrative of the Progress of the Gospel Amongst the Indians in New England" (1653), Massachusetts Historical Society, in Collections 4, 3rd series (1834):208 (hereafter cited as MHS Colls).

18. Eliot to Henry Whitfeld, in Henry Whitfeld, "The Light Appearing More and More towards the End of the Perfect Day . . . " (1651), MHS Colls. 4, 3d series (1834):131.

19. Cotton Mather, "Life of Eliot," in Magnalia Christi Americana, vol. 1, p. 556.

20. Roy Harvey Pearce, Savagism and Civilization (Baltimore, 1965), p. 31.

21. See Joseph Caldwell, "Trend and Tradition in the Prehistory of the Eastern United States," Memoir 88, American Anthropological Association, Scientific Papers, vol. 10; William A. Ritchie, "Archaeological Manifestations and Relative Chronology in the Northeast," in "Man in Northeastern North America," ed. Frederick Johnson, Papers of the Robert S. Peabody Foundation for Archaeology, vol. 3 (Andover, Mass., 1946). For an assessment of the economic system of the southern New England Algonquian, see Salisbury, Manitou and Providence, pp. 30–39.

22. Corporation to commissioners, April 30, 1658, in Hazard, Historical Collections, vol. 2, p. 390.

23. Mather to Sir William Ashurst (probably)—Ashurst was governor of the New England Company, 1696–1712—in Selected Letters of Cotton Mather, ed. Kenneth Silverman (Baton Rouge, 1971), p. 128.

24. Gookin's figures were based on populations for five confederacies: Pequot, Narragansett, Pawkunnawkut (later known as Wampanoag), Massachusett and Pawtuckett (Penacook or Namesitt). Daniel Gookin, "Historical Collections of the Indians of New England" (1674), MHS Colls. 1 1st ser. (1792):7–12.

25. W. Vernon Kinietz, The Indians of the Western Great Lakes, 1615–1760 (Occasional Contributors of the Museum of Anthropology, University of Michigan, no. 10, 1940), p. 167, as quoted by A. Irving Hallowell, "Some Psychological Characteristics of the Northeastern Indians," in "Man in Northeastern North America," ed. Frederick Johnson, Papers of the Robert S. Peabody Foundation for Archaeology, vol. 3 p. 198.

26. "The Relation of John Verarzanus, a Florentine; of the lande by him discovered in the name of his Majestie, written in Diepe the eight of July 1524," in Richard Hakluyt, Divers Voyages Touching the Discovery of America and the Islands Adjacent, ed. John Winter Jones (London, 1850), vol. 7, p. 65.

27. William Wood, "New England's Prospect" (1631), in Morison, Founding of Harvard College, p. 77.

28. Roger Williams, A Key into the Language of America (1653), ed. John J. Teuniessen and Evelyn J. Hinz (Detroit, 1973), p. 104.

29. Wood, "New England's Prospect," pp. 100, 106.

30. Frank G. Speck, "The Family Hunting Band as the Basis of Algonquian Social Organization," American Anthropologist 17, new ser. (April–June, 1915):289–94.

31. William Cronon, Changes in the Land (New York, 1983), pp. 51, 165–70.

32. Salisbury, Manitou and Providence, p. 109.

33. Salisbury, "Conquest of the 'Savage,'" p. 167. Population figures are from Gookin, "Historical Collections of Indians in New England," pp. 7–12. The most reliable synthesis of population statistics in this area is in Salisbury, *Manitou and Providence*, pp. 22–30.

34. John Eliot, "The Day Breaking, if not the Sun-Rising of the Gospell with the Indians in New England" (1647), *MHS Colls.* 4, 3d ser. (1834).

35. *New England Company 1649–1776*, p. 116.

36. Edward Winslow, "Glorious Progress of the Gospel," *MHS Colls.* 4, 3d ser. (1834), p. 90. This was probably more like an indentured servitude, or perhaps even similar to the position of a slave. See Jennings, *Invasion of America*, p. 233.

37. The population estimate for the praying villages is in Gookin, "Historical Collections of Indians in New England," p. 87. For reassessment of Eliot see Pearce, *Savagism and Civilization*, pp. 19–35; Jennings, "Goals and Functions of Puritan Missions to the Indians," *Ethnohistory* 18 (Summer, 1971):197–212; Jennings, *Invasion of America*, pp. 233–53; Salisbury, "Red Puritans"; Salisbury, "Conquest of the 'Savage'"; Simmons, "Cultural Bias in the New England Puritans' Perception of Indians"; and Bowden and Ronda, "Introduction," *John Eliot's Indian Dialogues*.

38. Cockenoe's biographer, William Wallace Tooker, suggests that the Montauk and Massachusett were closely related, but others place Montauk in a grouping with Mohegan–Pequot and Quinnipiac. See William Wallace Tooker, *John Eliot's First Indian Teacher and Interpreter: Cockenoe-de Long Island* . . . (New York, 1896), p. 16; Carl F. Voegelin and E. W. Voegelin, "Linguistic Considerations of Northeastern North America," ed. Frederick Johnson, *Papers of the Robert S. Peabody Foundation for Archaeology*, vol. 3, p. 189.

39. Eliot to Winslow (?), December 2, 1648, in "Glorious Progress of the Gospel," p. 90.

40. Tooker, *John Eliot's First Indian Teacher*, p. 21.

41. Huntington Records, vol. 1, pp. 16, 17, as cited in ibid., p. 37.

42. Ibid., pp. 26–28.

43. See "Glorious Progress of the Gospel," p. 90.

44. See "The Day-Breaking, if not the Sun-Rising of the Gospell with the Indians in New England" (1647) *MHS Colls.* 4, 3d ser. (1834), pp. 1–23. See also Jennings, *The Invasion of America*, pp. 238–40, for a discussion of Eliot's first two meetings with the Massachusett; and Jennings, "Goals and Functions of Puritan Missions to the Indians," 203–5.

45. Henry Whitfeld, "The Light Appearing More and More toward the End of the Perfect Day . . . " (1651), in *MHS Colls.* 4, 3d ser. (1834), p. 144 (hereafter cited as "The Light Appearing").

46. Eliot to Corporation, April 28, 1651, in Henry Whitfeld, "Strength out of Weaknesse . . . " (1652), *MHS Colls.* 4, 3d ser. (1834), pp. 4–5.

47. Ibid., p. 7; Eliot to Winslow, August 20, 1651, in "Letters of the Reverend John Eliot, Apostle to the Indians, *New England Historical and Genealogical Register* 36 (1882), 292.

48. Wilson to corporation, October 17, 1651, in Whitfeld, "Strength out of Weakness," p. 17.

49. One author suggested that Montequassum died of consumption, but I found no evidence to support this. See Walter T. Meserve, "English Works of Seventeenth Century Indians," *American Quarterly* 8 (Fall 1956), 267. Meserve quoted George Ellis, *The Red Man and the White Man in North America* . . . (Boston, 1882), p. 448.

50. Hazard, *Historical Collections*, vol. 2, pp. 359–531.

51. Eliot to corporation, April 28, 1651, in Whitfeld, "Strength out of Weakness," p. 7.

52. A copy is available at the Congregational Library in Boston.

53. John Small, "Introduction" to *The Indian Primer* (1668), by John Eliot (Edinburgh, 1880), p. xxvi.

54. Neal Salisbury, "Red Puritans," p. 43.

55. On the Nipmuc, see Frank G. Speck, "A Note on the Hassenamisco Band of Nipmuc," *Massachusetts Archaeological Society Bulletin* 4 (1944); Eva L. Butler, "Some Early Indian

Basket Makers of Southern New England," in Frank G. Speck, *Eastern Algonkian Block-Stamp Decoration: A New World Original or an Acculturated Art* (Trenton, N.J., 1947), pp. 50–52; Harriet Merrifield Forbes, *The Hundredth Town, Glimpses of Life in Westborough, 1717–1817* (Boston, 1889), chap. 10.

56. Eliot recalled it as the fourth. See Eliot to Robert Boyle, July 6, 1669, in *Some Correspondence between Governor and Treasurers of the New England Company . . . to which are added the Journals of the Rev. Experience Mayhew* (London, 1896), p. 29. But Gookin, in 1674, remembered it as the third. See Eliot to Robert Boyle, Gookin, "Historical Collections of Indians in New England," p. 72.

57. See Samuel Drake, *The Book of Indians of North America* (Boston, 1844), p. 56.

58. *Massachusetts Archives*, vol. 30, p. 9; as quoted by Morison, *Founding of Harvard College*, p. 313.

59. George Parker Winship, *The Cambridge Press, 1638–1692* (Philadelphia, 1945), p. 201.

60. Commissioners to corporation, September 10, 1660, in Hazard, *Historical Collections*, vol. 2, p. 429.

61. So-named because the youngest apprentices or work-boys became so black with ink they were likened to the 'devil.' *The New English Dictionary* (Oxford, 1897), vol. 3, pt. 1, p. 284.

62. Winship, *Cambridge Press*, pp. 112–16; George Emery Littlefield, *The Early Massachusetts Press, 1638–1711*, (Boston, 1907), vol. 1, pp. 200–201.

63. John T. Winterich, *Early American Books and Printing* (Boston, 1935), p. 35.

64. See Winship, *Cambridge Press*, chap. 10.

65. Commissioners to corporation, September 10, 1660, in Hazard, *Historical Collections*, vol. 2, p. 429.

66. On Marmaduke Johnson's appointment, see Records of the Corporation for New England, April 14, 1660, in Kellaway, *New England Company*, pp. 71–72; Winship, *Cambridge Press*, pp. 205–6.

67. See Winship, *Cambridge Press*, chaps. 12 and 18.

68. The stormy life of Marmaduke Johnson is treated in Littlefield, *Early Massachusetts Press*, pp. 209–69; Winship, *Cambridge Press*, chaps. 10, 12, and 13; and Kellaway, *New England Company*, p. 1.

69. William B. Weeden, *Economic and Social History of New England*, vol. 1 (Boston, 1880), p. 274; on Benjamin Franklin's apprenticeship, see Arthur Berman Tourtellot, *Benjamin Franklin, The Shaping Genius, Boston Years* (Garden City, N.Y., 1977), pp. 204, 214.

70. See Drake, *Book of the Indians of North America*, p. 56.

71. Increase Mather, July 8, 1676, as quoted in ibid. On the Nipmuc who returned with James, see Speck, "A Note on the Hassenamisco Band of Nipmuc," p. 53. *The Diary of Samuel Sewall*, ed. M. Halsey Thomas (1676; repr. New York, 1973), vol. 1, p. 18.

72. Daniel Gookin, "An Historical Account of the Doings and Sufferings of the Christian Indians in New England" (1677), *Transactions and Collections of the American Antiquarian Society*, vol. 2 (1836), p. 444.

73. Eliot to Robert Boyle, March 15, 1682/83, in *Life of the Honourable Robert Boyle*, Appendix to Robert Boyle, *Works*, ed. Thomas Birch (Darmstadt, 1965), vol. 1, p. ccviii.

74. Winship, *Cambridge Press*, pp. 355–56.

75. Tourtellot, *Benjamin Franklin*, p. 205.

76. Drake, *Book of the Indians*, vol. 2, p. 57. See also the Grindal Rawson–Samuel Danforth trip of 1698, attached to Nicholas Noyes, in *New England's Duty and Interest* (Boston, 1698), p. 98.

77. John Clyde Oswald, *Printing in America* (New York, 1968), p. 72.

78. J. Hammond Trumbull, "The Indian Tongue and Its Literature as Fashioned by Eliot and Others," in *The Memorial History of Boston*, ed. Justin Winsor (Boston, 1881), vol. 1, pp. 476–477.

79. The date of James Printer's death has not been verified, but he had died by 1714–15, when Samuel Sewall, secretary for the Boston Commissioners of the New England Company, recorded a payment of £1 for "the Widow Printer and the Widow Unkalolet's sister." See George Parker Winship, "Samuel Sewall and the New England Company," MHS *Proceedings* 67 (1945), 82.

80. Speck, "A Note on the Hassenamisco Band of Nipmuc," p. 31. Speck also points out that descendants of James bearing the name of Printer lived in the Grafton area into the early nineteenth century. In the 1940s, there were still descendants in the area, but they no longer bore the name of Printer (p. 54).

81. Speck, *Eastern Algonkian Block-Stamp Decoration*, p. 30. For another dimension of the impact of printing on Indians, see James Axtell, "The Power of Print in the Eastern Woodlands," *WMQ* 44, 3d ser. (April 1987):300–309.

82. The best history of Martha's Vineyard is Charles Edward Banks, *History of Martha's Vineyard*, 3 vols. (Edgartown, Mass., 1966); see also Lloyd C. M. Hare, *Thomas Mayhew, Patriarch to the Indians* (New York, 1932).

83. Matthew Mayhew, "A Brief Narrative of the Success which the Gospel hath had among the Indians on Martha's Vineyard . . . , " in Mather, *Magnalia Christi Americana*, vol. 2, p. 427 (hereafter cited as "A Brief Narrative").

84. Banks, *Martha's Vineyard*, vol. 1, p. 32.

85. Matthew Mayhew, "A Brief Narrative," p. 424.

86. Mather, *Magnalia Christi Americana*, vol. 2, pp. 430, 432.

87. Thomas Mayhew, Jr., to Henry Whitfeld, September 7, 1650, in Whitfeld, "The Light Appearing," p. 109.

88. Experience Mayhew, *Indian Narratives of Pious Indian Chiefs, and Others of Martha's Vineyard* (1735; Boston, 1829), p. 9.

89. Mayhew, Jr., to Whitfeld, September 7, 1650, in Whitfeld, "The Light Appearing," p. 109.

90. Ibid., p. 116.

91. William S. Simmons, "Conversion from Indian to Puritan," p. 208.

92. Gookin, "Historical Collections of Indians in New England," p. 21.

93. Banks, *Martha's Vineyard*, vol. 1, pp. 240–41; Eliot, "A Brief Narrative of the Progress of the Gospel amongst the Indians in New-England in the Year 1670" (1671; Boston, 1868), p. 4.

94. Salisbury, "Conquest of the 'Savage,'" pp. 172–73; Simmons, "Conversion from Indian to Puritan," pp. 215, 217; Jennings, *Invasion of America*, pp. 230–32. See Ronda, "Generations of Faith: The Christian Indians of Martha's Vineyard."

95. Eliot to Reverend Jonathan Hanmer, July 19, 1652, in *John Eliot and the Indians, Being Letters addressed to Jonathan Hanmer of Barnstaple, England*, ed. Wilberforce Eames (New York, 1915), p. 7.

96. Mayhew to Whitfeld, October 16, 1651, in Whitfeld, "Strength out of Weakness," p. 31.

97. Mayhew to Corporation, October 22, 1652, in John Eliot and Thomas Mayhew, Jr., "Tears of Repentance" (1653); *MHS Colls* 4, 3d ser. (1834), p. 208; Mayhew, Jr., to Whitfeld, in Whitfeld, "The Light Appearing," p. 118; Ronda, "Generations of Faith: The Christian Indians of Martha's Vineyard," p. 392.

98. Commissioners to Mayhew, September 18, 1654, in Hazard, *Historical Collections*, vol. 2, p. 317.

99. For accounts of Folger, see Banks, *History of Martha's Vineyard*, vol. 2, pp. 67–70;

Alexander Starbuck, *The History of Nantucket* (Boston, 1924), pp. 21–22, 24–25, 52–55, 595–96, 740–41; *Dictionary of American Biography*, vol. 4 (New York, 1943), p. 488; Frederick Lewis Weiss, *The Colonial Clergy and the Colonial Churches of New England* (Lancaster, Mass., 1936), p. 86.

100. Corporation to Commissioners, April 30, 1658, in Hazard, *Historical Collections*, vol. 2, p. 390.

101. Commissioners to Corporation, September 16, 1658, in ibid., p. 391.

102. Ibid., p. 392.

103. This figure is compiled from financial records for 1658–63, in ibid., pp. 391–475.

104. Banks, *Martha's Vineyard*, vol. 2, p. 81.

105. For a sketch of Matthew Mayhew, see Banks, *Martha's Vineyard*, vol. 2, pp. 79–84.

106. Spelling of Caleb's name varies. The 1658 deed signed by his father was written "Cheeschamuck." I am using the spelling used by Caleb for the Latin address written for the New England Company in 1663. See Samuel Eliot Morison, *Harvard College in the Seventeenth Century* (Cambridge, Mass., 1936), pt. I, pp. 354–55.

107. See Speck, "Notes of the Hassenamisco Band of Nipmuc," p. 54.

108. See Banks, *Martha's Vineyard*, vol. 1, p. 39; vol. 2, p. 134.

109. Sheldon S. Cohen, *A History of Colonial Education, 1607–1776* (New York, 1974), p. 66.

110. *Publications of Colonial Society of Massachusetts Collections* 31 (1935), p. 329.

111. Commissioners to Thomas Mayhew, September 16, 1658, in Hazard, *Historical Collections*, vol. 2, p. 398.

112. Lawrence A. Cremin, *American Education: The Colonial Experience* (New York, 1970), p. 186; Morison, *Harvard College in the Seventeenth Century*, pt. I, p. 334 n.

113. Lucius Robinson Paige, *History of Cambridge, Massachusetts, 1630–1877* (Boston, 1877), p. 366.

114. Ibid., p. 373.

115. John Leverett to Henry Newman, Leverett Saltonstall MSS, as quoted in Samuel Eliot Morison, *The Intellectual Life of Colonial New England* (1936; repr., Ithaca, N.Y., 1961), p. 102.

116. Cotton Mather, *Corderius Americanus, An Essay upon the Good Education of Children . . .* (Boston, 1708), p. 28.

117. Commissioners to Edward Winslow, September 24, 1653, in Hazard, *Historical Collections*, vol. 2, p. 299; see also Kellaway, *New England Company*, pp. 109–11.

118. A sometime teacher at Natick, Sassamon's divided loyalties apparently led to his murder, which, in turn, lighted the fuse for King Philip's War. See William J. Miller, *Notes Concerning the Wampanoag Tribe of Indians* (Providence, 1880), p. 62; Morison, *Harvard College in the Seventeenth Century*, pt. I, pp. 352–53.

119. Meeting of Commissioners, September 23, 1654, in Hazard, *Historical Collections*, vol. 2, p. 321.

120. By at least 1667, and possibly earlier, two Indian schoolmasters taught at Mashpee under the supervision of the Reverend Richard Bourne, missionary there from 1670 until his death in 1682. Bourne's granddaughter, Remember, later married Experience Mayhew, thus cementing two missionary families. See Gookin, "Historical Collections of the Indians of New England," p. 51; Weiss, *Colonial Clergy*, pp. 36–37; Paul Brodeur, "A Reporter at Large, The Mashpee," *New Yorker* 54 (October 30, 1978):62–250. See also Norman Earl Tannis, "Education in John Eliot's Indian Utopia, 1646–1675," *History of Education Quarterly* 10 (Fall 1970), 318.

121. Richard Walden Hale, Jr., *Tercentenary History of the Roxbury Latin School, 1645–1945* (Cambridge, Mass., 1946), pp. 16, 26, 28.

122. Meeting of Commissioners, September 19 (?), 1657, in Hazard, *Historical Collec-*

tions, vol. 2, p. 379. Morison estimated that Corlet and Weld taught a total of twenty Indian pupils. See *Harvard College in the Seventeenth Century*, pt. 1, p. 353.

123. See accounts for these years in Hazard, *Historical Collections*, vol. 2 (1656–72), pp. 359–531.

124. Commissioners to Corporation, September 28, 1658, in ibid., p. 395; Meeting of Commissioners, September 15, 1656, in ibid., p. 356.

125. Gookin, "Historical Collections of Indians in New England," pp. 53–54.

126. Elijah Corlet and Charles Chauncy, September 6, 1659, as quoted by John Eliot, *A Further Account of the Progress of the Gospel amongst the Indians in New England . . .* (London, 1660), pp. 77–78.

127. Charles Chauncy to Robert Boyle, October 2, 1684, in *Some Correspondence between Governors and Treasurers of the New England Company*, p. 10.

128. Goodkin, "Historical Collections of Indians in New England," p. 53.

129. On Wampas, see Commissioners to Robert Boyle, September 10, 1668, in ibid., p. 21. Morison gives the most detailed description of these two students in *Harvard College in the Seventeenth Century*, pt. I, pp. 356–57.

130. Speck, "A Note on the Hassenamisco Band of Nipmuc," p. 49.

CHAPTER 5

1. Evelyn Adams, *American Indian Education* (New York, 1946), p. 17; Harold Morris, "A History of Indian Education in the United States" (Ph.D. diss., Oregon State University, 1954), p. 24.

2. Hugh T. Lefler and William S. Powell, *Colonial North Carolina, A History* (New York, 1973), p. 32.

3. Verner W. Crane, *The Southern Frontier, 1670–1732* (Ann Arbor, 1959; 1929), p. 110.

4. Ibid., p. 108.

5. Ibid., chap. 2. See also Charles Hudson, *The Southeastern Indians* (Knoxville, Tennessee, 1976), pp. 435–36; and David H. Corkran, *The Creek Frontier, 1540–1783* (Norman, Okla., 1967), pp. 3–7.

6. Crane, *Southern Frontier*, p. 38.

7. Dr. Bray was rector of St. Botolph, Without, Aldgate; see ibid., p. 304. For Bray's strong influence on the church societies formed in this period, see Benjamin Kirkman Gray, *A History of English Philanthropy* (New York, 1967), pp. 87–89, 91–96, 175.

8. John Calam, *Parsons and Pedagogues: The SPG Adventure in American Education* (New York, 1971). On the SPG in the American colonies, see: David Humphreys, *An Historical Account of the Incorporated Society for the Propagation of the Gospel in Foreign Parts* (New York, 1969; 1728); C. F. Pascoe, *Two Hundred Years of the S.P.G.: An Historical Account of the Society for the Propagation of the Gospel in Foreign Parts, 1701–1900* (London, 1901); William Wilson Manross, *A History of the American Episcopal Church* (New York, 1950), pp. 46–64, and passim; Carson I. A. Ritchie, *Frontier Parish* (Cranbury, N.J., 1976); Frank J. Klingberg, ed., *The Carolina Chronicle of Dr. Francis Le Jau, 1706–1717* (Berkeley and Los Angeles, 1956).

9. Brenda Hough, "The Archives of the Society for the Propagation of the Gospel," *Historical Magazine of the Protestant Episcopal Church* 46 (September 1977), 310.

10. Everts B. Greene, "The Anglican Outlook on the American Colonies in the Early Eighteenth Century," *AHR* 20 (October 1914), 72.

11. SPG, Letters Received, A II, no. 22, as quoted by Greene in ibid., p. 73.

12. Ritchie, *Frontier Parish*, p. 89.

13. Pascoe, *Two Hundred Years of the SPG*, p. 38.

14. Lawrence A. Cremin, *American Education: The Colonial Experience, 1607–1783* (New York, 1970), p. 342; see also John Calam, *Parsons and Pedagogues: The SPG Adventure in American Education.*

15. Ibid., p. 120.

16. John R. Swanton, "Indians of the Southeastern United States," *BAE Bulletin*, no. 137 (Washington, D.C., 1946), p. 129.

17. For Spanish population estimate, see ibid., p. 210. Crane discusses the Yamasee settlements on the Carolina frontier in *Southern Frontier*, pp. 162–65.

18. Swanton, ibid, pp. 104–5; Hudson, *Southeastern Indians*, pp. 23, 435, 478, 480, 496.

19. On the Presbyterian among the Cherokee, see Samuel C. Williams, "An Account of the Presbyterian Mission to the Cherokees, 1757–1758," *Tennessee Historical Magazine* 1, 2d ser. (1951):125–38; A. Mark Conrad, "The Cherokee Mission of Virginia Presbyterians," *Journal of Presbyterian History* 58 (Spring 1980).

20. Michael D. Green, *The Politics of Indian Removal, Creek Government and Society in Crisis* (Lincoln, Nebr., 1982), p. 192. In a discussion of the Muskogee themselves, John Swanton has suggested that "this process of aggregation . . . had been operating through a much longer period and had brought extraneous elements in even earlier." Swanton, "Early History of the Creek Indians and Their Neighbors," *BAE Bulletin* 73 (Washington, D.C., 1922), 215.

21. Swanton, "Indians of the Southeastern United States," p. 199.

22. Crane, *Southern Frontier*, pp. 5–6. On the Yuchi, see also Swanton, "Indians of the Southeastern United States," pp. 212–15; Hudson, *Southeastern Indians*, p. 24.

23. Crane, *Southern Frontier*, pp. 19–20; Swanton, "Indians of the Southeastern United States," pp. 184, 213.

24. Le Jau to the Secretary, May 10, 1715, in Frank J. Klingberg, ed., *The Carolina Chronicle of Francis Le Jau, 1706–1717* (Berkeley and Los Angeles, 1956), p. 152.

25. Le Jau to John Chamberlayne, August 22, 1715, microfilm, p. 43, Series C, South Carolina, Records of the Society for the Propagation of the Gospel in Foreign Parts, Manuscript Division, Library of Congress (hereafter cited as SPG LC). On the reaction of ministers to the war, see also Edgar Lee Pennington, "The South Carolina Indian War of 1715, As Seen by the Clergymen," *Carolina Historical and Genealogical Magazine* 32, no. 4 (October 1931):251–269.

26. Klingberg, *Carolina Chronicle of Dr. Francis Le Jau*, p. 188.

27. Pennington, "South Carolina Indian War of 1718 . . . ," p. 267.

28. Klingberg, *Carolina Chronicle of Dr. Francis Le Jau*, p. 202. The peace between South Carolina and the Creek was finally concluded near the end of 1717, but even then it was an uncertain agreement. See Crane, *Southern Frontier*, p. 184.

29. Pennington, "South Carolina Indian War of 1715," p. 267.

30. Marion Eugene Sirmans, *Colonial South Carolina, A Political History: 1663–1763* (Chapel Hill, 1966), pp. 114–15.

31. Klingberg, *Carolina Chronicle of Dr. Francis Le Jau*, p. 202.

32. Ibid., p. 170.

33. Ibid., p. 41.

34. Pascoe, *Two Hundred Years of the SPG*, p. 13.

35. Ibid., p. 13. J. Leitch Wright contends that the Yamasee villages were "almost as populous and as safe during Queene Anne's War as ever, though considering all the wartime rumors Thomas may not have believed this." *The Only Land They Knew: The Tragic Story of the American Indians in the Old South* (New York and London, 1981), p. 192.

36. Report by Governor Nathaniel Johnson to the royal government in Frank J. Klingberg, *Carolina Chronicle, The Papers of Commissary Gideon Johnston, 1707–1716*, University of California Publications in History, vol. 35 (Berkeley and Los Angeles, 1946), p. 173.

37. John Norris to Sir John Philips, January 13, 1711, as quoted by Frank J. Klingberg in "Early Attempts at Indian Education in South Carolina, A Documentary," *South Carolina Historical Magazine* 61 (1960), 5.

38. Ibid.

39. Norris to John Chamberlayne, March 20, 1711, as quoted in ibid., p. 6.

40. Le Jau to Secretary, September 5, 1711, as quoted in *Carolina Chronicle of Dr. Francis L. Jau,* p. 97.

41. Klingberg, "Early Attempts at Indian Education in South Carolina," p. 9.

42. Le Jau to the Secretary, January 4, 1712, in Klingberg, *Carolina Chronicle of Dr. Francis Le Jau,* p. 105.

43. Le Jau to the Secretary, May 26, 1712, in ibid., p. 114.

44. Le Jau to the Secretary, August 12, 1712, in ibid., p. 118.

45. Ibid., November 28, 1715, in ibid., p. 170.

46. Klingberg, "Early Attempts at Indian Education in South Carolina," p. 10.

47. Ibid.

48. Klingberg mentions several examples of this type of schooling in "Early Attempts at Indian Education in South Carolina," pp. 4–10. Also see Pascoe, *Two Hundred Years of the SPG,* pp. 18, 22, 47, 48, 63–66.

49. See, for example: Pascoe, *Two Hundred Years of the SPG,* p. 13; Crane, *Southern Frontier,* p. 166; Wright, *Only Land They Knew,* pp. 163–94; Klingberg, *Carolina Chronicle of Francis Le Jau,* pp. 155, 165, and passim.

50. Most of the material on Johnston is drawn from Klingberg, *Carolina Chronicle: The Papers of Commissary Gideon Johnston, 1706–1716,* pp. 4–16, 112–35, 172–76.

51. Series C, South Carolina, p. 30, SPG LC.

52. Ibid. See also Frank J. Klingberg, "The Mystery of the Lost Yamasee Prince," *South Carolina Historical Magazine* 63 (1962), 18.

53. Account by William Brooks [Prince George's third tutor], Series C, South Carolina, p. 107, SPG LC.

54. Klingberg, "Mystery of the Lost Yamasee Prince," p. 21.

55. Ibid., p. 27.

56. Ibid.

57. Le Jau to John Robertson, April 25, 1716; Klingberg, *Carolina Chronicle of Dr. Francis Le Jau,* p. 179.

58. Swanton, "Indians of the Southeastern United States," p. 210.

59. Thomas Nairne to the Reverend Edward Marston, August 20, 1705, in Klingberg, "Early Attempts at Indian Education in South Carolina," p. 3.

60. Ibid., p. 4.

61. Crane, *Southern Frontier,* p. 169.

CHAPTER 6

1. Kenneth Coleman, *Colonial Georgia, A History* (New York, 1976), pp. 22–23; Henry T. Malone, *The Episcopal Church in Georgia, 1733–1957* (Atlanta, 1960), pp. 6–7; C. F. Pascoe, *Two Hundred Years of the SPG* (London, 1901), p. 26.

2. John Wesley, *Journal,* abridged by Nehemiah Curnock (New York, 1963), p. 7.

3. Euerette–Tyerman MSS, vol. 1, NAM P11 657 A, p. 11. Methodist Archives, John Rylands University Library of Manchester, Manchester, England (hereafter cited as Euerette–Tyerman MSS, MA, JRL). For a brief biography of Delamotte, see John Naylor, *Charles Delamotte* (London. 1938).

4. Luke Tyerman, *The Oxford Methodists* (London, 1873). p. vii. On the Oxford Methodists, see also Arnold A. Dallimore, *George Whitefield* (Westchester, Ill., 1979; 1970) vol. 1,

chap. 3; and Richard P. Heizenrater, ed., *Diary of an Oxford Methodist Benjamin Ingham, 1733–1734* (Durham, North Carolina, 1985), pp. 7–11.

5. See Maldwyn Edwards, *Family Circle: A Study of the Epwourth Household in Relation to John and Charles Wesley* (London, 1961), see especially chaps. 2 and 4.

6. Tyerman, *Oxford Methodists*, p. v.

7. See Clifton E. Olmstead, *History of Religion in the United States* (Englewood Cliffs, N.J., 1960), pp. 133–36. William Warren Sweet, *Religion in Colonial America* (New York, 1943), pp. 211–12.

8. Zinzendorf's Instructions are quoted in Adelaide L. Fries, *The Moravians in Georgia, 1735–1740* (Raleigh, N.C., 1905), p. 71.

9. Fries has included portions of all four diaries. John Wesley's account can be found in Nehemiah Curnock, ed. *The Journal of the Rev. John Wesley, A.M.*, (London, 1938), vol. 1 (hereafter cited as *John Wesley's Journal*]. Ingham's journal is in the Euerette–Tyerman MSS, MA, JRL; it has also been published by Tyerman in *The Oxford Methodists*, pp. 63–80.

10. Euerette–Tyerman MSS, MA, JRL, p. 11.

11. Fries, *Moravians in Georgia*, pp. 48–50.

12. Ibid., pp. 123, 130.

13. Frank Baker, *From Wesley to Asbury: Studies in Early American Methodism* (Durham, N.C., 1976), p. 7. For a further assessment of the Georgia experience, see Frederick A. Norwood, *The Story of American Methodism* (Nashville and N.Y., 1974), pp. 25–26: William Warren Sweet, *Methodism in American History* (Nashville and N.Y., 1974). pp. 31–35; Edgar Legere Pennington, "John Wesley's Georgia Ministry," *Church History* 8 (1939):251–54; David T. Morgan, "John Wesley's Sojourn in Georgia Revisited," *Georgia Historical Quarterly* 64 (Fall. 1980):253–62.

14. Euerette–Tyerman MSS, MA, JRL, p. 7.

15. Pascoe, *Two Hundred Years of the SPG*, pp. 26–27. Upon the request of the Georgia trustees, the SPG agreed to pay John Wesley the salary of £50 formerly paid to Reverend Quincy. Originally designated as missionary to the Indians, John Wesley's position was then changed to minister at Savannah. In the Proceedings of the Trustees, John Wesley is described as "Our Minister in Savannah." See Robert G. McPherson, ed., *The Journal of the Earl of Egmont* (Athens, Georgia, 1962), pp. 114, 120, 124, 306. However, Wesley commented later, when asked if the Trustees appointed him to be minister of Savannah, "I replied. They did; but it was not done by my solicitation; it was done without either my desire or my knowledge." *John Wesley's Journal*, vol. 1, p. 298.

16. Euerette–Tyerman MSS, MA, JRL, p. 18.

17. This population figure is borrowed from David H. Corkran, *The Creek Frontier, 1540–1783* (Norman, Okla., 1967), p. 82. Swanton's estimates are more conservative. He suggests that when Yamacraw was settled in 1730, it included seventeen or eighteen families and thirty or forty men. John R. Swanton, "Early History of the Creek Indians and Their Neighbors," *BAE Bulletin*, no. 137 (Washington, D.C., 1946), p. 108. During Tomochichi's visit to England in 1734, the Earl of Egmont reported the Yamacraw population as "not above 50 fighting men." See *Journal of the Earl of Egmont*, p. 57.

18. Recalling the settlement of Apalachicola, a group of Lower Creek who had lived fifty miles upriver from Yamacraw before the Yamasee War, Swanton suggests that Tomochichi may have "belonged to some refugee Yamasee among the Apalachicola." Swanton, "Early History of the Creek Indians and Their Neighbors," pp. 109, 131. Since this group migrated to the Chatahoochee after the Yamasee War, they may well have been those banished in 1728, including Tomochichi and his followers. On Tomochichi, see also Charles Colcock Jones, Jr., *Historical Sketch of Tumo-Chi-Chi. Mico of the Yamacraws* (Albany, N.Y., 1868).

19. Ibid., pp. 108–9. Verner Winston Crane, *The Southern Frontier, 1670–1732* (Ann Arbor, 1959), pp. 270–72; Corkran, *Creek Frontier*, pp. 82–83.

20. For biographical background on Mary Musgrove, I have relied on: E. Merton Coulter, "Mary Musgrove, 'Queen of the Creeks': A Chapter of Early Georgia Troubles," *Georgia Historical Quarterly*, 11 (March, 1927):2–3.

21. Coulter, "Mary Musgrove, Queen of the Creeks," p. 3.

22. Samuel Eveleigh to the Trustees, April 6, 1733, as quoted in Mills Lane, ed., *General Oglethorpe's Georgia: Colonial Letters. 1733–1743*, (Savannah, 1975), vol. 1, p. 12.

23. Coulter, "Mary Musgrove, Queen of the Creeks," p. 2.

24. Cockran points out that the South Carolina assembly alerted Johnny Musgrove as to Oglethorpe's arrival, and that he and Mary were thus prepared for the encounter. *Creek Frontier*, p. 83.

25. "Oglethorpe's Treaty with the Lower Creek Indians," *Georgia Historical Quarterly*, 4 (1920): 13.

26. For an assessment of Oglethorpe's Indian policy, see Phinizy Spalding, *Oglethorpe in America* (Chicago, 1977), chap. 6.

27. Ibid., pp. 78–79.

28. *Journal of the Earl of Egmont*, pp. 61–62. The visit is also described in Corkran, *Creek Frontier*, pp. 85–88; T. R. Reese, "A Red Indian's Visit to Eighteenth-Century England," *History Today* 4 (May 1954):334–37. A perceptive analysis of the visit is by Spalding, *Oglethorpe and the Indians*, pp. 80–83. A detailed account can be found in Jones, *Historical Sketch of Tomo-Chi-Chi*, pp. 54–72.

29. Oglethorpe to Samuel Wesley, December 25, 1734, as quoted in *Henry Newman's Salzburger Letter Books*, trans. by George Fenwick Jones (Athens, 1966), pp. 519–20.

30. Both John Wesley and Ingham had studied shorthand, and each recorded a variation of their impressions of the visit. See *John Wesley's Journal*, vol. 1, pp. 159–61; Euerette–Tyerman MSS, MA, JRL, pp. 19.

31. Euorette–Tyerman MSS, MA, JRL, p. 17.

32. Ibid., p. 19.

33. *John Wesley's Journal*, vol. 1, p. 159.

34. Ibid., pp. 168, 180. It is unclear whether John Wesley includes the Moravians when he speaks of the house Oglethorpe promised to build for "us." Also see Fries, *Moravians in Georgia*, p. 131.

35. Coulter, "Mary Musgrove, Queen of the Creeks," pp. 3–4.

36. Euerette–Tyerman MSS, MA, JRL, p. 24. In April, Ingham expressed an interest in going as missionary to the Cherokee. He invited Seifert and one other Moravians to join him and Wesley. The Moravians hesitated, and Oglethorpe objected, so the plan disintegrated. See Fries, *Moravians in Georgia*, p. 149. In June, Wesley broached to Oglethorpe the idea of going to the Cherokee. Oglethorpe objected, "Not only the danger of being intercepted or being killed by the French there; but much more the inexpediency of leaving Savannah destitute of a minister" (*John Wesley's Journal*, vol. 1, pp. 238, 239).

37. See Fries, *Moravians in Georgia*, p. 150.

38. *John Wesley's Journal*, vol. 1, p. 242.

39. Euerette–Tyerman, MSS, MA, JRL, p. 24.

40. *John Wesley's Journal*, vol. 1, p. 237. For a discussion of Oglethorpe's meetings with the Chickasaw and Creek delegation in the summer of 1736, see Spalding, *Oglethorpe in America*, pp. 86–88.

41. *John Wesley's Journal*, vol. 1, p. 250. Wesley wrote of this dialogue to the Trustees; see *Journal of the Earl of Egmont*, pp. 177–78. During their visit, the Chickasaw told Oglethorpe that they were being surrounded by the French, and he provided them with powder and shot. See Spalding, *Oglethorpe in America*, pp. 87–88.

42. Fries, *Moravians in Georgia*, p. 144.

43. Benjamin Ingham to Sir John Phillips, September 15, 1736, as quoted in Lane, *General Oglethorpe's Georgia*, p. 278.

44. Ibid. Fries quotes a document from the Herrnhut Archives that suggests it was "on an island in the Savannah River which was occupied by the Creeks" (*Moravians in Georgia*, p. 152). By the 1730s the Irene site had become an "internment island." During high tides and seasonal floods, it was surrounded by water. See Joseph Caldwell and Catherine McCann, *Irene Mound Site, Chatham County, Georgia* (Athens, Ga., 1941).

45. See Hudson, *Southeastern Indians*, pp. 327–36. During the Great Depression, WPA funding enabled archaeologists to excavate the site between 1937 and 1940. They discovered that the large mound consisted of eight superimposed mounds. Adjacent to this large mound—the school site itself—they located a burial mound, a mortuary structure, a rotunda or winter council house, and several other small buildings. In historic times the Creek used the rotunda, which was an important feature of their public grounds. The archaeologists postulated that the people of Irene may have been Guale Indians, who spoke a language somewhat different from the Yamasee but were later identified with them, or with Cusabo, who lived just north of the Savannah River. Fries also argues that the schoolhouse was built on a burial mound. See *Moravians in Georgia*, pp. 152–53. John Wesley suggested the site of Irene was named after the first ship that brought settlers, which is puzzling, since the earliest ship of 1733 that carried Oglethorpe and the others was the *Ann(e)*. See *John Wesley's Journal*, p. 405. See also Caldwell and McCann, *Irene Mound Site*, pp. 3, 8–37 and passim, 73; Swanton, "Early History of the Creek Indians," pp. 94–95, 128.

46. Ingham to Sir John Phillips, September 15, 1736, p. 279. Also found in Allen D. Gendler, et al., eds., *The Colonial Records of the State of Georgia* (Atlanta, 1904–16), vol. 21, p. 222 (hereafter cited as *CRSG*).

47. Ingham to Phillips, September 15, 1736, p. 279; *CRSG*, vol. 21, p. 223. George H. Loskiel argues that the Moravians were the motivating group in the school at Irene, but this refutes the primary sources on the subject. See George Henry Loskiel, *History of the Mission of the United Brethren among Indians in North America* (London, 1794), pp. 3–4. For a more favorable opinion of Ingham, see Fries, *Moravians in Georgia*, p. 144.

48. *John Wesley's Journal*, vol. 1, p. 244.

49. Ingham to Phillips, p. 279; *CRSG*, vol. 21, p. 223. The comment attributed to Tomochichi can be found in Jones, *Historical Sketch of Tomo-Chi-Chi*, p. 96. Jones, however, cites no source.

50. *John Wesley's Journal*, vol. 1, pp. 297–98.

51. In the fall of 1737, Anton Seifert and Bohner moved to the Yamacraw village where they improved their command of Muskogee and began missionary work. In January, Peter and Catherine Rose and their infant daughter joined them there. The Moravians wanted to leave a few of their number in Georgia to serve as missionaries to the Indians, but the trustees stipulated that any Moravian missionaries also had to be citizens. Since they could not comply with the military service required for citizenry, they saw they could not remain. Probably late in 1738, ill health had forced Seifert to return to Savannah. In January 1739 the Rose family also returned. In October 1739, Tomochichi died and further efforts of schoolmasters at Irene died with him. Fries, *Moravians in Georgia*, pp. 154–55, 185–87, 213–14.

52. *John Wesley's Journal*, vol. 1, pp. 320–21.

53. Tyerman, *Oxford Methodists*, p. 86.

54. *John Wesley's Journal*, vol. 1, p. 400.

55. Ibid., p. 418.

56. Ibid., p. 422.

57. For a description of the funeral of Tomochichi, see Spalding, *Oglethorpe in America*, p. 93. After the death of the old *mico*, Samuel Wesley (older brother) wrote an ode in his honor, which appeared in *The Gentleman's Magazine*, vol. 9 (1739), 21. See Leslie F.

Church, *Oglethorpe: A Study of Philanthropy in England and Georgia* (London, 1932), p. 116.

58. Charles C. Jones argues that Toonahowi died fighting the Yamasee, but it is likely that both the Yamasee and the Spanish were involved. See *Historical Sketch of Tomo-Chi-Chi*, p. 108. Swanton, "Indians of the Southeastern United States," p. 210.

59. Tyerman, *Oxford Methodists*, p. 83.

60. Thaddeus Mason Harris, *Biographical Memoirs of James Oglethorpe* (Boston, 1841), p. 177.

CHAPTER 7

1. These names represent only a small number of employees of the Company. George Parker Winship, "Samuel Sewall and the New England Company," MHS *Proceedings* 68 (1945), pp. 78–110.

2. William Kellaway, *The New England Company, 1649–1776* (London, 1961), p. 173.

3. Ibid., p. 174.

4. Winship, "Samuel Sewall and the New England Company," p. 90.

5. On Larnell, see Cotton Mather to William Ashurst, June 1, 1714, in Kenneth Silverman, ed., *Selected Letters of Cotton Mather* (Baton Rouge, 1971), p. 151; and Samuel Sewall, *Diary of Samuel Sewall*, ed. M. Halsey Thomas (New York, 1973), vol. 2, pp. 651–52, 763. On Larnell and Peabody, see Kellaway, *New England Company*, pp. 231, 237–39. On Peabody, see William Biglow, *History of the Town of Natick, Massachusetts* (Boston, 1830), pp. 53–58.

6. Increase Mather to Ashurst, January 20, 1697, in *Some Correspondence between Governor and Treasurers of the New England Company . . . to which are added the Journals of the Rev. Experience Mayhew in 1713 and 1714* (London, 1896), pp. 80–81 (hereafter cited *New England Company Correspondence*). See also Kellaway, *The New England Company*, pp. 201–03.

7. *Diary of Samuel Sewall*, vol. 1, p. 415. On the new appointments, see also WA to Gentlemen, London, 8 March 1698–99, "Letter Book of the New England Company, 1688–1761," University of Virginia Microfilm Publication, no. 8, p. 25 (hereafter cited as New England Company Letterbook, VMP). See also Winship, "Samuel Sewall and the New England Company," p. 62.

8. Cotton Mather, *Diary of Cotton Mather*, Worthington Chauncey Ford (New York, 1957), vol. 1, p. 304. On Mather's stormy relationship with the London officers of the company, see New England Company Letterbook pp. 55–56. Mather offered to resign in 1702–3, 1713, 1721–22, and 1724.

9. James Hammond Trumbull, "The Indian Tongue and Its Literature as Fashioned by Eliot and Others," in Trumbull, *The Memorial History of Boston*, 4 vols., ed. Justin Winsor (Boston, 1881), vol. 1, p. 430.

10. This was the Company's sole attempt at publishing in Iroquois. A sixteen-page instruction booklet, it appeared in Iroquois, Latin, and Dutch. See Kellaway, *New England Company*, pp. 149–50.

11. Ibid., pp. 156–57. For Mayhew's description of the need for Bibles, see *A Brief Account of the State of the Indians on Martha's Vineyard . . . 1694–1720* (Boston, 1720), pp. 8–10.

12. Increase Mather, et al., to Sir William Ashurst, March 2, 1705/06 New England Company Correspondence, p. 84.

13. A later survey was made by Nathan Prince in 1725, but the report on this survey has not been found. See Kellaway, *New England Company*, p. 234. However, Prince's *Some*

Account of those English Ministers who have successfully presided over . . . the Indians on Martha's Vineyard and the adjacent Islands (appended to Experience Mayhew, Indian Converts . . .) was printed in London in 1725.

14. The Reverend Mr. Grindal Rawsom . . . and the Reverend Mr. Samuel Danforth . . . May 30 to June 24, 1698, in viewing the several Plantations of Indians, within this Province, attached to Nicholas Noyes, New England's Duty and Interest (Boston, 1698), p. 99 (hereafter cited as Rawson–Danforth Report). Descriptions of Rawson and Danforth are in ibid., pp. 233–34.

15. Sewall gave Japhet "two Arabian pieces gold . . . to buy corn." Diary of Samuel Sewall, vol. 2, p. 465.

16. The commissioners' observations on the Mohegan and Narragansett are in Increase Mather, Cotton Mather, Nehemiah Walker, A Letter about the Present State of Christianity among the Indians (Boston, 1705), p. 13. For further background on Japhet, see Rawson–Danforth Report, pp. 91, 93; and Winship, Samuel Sewall and the New England Company, p. 90. Sewall recorded payments made to "Japheth" by the New England Company between 1708 and 1712–13. However, the latter citation was a payment of £12 made to his widow.

17. Kellaway, New England Company, p. 251.

18. Ashurst to ? (unreadable), May 12, 1707, New England Company Letter Book, VMP, p. 81.

19. Diary of Cotton Mather, vol. 2, p. 133. Harold Clayton Bradshaw notes that Mather himself sent two missionaries to the Mohegans and their neighbors, but with little effect. Bradshaw, The Indians of Connecticut (Deep River, Conn., 1935), p. 554.

20. Cotton Mather (probably) to Sir William Ashurst, December 10, 1712, in Silverman, Selected Letters of Cotton Mather, p. 128.

21. On Mayhew's contributions, see Charles Edward Banks, The History of Martha's Vineyard, Dukes County, Massachusetts (Edgartown, Mass., 1966), vol. 1, pp. 249, 253.

22. Journals of the Rev. Experience Mayhew, p. 99.

23. Ibid., p. 102.

24. Ibid., p. 103.

25. Ibid., p. 127.

26. Ibid.

27. Ibid., p. 114.

28. Ibid., p. 120.

29. Kellaway, New England Company, p. 251.

30. Charles J. Hoadly, ed., The Public Records of the Colony of Connecticut (Hartford, 1850–90), vol. 6, pp. 31–32.

31. Ibid. Also see W. DeLoss Love, Samson Occom and the Christian Indians of New England (Boston, 1899), p. 27 (hereafter cited as Occom and the Christian Indians.)

32. Journals of the Rev. Experience Mayhew, p. 121.

33. For a biographical sketch of Fitch, see Frederick Lewis Weiss, The Colonial Clergy and the Colonial Churches of New England (Lancaster, Mass., 1936), p. 85 (hereafter cited Colonial Clergy of New England).

34. Eliot to Commissioners, September 4, 1671, in "Letters of John Eliot the Apostle," MHS Proceedings 27 (1879–80), p. 248.

35. Francis Mainwaring Caulkins, History of Norwich, Connecticut, from its possession by the Indians to the year 1866 (Hartford, Conn., 1866), pp. 105–15.

36. Journals of the Rev. Experience Mayhew, p. 120.

37. Ibid.

38. Ibid., p. 109.

39. On Adams's life, see Colonial Clergy of New England, p. 17.

40. On Mason's school, see Kellaway, *New England Company*, pp. 253–55; Harold Blodgett, *Samson Occum* (Hanover, N.H., 1935), p. 25.

41. Mason also budgeted "27 blankets for the Councellours & other Chiefs or such as send their Children." Kellaway, *New England Company*, p. 253. Indian trade goods information is from Wilbur R. Jacobs, *Wilderness Politics and Indian Gifts: The Northern Colonial Frontier, 1748–1763* (Lincoln: University of Nebraska Press, 1967; 1950), pp. 49, 69.

42. Kellaway, *New England Company*, pp. 253–54.

43. On the trip to England, see ibid., p. 255; John W. DeForest, *History of the Indians of Connecticut from the Earliest Known Period to 1850* (Hartford, Conn., 1852), p. 323 (hereafter cited as *History of the Indians of Connecticut*.) The Rev. Isaac Watts met Mason and recorded his impressions in a letter to the Rev. Benjamin Colman of Boston, September 13, 1736; see "Letters of Dr. Watts," MHS *Proceedings* 9, 2d ser. (1895), pp. 348–355.

44. James Dow McCallum, ed., *The Letters of Eleazar Wheelock's Indians* (Hanover, N.H., 1932), p. 13.

45. Ibid., p. 256. The information on Farmington is drawn from Kellaway and Love, *Occom and the Christian Indians*, p. 202. On the Indians of this general area, see Samuel Orcutt, *The Indians of the Housatonic and Naugatuck Valleys* (Hartford, Conn., 1882; Stratford reprint 1972), pp. 7–10, 48–49; and DeForest, *History of the Indians of Connecticut*, pp. 360–76.

46. On David Jewitt, see McCallum, *Letters of Eleazar Wheelock*, pp. 13, 37. For a sketch of Jacob Johnson, see Kellaway, *New England Company*, pp. 256–57.

CHAPTER 8

1. Edwin Scott Gaustad, *The Great Awakening in New England* (Chicago, 1968), pp. 2–3.

2. *Diary of Cotton Mather*, vol. 2, p. 804.

3. When Sewall lodged John Neesnummin of Natick in his home, the MHS editors noted the unusual nature of this action. "[I]n his, gentle kindness of spirit and humanity of righteousness, [Sewall] proved himself far in advance of his contemporaries in his sympathies with negroes and Indians." *Diary of Samuel Sewall*, vol. 2, p. 586. Sewall published the first antislavery tract in America in 1700: Samuel Sewall, *The Selling of Joseph, A Memorial*, ed. Sidney Kaplan (Amherst, Mass., 1969; 1700).

4. For sources on Occom's background, I have relied on Love, *Occom and the Christian Indians*, pp. 21–22, and Blodgett, *Samson Occom*, pp. 27–28.

5. Samson Occom, "Diary," vol. 1, p. 82, in Dartmouth College Archives (hereafter cited as DCA).

6. Jewitt served as minister of the North Parish, New London, 1739–83. For further sources on Jewitt, see Frances Mainwaring Caulkins, *History of New London, Connecticut, 1612–1852* (Hartford, Conn., 1852), p. 434; Blodgett, *Samson Occom*, pp. 78–79, 82, and passim; and Leon Burr Richardson, *An Indian Preacher in England* (Hanover, N.H., 1933), pp. 23, 28–31.

7. Jonathan Edwards, *The Works of President Edwards, in Four Volumes* (New York, 1843), p. 328, as cited in Gaustad, *Great Awakening in New England*, p. 15.

8. A contemporary description quoted in Harry S. Stout and Peter Onuf, "James Davenport and the Great Awakening in New London," *JAH* 70 (December 1983), 559.

9. Ibid., pp. 560–61.

10. Ibid., p. 557.

11. For Davenport's confession and retractions, see Alan Heimert and Perry Miller, eds., *The Great Awakening* (Indianapolis and New York, 1967), pp. 257–62.

12. Occom, "Diary," vol. 1, p. 83. William Simmons suggests that the Great Awakening appealed to the New England Algonquians because it "most resembled their ancestral Indian religion. See Simmons, "Narragansett Conversion in the Great Awakening," *American Ethnologist* 10 (1983), 266–267.

13. Occom, "Diary," p. 84.

14. The earliest biography of Wheelock is David McClure and Elijah Parish, *Memoirs of the Rev. Eleazar Wheelock* (Newburyport, Mass., 1811). The description quoted is in James Dow McCallum, *Eleazar Wheelock, Founder of Dartmouth College* (Hanover, N.H., 1939), p. 7.

15. Gaustad, *Great Awakening*, p. 45.

16. McCallum, *Eleazar Wheelock*, p. 15.

17. Gaustad, *Great Awakening*, p. 45.

18. Occom, "Diary," vol. 1, p. 84.

19. Occom signed his name; most of the others affixed their "mark." Mohegan Councillors to General Assembly, Indians, Series I, I, 247, in Connecticut State Archives (hereafter cited as CA).

20. John W. DeForest, *History of the Indians of Connecticut from the Earliest Known Period to 1850* (Hartford, Conn., 1852), p. 346.

21. Blodgett, *Samson Occom*, p. 36.

22. *Diary of Joshua Hempstead of New London, Connecticut* (New London, 1901), p. 447; Caulkins, *History of New London*, p. 321.

23. Samuel Buell, *The Excellence and Importance of the Saving Knowledge of the Lord Jesus Christ . . . A Sermon . . . at the Ordination of Mr. Samson Occom* (New York, 1761), as quoted in Caulkins, *History of New London*, p. 35.

24. See, for example, another Mohegan plea for the General Assembly, May 8, 1745, Indians, Series I, I, 256b, CA.

25. See Love, *Occom and the Christian Indians*, p. 40.

26. Wheelock to Occom, September 6, 1749, file 749506, DCA.

27. Wheelock to Col. Henchman and the Boston Commissioners, February 5, 1756, file 756190, DCA.

28. According to a 1741 census, they numbered only 34 families or 162 persons. Blodgett, *Samson Occom*, p. 38.

29. On the salary issue, see ibid., pp. 40–44; Occom, "Diary," vol. 1, p. 91; Love, *Occom and the Christian Indians*, p. 45. On his supporters, much correspondence is available in the Dartmouth College archives. See, for example, Benjamin Pomeroy to Solomon Williams, July 14, 1751, file 751424, DCA. On Occom's ordination as a Presbyterian minister see Occom, "Diary," vol. 1, p. 19, DCA.

30. Eleazar Wheelock, *A Plain and Faithful Narrative of the Original Design, Rise, Progress and Present State of the Indian Charity School in Lebanon* (Boston, 1763; repr. Rochester, n.d.), p. 29 (hereafter cited as Wheelock *Narratives*, 1763).

31. On this theme, see Love, *Occom and the Christian Indians*, p. 56; McClure and Parish, *Memoirs of the Rev. Eleazar Wheelock*, p. 15.

32. Joseph Mortimer Levering, *A History of Bethlehem, Pennsylvania, 1741–1892* (New York, 1971; 1903).

33. Paul A. W. Wallace, *Conrad Weiser, 1696–1760, Friend of Colonist and Mohawk* (Philadelphia and London, 1945), p. 117.

34. Charles Hartshorn Maxson, *The Great Awakening in the Middle Colonies* (Gloucester, Mass., 1958), pp. 80–83.

35. John Joseph Stout, "Count Zinzendorf and the Pennsylvania Congregation of God in the Spirit," *Church History* 9 (1940), 376.

36. See Harold Clayton Bradshaw, *The Indians of Connecticut . . .* (Deep River, Conn.,

1935), pp. 46–50; William M. Beauchamp, ed., *Moravian Journals Relating to Central New York, 1745–66* (Syracuse, 1916), pp. 3–17; Glenn Weaver, "The Moravians during the French and Indian War," *Church History* 24 (1955), 243.

37. The tract of land for Nazareth was purchased from George Whitefield. For details on this event, see Arnold A. Dallimore, *George Whitefield*, (Westchester, Ill., 1980), vol. 1, pp. 503–8.

38. On Zeisberger's arrival in Georgia, see Adelaide Fries, *The Moravians in Georgia, 1735–1740* (Raleigh, N.C., 1905), pp. 188–89.

39. Marie J. Kohnova, "The Moravians and Their Missionaries, A Problem in Americanization," *Mississippi Valley Historical Review* 19 (December 1932), 359. For a biography of Zeisberger, see Edmund De Schweinitz, *The Life and Times of David Zeisberger* (Philadelphia, 1871).

40. For a representative list of these statutes and rules, which is located in the Moravian Archives (Bethlehem, Pa.), see Kenneth G. Hamilton, "Cultural Contributions of Moravian Missions among the Indians," *Pennsylvania History* 18 (January 1951), 12–13. See also David Zeisberger, *Diary of David Zeisberger, A Moravian Missionary among the Indians of Ohio*, ed. and trans. Eugene F. Bliss (Cincinnati, 1885), vol. 1, pp. xxviii, xxix.

41. Kohnova, "Moravians and Their Missionaries," 357.

42. Ibid., 359; Hamilton, "Cultural Contributions of Moravian Missions," 6–7; Elma E. Gray, *Wilderness Christians* (Ithaca, N.Y., 1956), pp. 27–28.

43. Kohnova, "Moravians and Their Missionaries," 359.

44. Gaustad, *Great Awakening in New England*, p. 17.

45. On the Mahican, see Allen W. Trelease, *Indian Affairs in Colonial New York: The Seventeenth Century* (Ithaca, N.Y., 1960), pp. 46–48, 129–30, 157–58, and passim; T. J. Brasser, "Mahican," in *Handbook of North American Indians, Northeast*, vol. 15, ed. Bruce G. Trigger (Washington, D.C., 1978), pp. 198–212; Douglas Edward Leach, *The Northern Colonial Frontier, 1607–1763* (New York, 1966), p. 97; T. J. Brasser, *Riding on the Frontier's Crest: Mahican Indian Culture* (Ottawa, 1974), p. 2; and a critique of Brasser by Ives Goddard in *Ethnohistory* 22 (Spring 1975):185–87. Goddard suggests that some of the early Housatonic Indians probably came from Paugusset and other groups of western Connecticut, rather than from the Mahican. For support of this theme, see Samuel Orcutt, *The Indians of the Housatonic and Naugatuck Valleys* (Hartford, Conn., 1882; repr., 1972), p. 35. The name Muhhakaneok is found in Electa Fidelia Jones, *Stockbridge, Past and Present* (Springfield, Mass., 1854), p. 14; and in Brasser, "Mahican," 211.

46. Samuel Hopkins, *Historical Memoir Relating to the Housatonic Indians* (Boston, 1753; repr., 1912), p. 3 (hereafter cited as *Historical Memoir*).

47. Hopkins planned to make the journey, but he was forced to remain home because of illness. Hopkins, *Historical Memoir*, p. 4. The choice of Williams was appropriate. During one of many raids on Deerfield, Indians from Canada had taken him captive at age eleven. He was not returned for almost two years. Williams later studied for the ministry at Harvard and ministered at Longmeadow for the remainder of his life. William B. Sprague, *Annals of the American Pulpit*, I (New York, 1969; 1866), pp. 284–88. On the initiation of the mission, also see William Kellaway, *New England Company, 1649–1776*, pp. 270–71.

48. For an overview of Stockbridge, see Sarah Cabot Sedgwick and Christina Sedgwick Marquand, *Stockbridge, 1739–1974* (Stockbridge, Mass., 1974). See also Jones, *Stockbridge*, pp. 76–77; Love, *Occom and the Christian Indians*, p. 236.

49. Hopkins, *Historical Memoir*, pp. 3, 5. See also Jones, *Stockbridge*, p. 41.

50. John Sergeant's Journal, quoted in Hopkins, *Historical Memoirs*, p. 8.

51. Sergeant's Journal, quoted in Jones, *Stockbridge*, p. 41.

52. For the sketch of the Muhhakaneok, I have relied on Jones, *Stockbridge*, pp. 15–20; and Hopkins, *Historical Memoir*, p. iii. Another version of these people's past can be found

in a reminiscence by Wannuaucon in J. W. Davidson, *Muh-he-ka-ne-ok, A History of the Stockbridge Nation* (Milwaukee, Wisc., 1893), pp. vii–ix, 16. See also Brasser, "Mahican," pp. 198–200, 206.

53. James Russell Trumbull, "The Indian Tongue and Its Literature," in Justin Winsor, ed., *The Memorial History of Boston* (Boston, 1881), p. 480. See also Jonathan Edwards, *Observations on the Language of the Muhhekaneew Indians* (New Haven, Conn., 1783) and Davidson, *Muh-he-ka-ne-ok*, p. 6.

54. Sergeant to the Indians, December 19, 1734, as quoted in Jones, *Stockbridge*, p. 45. Full letter is in Hopkins, *Historical Memoir*, p. 33.

55. See Sedgwick and Marquand, *Stockbridge*, pp. 22–23; Love, *Samson Occom and the Christian Indians*, p. 236; and Richard Davenport Birdsall, *Berkshire County: A Cultural History* (New Haven, Conn., 1959), p. 37.

56. On the boarding school see: Davidson, *Muh-he-ka-ne-ok*, pp. 7, 9–10; Sedgwick and Marquand, *Stockbridge*, pp. 27–28, 35–39, and passim; Hopkins, *Historical Memoirs*, pp. 73–76, and passim; Benjamin Colman to John Sergeant, August 11, 1743, in John Sergeant, *A Letter from the Rev. Mr. Sergeant of Stockbridge to Dr. Colman of Boston* (Lancaster, Pa., 1929; 1743), pp. 10–16.

57. Davidson, *Muh-he-ka-ne-ok*, p. 12.

58. Morgan recounts the Stiles episode in Edmund S. Morgan, *The Gentle Puritan: A Life of Ezra Stiles, 1727–1795* (New Haven, Conn., 1962), pp. 79–89.

59. Edwards to Rev. Timothy Edwards, January 27, 1752, Folder 1752, B no. 2, Jonathan Edwards Transcripts, Hills Library, Andover Newton Theological School, Newton Centre, Mass. (hereafter cited as JE, HL, ANTS).

60. Edwards to Secretary Willard, July 17, 1752, folder 1752-D, in ibid.

61. Edwards to John Erskine, November 23, 1752, folder 1752-D, in ibid.

62. Gideon Hawley served briefly as a missionary among the Iroquois, but was forced to withdraw because of the war. Ordained in 1754 after he left Stockbridge, he was appointed later as missionary to the Indians at Mashpee, where he remained for the rest of his life (1727–1807). See Sprague, *Annals of the American Pulpit*, vol. 1, pp. 497–99. See also Gideon Hawley papers, Congregational Library, Boston (hereafter cited as Hawley papers, CL).

63. See Edwards Transcripts, HL, ANTS.

64. Hawley to unknown correspondent, October 10, 1753, Hawley papers, CL.

65. Thomas Brainerd, *The Life of John Brainerd* (Philadelphia, 1865), p. 77.

66. Sedgwick and Marquand, *Stockbridge*, p. 34.

67. See David Brainerd's Journal, in Edward Parsons and Edward Williams, *The Works of President Edwards in Eight Volumes*, (New York, 1968 [1817]), vol. 8, pp. 436–64.

68. Brainerd, *Life of John Brainerd*, pp. 51–54.

69. Ibid., pp. 348, 404.

70. Hawley to unknown correspondent, June 13, 1753, Hawley papers, CL.

71. Brainerd to a friend in England, October 4, 1752, in Brainerd, *The Life of John Brainerd*, p. 255.

72. Ibid.

73. Ibid., p. 268.

74. On Wooley, see Brainerd to Wheelock, December 17, 1757, in ibid., p. 299.

75. In 1832, Bartholomew signed the claim against New Jersey as agent for this group of Delaware. The state awarded the New Jersey tribe two thousand dollars. See ibid., pp. 415–17. On the migration and establishment of the Wisconsin community, see C. A. Weslager, *The Delaware Indian Westward Migration* (Wallingford, Pa., 1978), pp. 10, 15–16. Weslager points out that the Stockbridge–Munsee Community of Wisconsin has achieved tribal recognition by the federal government. On the Stockbridge–Munsee in the recent century, see Brasser, "Mahican," pp. 210–11.

CHAPTER 9

1. "[A] memorandum of the things Meriam has had. . . , " file 000050, Dartmouth College Archives (hereafter cited as DCA). As a source for terminology of eighteenth-century fashions, see Mary Brooks Picken, *The Fashion Dictionary* (New York, 1939).

2. Frederick Chase, *History of Dartmouth College and the Town of Hanover, New Hampshire (to 1815)* (Brattleboro, 1928).

3. W. DeLoss Love, *Samson Occom and the Christian Indians of New England* (Boston, 1899), pp. 21–41; Blodgett, *Samson Occom*, pp. 17–35; Richardson, *An Indian Preacher in England*, pp. 70–71; Occom, "Diary," I, DCA.

4. Wheelock *Narratives*, p. 82.

5. Franklin Bowditch Dexter, ed., *The Literary Diary of Ezra Stiles*, vol. 3 (New York, 1901), p. 338.

6. Wheelock, *Narratives*, 1763, pp. 10, 13.

7. Ibid., p. 11.

8. Wheelock to General Thomas Gage, February 22, 1764, file 764172.2, DCA.

9. Wheelock to George Whitefield, November 11, 1765, file 765611, DCA. The Wheelock–Whitefield correspondence reveals an unusual relationship, one of revivalist enthusiasm tempered by an acute business awareness.

10. Wheelock, *Narratives*, 1763, p. 15.

11. Ibid., p. 17.

12. On Wheelock and the SSPCK, see *An Account of the Society in Scotland for Propagating Christian Knowledge* (Edinburgh, 1774), pp. 16–17.

13. *A Continuation of the Narrative of the State, &c, of the Indian Charity-School, at Lebanon, In Connecticut . . .* (Boston, 1765); *A Brief Narrative of the Indian Charity-School, in Lebanon in Connecticut, New England* (London, 1766); *A Brief Narrative of the Indian Charity-School, in Lebanon in Connecticut, New England* (London, 1767); *A Continuation of the Narrative of the Indian Charity-School in Lebanon . . .* (London, 1769); *A Continuation of the Narrative of the Indian Charity-School, in Lebanon, in Connecticut; From the Year 1768 to the Incorportion of It with Dartmouth-College, etc.* (Hartford, 1771); *A Continuation of the Narrative of the Indian Charity-School, etc.* (Portsmouth, N.H., 1773); *A Continuation of the Narrative of the Indian Charity-School, etc.* (Hartford, 1773); *A Continuation of the Narrative of the Indian Charity-School, etc.* (Hartford, 1775).

14. John Sergeant to Benjamin Colman, May 6, 1743, "Dr. Colman's Return," August 22, 1743, in *A Letter From the Rev'd Mr. Sergeant of Stockbridge to Dr. Colman of Boston . . .* (1743); repr., Lancaster, Pa., 1929, p. 15. On John Sergeant, see Samuel Hopkins, *Historical Memoirs Relating to the Housatonic Indians* (Boston, 1753); Edmund S. Morgan, *The Gentle Puritan: A Life of Ezra Stiles, 1727–1795* (New Haven, Conn., 1962), pp. 78–89; and Sarah Cabot Sedgwick and Christina Sedgwick Marquand, *Stockbridge, 1739–1974* (Stockbridge, Mass., 1974), pp. 1–52.

15. John Brainerd succeeded his brother, David Brainerd. See Jonathan Edwards, ed., *The Life and Diary of David Brainerd* (Chicago, 1949), and Thomas Brainerd, *The Life of John Brainerd* (Philadelphia, 1865).

16. John Brainerd to Ebenezer Pemberton, August 20, 1751, in Thomas Brainerd, *Life of John Brainerd*, pp. 247–49.

17. Enrollment figures for Indian pupils at the school vary. A conservative estimate, including both boys and girls, is about sixty. Wheelock's own figures were much higher.

18. Thomas Moody, *Women's Education in the United States*, vol. 1 (New York, 1929), p. 129. For a discussion on education for women in colonial New England, see Edmund S. Morgan, *The Puritan Family* (New York, 1966); Robert Middlekauff, *Ancients and Axioms: Secondary Education in Eighteenth-Century New England* (New Haven and Lon-

don, 1963), pp. 103–9; Walter Herbert Small, *Early New England Schools* (Boston and London, 1914; repr., New York, 1969), pp. 162–86, 275–89; Sheldon S. Cohen, *A History of Colonial Education, 1607–1776* (New York, 1974), pp. 67–69, 101–3; John Demos, *A Little Commonwealth: Family Life in Plymouth Colony* (New York, 1970), pp. 120–22, 142, 183–84; James Axtell, *The School upon a Hill* (New York, 1976), pp. 59–60, 116–18, 175, 178–79.

19. On Indian slavery, see Henry C. Dorr, "The Narragansetts," in *Collections of the Rhode Island Historical Society* 7 (1885), 233; James P. Ronda, "Red and White at the Bench: Indians and the Law in Plymouth County, 1680–1691," *Essex Institute Historical Collections* 110 (1974):200–215.

20. Wheelock, *Narratives*, 1763, p. 34.

21. Wheelock to Sir William Johnson, December 11, 1761, file 761661 DCA.

22. Wheelock, *Narratives*, 1763, p. 34.

23. Jonathan Mitchell, *Nehamiah on the Wall in Troublesome Times* (Cambridge, 1671), p. 6, as quoted in Morgan, *Puritan Family*, 20.

24. Wheelock, *Narratives*, 1763, p. 34.

25. John Norton, *Abel Being Dead Yet Speaketh* (London, 1658), p. 9, as quoted in Morgan, *Puritan Family*, 66.

26. Wheelock to Andrew Oliver [Treasurer of the Boston Board of the New England Company], October 15, 1760, file 760565 DCA. Wheelock, *Narratives*, 1763, p. 15.

27. Hannah Nonesuch Confession, March 11, 1768, file 768211.1, DCA.

28. Miram's family name, like the names of many of Wheelock's students, was spelled several ways. I have chosen the spelling used by the students themselves.

29. For a description of the Delaware in New Jersey at this time, see Clinton A. Weslager, *The Delaware Indians: A History* (New Brunswick, N.J., 1972), pp. 261–81; Anthony F. C. Wallace, *King of the Delawares: Teedyuscung, 1700–1763* (Philadelphia, 1949), pp. 1–17; Edward Jacob Fisher, *New Jersey as a Royal Province, 1738–1776* (New York, 1967), pp. 330–32, 348–51; Brainerd, *Life of John Brainerd*, pp. 118, 246–48, 255–56, 370–73; William W. Newcomb, Jr., "The Culture and Acculturation of the Delaware Indians," *Anthropological Papers*, no. 10 (Ann Arbor, 1965), 84–97. From Newcomb's description (pp. 5–9), I have tentatively concluded that the Delaware brought together by the Brainerds were a combination of the Unami and Unalachtigo groups.

30. John Brainerd to Wheelock, September 14, 1761, in Brainerd, *Life of John Brainerd*, p. 332.

31. Wheelock to Dennys de Berdt, November 16, 1761, file 761616, DCA. De Berdt was a friend to the school and a frequent correspondent of Wheelock. See Albert Matthews, ed., *Letters of Dennys De Berdt, 1757–1770* (Freeport, N.Y., 1971).

32. For the girls, Wheelock noted that "Expence for their Education will be but Little more than their Cloathing" (*Narratives*, 1763, p. 42). For his own records, he "charged for the Girls but 4d. per Week, i.e. for one Day's Schooling and Dinner" (ibid., p. 46). In his "payments on account" from February 1766 to March 8, 1768, he recorded an expenditure of approximately 55 pounds for his female students, compared with about 434 pounds for his male students (ibid., 1769, p. 132).

33. Wheelock to Sir William Johnson, December 11, 1761, file 761661, DCA.

34. Elizabeth Huntingdon to Wheelock, February 21, 1766, file 766171, DCA.

35. Cotton Mather, *Cares about the Nurseries* (Boston, 1702), p. 34, as quoted in Morgan, *Puritan Family*, p. 89.

36. Wheelock to Andrew Gifford, February 24, 1763, in McCallum, *Letters*, p. 70.

37. Hezekiah Calvin to Wheelock, June 10, 1767, in ibid., 55.

38. Storrs to Wheelock, New York, n.d., file 768624, DCA.

39. Brainerd to Wheelock, February 3, 1769, in Brainerd, *Life of John Brainerd*, p. 382.

40. Brainerd to Wheelock, June 22, 1769, in ibid., p. 383.

41. Brainerd to Wheelock, December 25, 1772, in ibid., p. 396.

42. For information on Pequot survivors, see Howard Bradstreet, "The Story of the War with the Pequots Re-Told," *Tercentenary Commission for the State of Connecticut* 5 (New Haven, 1933), 27, 29–30; Dorothy Deming, "The Settlement of the Connecticut Towns," *Tercentenary Commission for the State of Connecticut* 6 (New Haven, 1933), 18, 37; Mathias Spies, "The Indians of Connecticut," *Tercentenary Commission for the State of Connecticut* 9 (New Haven, 1933), 6–7; Samuel Hugh Brockunier, *The Irrepressible Democrat: Roger Williams* (New York, 1940), pp. 99–100, 101; Frances M. Caulkins, *History of New London* (Hartford, Conn., 1852), p. 30; Frank G. Speck, "Native Tribes and Dialects of Connecticut," *BAE Annual Report*, No. 43 (Washington, D.C., 1928), pp. 207–8, 212–13; Jennings, *Invasion of America*, pp. 254–81; William S. Simmons, "Red Yankees: Narragansett Conversion in the Great Awakening," *American Ethnologist* 10 (1983):253–61.

43. For accounts of the Narragansett in the eighteenth century, see: Henry C. Dorr, "The Narragansetts," 135–237; Ethel Boissevain, *The Narragansett People* (Phoenix, 1975); Ethel Boissevain, "Narragansett Survival: A Study of Group Persistence through Adapted Traits," *Ethnohistory* 6 (Summer 1959), 347–62; Howard Chapin, *Sachems of the Narragansetts* (Providence, 1931); John W. DeForest, *History of the Indians of Connecticut from the Earliest Known Period to 1850* (Hartford, 1853); "Journals of the Rev. Experience Mayhew in 1713 and 1714," in *Some Correspondence between the Governors . . . of the New England Company and the Commissioners . . . in America* (London, 1896), pp. 98–127. Also essential to an understanding of the Narragansett is Roger Williams, *A Key into the Language of America*, ed. John J. Teunissen and Evelyn J. Hinz (Detroit, 1973).

44. Joseph Woolley to Wheelock, August 17 (probably 1764), in James Dow McCallum, *The Letters of Eleazar Wheeler's Indians* (Hanover, N.H., 1932), p. 270.

45. David Fowler to Wheelock, May 2, 1765, file 765302.2, DCA. Amy Johnson was the sister of Joseph Johnson, who was already at the school; and these two young people may have been the children of a Joseph Johnson, member of the Mohegan tribal council with Samson Occom. Indians, series 1, vol. 2, 35, CA.

46. Fowler to Wheelock, June 15, 1765, file 765365, DCA.

47. In this letter, the word "get" is crossed out and replaced with "pick." Fowler to Wheelock, May 13, 1766, file 766313.1, DCA.

48. One of the reasons why so much of the Wheelock correspondence has survived is because of Wheelock's habit of making copies in his own shorthand. This letter is an example. Wheelock to Fowler, August 26, 1766, file 766476.1, DCA.

49. Fowler to Wheelock, December 2, 1766, file 766652.2, DCA.

50. For accounts of the Brothertown settlement, see Love, *Occom and the Christian Indians*, pp. 247–315; Blodgett, *Samson Occom*, pp. 172–214; Occom, "Diary," 2, 3, DCA.

51. Wheelock to Brainerd, July 8, 1767, file 767408.1, DCA.

52. Calvin to Wheelock, March, 1768, in McCallum, *Letters*, pp. 62–63.

53. John Secutor to Wheelock, March 31, 1767, in ibid., pp. 53–54.

54. Mary Secutor to Wheelock, November 16, 1768, file 768616, DCA.

55. Mary's first confession, in McCallum, *Letters*, pp. 236–37; Mary's second confession, March 11, 1768, file 768211.2, DCA.

56. Secutor to Wheelock, November 16, 1768, file 768616, DCA.

57. Wheelock, *Narratives*, 1771, p. 20.

58. Sarah Simon's mother sent five children to Wheelock. Of these five, Abraham and Daniel were the only Indian pupils who moved from Lebanon to Hanover with Wheelock. Daniel graduated from Dartmouth in 1777; during the American Revolution, he was a teacher and preacher at Stockbridge (see Indians, series 1, vol. 2, 226, CA); he eventually succeeded John Brainerd as missionary to the Delaware in New Jersey. Abraham taught

school at Groton, Connecticut; after the revolution he became one of the original trustees at Brothertown.

59. John Adams to Abigail Adams, August 28, 1774, Lyman Butterfield, et al., eds., *The Book of Abigail and John, Selected Letters of the Adams Family, 1762–1784* (Cambridge, Mass., 1975), p. 69.

60. Wheelock, *Narratives*, 1763, p. 25.

61. Boissevain, *Narragansett People*, p. 57; Wallace, *King of the Delawares: Teedyuscung*, p. 16.

62. John Brainerd, "To his Friend in England," October 4, 1752, in Brainerd, *Life of John Brainerd*, p. 256; Wheelock *Narratives*, 1771, pp. 15–23.

63. Wheelock to Whitefield, July 4, 1761, file 761404, DCA; Occom, "Diary," 82–92, DCA.

64. Edward Deake to Wheelock, June 21, 1768, 76371.2, DCA; Deake to Wheelock, August 18, 1768, 768268.5, DCA.

65. David Crosby to Wheelock, November 4, 1767, 767604.1, DCA.

66. Caulkins, *History of New London*, p. 429.

67. Wheelock to Mrs. Symons, June 27, 1768, in McCallum, *Letters*, pp. 225–26.

CHAPTER 10

1. Wheelock. *Narrative*, 1763, pp. 19–20.

2. Ibid., p. 20.

3. Ibid., p. 21.

4. Ibid., p. 26.

5. Wheelock to William Johnson, April 30, 1762, file 762280.2, DCA.

6. Wheelock. *Narrative*, 1763, pp. 16, 17, 27.

7. William Johnson to Wheelock, August 8, 1765, file 765458.1, DCA. A copy of this letter is in *The Papers of William Johnson*, vol. 4 (Albany, N.Y., 1925), pp. 812–14.

8. On William Johnson, the SPG, and Indian schooling, see John Wolfe Lydekker, *The Faithful Mohawks* (Long Island, N.Y., 1968), p. 115; *Papers of William Johnson*, vol. 4, pp. 236, 383, 388–91, and passim.

9. On Wheelock's search for sites and the founding of Dartmouth, see: James Dow McCallum, *Eleazar Wheelock* (Hanover, N.H., 1939), chapter 11; James Axtell, "Dr. Wheelock's Little Red School," in James Axtell, *The European and the Indian* (New York, 1981), pp. 106–9; Jere B. Daniell, "Eleazar Wheelock and the Dartmouth College Charter" (Hanover, N.H., 1969).

10. On the Wheelock–Kirkland dispute, see *The Journals of Samuel Kirkland*, ed. Walter Pilkington (Clinton, N.Y., 1980), p. 41; McCallum, *Letters*, p. 92; Kirkland–Wheelock correspondence, DCA; correspondence files, 1769–73, Samuel Kirkland Papers, Hamilton College Library (hereafter cited as SKP-HCL).

11. On Mundius, see "Tagawaron Speaker," in "Speech to Chiefs of the Oneida Tribe," February 24, 1772, in February 1772 folder, correspondence, SKP-HCL; on Abraham, a Mohawk schoolmaster, see Wheelock to Kirkland, February 26, 1772, in SKP-HCL.

12. Of the twenty-four Iroquois pupils who attended the school in Lebanon between 1761 and 1769, twelve stayed less than a year (six of these were at the school less than three months); one stayed a year; six remained for two years; three remained for three years; and two were there for four years. See McCallum, *Letters*, pp. 293–96, which gives the arrival dates and some of the departure dates.

13. Eleazar Wheelock, *A Continuation of the Narrative of . . . the Indian Charity-School, at Lebanon . . . From Nov. 27, 1762 to Sept. 3d, 1765* (Boston, 1765), p. 17.

14. Hezekiah Calvin to Wheelock, August 11, 1766, file 766461.2, DCA; Joseph Wooley to Wheelock, July 16, 1765, file 765440.2, DCA.

15. Lydekker, *Faithful Mohawks*, p. 55. On the SPG and the Mohawk, see also: Lydekker, *The Life and Letters of Charles Inglis* (London, 1936), pp. 91–134; Frank J. Klingberg, *Anglican Humanitarianism in Colonial New York* (Philadelphia, 1940), pp. 52–120; Francis E. Wakely, "Mission Activity among the Iroquois, 1642–1719," *Rochester History* 38 (October 1976), 15–19.

16. Milton W. Hamilton, *Sir William Johnson, Colonial American, 1715–1763* (Port Washington, N.Y., 1976), chap. 24; Milton W. Hamilton, "Sir William Johnson: Interpreter of the Iroquois," *Ethnohistory* 10 (Summer 1963):270–86.

17. See Hamilton, *Sir William Johnson*, chap. 25.

18. On the SSPCK, see *Society in Scotland for Propagating Christian Knowledge, An Account of, From its Commencement in 1709* (Edinburgh, 1774).

19. On Peter's return to the Oneida, see Titus Smith to Wheelock, August 3, 1765, file 765453.1, DCA.

20. Wheelock, *A Brief Narrative of the Indian Charity School* (1766; repr., Rochester, n.d.), p. 30.

21. Wheelock, *Narrative*, 1765, p. 8.

22. Wheelock to Whitefield, May 4, 1765, file 765304, DCA.

23. The Narragansett Simon family illustrates the importance of familial ties. Between 1763 and 1769, widow Sarah Simon sent five children to the school; two graduated from Dartmouth College; most settled in the Brothertown community in New York. W. DeLoss Love, *Samson Occom and the Christian Indians of New England* (Syracuse: Syracuse University Press, 2000 [1899]), 71–72, passim.

24. Wheelock, *Narrative*, 1763, p. 39. For the most recent biography of Brant see: Isabel Thompson Kelsey, *Joseph Brant, 1743–1807, Man of Two Worlds* (Syracuse, 1984).

25. Wheelock to William Johnson, April 29, 1765, file 765279.1, DCA.

26. McCallum gives a short biographical sketch of Fowler in *Letters*, p. 85.

27. David Fowler to Wheelock, May 29, 1765, file 765329.2, DCA.

28. David Fowler to Wheelock, June 24, 1765, file 765374.2, DCA.

29. Wheelock, *Narrative*, 1765, pp. 17–18.

30. Wheelock, *A Continuation of the Narrative of the Indian Charity School . . . From the Year 1768, to the Incorporation of it with Dartmouth-College . . .* (1771; repr., Rochester, n.d.), p. 23.

31. Wheelock, *Narrative*, 1763, p. 33.

32. Fowler to Wheelock, December 2, 1766, file 766167.1, DCA.

33. Fowler to Wheelock, September 23, 1765, file 765523.5, DCA.

34. Fowler to Wheelock, January 21, 1766, file 766121.2, DCA.

35. See McCallum, *Eleazar Wheelock*, p. 85.

36. The shortage of supplies necessitated additional trips to Lebanon. Fowler returned for provisions in the late summer of 1765, but by January 1766 he was in such need that he appealed to William Johnson, who made arrangements for Fowler to receive provisions from the "Royal Block House." Fowler to Wheelock, January 21, 1766, file 766121.2, DCA.

37. Fowler to Wheelock, February 17, 1766, file 766167.1, DCA. Canowaroghere was an Oneida town, and should not be confused with Canajoharie, one of the principal Mohawk settlements near Johnson Hall.

38. Hezekiah Calvin to Wheelock, August 11, 1766, file 766461.2, DCA.

39. Joseph Wooley to Samuel Kirkland, February 11, 1765, in March 31, 1765 entry in *The Journals of Samuel Kirkland*, ed. Walter Pilkington (Clinton, N.Y., 1980), p. 17.

40. Fowler to Wheelock, June 15, 1765, file 765565, DCA.

41. "Books that David Fowler carried into the Mohawk Country from the Liebery [sic] to

distribute among the Boys that are keeping School there, & for himself," file 768900.2, DCA.

42. Fowler to Wheelock, June 24, 1765, DCA.

43. Ibid.

44. Jacob Fowler to Wheelock, November 28, 1766, file 766628.1, DCA.

45. Wooley to Wheelock, July 6, 1766, in McCallum, *Letters,* p. 268.

46. David Avery to Wheelock, June 6, 1771, reel 8, David Avery Papers, Princeton Theological Seminary (hereafter cited as DAP-PTS). Original letter is in file 771356, DCA.

47. Fowler to Wheelock, February 17, 1766, file 766167.1, DCA.

48. Amy Johnson enrolled at the school in 1761 and left in 1766, the same year that her brother Joseph became Fowler's assistant at Oneida. When Fowler courted her, she was employed at Captain Bull's tavern, the "Bunch of Grapes," in Hartford. See Fowler to Amy Johnson, May 2, 1765, file 765302.2, DCA.

49. Wheelock, *Narrative,* 1763, p. 15.

50. Fowler to Wheelock, June 15, 1765, DCA.

51. On Fowler's marriage to Hannah Garret, see Wheelock, *Narrative,* 1767, p. 58.

52. Joseph Johnson to Wheelock, December 1, 1766, file 766651.3, DCA; see also Wheelock to William Johnson, July 4, 1766, file 766404, DCA.

53. Wheelock, *Narrative,* 1763, p. 18.

54. Fowler to Wheelock, December 2, 1766, file 766662.2, DCA.

55. The Kirkland–Fowler analysis is based on the following sources: their correspondence with Wheelock in the Dartmouth College Archives; the Samuel Kirkland Papers, Hamilton College Library, Clinton, New York (see especially 1768 folder—Correspondence files); McCallum, *Letters,* pp. 85–113; Pilkington, *Journals of Samuel Kirkland,* p. 40.

56. March 31, 1765 entry in Pilkington, *Journals of Samuel Kirkland,* p. 19.

57. David Fowler to Wheelock, March 17, 1767; McCallum, *Letters,* pp. 108–9.

58. See 1770–71 correspondence between David Avery and Wheelock, reel 8, DAP-PTS.

59. Fowler to Wheelock, February 26, 1767, file 767176.3, DCA.

60. Fowler to Wheelock, May 28, 1767, McCallum, *Letters,* p. 110.

61. In the spring of 1765, the Montauk had asked Wheelock to send David Fowler to "keep a School" for their children. Indians of Long Island to Wheelock, March 4, 1765, file 765204, DCA.

62. Fowler's return to Montauk is noted in Wheelock, *A Continuation of the Narrative . . .* (1769; repr.: Rochester, n.d.), p. 30.

63. The following spring, Wheelock wrote to the Reverend Nathaniel Whitaker (who was in Britain with Occom): "I have nothing new to [blurred] excepting the Death of My dear Joseph Wooley . . . his death is much lamented by the Indians . . . " (April 5, 1766, file 766255, DCA).

64. Wheelock to Whitaker, February 12, 1766, file 766162, DCA.

65. Calvin to Wheelock, February 19, 1766, file 766169, DCA.

66. Calvin's family was both Christianized and educated, but his experiences at Moor's School and among the Mohawk turned him away from teaching. Although he eventually returned to his people, as of 1772, he had not accepted the position of schoolmaster. John Brainerd to Wheelock, December 25, 1772, in Thomas Brainerd, *The Life of John Brainerd,* p. 295.

67. Calvin to Wheelock, August 14, 1767, McCallum, *Letters,* p. 58.

68. Samuel Johnson to David Avery, October 27, 1766, reel 8, DAP, p. 85.

69. Calvin to Wheelock, August 14, 1767, in McCallum, *Letters,* p. 58.

70. Samuel Johnson to David Avery, October 27, 1766, reel 8, DAP-PTS.

71. Joseph Johnson to Wheelock, February 10, 1768, file 768160, DCA.

72. Ibid. "Samps" was "coarsely ground Indian corn; also a kind of porridge made from

it," according to McCallum, *Letters*, p. 130. It was also mixed with berries or meat. See Arthur C. Parker, "Iroquois Uses of Maize and Other Food Plants," in *Parker on the Iroquois*, ed. William N. Fenton (Syracuse, N.Y., 1968), p. 75.

73. The Reverend Jacob Johnson, Wheelock's representative at the treaty negotiations, virtually destroyed Wheelock's standing with Sir William Johnson and the Iroquois. See correspondence between Avery and Wheelock of October, 1768, and Jacob Johnson and Wheelock of October and November 1768, in DCA.

74. Joseph Johnson to Wheelock, May 2, 1768, file 768302, DCA.

75. Kirkland to Wheelock, December 29, 1768, in McCallum, *Letters*, p. 141.

76. Johnson to Wheelock, May 2, 1768.

77. The Onondaga reply to Ralph Wheelock was delivered in 1768 and is here summarized by Thomas, an Oneida, and recorded by David Avery in the final negotiations between Wheelock and the Iroquois, June, 1772. McCallum, *Letters*, p. 287.

78. Aaron Kinne to Wheelock, June 13, 1768, file 768363.1, DCA.

79. Wheelock to Kirkland, November 21, 1768, 1768 folder, correspondence files, SKP-HCL.

80. Joseph Johnson to Wheelock March (1769?), file 769240.2, DCA. See also Johnson to "Enquiring Friends," February 1772, file 792900.2, DCA.

81. Wheelock to Whitefield, April 24, 1769, file 769274.2, DCA.

82. Of the seven Algonquian schoolmasters who taught among the Iroquois, one died, two disappeared, and four returned to teach among their people of southern New England. Moreover, four additional students from Moor's School served as schoolmasters among the Algonquian. When Occom is added to this list, a total of nine students influenced by Wheelock taught among the Algonquian.

83. Love, *Samson Occom*, pp. 65–66.

84. Joseph Johnson to Wheelock, April 20, 1768, file 768270, DCA.

85. Johnson received a commission from the Boston commissioners of the New England Company for the Farmington position. These Algonquian included the Tunxis (John Mettawan's group), who had been joined by remnant families of Quinnipiac, Wangunk, and possibly Paugasuck. On the Indians of this area, see Samuel Orcutt, *The Indians of the Housatonic and Naugatuck Valleys* (1882; repr., Stratford, Conn., 1972); and Love, *Samson Occom*, p. 202.

86. Joseph Johnson to "All Enquiring Friends," ca. February 1772, file 772900.2, DCA.

87. Joseph Johnson's speech to the Oneida, January 20, 1774, in Love, *Occom*, pp. 212–13.

88. Wheelock to Occom, January 25, 1769, file 769125, DCA.

89. Wheelock to Whitefield, April 24, 1769.

90. David Fowler to Wheelock, May 25, 1768, file 768325, DCA.

91. David Avery to Wheelock, December 25, 1770, file 770675.1, DCA; Avery to Wheelock, June 6, 1771, file 771356, DCA.

92. Occom to Wheelock, July 24, 1771, in Blodgett, *Samson Occom*, p. 122.

93. For Occom's role in the contest, see: "Indians," ser. I, vol. 2, 286-a, 276-a, Connecticut State Archives, Hartford. For some clarification of this complex land issue, see Love, *Occom*, pp. 119–29.

94. Occom realized no financial relief until 1772, when his plight was finally recognized, and he began to receive some funds from both England and Scotland.

95. Occom to "Honorable Board of Correspondents," January 4, 1769, file 769104, DCA.

96. David McClure to Wheelock, May 21, 1770, file 770321, DCA.

97. See Love, *Occom*, pp. 160–62.

98. Occom to Wheelock, July 24, 1771, in Blodgett, *Occom*, p. 122.

99. Wheelock, *A Continuation of the Narrative of the Indian Charity School . . .* (1775; repr., Rochester, n.d.), p. 16.

100. Joseph Johnson speech to the Indians (Oneida), January 20, 1774, File 774120, DCA; Love, 212–213.

101. These "Brothertown" Indians were joined later by a scattering of New Jersey Delaware.

102. Wheelock described the land as fifteen or twenty miles square. Wheelock, *Narrative*, 1775, p. 16.

103. Ibid.

104. George Washington to Joseph Johnson, February 10, 1776, file 776170.1, DCA.

105. Occom, "Diary," 2, 166–67. The Algonquian who remained in southern New England and whose descendants live there today are discussed in Laura E. Conkey, Ethel Boissevain, and Ives Goddard, "Indians of Southern New England and Long Island: Late Period," *Handbook of North American Indians, Northeast,* vol. 15, ed. Bruce G. Trigger; and William S. Simmons, *Spirit of the New England Tribes* (Hanover and London, 1986).

106. Tagawaron speaker, reply to "Speech to the Chiefs of the Oneida Tribe (in the Name of Mr. Avery)," February 24, 1772, February 1772 folder, correspondence files, SKP-HCL.

107. Wheelock, *A Continuation of the Narrative of the Indian Charity School* . . . (1773; repr., Rochester, n.d.), p. 16.

CHAPTER 11

1. Samuel Orcutt, *Indians of the Housatonic and Naugatuck Valleys* (Stratford, Ct., 1972; 1872), p. 34.

BIBLIOGRAPHY

MANUSCRIPT SOURCES

Alderman Library, University of Virginia.
  Letter Book of the New England Company, 1688–1761 (microfilm).
Baker Library, Dartmouth College, Hanover, N.H.
  Eleazar Wheelock Papers.
  Samson Occom Papers.
  Records of Moor's Indian Charity School.
  Nathaniel Whitaker Papers.
Connecticut State Archives, Hartford, Conn.
Congregational Library, Boston, Mass.
  Gideon Hawley Papers.
  Correspondence of the New England Company and the Mayhew Family
Hamilton College Library, Clinton, N.Y.
  Samuel Kirkland Papers.
Hills Library, Andover-Newton Theological School, Newton Centre, Mass.
  Jonathan Edwards Transcripts
The John Rylands University Library of Manchester, Manchester, United Kingdom.
  Methodist Archives
  Euerette–Tyerman Manuscript, Vol. 1.
Library of Congress, Manuscript Division.
  Records of the Society for the Propagation of the Gospel in Foreign Parts.
Speer Library, Princeton Theological Seminary, Princeton, N.J.
  David Avery Papers.

BOOKS

An Account of the Society in Scotland for Propagating Christian Knowledge. Edinburgh:
  A. Murray and J. Cochrane, 1774.

Adair, James. The History of the American Indians, particularly those nations adjoining to the Mississippi . . . Edited by Samuel C. Williams, London: E. and C. Dilly, 1775.

Adams, Evelyn C. American Indian Education: Government Schools and Economic Progress. 1946. Reprint. New York: Arno, 1971.

Adams, Nehemiah. The Life of John Eliot: With an Account of the Early Missionary Efforts among the Indians of New England. Boston: Massachusetts Sabbath School Society, 1847.

Arber, Edward, and A. G. Bradley. Travels and Works of Captain John Smith. Vol. 2, pp. 383–984. Edinburgh: John Grant, 1910.

Ariès, Philippe. Centuries of Childhood: A Social History of Family Life. New York: Knopf, 1962.

Axtell, James. The European and the Indian: Essays in the Ethnohistory of Colonial America. New York: Oxford University Press, 1981.

———. The Invasion Within: The Contest of Cultures in Colonial North America. New York and Oxford: Oxford University Press, 1985.

———. The School upon a Hill: Education and Society in Colonial New England. New York: W. W. Norton and Co., 1976.

———, ed. The Educational Writings of John Locke. Cambridge: Cambridge University Press, 1968.

Ayling, Stanley. John Wesley. London: William Collins and Co., 1979.

Bailyn, Bernard. Education in the Forming of American Society. New York: Vintage Books, 1963.

Baker, Frank. From Wesley to Asbury: Studies in Early American Methodism. Durham, N.C.: Duke University Press, 1976.

———. John Wesley and the Church of England. London: Epworth Press, 1970.

———, ed. The Works of John Wesley, Vol. 25, Letters, I, 1721–1739. Oxford: Clarendon Press, 1980.

Banks, Charles Edward. The History of Martha's Vineyard, Dukes County, Massachusetts. 1911. Reprint. 3 vols. Edgartown, Mass.: Dukes County Historical Society, 1966.

Barbour, Philip L. Pocahontas and Her World. Boston: Houghton Mifflin Co., 1970.

———. The Three Worlds of Captain John Smith. Boston: Houghton Mifflin Co., 1964.

Beaver, R. Pierce. Church, State, and the American Indians. St. Louis: Concordia, 1966.

Bell, Sadie. The Church, the State, and Education in Virginia. Philadelphia: Science Press Printing Co., 1930.

Best, John Hardin. Benjamin Franklin on Education. New York: Bureau of Publications, Teachers College, Columbia University, 1962.

Beverly, Robert. The History and Present State of Virginia. 1705; rev., 1722. Reprint edited by Louis B. Wright. Chapel Hill: University of North Carolina Press, 1947.

Biglow, William. History of the Town of Natick, Massachusetts. Boston: Marsh, Capen, and Lyon, 1830.

Billings, Warren M., ed. The Old Dominion in the Seventeenth Century: A Documentary History of Virginia, 1606–1689. Chapel Hill: University of North Carolina Press, 1975.

Birdsall, Richard Davenport. Berkshire County: A Cultural History. New Haven, Conn.: Yale University Press, 1959.

Blodgett, Harold. Samson Occom. Hanover, N.H.: Dartmouth College, 1935.

Boissevain, Ethel. The Narragansett People. Phoenix: Indian Tribal Series, 1975.

Book for the copying of Letters & other Things Relating to ye Compª for propagating of the Gospel in New England &c, 1688. New England Company; 322 pp. Reprint. University of Virginia Library Microfilm Publications.

Boyle, Robert. The Works. Vol. 1. Edited by Thomas Birch. London: 2d ed., 1772. Reprint. Darmstadt, Germany, 1965.

Bradshaw, Harold Clayton. The Indians of Connecticut: The Effect of English Colonization and of Missionary Activity on Indian Life in Connecticut. Deep River, Conn.: New Era Press, 1935.

Brainerd, Thomas. The Life of John Brainerd. Philadelphia: Presbyterian Publication Committee, 1865.

Brasser, Ted J. Riding on the Frontier's Crest: Mahican Indian Culture. Ottawa: National Museum of Canada, 1974.

Bridenbaugh, Carl. Cities in Revolt: Urban Life in America, 1743–1776. 1955. Reprint. London, Oxford, and New York: Oxford University Press 1971.

———. The Colonial Craftsman. 1956. Reprint. Chicago: University of Chicago Press, 1961.

———. The Spirit of '76: The Growth of American Patriotism before Independence. New York: Oxford University Press, 1975.

Brinisfield, John W. Religion and Politics in Colonial South Carolina. Easley, S.C.: Southern Historical Press, 1983.

Brock, R. A., ed. The Official Records of Robert Dinwiddie, Lieutenant-Governor of the Colony of Virginia, 1751–1758. Richmond: Virginia Historical Society, new ser., 3–4, 1883–84.

Brookes, George S. Friend Anthony Benezet. Philadelphia: University of Pennsylvania Press, 1937.

Bruce, Philip Alexander. Economic History of Virginia in the Seventeenth Century. 1896. Reprint. 2 vols. New York: Johnson Reprint Co., 1966.

———. Social Life in Old Virginia, from the Institutional History of Virginia in the Seventeenth Century. 1940. Reprint. New York: Capricorn Books, 1965.

Bushman, Richard L., ed. The Great Awakening: Documents on the Revival of Religion, 1740–45. New York: Atheneum, 1970.

Butterfield, Lyman H. John Witherspoon Comes to America. Princeton, N.J.: Princeton University Library, 1953.

Byrd, William. The Secret Diary of William Byrd of Westover. Edited by Louis B. Wright and Marion Tinling. Richmond: Dietz Press, 1941.

Calam, John. Parsons and Pedagogues: The SPG Adventure in American Education. New York: Columbia University Press, 1971.

Caldwell, Joseph, and Catherine McCann. Irene Mound Site, Chatham County, Georgia. Athens: University of Georgia Press, 1941.

Candler, Allen D., et al., eds. Colonial Records of the State of Georgia. 26 vols. Atlanta: C. P. Byrd, 1904–16.

Calhoun, Arthur W. A Social History of the American Family. Vol. 3: From 1865 to 1919. New York: Barnes and Noble, 1960.

Caulkins, Frances Mainwaring. History of New London, Connecticut, 1612–1852. Hartford: Press of Case Tiffany and Co., 1852.

———. History of Norwich, Connecticut, from its possession by the Indians to the year 1866. 1845. Reprint. Hartford, Conn.: printed by the author, 1866.

Chapin Howard. Sachems of the Narragansetts. Providence: Rhode Island Historical Society, 1931.

Church, Leslie F. Oglethorpe: A Study of Philanthropy in England and Georgia. London: Epworth Press, 1932.

Cohen, Sheldon S. A History of Colonial Education; 1607–1776. New York: John Wiley and Sons, 1974.

Coleman, Kenneth. Colonial Georgia, A History. New York: Charles Scribner's Sons, 1976.

Commager, Henry Steele, ed. Documents of American History. New York: F. S. Crofts and Co., 1934.

Corkran, David H. The Creek Frontier, 1540–1783. Norman: University of Oklahoma Press, 1967.

Corner, George W., ed. *The Autobiography of Benjamin Rush: His "Travels through Life,"* *Together with his Commonplace Book for 1789–1813*. Princeton: Princeton University Press, 1948.

Corry, John Pitts. *Indian Affairs in Georgia, 1732–1756*. Philadelphia: Privately printed by author, 1936.

Crane, Verner W. *The Southern Frontier, 1670–1732*. 1929. Ann Arbor: University of Michigan Press 1959.

Craven, Wesley Frank. *Dissolution of the Virginia Co*. New York: Oxford University Press, 1932.

———. *The Southern Colonies in the Seventeenth Century*. Baton Rouge, La.: Louisiana State University Press, 1949.

———. *White, Red, and Black: The Seventeenth-Century Virginian*. Charlottesville: University Press of Virginia, 1971.

Cremin, Lawrence A. *American Education: The Colonial Experience, 1607–1783*. New York: Harper and Row, 1970.

Cronon, William. *Changes in the Land*. New York: Hill and Wang, 1983.

Cross, Arthur Lyon. *The Anglican Episcopate and the American Colonies*. Cambridge: Harvard University Press, 1924.

Dallimore, Arnold A. *George Whitefield: The Life and Times of the Great Evangelist of the Eighteenth Century Revival*. 2 vols. Edinburgh, Scotland: Banner of Truth Trust, 1979. Reprint. Westchester, Ill.: Cornerstone Books, 1980.

Davidson, J. N. *Muh-he-ka-ne-ok, A History of the Stockbridge Nation*. Milwaukee, Wisc.: Silas Chapman, 1893.

Davis, Richard Beale. *Intellectual Life in the Colonial South, 1585–1763*. 3 vols. Knoxville: University of Tennessee Press, 1978.

De Schweinitz, Edmund. *The History of the Church Known as the Unitas Fratrum*. 1885. Reprint. Bethlehem, Pa.: Moravian Publications Concern, 1901.

———. *The Life and Times of David Zeisberger*. Philadelphia: Lippincott, 1871.

Demos, John. *A Little Commonwealth: Family Life in Plymouth Colony*. London, New York: Oxford University Press, 1971.

Dexter, Franklin Bowditch. *Biographical Sketches of the Graduates of Yale College*. Vol. I, 1885. New York: H. Holt and Co., 1885–1912.

———, ed. *The Literary Diary of Ezra Stiles*. 3 vols. New York: Charles Scribner's Sons, 1901.

Dickey, John Sloan. *Eleazar Wheelock, 1711–1779, Daniel Webster, 1782–1852 and Their Pioneer Dartmouth College*. New York: Newcomb Society in North America, 1954.

Dobyns, Henry F. *Native American Historical Demography: A Critical Bibliography*. Newberry Library American Indian Bibliographical Series. Bloomington: University of Indiana Press, 1976.

Drake, Francis S. *The Town of Roxbury: Its Memorable Persons and Places. . . .* Roxbury, Mass.: Published by the author, 1878.

Drake, Samuel G. *The Book of the Indians of North America*. Boston: Josiah Drake, 1833.

Eames, Wilberforce, ed. *John Eliot and the Indians, Being Letters addressed to Jonathan Hanmer of Barnstable, England*. New York: Adams and Grace Press, 1915.

Edwards, Jonathan. *Observations on the Language of the Muhhekaneew Indians*. New Haven: Printed by Josiah Meigs, 1783. Reprint. London: W. Justins, 1788.

———. *The Works of President Edwards, in Eight Volumes*. Edited by Edward Parsons and Edward Williams. London: James Black and Son, 1817. Reprint. New York: Burt Franklin, 1968.

Edwards, Maldwyn. *Family Circle: A Study of the Epwourth Household in Relation to John and Charles Wesley*. London: Epwourth Press, 1961.

Egmont, Earl of. *Journal of the Earl of Egmont.* Edited by Robert G. McPherson. Athens: University of Georgia Press, 1962.

Eliot, John. *A Brief Narrative of the Progress of the Gospel amongst the Indians in New-England in the Year 1670.* London: Printed for John Allen, 1671.

———. *The Day Breaking, if not the Sun-Rising of the Gospell with the Indians in New-England.* Boston: Old South Association, n.d. Reprint. London: Richard Cotes, 1647.

———. *A Further Account of the Progress of the Gospel Amongst the Indians in New England, Being a Relation of the Confessions made by several Indians (in the presence of the Elders and Members of several Churches) in order to their Admission into Church-fellowship.* London: Printed by John Macook, 1660.

———. *Indian Dialogues, for their Instruction in that great Service of Christ . . .* Printed at Cambridge, Mass., 1671.

———. *The Indian Grammar Begun: or, an Essay to Bring the Indian Language into Rules.* Cambridge: Marmaduke Johnson, 1666.

———. *The Indian Primer, or The Way of Training up our Indian Youth in the Good Knowledge of God.* 1669. Edinburgh: Andrew Elliot, 1880.

———. *The Logic Primer.* 1672. Reprint. Edited by Wilberfore Eames, Cleveland: Burrows Brothers, 1904.

———, and Thomas Mayhew, Jr. *Tears of Repentance: Or, a further Narrative of the Progress of the Gospel Amongst the Indians in New-England.* London, 1653.

Ellis, George. *The Red Man and the White Man in North America . . .* Boston: Little, Brown and Co., 1882.

Farish, Hunter Dickinson. *Journal and Letters of Philip Vickers Fithian, 1773–1774: A Plantation Tutor of the Old Dominion.* Princeton: Princeton University Press, 1943.

Fausz, J. Frederick. "Opechancanough: Indian Resistance Leader." In *Struggle and Survival in Colonial America,* edited by David G. Sweet and Gary B. Nash. Berkeley, Los Angeles, and London: University of California Press, 1981.

Flannery, Regina. *An Analysis of Coastal Algonquian Culture.* Washington, D.C.: Catholic University of America Press, 1939.

Flexner, James Thomas. *Lord of the Mohawks, A Biography of Sir William Johnson.* Boston: Little, Brown and Co., 1979.

Forbes, Harriet Merrifield. *The Hundredth Town: Glimpses of Life in Westborough, 1717–1817.* Boston: Press of Rockwell and Churchill, 1889.

Ford, Paul Leicester, ed. *The New England Primer.* 1897. Reprint. New York: Teachers College, Columbia University, 1962.

Franklin, Benjamin. *Proposals Relating to the Education of Youth in Pennsylvania.* Philadelphia: University of Pennsylvania Press, 1931.

Fries, Adelaide Lisette. *The Moravians in Georgia, 1735–1740.* Raleigh, N.C.: Edwards and Broughton, 1905.

Frost, J. William. *The Quaker Family in Colonial America.* New York: St. Martin's Press, 1973.

Gaustad, Edwin Scott. *The Great Awakening in New England.* 1957. Reprint. Chicago: Quadrangle Books, 1968.

George, Charles H. and Katherine George. *The Protestant Mind of the English Reformation, 1570–1640.* Princeton, N.J.: Princeton University Press, 1961.

Gollin, Lindt Gillian. *Moravians in Two Worlds: A Study of Changing Communities.* New York: Columbia University Press, 1967.

Gray, Benjamin Kirkman. *A History of English Philanthropy.* New York: A. M. Kelley, 1967.

Gray, Elma E. *Wilderness Christians, the Moravian Mission to the Delaware Indians.* Ithaca, N.Y.: Cornell University Press, 1956.

308   BIBLIOGRAPHY

Greaves, Richard L. *The Puritan Revolution and Educational Thought.* New Brunswick, N.J.: Rutgers University Press, 1969.

Green, Fletcher Melvin. "Higher Education of Women in the South before 1860." In *Democracy in the Old South and Other Essays,* edited by J. Isaac Copland. Memphis: Vanderbilt University Press, 1969.

Green, Michael D. *The Creeks.* Newberry Library American Indian Bibliographical Series. Bloomington: University of Indiana Press, 1979.

Greene, Lorenzo Johnson. *The Negro in Colonial New England.* 1942. Reprint. New York: Athenaeum, 1971.

Greven, Philip J., Jr., ed. *Child-Rearing Concepts, 1628–1861.* Itasca, Il.: F. E. Peacock Publishers, 1973.

Hale, Richard Walden, Jr. *Tercentenary History of the Roxbury Latin School, 1645–1945.* Cambridge: Riverside Press, 1946.

Hall, Clayton C., ed. *Narratives of Early Maryland, 1633–1684.* New York: Charles Scribner's Sons, 1910.

Hamilton, Milton W. *Sir William Johnson, Colonial American, 1715–1763.* Port Washington, N.Y.: Kennikat Press, 1976.

Handbook of North American Indians, vol 15: *Northeast.* Edited by Bruce G. Trigger. Washington, D.C.: Smithsonian Institution, 1978.

Hare, Lloyd C. M. *Thomas Mayhew, Patriarch to the Indians.* New York: D. Appleton and Company, 1932.

Harris, Thaddeus Mason. *Biographical Memorials of James Oglethorpe.* Boston: Printed for the author, 1841.

Hawke, David Freeman, ed. *Captain John Smith's History of Virginia.* Indianapolis and New York: Bobbs Merrill Co., 1970.

Hazard, Ebenezer. *Historical Collection, Consisting of State Papers.* Vol. 1, 1792; Vol. 2, 1794. Philadelphia: T. Dobson.

Heimert, Alan. *Religion and the American Mind, From the Great Awakening to the Revolution.* Cambridge: Harvard University Press, 1966.

———, and Perry Miller, eds. *The Great Awakening.* Indianapolis and New York: Bobbs-Merrill Co., 1967.

Heizenrater, Richard P., ed. *Diary of an Oxford Methodist Benjamin Ingham, 1733–1734.* Durham, North Carolina: Duke University Press, 1985.

Hempstead, Joshua. *Diary of Joshua Hempstead of New London, Connecticut.* New London, Ct.: New London Historical Society, 1901.

Hening, William W., ed. *The Statutes at Large; Being a Collection of All the Laws of Virginia, 1619–1792.* 13 vols. Vol 3: Philadelphia: Printed for the editor by Thomas DeSilver, 1823.

The History of the College of William and Mary from Its Foundation, 1660 to 1874. Richmond: J. W. Randolph and English, 1874.

Hoadly, Charles J., ed. *The Public Records of the Colony of Connecticut.* Hartford: Press of the Case, Lockwood and Brainerd Co., 1850–90.

Hopkins, Samuel. *Historical Memoirs Relating to the Housatonic Indians.* Boston: S. Kneeland, 1753. Reprint. *The Magazine of History,* 5, no. 17 (1912):7–198.

Hudson, Charles M. *The Southeastern Indians.* Knoxville: University of Tennessee Press, 1976.

Humphreys, David. *An Historical Account of the Incorporated Society for the Propagation of the Gospel in Foreign Parts.* 1728. Reprint. Arno Press and the New York *Times,* 1969.

Jefferson, Thomas. *Notes on the State of Virginia.* Edited by William Peden. Chapel Hill: University of North Carolina Press, 1955.

Jennings, Francis. *The Invasion of America: Indians, Colonialism, and the Cant of Conquest.* New York: Norton Library and University of North Carolina Press, 1976.

Jernegan, Marcus W. *Laboring and Dependent Classes in Colonial America: 1607–1783.* Chicago: University of Chicago Press, 1931.

Jones, Charles Colcock, Jr. *Historical Sketch of Tomo-Chi-Chi, Mico of the Yamacraws.* Albany, N.Y.: Joel Munsell, 1868.

Jones, Electa Fidelia. *Stockbridge, Past and Present or Records of an old Mission Station.* Springfield, Mass.: S. Bowles and Co., 1854.

Jones, Hugh. *The Present State of Virginia.* 1724. Reprint. Edited by Richard L. Morton. Chapel Hill: University of North Carolina Press, 1956.

Kellaway, William. *The New England Company, 1649–1776.* London: Longman, Green and Co., 1961.

Kelsey, Isabel Thompson. *Joseph Brant, 1743–1807, Man of Two Worlds.* Syracuse, N.Y.: Syracuse University Press, 1984.

Kemp, William Webb. *The Support of Schools in Colonial New York by the Society for the Propagation of the Gospel in Foreign Parts.* New York: Teacher's College, Columbia University, 1913.

Kingsbury, Susan Myra, ed. *The Records of the Virginia Company of London.* 4 vols. Washington, D.C.: U.S. Government Printing Office, 1906–35.

Klingberg, Frank J. *Anglican Humanitarianism in Colonial New York.* Philadelphia: Church Historical Society, vol. 11, 1940.

———, ed. *The Carolina Chronicle of Dr. Francis Le Jau, 1706–1717.* Berkeley and Los Angeles: University of California Press, 1956.

———. *Carolina Chronicle: The Papers of Commissary Gideon Johnston, 1707–1716.* Berkeley and Los Angeles: University of California Press, 1946.

Knight, Edgar W. ed. *A Documentary History of Education in the South before 1860.* 5 vols. Chapel Hill: University of North Carolina Press, 1949–53.

Lane, Mills, ed. *General Oglethorpe's Georgia: Colonial Letters, 1733–1743.* 2 vols. Savannah: Beehive Press, 1975.

Laslett, Peter. *The World We Have Lost.* New York: Charles Scribner's Sons, 1965.

Lefler, Hugh T., and William S. Powell. *Colonial North Carolina, A History.* New York: Charles Scribner's Sons, 1973.

———, and Albert Ray Newsome. *North Carolina, The History of a Southern State.* Chapel Hill: University of North Carolina Press, 1973.

Levering, Joseph Mortimer. *A History of Bethlehem, Pennsylvania, 1741–1892.* Bethlehem: Times Pub. Co., 1903. Reprint. New York: AMS Press, 1971.

Levin, David. *Cotton Mather: The Young Life of the Lord's Remembrancer, 1663–1705.* Cambridge, Mass.: Harvard University Press, 1978.

Lewis, Clifford M., and Albert J. Loomie. *The Spanish Jesuit Mission in Virginia, 1570–1572.* Chapel Hill: University of North Carolina Press, 1953.

Littlefield, George Emery. *The Early Massachusetts Press, 1638–1711.* 2 vols. Boston, Mass.: Cambridge University Press, 1907.

Lockridge, Kenneth A. *Literacy in Colonial New England.* New York: W. W. Norton and Co., 1974.

Loskiel, George Henry. *History of the Mission of the United Brethren among the Indians of North America.* London: Brethren Society for the Furtherance of the Gospel, 1794.

Lothrop, Samuel K. *Life of Samuel Kirkland, Missionary to the Indians.* In Jared Sparks, *Library of American Biography* Vol. 15, 2d ser. New York: Harper, 1848.

Love, William DeLoss. *Samson Occom and the Christian Indians of New England.* Boston: Pilgrim Press, 1899.

Lydekker, John Wolfe. *The Faithful Mohawks.* London: Society for Promoting Christian Knowledge, 1938. Reprint. Long Island, N.Y.: Ira J. Friedman, 1968.

———. *The Life and Letters of Charles Inglis.* London: Society for Promoting Christian Knowledge, 1936.

McCain, James Rose. *Georgia as a Proprietary Province.* Boston: R. G. Badger, 1917.

McCallum, James Dow. *Eleazar Wheelock, Founder of Dartmouth College.* Hanover, N.H.: Dartmouth College Publications, 1939.

———, ed. *The Letters of Eleazar Wheelock's Indians.* Hanover, N.H.: Dartmouth College Publications, 1932.

McClure, David, and Elijah Parish. *Memoirs of the Rev. Eleazar Wheelock.* Newburyport, Mass.: Edward Norris and Co., 1811.

McCulloch, Samuel C., ed. *British Humanitarianism: Essays Honoring Frank J. Klingberg.* Philadelphia: Church Historical Society, 1950.

Malone, Henry Thompson. *The Episcopal Church in Georgia, 1733–1957.* Atlanta: Protestant Episcopal Church in the Diocese of Atlanta, 1960.

Manross, William Wilson. *A History of the American Episcopal Church.* New York: Morehouse-Gorham Co., 1950.

———. *The Fulham Papers in the Lambeth Palace Library.* London: Oxford University Press, 1965.

———. *SPG Papers in the Lambeth Palace Library.* Oxford: Clarendon Press, 1974.

Marambaud, Pierre. *William Byrd of Westover, 1674–1744.* Charlottesville: University Press of Virginia, 1971.

Mather, Cotton. *Cares about the Nurseries.* Boston, 1702. Excerpts reprinted in *Theories of Education in Early America, 1655–1819,* edited by Wilson Smith. Indianapolis and New York, 1973.

———. *The Diary of Cotton Mather, 1681–1708.* 2 vols. Massachusetts Historical Society *Collections,* Vols. 7 & 8, 7th ser. Boston: Massachusetts Historical Society.

———. *Corderius Americanus, An Essay upon the Good Education of Children and what may Hopefully be Attempted, for the Hope of the Flock in a Funeral Sermon upon Mr. Ezekial Cheever.* Boston: John Allen, 1708.

Matthews, Albert, ed. *Letters of Dennys De Berdt, 1757–1770.* Freeport, N.Y.: Books for Libraries Press, 1971.

Maxson, Charles Hartshorn. *The Great Awakening in the Middle Colonies.* Chicago: University of Chicago, 1920. Reprint. Gloucester, Mass.: Peter Smith, 1958.

May, Henry F. *The Enlightenment in America.* New York: Oxford University Press, 1977.

Mayhew, Experience. *A Brief Account of the State of the Indians on Martha's Vineyard and the small islands adjacent in Dukes county, from the year 1694–1720.* Boston: B. Green for Samuel Gerrish, 1720.

———. *Indian Converts: or, Some account of the lives and dying speeches of a considerable number of the Christianized Indians of Martha's Vineyard, in New England.* London: printed for S. Gerrish, bookseller in Boston, in New England and sold by J. Osborn, 1727.

———. *Narratives of the Lives of Pious Indian Women who lived on Martha's Vineyard More than One Hundred Years Since.* 1727. Reprint. Boston: James Loring, 1830.

———. *Narratives of Pious Indian Children.* 1727. Reprint. Boston: James Loring, 1829.

———. *Observations on the Indian Language.* Boston: David Clapp and Son, 1884.

———. "Brief Narrative of the Success which the Gospel hath had among the Indians, of Martha's Vineyard (and the Places Adjacent) in New-England." 1694. In Cotton Mather, *Magnalia Christi Americana; or, The Ecclesiastical History of New-England,* 2 vols. Hartford: Silas Andrus and Son, 1853.

Middlekauff, Robert. *Ancients and Axioms: Secondary Education in Eighteenth-Century New England.* New Haven and London: Yale University Press, 1963.

Miller, Perry. *Errand into the Wilderness.* 1934. Reprint. New York: Harper and Row, 1956.

———. *Jonathan Edwards.* Cleveland and New York: World Publishing Company, 1965.

Morgan, Edmund S. *American Slavery, American Freedom: The Ordeal of Colonial Virginia.* New York: W. W. Norton and Co., 1975.

———. *The Gentle Puritan: A Life of Ezra Stiles, 1727–1795.* New Haven, Conn.: Yale University Press, 1962.

———. *The Puritan Family.* New York: Harper and Row, 1966.

———. *Virginians at Home: Family Life in the Eighteenth Century.* Chapel Hill: University of North Carolina Press, 1952.

Morison, Samuel Eliot. *The Founding of Harvard College.* Cambridge, Mass.: Harvard University Press, 1935.

———. *Harvard College in the Seventeenth Century,* 2 vols. Cambridge: Harvard University Press, 1936.

———. *The Intellectual Life of Colonial New England.* 1936. Reprint. Ithaca, N.Y.: Cornell University Press, 1961.

Naylor, John. *Charles Delamotte.* London: Epworth Press, 1938.

Nelson, William. *The Indians of New Jersey: Their Origin and Development; Manners and Customs; Language, Religion and Government, with Notices of Some Indian Place Names.* Paterson, N.J.: Press Printing and Publishing Co., 1894.

Newman, Henry. *Henry Newman's Saltzburger Letterbooks.* Transcribed and edited by George Fenwick Jones. Athens: University of Georgia Press, 1966.

Norwood, Frederick A. *The Story of American Methodism.* Nashville and New York: Abingdon Press, 1974.

O'Callaghan, Edmund Bailey. *Documentary History of New York.* Albany: New York Historical Society Collections, 1849–51.

Occom, Samson. *Sermon at the Execution of Moses Paul, An Indian; Who had been guilty of murder.* New Haven, Ct., 1788. Reprint. London: Buckland, Paternoster Row, 1789.

Official Letters of Alexander Spotswood. Richmond: Virginia Historical Society, 1973.

Orcutt, Samuel. *The Indians of the Housatonic and Naugatuck Valleys.* Hartford, Ct., 1882. Reprint. Stratford, Conn.: John E. Edwards, 1972.

Oswald, John Clyde. *Printing in the Americas.* 1937. Reprint. New York: Hacker Art Books, 1968.

Paige, Lucius Robinson. *History of Cambridge, Massachusetts, 1630–1877.* Boston: H. O. Houghton and Company; Cambridge: Riverside Press, 1877.

Papers of Sir William Johnson. 12 vols. Albany: University of State of New York, 1921–1957.

Pascoe, C. F. *Two Hundred Years of the S.P.G.: An Historical Account of the Society for the Propagation of the Gospel in Foreign Parts, 1701–1900.* London: Published at the Society's Office, 1901.

Pearce, Roy Harvey. *Savagism and Civilization.* 1953. Reprint. Baltimore and London: Johns Hopkins Press, 1965.

Pettitt, George A. *Primitive Education in North America.* Berkeley: University of California Publications in American Archaeology and Ethnology, 1946.

Pilcher, George William. *Samuel Davies, Apostle of Dissent in Colonial Virginia.* Knoxville: University of Tennessee Press, 1971.

Potter, Elisha R., Jr. *The Early History of Narragansett.* Providence: Collections of the Rhode Island Historical Society, 1835.

Quinn, David B. *North America from Earliest Discovery to First Settlements, The Norse Voyages to 1612.* New York: Harper and Row, 1975.

Randolph Edmund. *History of Virginia.* Edited by Arthur H. Shaffer. Charlottesville: University Press of Virginia, 1970.

Richardson, Leon Burr. *An Indian Preacher in England.* 1933. Reprint. Hanover, N.H.: Dartmouth College Publications, 1939.

———. *History of Dartmouth College.* 2 vols. Hanover: Dartmouth College Publications, 1932.

Riley, Edward Miles, ed. *The Journal of John Harrower, An Indentured Servant in the Colony of Virginia, 1773–1776.* Williamsburg and New York: Colonial Williamsburg; Holt, Rinehart and Winston, 1963.

Ritchie, Carson I. A. *Frontier Parish: An Account of the SPG and the Anglican Church in America, Drawn from the Records of the Bishop of London.* Cranbury, N.J.: Associated University Presses, 1976.

Ronda, James P. and James Axtell. *Indian Missions: A Critical Bibliography.* Newberry Library American Indian Bibliographical Series. Bloomington: University of Indiana Press, 1978.

Rush, Benjamin. *The Autobiography of Benjamin Rush.* Edited by George W. Corner. Princeton: Princeton University Press, 1948.

Rutman, Darrett B. *American Puritanism.* New York: J. P. Lippincott Co., 1970.

Salisbury, Neal. *Manitou and Providence: Europeans and the Making of New England, 1500–1643.* New York and Oxford: Oxford University Press, 1982.

Sedgwick, Sarah Cabot and Christina Sedgwick Marquand. *Stockbridge, 1739–1974.* Stockbridge, Mass.: Berkshire Traveller Press, 1974.

Sergeant, John. *A Letter from the Rev. Mr. Sergeant of Stockbridge to Dr. Colman of Boston.* Boston: Printed by Rogers and Fowle for D. Henchman in Cornhill, 1743. Reprint. Lancaster, Pa.: Lancaster Press, May 1929.

Sewall, Samuel. *Diary of Samuel Sewall.* 2 vols. Edited by M. Halsey Thomas. New York: Farrar, Straus and Giroux, 1973.

[Seymour, A. C. H.]. *The Life and Times of Selina, Countess of Huntingdon.* 2 vols. London: William Edward Painter, Strand; and John Snow, Paternoster Row, 1844.

Shea, John D. G. *History of the Catholic Missions among the Indian Tribes of the United States, 1529–1854.* 1855. Reprint. New York: Arno, 1969.

Sheehan, Bernard W. *Savagism and Civility: Indians and Englishmen in Colonial Virginia.* Cambridge: Cambridge University Press, 1980.

Silverman, Kenneth, ed. *Selected Letters of Cotton Mather.* Baton Rouge: Louisiana State University Press, 1971.

Sirmans, Marion Eugene. *Colonial South Carolina, A Political History, 1663–1763.* Chapel Hill: University of North Carolina Press, 1966.

Sloan, Douglas, ed. *The Great Awakening and American Education: A Documentary History.* New York: Teachers College Press, 1973.

Small, Walter Herbert. *Early New England Schools.* Boston and London: Ginn and Company Publishers, 1914. Reprint. New York: Arno Press and the New York Times, 1969.

Smith, Wilson, ed. *Theories of Education in Early America, 1655–1819.* Indianapolis and New York: Bobbs-Merrill Company, 1973.

Some Correspondence between the Governors and Treasurers of the New Eng Co . . . & the Commissioners of the United Colonies in America . . . Between the years 1657 and 1712 to which are added the Journals of the Rev. Experience Mayhew in 1713–1714. London: Spottiswoode and Co., 1896.

Spalding, Phinizy. *Oglethorpe in America.* Chicago: University of Chicago Press, 1977.

Sprague, William B. *Annals of the American Pulpit.* Vol. 1: Trinitarian Congregational. Reprint. New York: Arno Press and the New York Times, 1969.

Spruill, Julia Cherry. *Women's Life and Work in the Southern Colonies.* New York: W. W. Norton and Co., 1972.

Stanard, Mary Newton. *Colonial Virginia: Its People & Customs.* Philadelphia: Lippincott, 1917.

Starbuck, Alexander. *The History of Nantucket.* Boston: C. E. Goodspeed and Co., 1924.

Stewart, Frank H. *Indians of Southern New Jersey.* 1932. Reprint. Port Washington, N.Y.: Kennikat Press, 1972.

Stiles, Ezra. *The Literary Diary of Ezra Stiles.* 3 vols. New York: Charles Scribner's Sons, 1901.

Stith, William. *History of the First Discovery and Settlement of Virginia.* Williamsburg, 1747. Reprint. New York: Johnson Reprint Co., 1969.

Stone, Lawrence. *The Family, Sex and Marriage in England, 1500–1800.* London: Weidenfeld and Nicholson, 1977.

Strachey, William. *The Historie of travaile into Virginia Britannia.* Edited by R. H. Major. London: Printed for the Hakluyt Society, 1849.

———. *The Historie of travaile into Virginia Britannia.* Edited by Louis B. Wright and Virginia Freund. London: Printed for the Hakluyt Society, 1953.

Thomas, Isaiah. *The History of Printing in America.* 2 vols. New York: Burt Franklin, 1874. Reprint, 1972.

Thwaites, Reuben Gold. *The Jesuit Relations and Allied Documents.* 73 vols. Cleveland, Ohio: The Burrow Brothers Company, 1876.

Tooker, Elisabeth. *The Indians of the Northeast.* Newberry Library American Indian Bibliographical Series. Bloomington: University of Indiana Press, 1976.

Tooker, William Wallace. *John Eliot's First Indian Teacher and Interpreter: Cockenoe-de-Long Island and the Story of his Career from the Early Records.* New York: F. P. Harper, 1896.

Trelease, Allen W. *Indian Affairs in Colonial New York: The Seventeenth Century.* Ithaca, N.Y.: Cornell University Press, 1960.

Trumbull, Benjamin. *A Complete History of Connecticut, Civil & Ecclesiastical.* New London, Ct.: Utley, 1898.

Tryon, Rolla Milton. *Household Manufactures in the United States, 1640–1860.* 1917. Reprint. New York: Johnson Reprint Co., 1966.

Tyerman, Luke. *The Life and Times of the Rev. John Wesley, M.A., founder of the Methodists.* 3 vols. New York: Harper and Brothers, Publishers, 1872.

Tyerman, Luke. *The Oxford Methodists: Memoirs of the Rev. Messrs. Clayton, Ingham, Gambold, Hervey, and Broughton, with Biographical Notices of Others.* London: Hodder and Stoughton, 1873.

Tyler, Lyon Gardiner. *Williamsburg, The Old Colonial Capital.* Richmond: Whittet and Shepperson, 1907.

Vassar, Rena L., ed. *Social History of American Education.* Vol. 1: *Colonial Times to 1860.* Chicago: Rand McNally and Co., 1966.

Velarde, Pablita. *Old Father, the Story Teller.* Globe, Arizona: Dale Stuart King, 1969.

Wallace, Anthony F. C. *King of the Delawares: Teedyuscung, 1700–1763.* Philadelphia: University of Pennsylvania Press, 1949.

Wallace, Paul A. W. *Conrad Weiser, 1696–1760, Friend of Colonist and Mohawk.* Philadelphia: University of Pennsylvania Press; London: Humphrey Milford, Oxford University Press, 1945.

Weiss, Frederick Lewis. *The Colonial Clergy and the Colonial Churches of New England.* Lancaster, Mass.: Society of the Descendents of the Colonial Clergy, 1936.

Weslager, Clinton Alfred. *The Delaware Indians: A History.* New Brunswick, N.J., 1972.

———. *The Delawares: A Critical Bibliography.* Newberry Library American Indian Bibliographical Series. Bloomington: University of Indiana Press, 1978.

———. *Delaware's Forgotten Folk: The Story of the Moors and Nanticokes.* Philadelphia: University of Pennsylvania Press, 1943.

———. *The Nanticoke Indians—Past and Present.* Newark: University of Delaware Press; London and Toronto: Associated University Presses, 1983.

Wesley, John. *The Journal of the Rev. John Wesley, A.M..* 8 vols. Edited by Nehemiah Curnock. London: The Epworth Press, 1938.

Wheelock, Eleazar. *A Plain and Faithful Narrative of the Original Design, Rise, Progress & Present State of the Indian Charity-School at Lebanon, In Connecticut.* Boston: Printed by Richard and Samuel Draper, in Newberry Street, 1763.

———. *A Narrative of the Indian Charity School . . .* Boston: Printed by Richard and Samuel Draper, 1763.

———. *A Continuation of the Narrative of the State, &C, of the Indian Charity-School, at Lebanon, In Connecticut, From Nov. 27th, 1762 to Sept 3d, 1765.* Boston: Printed by Richard and Samuel Draper, 1765.

———. *A Brief Narrative of the Indian Charity-School, in Lebanon in Connecticut, New England.* London: Printed by J. and W. Oliver, in Bartholomew Close. . . , 1766.

———. *A Brief Narrative of the Indian Charity-School, in Lebanon in Connecticut, New England.* 2d edition, with an appendix. London: Printed by J. and W. Oliver, in Bartholomew Close. . . , 1767.

———. *A Continuation of the Narrative of the Indian Charity-School in Lebanon in Connecticut, New England, etc.* London: Printed by J. and W. Oliver in Bartholomew Close. . . , 1769.

———. *A Continuation of the Narrative of the Indian Charity-School, in Lebanon, in Connecticut; From the Year 1768 to the Incorporation of It with Dartmouth-College, etc..* Hartford: N.P. 1771.

———. *A Continuation of the Narrative of the Indian Charity-School, etc..* Hartford, Conn.: Printed by Ebenezer Watson, 1773.

———. *A Continuation of the Narrative of the Indian Charity-School, etc..* Hartford, Conn.: Printed by Ebenezer Watson, 1775.

Williams, Roger. *A Key into the Language of America.* 1653. Reprint. Edited by John J. Teunissen and Evelyn J. Hinz. Detroit: Wayne State University Press, 1973.

Willoughby, Charles C. *Antiquities of the New England Indians with Notes on the ancient cultures of the adjacent territories.* Cambridge, Mass.: Peabody Museum of American Archaeology and Ethnology, 1935.

Winship, George Parker. *The Cambridge Press, 1638–1692.* Philadelphia: University of Pennsylvania Press, 1945.

———. *The New England Company of 1649 and John Eliot.* Boston: Prince Society Publications, 1920; Reprint. New York: Burt Franklin, 1960.

Winslow, Ola Elizabeth. *John Eliot, "Apostle to the Indians".* Boston: Houghton Mifflin Co., 1962.

Winsor, Justin, ed. *The Memorial History of Boston.* 4 vols. Boston: James R. Osgood and Co., 1880–81.

Winterich, John T. *Early American Books and Printing.* Boston and New York: Houghton Mifflin Co., 1935.

Woody, Thomas. *Early Quaker Education in Pennsylvania.* New York: Teachers College, Columbia University, 1920.

———. *A History of Women's Education in the United States.* Vol. 1. New York: Science Press, 1929.

———, ed. *Educational Views of Benjamin Franklin.* New York and London: McGraw-Hill, 1931.

Wright, J. Leitch, Jr. *Anglo–Spanish Rivalry in North America.* Athens: University of Georgia Press, 1971.

———. *The Only Land They Knew: The Tragic Story of the American Indians in the Old South.* New York: Free Press; London: Collier Macmillan Publishers, 1981.

Wright, Louis B. *Culture on the Moving Frontier.* Bloomington: Indiana University Press, 1955.

———. *Middle-Class Culture in Elizabethan England.* Chapel Hill: University of North Carolina Press, 1935.

————, ed. *The Prose Works of William Byrd of Westover.* Cambridge, Mass.: Belknap Press of Harvard University Press, 1966.

ARTICLES

Alexander, Edward P. "An Indian Vocabulary from Fort Christanna, 1716." *Virginia Magazine of History and Biography* 79 (July 1971):303–12.

Axtell, James. "Dr. Wheelock's Little Red School." In James Axtell, *The European and the Indian: Essays in the Ethnohistory of Colonial North America,* pp. 87–109. New York: Oxford University Press, 1981.

Beaver, R. Pierce. "Methods in American Missions to the Indians in the Seventeenth and Eighteenth Centuries: Calvinist Models for Protestant Foreign Missions." *Journal of Presbyterian History* 47 (1969):124–48.

Berkhofer, Robert K., Jr. "Protestants, Pagans, and Sequences Among the North American Indians, 1760–1860." *Ethnohistory* 10 (1963):201–69.

Boissevain, Ethel. "The Detribalization of the Narragansett Indians: A Case Study." *Ethnohistory* 3 (Summer 1956):225–45.

————. "Narragansett Survival: A Study of Group Persistence through Adapted Traits." *Ethnohistory* 6 (Summer 1959):347–362.

Bradstreet, Howard. "The Story of the War with the Pequots, Re-Told." *Tercentenary Commission for the State of Connecticut* 5. New Haven: Yale University Press, 1933.

Brasser, T. J. C. "The Coastal Algonkians: People of the First Frontiers." In *North American Indians in Historical Perspective.* Edited by Eleanor B. Leacock and Nancy O. Lurie. New York: Random House, 1971.

Bridenbaugh, Carl. "Opechancanough: A Native American Patriot." In Bridenbaugh, *Early Americans.* New York and Oxford: Oxford University Press, 1981.

Brodeur, Paul. "A Reporter at Large, The Mashpee." *New Yorker* 54 (October 30, 1978):62–250.

Campbell, Bernard Ulysses. "Early Missions among the Indians of Maryland." *Maryland Historical Magazine* 1 (December 1906):293–316.

Campisi, Jack C. "Oneida." In *Handbook of North American Indians,* Vol. 15: *Northeast,* pp. 481–90. Edited by Bruce C. Trigger. Washington, D.C.: Smithsonian Institution, 1978.

Cleaveland, George J. "At Henrico." *William and Mary Alumni Gazette* 37 (March 1970):4–10.

Conrad, A. Mark. "The Cherokee Mission of Virginia Presbyterians." *Journal of Presbyterian History* 58 (Spring 1980):35–48.

Corry, John Pitts. "Education in Colonial Georgia." *Georgia Historical Quarterly* 16 (1932):136–45.

Coulter, Ellis Merton. "Mary Musgrove, Queen of the Creeks." *Georgia Historical Quarterly* 11 (1927).

Cramer, Kenneth C. "Notes from the Special Collections The American Indian and Eleazar Wheelock." *Dartmouth College Library Bulletin* 17, new ser. (November 1976):27–31.

Deming, Dorothy. "The Settlement of the Connecticut Towns." *Tercentenary Commission of the State of Connecticut* 6. New Haven, Ct.: Commission on Historical Publications, Yale University Press, 1933.

"Description of New England, or the Observations, and discoveries of Captain John Smith (Admirall of that Country) in the North of America, in the year of our Lord 1614; w/the successe of sixe Ships, that went the next yeare 1615; and the accidents befell him among the French men of Warre. . . . " In Arber and Bradley, *Travels and Works of Captain John Smith*, Part I, pp. 175–229. London: Printed by Humfrey Lawnes for Robert Clerke, 1616.

Dobyns, Henry F. "Estimating Aboriginal American Population: An Appraisal of Techniques with a new Hemispheric Estimate." *Current Anthropology* 7 (October 1966): 395–416.

Dorr, Henry C. "The Narragansetts." *Collections of the Rhode Island Historical Society* 7 (1885):137–237.

Drake, Francis S. "Roxbury in the Colonial Period." In *Memorial History of Boston*, Vol. 1, pp. 401–22. Edited by Justin Winsor. Boston: James R. Osgood and Co., 1881.

East, Robert A. "Puritanism and New Settlement." *New England Quarterly* 17 (June 1944):255–64.

Eliot, John. "A Late and Further Manifestation of the Progress of the Gospel amongst the Indians in New-England." Massachusetts Historical Society *Collections* 4, 3d ser. (1834):261–87.

———. "An Account of Indian Churches in New-England." Massachusetts Historical Society *Collections* 10, 1st ser. (1809):124–29.

———. "The Christian Commonwealth: or, The Civil Policy of the Rising Kingdom of Jesus Christ." 1659. Massachusetts Historical Society *Collections*, 9, 3d ser. (1846):127–164.

Fausz, J. Frederick. "The Invasion of Virginia: Indians, Colonialism and the Conquest of Cant: A Review Essay on Anglo-Indian Relations in the Chesapeake." *Virginia Magazine of History and Biography* 95 (April 1987):133–56.

———. "Middlemen in Peace and War: Virginia's Earliest Interpreters, 1608–1632." *Virginia Magazine of History and Biography* 95 (January 1987):41–64.

Feest, Christian F. "Nanticoke and Neighboring Tribes." In *Handbook of North American Indians*. Vol. 15: *Northeast*, pp. 240–52. Edited by Bruce C. Trigger. Washington, D.C.: Smithsonian Institution, 1978.

Fenton, William N. "Northern Iroquoian Culture Patterns." In *Handbook of North American Indians*. Vol. 15: *Northeast*, pp. 296–321. Edited by Bruce Trigger. Washington, D.C.: Smithsonian Institution, 1978.

Fenton, William N., and Elisabeth Tooker. "Mohawk." In *Handbook of North American Indians*. Vol. 15: *Northeast*, pp. 466–80. Edited by Bruce G. Trigger. Washington, D.C.: Smithsonian Institution, 1978.

Franklin, W. Neil, ed. "Act for the Better Regulation of the Indian Trade." *Virginia Magazine of History and Biography* 72 (April 1964):141–51.

Ganter, Herbert Lawrence. "Some notes on 'The Charity of the Honorable Robert Boyle Esq., of the City of London, deceased.'" *William and Mary College Quarterly Historical Magazine* 15, 2d ser. (1935):1–39, 207–28, 346–84.

Goodwin, J. "Christianity, Civilization, and the Savage: The Anglican Mission to the American Indian." *Historical Magazine of the Protestant Episcopal Church* 42 (1973): 93–110.

Gookin, Daniel. "An Historical Account of the Doings and Sufferings of the Christian Indians in New England." (1677). *Transactions and Collections of the American Antiquarian Society* 2 (1836):423–534.

———. "Historical Collections of the Indians in New England (1674)." Massachusetts Historical Society *Collections*, 1, 1st ser. (1792):141–227.

Greene, Evarts B. "The Anglican Outlook on the American Colonies in the Early Eighteenth Century." *American Historical Review* 20 (October 1914):64–85.

Guernsey, S. J. "Notes on Explorations of Martha's Vineyard." *American Anthropologist* 18, new ser., (January–March 1916):81–97.

Hallowell, A. Irving. "Some Psychological Characteristics of the Northeastern Indians." In "Man in Northeastern North America." Edited by Frederick Johnson. *Papers of the Robt. S. Peabody Foundation for Archaeology*, Vol. 3. Andover, Mass.: Phillips Academy, 1946.

Hamilton, Kenneth G. "Cultural Contributions of Moravian Missions among the Indians." *Pennsylvania History* 18 (January 1951):1–15.

Hamilton, Milton W. "Sir William Johnson: Interpreter of the Iroquois." *Ethnohistory* 10 (Summer 1963):270–86.

Harrower, John. "Documents of John Harrower, 1773–1776." *American Historical Review* 6 (October 1900):65–107.

Harvard College Records, Part 1, Corporation Records, 1656–1750, College Buildings: 1637–1750, Indian College, 1655–1698. *Publications of the Colonial Society of Massachusetts* Vol. 15, *Collections*. Boston: University Press, 1925.

Jacobs, Wilbur F. "The Tip of an Iceberg: Pre-Columbian Indian Demography and Some Implications for Revisionism." *William and Mary Quarterly*, 31, 3d ser. (January 1974):123–32.

Jennings, Francis. "Goals and Functions of Puritan Missions to the Indians." *Ethnohistory* 18 (Summer 1971):197–212.

Jernegan, Marcus W. "Slavery and Conversion in the American Colonies." *American Historical Review* 21 (1915–16):504–17.

"John Wesley's Journal from October 14, 1735 to February 1, 1937 Covering his Visit to America." Published for the first time by the New Orleans *Picayune* through the courtesy of Bishop E. R. Hendrix of Missouri. Picayune Print, 1901.

Johnson, Frederick, ed. "Man in Northeastern North America." *Papers of the Robert S. Peabody Foundation for Archaeology*. Vol. 3. Andover, Mass.: Phillips Academy, 1946.

Johnson, Richard R. "The Search for a Usable Indian: an Aspect of the Defense of Colonial New England." *Journal of American History* 64 (December 1977):623–51.

Kammen, Michael G., ed. "Virginia at the Close of the Seventeenth Century: An Appraisal by James Blair and John Locke." *Virginia Magazine of History and Biography* 74 (January 1966):141–69.

Kenney, William Howland. "George Whitefield, Dissenter Priest of the Great Awakening, 1739–1741." *William and Mary Quarterly* 26, 3d ser. (January 1969):75–93.

Klingberg, Frank J. "Early Attempts at Indian Education in South Carolina: A Documentary." *South Carolina Historical Magazine* 61 (1960):1–10.

———. "Indian Frontier in South Carolina as Seen by SPG Missionaries." *Journal of Southern History* 5 (November 1939):478–500.

———. "The Mystery of the Lost Yamassee Prince." *South Carolina Historical Magazine* 63 (1962):18–32.

Kohnova, Marie J. "The Moravians and Their Missionaries, A Problem in Americanization." *Mississippi Valley Historical Review* 19 (December 1932):348–61.

Land, Robert O. "Henrico and Its College." *William and Mary Quarterly* 18, 2d ser. (1938):453–98.

Landy, David. "Tuscarora among the Iroquois." In *Handbook of North American Indians*. Vol. 15: *Northeast*, pp. 518–24. Edited by Bruce G. Trigger. Washington, D.C.: Smithsonian Institution, 1978.

"Letters from Mr. John Eliot of New-England to Mr. Boyle . . . " In Robert Boyle, *The Works*. Vol. 1. Edited by Thomas Birch. London, 1792. Reprint. Darmstadt, Germany, 1965.

"Letters of Isaac Watts." *Massachusetts Historical Society Proceedings*, 9, 2d ser. Boston: Published by the Society, 1895.

"Letters of John Eliot the Apostle." *Massachusetts Historical Society Proceedings* 17 (1879–1880):245–53.

"Letters of the Rev. John Eliot, Apostle to the Indians." *New England Historical and Genealogical Register* 36 (1882):291–299.

"Letters of Samuel Lee and Samuel Sewall Relating to New England and the Indians." Colonial Society of Massachusetts *Publications* 14 (1913):142–86.

Lounsbury, Floyd G. "Iroquoian Languages." In *Handbook of North American Indians*. Vol. 15: *Northeast*. pp. 324–43. Edited by Bruce G. Trigger. Washington, D.C.: Smithsonian Institution, 1978.

Lurie, Nancy Oestreich. "Indian Cultural Adjustment to European Civilization." In *Seventeenth Century America: Essays in Colonial History*, pp. 33–60. 1959. Reprint. Edited by James Morton Smith. New York: W. W. Norton and Co., 1972.

McCabe, W. Gordon. "The First University in America, 1619–1622." *Virginia Magazine of History and Biography* 30 (1922):133–56.

Marshall, Peter. "Sir William Johnson and the Treaty of Fort Stanwix, 1768." *Journal of American Studies* 1 (October 1967):149–169.

Merrell, James H. "Cultural Continuity among the Piscataway Indians of Colonial Maryland." *William and Mary Quarterly* 36, 3d ser. (October 1979):548–70.

Meserve, Walter T. "English Works of Seventeenth-Century Indians." *American Quarterly* 8 (Fall 1956):264–76.

Michelson, Truman. "The Linguistic Classification of Powhatan." *American Anthropologist* 35 (1933):549.

Mook, Maurice. "Virginia Ethnology from an Early Relation." *William and Mary Quarterly* 23, 2d ser. (April 1943):101–29.

———. "The Aboriginal Population of Tidewater Virginia." *American Anthropologist* 46 (1944):193–208.

———. "The Anthropological Position of the Indian Tribes of Tidewater Virginia." *William and Mary Quarterly* 23, 2d ser. (January 1943):27–40.

Mooney, James. "The Powhatan Confederacy, Past and Present." *American Anthropologist* 9 (1907):129–52.

———. "The Siouan Tribes of the East." *Bureau of American Ethnology Bulletin*, No. 22. Washington, D.C.: Smithsonian Institution, 1894.

Morgan, David T. "John Wesley's Sojourn in Georgia Revisited." *Georgia Historical Quarterly* 64 (Fall 1980):253–62.

Newcomb, William W., Jr. "The Culture and Acculturation of the Delaware Indians"; *Anthropological Papers*, no. 10, Museum of Anthropology, University of Michigan. Ann Arbor: University of Michigan, 1956.

Occom, Samson. "An Account of the Montauk Indians, on Long Island." 1761. Massachusetts Historical Society *Collections* 10, 1st ser.: 106–11.

"Oglethorpe's Treaty with the Lower Creek Indians." *Georgia Historical Quarterly* 4 (1920):3–16.

Onuf, Peter S. "New Lights in New London: A Group Portrait of the Separatists." *William and Mary Quarterly* 37 (October 1980):627–43.

Pargellis, Stanley, ed. "An Account of the Indians in Virginia . . . 1689." *William and Mary Quarterly* 16, 3d ser. (April 1959):228–43.

Pearce, Roy Harvey. "The 'Ruines of Mankind': The Indian and the Puritan Mind." *Journal of the History of Ideas* 13 (1952):200–217.

Pennington, Edgar Legare. "John Wesley's Georgia Ministry." *Church History* 8 (1939): 231–54.

———. "The South Carolina Indian War of 1715, As Seen by the Clergymen." *South Carolina Historical and Genealogical Magazine* 32, no. 4 (October 1931):251–69.

Porter, Frank W. "A Century of Accommodation: The Nanticokes in Colonial Maryland." *Maryland Historical Magazine* 74 (June, 1979):175–92.

Powicke, J. F., ed. "Some Unpublished Correspondence of the Rev. Richard Baxter and the Rev. John Eliot." Manchester, England: Manchester University Press, 1931. Reprint. John Ryland Library Bulletin 15, no. 2 (July 1931):442–66.

Prince, J. Dyneley, and Frank G. Speck. "The Modern Pequots and Their Language." American Anthropologist 5, new. ser. (April–June 1903):193–212.

Randolph, J. Ralph. "John Wesley and the American Indian: A Study in Disillusionment." Methodist History 10 (April 1972):3–11.

Reese, Trevor R. "A Red Indian Visit to Eighteenth-Century England." History Today 4 (May 1954):334–37.

"Relation of John Verarzanus, a Florentine, of the lande by him discovered in the name of his Majestie, written in Diepe the eight of July 1524." In Richard Hakluyt, Divers Voyages Touching the Discovery of America and the Islands Adjacent. 1582. Reprint. Edited by John Winter Jones. London: Printed for the Hakluyt Society, 1850. In Works, Vol. 7, Hakluyt Society.

Robinson, Walter S., Jr. "Indian Education and Missions in Colonial Virginia." Journal of Southern History 18 (May 1952):152–68.

————. "The Legal Status of the Indian in Colonial Virginia." Virginia Magazine of History and Biography 61 (1953):249–59.

————. "Tributary Indians in Colonial Virginia." Virginia Magazine of History and Biography 67 (January 1959):49–64.

————. "Virginia and the Cherokees: Indian Policy from Spotswood to Dinwiddie." In The Old Dominion, Essays for Thomas Perkins Abernethy. Edited by Darrett B. Rutman. Charlottesville: University Press of Virginia, 1964.

Ronda, James P. "Generations of Faith: The Christian Indians of Martha's Vineyard." William and Mary Quarterly 38, 3d series (July 1981):369–94.

————. "Red and White at the Bench: Indians and the Law in Plymouth County, 1680–1691." Essex Institute Historical Collections 110 (1974):200–215.

————. "'We Are Well as We Are': An Indian Critique of Seventeenth-Century Christian Missions." William and Mary Quarterly 34, 3d ser. (January 1977):66–82.

Sainsbury, John A. "Indian Labor in Early Rhode Island." New England Quarterly 48 (September 1975):378–93.

Salisbury, Neal Emerson. "Red Puritans: The 'Praying Indians' of Massachusetts Bay and John Eliot." William and Mary Quarterly 31, 3d ser. (January 1974):27–54.

Shepard, Thomas. "The Clear Sun-Shine of the Gospel Breaking Forth upon the Indians in New England." London: Printed by R. Cotes for J. Bellamy, 1648. Massachusetts Historical Society Collections, 4, 3d ser. (1834):25–68.

Simmons, William S. "Southern New England Shamanism: An Ethnographic Reconstruction." In Papers of the Seventh Algonquian Conference, 1975. Reprint. Edited by William Cowan. Ottawa: Carleton University Press, 1976.

————. "Conversion from Indian to Puritan." New England Quarterly 52 (1979):197–218.

————. "Cultural Bias in the New England Puritans' Perception of Indians." William and Mary Quarterly 38, 3d ser. (January 1981):56–72.

————. "Narrangansett Conversion in the Great Awakening." American Ethnologist 10 (1983):253–71.

Speck, Frank G. "The Family Hunting Band as the Basis of Algonkian Social Organization." American Anthropologist 17, new ser. (April–June 1915):289–305.

————. "The Iroquois: A Study in Cultural Evolution." Cranbrook Institute of Science Bulletin 23. Bloomfield Hills, Mi., 1945.

————. "Native Tribes and Dialects of Connecticut." Bureau of American Ethnology Annual Report, No. 43. Washington, D.C.: Smithsonian Institution, 1928.

———. "Chapters on the Ethnology of the Powhatan Tribes of Virginia." *Indian Notes and Monographs* 1, no. 5. New York: Heye Foundation, 1928.

———. "The Ethnic Position of the Southeastern Algonquian." *American Anthropologist* 26 (April–June 1924):184–200.

———. "A Note on the Hassanamisco Band of Nipmuc." *Bulletin, Massachusetts Archaeological Society* 4, no. 4 (1944):49–56.

———. "Notes on the Mohegan and Niantic Indians." *Anthropological Papers of the American Museum of Natural History* 3. New York, 1909.

———. "The Rappahannock Indians of Virginia." *Indian Notes and Monographs* 5, no. 3. New York: Heye Foundation, 1925.

———. "The Wapanachki Delawares and the English: Their Part as Viewed by an Ethnologist." *Pennsylvania Magazine of History and Biography* 67 (1943):319–44.

Spiess, Mathias. "The Indians of Connecticut." *Tercentenary Commission of the State of Connecticut* 9. New Haven, Ct.: Yale University Press, 1933. Commission on Historical Publications.

Stern, Theodore. "Chicahominy: The Changing Culture of a Virginia Indian Community." *American Philosophical Society Proceedings*, 96 (1952):157–225.

Stern, Theodore. "The Creeks." In *The Native Americans, Ethnology and Background of the North American Indians*. 2d ed, pp. 424–44. Edited by Jesse D. Jennings. New York: Harper & Row, 1977.

Stone, Lawrence. "The Educational Revolution in England, 1560–1640." *Past and Present* 28 (July 1964):43–80.

Stout, Harry S., and Peter Onuf. "James Davenport and the Great Awakening in New London." *Journal of American History* 70 (December 1983):556–78.

Stout, John Joseph. "Count Zinzendorf and the Pennsylvania Congregation of God in the Spirit." *Church History* 9 (1940):366–80.

Swanton, John R. "Aboriginal culture of the Southeast." *Bureau of American Ethnology Annual Report*, no. 42. Washington, D.C.: Smithsonian Institution, 1928.

———. "Early History of the Creek Indians and Their Neighbors." *Bureau of American Ethnology Bulletin*, No. 73. Washington, D.C.: Smithsonian Institution, 1922.

———. "The Indians of the Southeastern United States." *Bureau of American Ethnology Bulletin*, No. 137. Washington, D.C.: Smithsonian Institution, 1946.

Tannis, Norman Earl. "Education in John Eliot's Indian Utopias, 1646–1675." *History of Education Quarterly* 10 (Fall 1970):308–23.

Tantaquidgeon, Gladys. "Notes on the Gay Head Indians of Massachusetts." *Indian Notes* 7 (January 1930):1–26.

Tennent, Gilbert. "The Necessity of Holding Fast the Truth . . . with an Appendix, Relating to Errors lately vented by some Moravians." Boston, 1743. In Alan Heimert, Perry Miller, eds. *The Great Awakening*. Indianapolis: Bobbs-Merrill Co., 1967.

Thomas, G. E. "Puritans, Indians, and the Concept of Race." *New England Quarterly* 48 (March 1975):3–27.

Tooker, Elisabeth. "The League of the Iroquois: Its History, Politics, and Ritual." In *Handbook of North American Indians*. Vol. 15: *Northeast*, pp. 418–441. Edited by Bruce G. Trigger. Washington, D.C.: Smithsonian Institution, 1978.

Trelease, Allen W. "Indian–White Contacts in Eastern North America." *Ethnohistory* 9 (Winter 1962):137–46.

Trigger, Bruce G. "Early Iroquoian Contacts with Europeans." In *Handbook of North American Indians*. Vol. 15: *Northeast*, pp. 344–461. Edited by Bruce G. Trigger. Washington, D.C.: Smithsonian Institution, 1978.

Trumbull, James Hammond. "Natick Dictionary." *Bureau of American Ethnology Bulletin*, No. 25. Washington, D.C.: Smithsonian Institution, 1903.

Trumbull, James Hammond. "The Indian Tongue and Its Literature as Fashioned by Eliot and Others." In Justin Winsor, ed., *The Memorial History of Boston*. 4 vols. Boston: James B. Osgood & Co., 1881.

Voegelin, Carl F., and E. W. Voegelin. "Linguistic Considerations of Northeastern North America." In Frederick Johnson, ed., "Man in Northeastern North America." *Papers of the Robert S. Peabody Foundation for Archaeology*. Vol. 3. Andover, Mass.: Phillips Academy Foundation, 1946.

Wakely, Francis E. "Mission Activity among the Iroquois, 1642–1719." *Rochester History* 38 (October 1976):1–24.

Walne, Peter. "The Collections for Henrico College, 1616–1618." *Virginia Magazine of History and Biography* 80 (1972):259–66.

Wallace, Anthony F. C. "Political Organization and Land Tenure among the Northeastern Indians, 1600–1830." *Southwestern Journal of Anthropology* 13 (Winter 1957):301–21.

Washburn, Wilcomb E. "Philanthropy and the American Indian: The Need for a Model." *Ethnohistory* 15 (1968):53–54.

Weaver, Glenn. "The Moravians during the French and Indian War." *Church History* 24 (1955):239–56.

Weiss, Frederick L. "The New England Company of 1649 and Its Missionary Enterprises." In Publications of the Colonial Society of Massachusetts, *Transactions* 38 (1947–51). Boston: Colonial Society of Massachusetts, 1959.

Weld, Thomas, and Hugh Peter. "New England's First Fruits in respect to the progress of learning, in the College at Cambridge in Massachusetts bay . . . " London, 1643. Massachusetts Historical Society *Collections* 1, 1st ser. (1792):242–50.

White, Andrew. "A Briefe Relation of the Voyage Unto Maryland." 1634. In Clayton C. Hall. *Narratives of Early Maryland*. New York: Charles Scribner's Sons, 1910.

Whitfield, Henry. *The Light Appearing More and More towards the End of the perfect Day, or a further Discovery of the present state of the Indians in (Present Day) New-England*. London, 1651. Massachusetts Historical Society *Collections* 4, 3d ser. (1834):100–148.

Whitfield, Henry. "Strength out of Weaknesse; or, a Glorious Manifestation of the further Progresses of the Gospel among the Indians in New-England." London: Printed by M. Simmons for John Blague and Samuel Howes, 1652. Massachusetts Historical Society *Collections* 4, 3d ser. (1834):149–96.

Williams, Samuel C. "An Account of the Presbyterian Mission to the Cherokees, 1757–1759." *Tennessee Historical Magazine* 1, 2d ser. (1931):125–38.

Willoughby, Charles C. "The Virginia Indians in the Seventeenth Century." *American Anthropologist* 9, new ser. (1907):57–86.

Winship, George Parker. "Samuel Sewall and the New England Company." Massachusetts Historical Society *Proceedings* 67 (1945):55–110.

Winslow, Edward. "The Glorious Progress of the Gospel, Amongst the Indians in New England . . . " (1649). In Massachusetts Historical Society *Collections* 4, 3d ser. (1834): 69–98.

THESES AND DISSERTATIONS

Bell, Sadie. "The Church, the State and Education in Virginia." Ph.D. dissertation, University of Pennsylvania, 1930.

Corry, John P., "Indian Affairs in Georgia, 1732–1756." Ph.D. dissertation, University of Pennsylvania, 1935.

Layman, Martha Elizabeth. "A History of Indian Education in the United States, 1542–1942." Ph.D. dissertation, University of Minnesota, 1942.

Morris, Harold W. "A History of Indian Education in the United States." Ph.D. dissertation,
  Oregon State University, 1954.
Salisbury, Neal. "Conquest of the 'Savage': Puritans, Puritan Missionaries, and Indians,
  1620–1680." Ph.D. dissertation, University of California, Los Angeles, 1972.
Stuart, Karen A. " 'So Good a Work,' The Brafferton School, 1691–1777." Masters Thesis,
  College of William and Mary, 1984.

Index

AE4.0

Julie Riggs

5 p.m. Saturday